THE CHILEAN ROAD
TO SOCIALISM

Dale L. Johnson is Associate Professor of Sociology, and Sociology Department Chairman, at Livingston College, Rutgers—The State University of New Jersey. Johnson has traveled to Chile a number of times since his residence there in 1964–65 to undertake research for his doctoral dissertation, "Industry and Industrialists in Chile" (Stanford University, 1967). He is coauthor with James D. Cockcroft and André Gunder Frank of another Doubleday Anchor Book, *Dependence and Underdevelopment: Latin America's Political Economy* (1972).

THE CHILEAN ROAD
TO SOCIALISM

EDITED
WITH AN INTRODUCTION

BY

DALE L. JOHNSON

Anchor Books
Anchor Press/Doubleday
Garden City, New York
1973

A Suni Paz, compañera,
ciudadana del Tercer Mundo

The Anchor Press edition is the first publication of
THE CHILEAN ROAD TO SOCIALISM

Anchor Press edition: 1973
ISBN: 0-385-03489-x
Library of Congress Catalog Card Number 72–76231
Copyright © 1973 by Dale L. Johnson
Copyright © 1973 by Doubleday & Company, Inc.
All Rights Reserved
Printed in the United States of America
First Edition

CONTENTS

INTRODUCTION

The Chilean Road to Socialism

Latin America's most visible revolutionary, Fidel Castro, spent nearly a month in late 1971 traveling to every corner of Chile. There he was enthusiastically greeted by large crowds, warmly embraced by the continent's most restrained revolutionary, Chilean President Salvador Allende, roundly pilloried by the opposition press, and frenetically followed everywhere by journalists from throughout the world. He gave daily impassioned, learned, and lengthy speeches and talked endlessly with hundreds of Chileans from all walks of life. Those in opposition to Chilean socialism became particularly upset when he conversed at length with the Church hierarchy and military officers. Shortly before and after his visit, the United States imposed stiff sanctions against Chile. Fidel's stay was climaxed by a large and violent anti-government and anti-Castro demonstration. Just before his departure, Fidel observed, "We have come to see something extraordinary. A unique process is taking place in Chile. Something more than unique: unusual! unusual! It is a process of a change. It is a revolutionary process in which the revolutionaries are trying to carry out changes peacefully."

Since Salvador Allende, backed by 36 per cent of the popular vote and the Popular Unity coalition of Marxist and left-of-center political parties, was officially proclaimed President on November 3, 1970, Chile has been flooded by visitors from all over the world: Régis Debray, famous French strategist of guerrilla warfare for Latin America, came directly from his Bolivian prison to reflect on the varieties of revolutionary strategy[1]; political exiles from repressive Latin American regimes settle to find refuge and employment; international bankers fly in to voice concern about Chile's nationalization policies; Russian, East European, and Chinese trade delegations and political observers come to talk; sophisticated West European tourists visit to reflect on the local political culture while sipping Chile's fine wines; Italian and French Communists come to learn about *la vía pacífica;* North American academicians travel to write endless books, theses, and articles; U.S. revolutionaries and reformers pass through to learn firsthand how imperialism works and how changes might be brought about nonviolently in another setting; multinational corporation executives return from New York to drive hard bargains or close up shop; American journalists stay to write misleading stories; and CIA agents sneak in to conspire with the local opposition to bring down the Allende regime.

Perhaps something unusual, something unique *is* happening in Chile! Chileans, on the other hand, while flattered by all the international attention, don't seem to consider *la vía chilena* to socialism so very unusual. The struggle for change there has been building up for decades within a context of underdeveloped capitalism, a socioeconomic system common to more than one hundred other countries and a political system borrowed from European parliamentary models by a pre-Allende ruling class with a taste for French culture, British ideology, and American business practice. That a plurality (now nearing a majority) of Chileans want to substitute a planned economic system for free enterprise, social leveling for rigid social inequality, development for stagnation, and social justice for social injustice, while retaining their constitutional system and "pluralist" democracy,

---

[1] In February 1971 Debray conducted a fascinating, lengthy interview with Allende and wrote an analysis of the Chilean process: *Conversations with Allende* (New York: Pantheon, 1971).

is not unique—or even unusual. It is logical. It is what Chile has been moving toward for at least thirty-four years. What does qualify as unique is that Chileans have a chance, certainly no more than that, of building a new Chile[2] without the bloodletting that has heretofore been associated with real social change.

The possibility of a new Chile cannot be fully appreciated apart from consideration of the constraints built into the situation that President Allende and the Popular Unity government face. The origin of these constraints is largely in Chile's relation to the rest of the world. While the country is geographically remote from the mainstream of world activity, it is by no means isolated. This is why so much of the book is devoted to analysis of Chile's situation as an *underdeveloped* and *dependent* society. Underdevelopment means having an economic system that perpetuates poverty and its attendant human misery and living with social structures based on gross inequalities in social well-being, privilege, and power. Dependence is an international structure that conditions underdevelopment. Chile is unable freely to make decisions that affect its economic, social, and political life, since the range of choice is constantly limited by external economic and political powers that do not have Chile's national interest as a primary concern. Thus, dependence leaves Chile faced with either the consequences of decisions it does not autonomously control, or the consequences of foreigners' adverse reactions and retaliatory measures against any choices Chile makes for itself. Moreover, Chile's dependence leaves the country very vulnerable to the consequences of decisions over which it has no control whatsoever—decisions by such external

---

[2] The North American Congress on Latin America has contributed a valuable addition to the literature available in English on Chile: NACLA, *New Chile* (P. O. Box 226, Berkeley, California, 94701).

forces as the World Bank and International Monetary Fund, agencies of the U. S. Government, the International Telephone & Telegraph Corp., and a hundred other "multinational" corporations that operate, or would like to operate, in Chile.

These structures of underdevelopment and dependence, inherited from four centuries of colonial and neocolonial domination, constitute the main problem that Salvador Allende and the Popular Unity face. These structures constrain Allende at every turn and limit the means of making the transition from the old to the new society, of making a better life for all Chileans and setting an example for the world. So far, Allende and the Socialists, Communists, and non-Marxist supporters of the Popular Unity have taken decisive steps in the direction of a new Chile and have been able to do so by strictly constitutional means. But the changes are reversible, and the situation of the government is tenuous. The Popular Unity could be simply boxed in and voted out in the next election. But a civil war, a bloody counterrevolution assisted by outside powers, or a total revolution brought about by armed workers and peasants must be included among the possibilities.

One can hope that a new society is in the making with minimum bloodshed and maximum democracy. Many Chilean Communists and Socialists are among the optimists who see a new historical process opening after a thousand years of violent struggle by antiquated social systems to maintain themselves against the threats from new social forces. Certainly the institutions and powers of old slave and feudal societies never stood conveniently aside to permit the next stage of social evolution peacefully to supersede the *ancien régime*. Nor has a socialist system ever been constructed following the rules established by the preceding, capitalist order. Fortunately, there are always new chapters in world history.

This book is several things: a record of an important historical process described and analyzed by participants; a compendium of information and analysis of imperialism, nationalism, and social change; a textbook reader in development and political sociology; a source book of theoretical debates, conveniently tied to a concrete case, on the nature and strategy of the transition to socialism. Most of all, however, the book is designed to bring American readers information, analysis, and perspective on what is happening in Chile. Mainly, the Chileans speak for themselves. Chilean intellectuals closely examine the economic problems and social structure of Chile; Chilean Socialists analyze Chilean politics and the process of socialist transformation; Chilean conservatives and Christian Democrats explain their opposition views. As editor, I have consciously chosen not to editorialize and have instead made my own contribution to the book, together with that of my North American colleagues, in the form of a series of articles, contained in Part I, on Chile's relation to and problems with the United States. The rationale for this is that Chileans are best equipped to explain what their struggle is about and that we, as Americans, have an obligation to take a close (and critical) look at how our institutions and leaders affect other peoples.

Appreciation is extended to *Compañera* Magaly Ortiz of the Center for Socioeconomic Studies of the University of Chile for her invaluable assistance in preparing this volume. To Theotonio dos Santos, Vania Bombirra, Gunder and Marta Frank, and many other *compañeros* in Chile I owe much of my intellectual formation. Sincere thanks are given to the many Chilean authors and to their publishers for their adherence to the socialist principle that the sphere of private property does not extend to intellectual work.

PART I

UNDERDEVELOPMENT
AND IMPERIALISM:

A View from the United States

CHAPTER 1

Multinational Corporations and Chile

THE MULTINATIONALS*

JAMES D. COCKCROFT, HENRY FRUNDT, and
DALE L. JOHNSON

How important is the multinational corporation?
Burton Teague, in a study published last September
by the Conference Board, a nonprofit, business-
sponsored research organization, put it this way:

"Of a gross world product of $3-trillion, approxi-
mately one-third is produced in the United States,
one-third in the industrial nations of Europe, Canada,
Japan and Australia, and the remaining one-third in
Russia, Eastern Europe, China and the developing
nations elsewhere in the world.

"About 15 per cent, or $450-billion, is accounted
for by multinational enterprises; $200-billion of this
by U.S.-based companies; $100-billion by foreign-
based companies which also operate in the U.S.,
and $150-billion by interproduction in other coun-
tries.

"The proportion contributed by multinational corporations is growing at a rate of 10 per cent per
year. At this rate the multinational companies will

* An original article for this volume based upon research by
the Chile Research Group of Rutgers University. James Cockcroft
is Associate Professor of Sociology at Rutgers; Henry Frundt is
a teaching assistant and graduate student at Rutgers.

generate one-half of the gross world product in less than 30 years."[1]

As important as copper may be to Chile, from the point of view of U.S. investors and the Chileans themselves the strategic sector affected by Chile's economic nationalism and incipient socialism is not mining but industry. For the Chileans, the question is one of achieving economic independence in order to promote national development. For the multinational corporate investors, the questions are the potential loss of a multimillion-dollar investment, the closure of opportunities to expand operations in a strategic South American location, and the effect that Chile's economic nationalism may have on other Third World countries.

At the time Allende assumed office, more than one hundred U.S. corporations had established themselves in Chile. Among these firms were twenty-four of the top thirty U.S.-based multinational corporations. These included the major auto producers, four of the biggest oil companies, Dow and DuPont chemicals, International Telephone & Telegraph (ITT), and other big industrials. In recent years the ranks of the industrials had been joined by multinational banks and corporations operating in the service sectors. Many of these foreign corporations entered Chile during the 1960s.

Thus Chile was very much affected by the most important phenomenon in international economics of the past two decades: the ascendance of multinational corporations in the secondary and tertiary sectors. These corporations are strongly attracted to foreign countries by the availability of cheap labor, penetrable markets, high returns, and other factors. At the same time, they have a strong incentive to expand abroad because of

[1] New York *Times,* March 12, 1972.

limitations on U.S. domestic markets, higher costs of labor, foreign restrictions on the importation of U.S. finished goods, and the growth and profit imperatives of corporate operations.[2] So intense has been the expansion of these corporations that, based on gross value of production, U.S. companies abroad now constitute the third-wealthiest "nation" in the world, behind the United States and the USSR.

While not as important as Brazil, Mexico, Argentina, and Puerto Rico for U.S. multinationals in Latin America, Chile nevertheless reflects this recent pattern of rapid economic expansion into foreign countries. After Eduardo Frei became President, in 1964, these corporations entered Chile with the full co-operation of the Chilean state. For example, all four of Chile's petrochemical companies arrived after 1967, as did two of the three rubber companies and three of the four manufacturers of electrical equipment. Most of the eighteen foreign automotive assembly plants were established in the 1960s. During these years foreign investments in manufacturing and commerce more than doubled.

Patterns of Corporate Expansion

There are three basic patterns of multinational expansion into the urban economies of underdeveloped countries that can be analyzed in the Chilean case. The traditional pattern is investment by long-established firms in utilities and transportation facilities. ITT's Chile Telephone Company is an example. But ITT's rapid ascendance as the world's number one "conglomerate" also serves to illustrate a second pattern: penetration into diverse sectors by modern conglomerates. In the specific case of Chile, the International Basic Economy Cor-

[2] The economic basis of corporate expansion is explained by Harry Magdoff, *The Age of Imperialism* (New York: Monthly Review Press, 1969).

poration serves as an even better example of this mode of expansion than ITT. A third pattern is direct investment by corporations in heavy and highly technological industries. We will use the 1967 investment of Dow Chemical in Chile to analyze this pattern.

ITT established itself in Chile in 1927 with an investment in the telephone company. Today, after Anaconda Copper ITT has the largest U.S. investment in Chile. The conglomerate owns 70 per cent of the telephone company, with declared assets of $153 million. The Chilean subsidiary is one of ITT's biggest earners abroad, making over $10 million annually. Other ITT properties in Chile include Standard Electric, which operates in twenty-four countries, All America Cables & Radio, two Sheraton hotels, ITT World Directories, and ITT World Communications.

Allende was elected on a platform that promised to socialize monopolies such as that of ITT. Negotiations for government purchase of the telephone company began early in 1971, after years of unbelievably bad service and abortive attempts by the Frei government (1964–70) to persuade the monopoly to provide adequate service.

Complaints about telephone service in Chile are legendary. Incomplete calls and wrong numbers are the norm. ITT's technology is obsolete. People wait for years in vain hope of installation, and there is practically no rural service. In 1967 the Frei regime concluded an agreement with the phone company to provide 147,000 lines by 1971. By the middle of 1971 only seventy thousand lines had been extended, and the vast amount of materials bought by the Chilean Government for telephone extension remained unused in warehouses.

During the 1971 negotiation period, the Popular Unity government prevented ITT from converting its assets into dollars. The negotiations broke down in August, and on September 2 the telephone company's bank accounts were blocked. On September 23 the Chilean state officially "intervened" the company—substituting state and worker-committee management for ITT management. After company records were examined, the former general manager of the company and three other officials were arrested on charges of fraud in company dealings.

Before the Chilean Government could determine the amount of compensation for the property, ITT filed a claim against its investment insurance held by the Overseas Private Investment Corporation (OPIC). This quasi-public agency of the U. S. Government, under *de facto* control of the corporate elite who sit on its advisory council, encourages overseas investment and reduces risks by insuring investors against expropriation and incovertibility of assets. (More details on ITT in Chile, its conflict with and attempt to undermine the Allende government, and the OPIC are provided in Chapter 2.)

The final episode in ITT's history in Chile is now being recorded. In March 1972 columnist Jack Anderson published secret papers from ITT files that document that the corporation applied considerable pressure on the U. S. Government and powers inside Chile to reverse the popular election of Salvador Allende as President of Chile in 1970.[3] The secret papers reveal that ITT co-operated with the CIA in the agency's plans to prevent Allende from taking office, including efforts to create economic chaos and provoke a military intervention. ITT, of course, is no longer welcome in Chile.

ITT is not the only "traditional" investor in Chile's non-mining economic sectors; Grace Lines began handling Chile's foreign trade in 1881. W. R. Grace expanded into textiles as early as 1914 and by 1918 into the export-import business. By the 1960s W. R. Grace, like ITT,

[3] "Secret Memos from ITT," *NACLA's Latin America and Empire Report,* VI, April 1972.

had become a huge conglomerate and was heavily involved in Chile in processed foods, petrochemicals, textiles, paints, electric lamps, and the import business.

Viewed in a world context, ITT is one of the best examples of the multinational conglomerate phenomenon. These are corporations that grow by taking control of and absorbing other firms. In the United States, ITT is the eighth-largest industrial concern. In ten years the corporation has grown from an $800-million communications company to a diversified giant worth $6.4 billion. This growth is a result of ITT's rapid expansion abroad and its take-over of about a hundred U.S. corporations, including Hartford Fire Insurance, Sheraton Hotels, Continental Baking, and Avis. This growth has also been facilitated by the U. S. Government's unwillingness to prevent most ITT take-overs through anti-trust-law enforcement and its awarding of large defense contracts to the corporation.

Revelations concerning ITT's friendly ties to the CIA in its Chile operations and to the Attorney General's office and the Republican Party (through ITT-Sheraton's offer of four hundred thousand dollars to subsidize the 1972 Republican Convention allegedly in return for a favorable settlement of an anti-trust suit) symbolize one aspect of the conglomerate's relationship to the U. S. Government. Moreover, with $233 million in defense business in 1971, ITT ranked number twenty-three on the Defense Department's list of prime contractors. Defense-related activities include the Ballistic Missile Early Warning System, various communications-satellite systems, an ITT space division working on top-secret Department of Defense contracts, electronic air-warfare devices being used in Indochina, and a major integrated communications system for U.S. military forces in South Vietnam. Former Senior Vice-President of ITT Charles Ireland is a retired lieutenant colonel of the U. S. Marine Corps.

ITT is among the very largest of U.S.-based multinational corporations. In 1970, 47 per cent of ITT's assets and sales were located abroad and 59 per cent of its profits flowed from foreign operations. Growth abroad proceeds at an even more rapid clip than ITT's sensational expansion inside the United States. With about $3 billion of its assets abroad, ITT operates in more than sixty countries, including twelve in Latin America. Like all multinationals, ITT views economic nationalism—especially when combined with efforts to construct socialism, as in Chile—as a fundamental threat to its interests.

ITT's expansion as a conglomerate in Chile, however, proceeded on a more modest scale than in the United States and Europe. Its operations were also more integrated, that is, related to its traditional communications business. After establishing the telephone company (1927), ITT began a plant (1942), Standard Electric, to manufacture telephone equipment, and opened international communications services. It got into non-communications business with its recent U.S. acquisition of the Sheraton Hotel chain. Given the revelations of the "ITT-Chile" papers released by Jack Anderson, it is not hard to imagine ITT officials in serious conversation with CIA agents and the Chilean equivalent of the Republican National Committee in a luxurious suite at Sheraton's Hotel Carrera in Santiago. Toward the end of the Frei regime, ITT began to establish links through an insurance company, La Trasandina, with a powerful and aggressive Chilean economic group that prospered under Frei and centered itself in the *Banco Hipotecario* (a group termed in Chile the *Pirañas,* after the ferocious South American fish). In Chile (as in the United States with ITT's successful take-over of Hartford Fire Insurance) insurance companies provide access to capital necessary for conglomerates to continue their acquisitions of penetrable companies.

Whatever plans ITT may have had for further expan-

sion in Chile were rudely interrupted by the Allende government's nationalization bill sent to Congress after the
scandal of ITT's interference in Chile's internal politics.

Another case of penetration by conglomerates is the
Rockefellers' International Basic Economy Corporation.
IBEC operates in thirty-three countries and in 1970 derived 60 per cent of its profits from Latin America, although only 33 per cent of its assets were in the region.
In Chile, IBEC has a ready-mix cement plant, a petro-
leum-products manufacturing and marketing concern, a
construction firm, a mining enterprise, and four investment and management companies. Through these investment companies Rockefeller interests have penetrated
many Chilean firms. IBEC now participates in thirteen of
the twenty-five largest Chilean corporations and controls
over 50 per cent of the stock in three of them. In short,
IBEC in Chile operates as ITT does everywhere: it grows
by achieving financial control of more and more independent firms.

One of the characteristics of conglomerates is that they
expand by financial manipulation rather than through
producing. The conglomerates do not usually bring any
significant capital of their own into an underdeveloped
country; their aim is to use other people's money to keep
expanding and to take capital out. Most new foreign investment, in Chile as in other Third World countries, has
been based on locally generated capital funds rather than
new direct investment or large external loans. As *The
Rockefeller Report on the Americas* candidly states, "The
United States is but one partner in a development effort
which is about 90 per cent financed by the other American republics."[4]

The third pattern of foreign investment evident in the

---

[4] *The Rockefeller Report on the Americas* (Chicago: Quadrangle Books, 1969).

Chilean case is the establishment of large industrials in chemicals, consumer durables, and machinery and equipment. These are all industries that require large initial investments and technological resources, investments that are very difficult for most underdeveloped countries to undertake without some form of dependence on foreign financing and expertise. The price—in terms of capital drains and loss of control over the economy—that an underdeveloped country has to pay for plants to produce automobiles, chemicals, electrical appliances and machinery, consumer niceties, pharmaceuticals, etc., is very high. Such investments are nevertheless facilitated by local business interests and governments in many underdeveloped countries, as well as by the U. S. Government.

An example of how both the Chilean Government and the U. S. Government facilitated this pattern of foreign investment is Dow Chemical's financing of a petrochemical complex. Dow Chemical, recently in ascendance as a multinational, came to Chile in 1967 to manufacture chemicals for the textile and paper industries in Chile. With an investment of $6.6 million, Dow provided but a fraction of the funds needed to finance its Chilean subsidiary. The U. S. Export-Import Bank—the chief function of which is to underwrite U.S. exports and corporate expansion overseas—together with the Bank of America provided the bulk of the capital, $17 million in credits. Chile provided $4.3 million, for a total investment of $31.3 million, including $2 million in value accorded Dow's technical know-how and a $1.4-million credit from the parent company. Petrodow Chilena must pay Dow Chemical Corporation 3.5 per cent to 4.5 per cent royalties on sales of specified products. While sales are in Chilean currency, royalties must be paid in dollars earned through copper exports. The Frei regime placed no restrictions on profit remissions, and Dow is entitled to amortize the total investment, including the loans and value arbitrarily placed on technical know-how, at the rate of 10 per cent per year. No customs duties are levied on Petrodow's imports. Tax stability is guaranteed for fifteen years. Dow Chemical retains 70 per cent of the stock and therefore control of decision making.

The long-range implications of this deal for capital transfers out of Chile are obvious. The investment came to Chile largely in the form of machinery and equipment (probably at inflated transfer prices from the parent corporation). The investment is amortized and profits repatriated, however, in hard currency. Chile must therefore dig into its scarce dollar reserves to repay Petrodow's loans and royalties and provide dollars for amortization allowances and profit transfers. With the sharp decline in copper prices since Allende took office, these reserves have all but disappeared.

Scope of Multinational Penetration

In general, by the time Allende became President most of Chile's important areas of industry and finance had passed into foreign hands. Of the eighteen largest non-banking corporations, all but two had participation of foreign capital. Two fifths of Chile's largest one hundred corporations were under foreign control, while many more were mixed ventures that allowed external influence or effective control.

As the cases of ITT, Dow, and IBEC suggest, some of the world's largest corporations are involved in Chile. By 1970 there were over a hundred U.S.-controlled corporations operating in the country, with investments worth more than $1 billion. The big U.S.-based multinationals (European and Japanese corporations are present but not greatly significant) dominate the most modern, dynamic areas of the Chilean economy. In addition to copper mining and nitrates, these areas include:

—machinery and equipment, 50% foreign control (including Xerox, National Cash Register, ITT, GE)
—iron, steel, and metal products, 60% foreign (including Bethlehem and ARMCO Steel, Koppers, Kaiser, Singer, Hoover)
—petroleum products and distribution, over 50% foreign (Standard Oil of N.J., IBEC, Gulf, Mobil)
—industrial and other chemicals, 60% foreign (Dow, Monsanto, W. R. Grace)
—rubber products, 45% foreign (General Tire, Firestone)
—automotive assembly, 100% foreign (including Ford, GM, Chrysler)
—radio and television, nearly 100% foreign (RCA, Phillips, General Telephone and Electronics)
—pharmaceuticals, nearly 100% foreign (American Cyanamid, Pfizer, Parke-Davis)
—office equipment, nearly 100% foreign (Sperry Rand, Remington, Xerox)
—copper fabricating, 100% foreign (Phelps Dodge, Northern Indiana Brass Co., General Cable)
—tobacco, 100% foreign (British-American Tobacco Co.)
—advertising, 90% foreign (J. Walter Thompson, McCann-Erickson, etc.)

Sectors of the economy developed over the course of a half century by Chilean entrepreneurs, such as processed foods and textiles, are now significantly penetrated by foreign capital. In manufactured foodstuffs, for example, W. R. Grace has a decided presence, along with CPC International, Ralston Purina (now nationalized), General Mills, and the inevitable Coca-Cola.

Of the top thirty U.S.-controlled multinational corporations, twenty-four operate in Chile (see table). These same twenty-four corporate giants are increasingly de-

TOP 30 U.S.-CONTROLLED MULTINATIONAL CORPORATIONS
(based on estimated foreign sales)

1970 RANK MULTINATIONAL	1970 RANK U.S. INDUSTRIAL	1970 NET INCOME (MILLIONS $)	1970 % INCOME FOREIGN	1971 RANK U.S. DEFENSE CONTRACTOR
1. +Standard Oil N.J.	2	1,310	52	27
2. +Ford Motor	3	516	24	24
3. +General Motors	1	609	19	17
4. +Mobil Oil	6	483	51	55
5. +IBM	5	1,018	50	19
6. +ITT	8	353	47	23
7. +Texaco	9	822	na	44
8. +Gulf Oil	11	550	21	—
9. Standard Oil Cal.	14	455	46	38
10. +Chrysler	7	d 7.6	na	33
11. +General Electric	4	329	20	5
12. +Caterpillar Tractor	42	144	na	84
13. F. W. Woolworth	na	77	61	—
14. +Eastman Kodak	27	404	19	69
15. Union Carbide	24	157	na	—
16. +Procter & Gamble	25	238	25	—

				d—deficit
17. +Singer	43	75	na	41
18. +Dow Chemical	51	103	45	—
19. +CPC International	74	61	51	—
20. +International Harvester	32	52	na	90
21. +Firestone Tire & Rubber	38	93	39	—
22. Colgate-Palmolive	81	40	na	—
23. Honeywell	49	58	na	22
24. +National Cash Register	89	30	51	—
25. +E. I. Du Pont	18	329	na	46
26. +W. R. Grace	50	30	39	—
27. Minnesota Mining & Manufacturing	65	188	na	—
28. +First National City Bank	na	139	40	—
29. +Sperry Rand	59	72	na	16
30. +Xerox	60	188	38	—

na—not available

+—multinational in Chile

Sources: *Fortune*, 500 Largest Industrial Corporations, 1970; *Forbes*, Nov. 15, 1971; *Economic Priorities Report*, Jan.–Feb. 1972.

pendent on foreign ventures: they now derive 40 per cent or more of their sales and income from foreign operations. With few exceptions, they rank among the principal contractors of the U. S. Department of Defense, thus turning over additional profits flowing from the U.S. military's defense of corporate interests overseas against the forces of nationalism and socialism.

Chilean Dependence

The essential impact of the increase in multinational corporate penetration in any given Third World economy is to exacerbate dependence at every level. By dependence we mean the inability to freely make decisions that affect one's economic, social, and political life and destiny; and, from a different angle, the suffering of the consequences of decisions that are made or significantly shaped by other parties. This can be seen in the Chilean case at the macroeconomic level and in terms of what we call the "denationalization of the national bourgeoisie."[5]

In the twentieth century, Chile's economy developed in two directions: On the one hand, the economy became heavily dependent upon copper exports. On the other hand, the collapse of the international economy during the Depression and World War II loosened the previous bonds of international dependence sufficiently to make possible a process of industrial development under the control of Chilean entrepreneurs.

In the non-mining sectors of the economy, development under control of Chilean entrepreneurs had come to a practical end by the mid-1950s. Since that period, Chile has suffered runaway inflation of over 25 per cent annu-

[5] For a theoretical clarification of the concept of dependence, and analysis of many questions raised by this paper, see James D. Cockcroft, André Gunder Frank, and Dale L. Johnson, *Dependence and Underdevelopment* (Garden City, N.Y.: Doubleday Anchor, 1972).

ally, combined with the virtual stagnation of the economy as a whole. The influx of foreign capital in the 1960s did not ameliorate any of the grave structural problems of the economy. In fact, during the period of greatest foreign investment, from 1967 to 1970, there was a negative per-capita rate of economic growth. Allende's successful economic policies in 1971 reversed the trend. Unemployment rates of up to 10 per cent, combined with disguised unemployment in the inflated services sector, have made real unemployment approach 30 per cent. The capital-intensive nature of foreign enterprise did not permit significant increases in employment. Moreover, production by foreign corporations of goods superfluous to the needs of three fourths of the consuming population (cars, durable consumer and luxury items, etc.) constitutes no real contribution to Chilean development, especially when one takes into account Chile's deficient food production, widespread undernourishment, inadequate housing, and lack of medical and social services. The Allende government will undoubtedly shift some investment away from heavy industry and consumer goods only the affluent can afford, toward meeting the basic needs of the Chilean people.

Foreign enterprise has created strong tendencies toward decapitalization. In the following article on copper, we document the very substantial flow of capital out of Chile due to foreign ownership of natural resources. In industry, U.S. investment approximately doubled during the 1960s, while profits went up sevenfold, of which part was repatriated and part reinvested in expanding Chilean operations. Chileans also paid out more and more for foreign licenses and patents, as illustrated in the case of Dow Chemical. Profit repatriation, payments for foreign licenses, and debt payments put enormous pressures upon available foreign exchange.

We do not have access to exact figures for Chile, but with respect to other Latin American nations, as much as

60 per cent of any given country's foreign exchange is consumed in repatriation of profits by foreign investors, debt and service payments to foreign creditors, and other charges and services on foreign transactions. The long-range effect of foreign investment in manufacturing, commerce, and services is the same as in mining—the transfer of wealth and decision making from the underdeveloped country to the home offices of the multinational corporations. Over the past two decades, U.S. corporations have concentrated more and more of the economic life of other countries in their hands, while taking out of the underdeveloped nations almost three times as much capital as they invested. At the same time, they increased threefold the value of their assets there.

Dependence is further accentuated by the integration of local businessmen with foreign capital. In the case of Chile, the business community contributed to what amounted to a virtual de-Chileanization of the economy in the 1960s. In part, this occurred because Chilean capitalists profited from business arrangements with foreigners; in other cases, Chileans could not compete with the greater assets possessed by foreigners in capital, technology, and credit. As a result, the Chilean bourgeoisie became a local partner of foreign capital, serving the interests of foreigners rather than those of national development. In this sense, the bourgeoisie was "denationalized."

One example is the association of the Yarur Chilean textile interests with W. R. Grace. Capital generated from that associative venture was used by Grace in the 1960s to acquire the Hucke Candy and Biscuit Company, the Eperva Fishmeal Company, COIA (Chile's largest paint producer and a major sugar refinery), and various sugar, wine, and distribution concerns. Another example is the Rockefellers' IBEC. The IBEC tactic in Chile has been to recruit close business associates from the local business elite, to buy into local businesses (using funds generated within the country from mutual funds, insurance companies, and other business), and then to put *their* men on the boards. This increases the concentration of decision making in the hands of local oligarchs serving foreign interests. Agustín Edwards of the oligarchic Edwards family, owners of the major Santiago newspaper and a wide assortment of other firms, is a stockholder and former president of a principal IBEC Chilean subsidiary. The Edwardses also had a 20 per cent participation in the Ralston Purina subsidiary intervened by the Popular Unity government in 1970. Shortly after Allende's election, Agustín Edwards went into voluntary exile in New York to become Vice-President of Pepsi-Cola Corporation, a firm he had also been associated with in Chile (see Chapter 21).

Yet another example is the First National City Bank, which made its ties to top Chilean businessmen and expanded its influence in the Chilean economy through National Finance, S.A. ("Finansa," 50 per cent First National City's), an investment firm linked to the Chilean economic group *Las Pirañas*.

The above examples are but a few among many. The *comprador,* dependent nature of the Chilean bourgeoisie is also revealed in the facts uncovered by Maurice Zeitlin, Lynda Ann Ewen, and Richard Ratcliff.[6] They studied the affiliations of 285 Chilean officers and directors of the fifty largest non-financial corporations during the mid-1960s. The researchers identified four interest groups of Chilean families, who controlled twenty-one of the top fifty corporations. Two thirds of the officers and directors of the top fifty had either personal or close family ties to foreign interests.

Moreover, dependence extends beyond the denational-

6 *Landlords and Capitalists* (New York: Harper & Row, forthcoming, 1973).

ized bourgeoisie to other strata of a Third World nation's society. A stratum of administrators and technicians recruited by foreigners from the upper and middle classes emerges to represent the interests of foreign capital. Until the Allende regime passed a law forbidding it, Chilean employees of some foreign firms were paid in dollars rather than *escudos,* which they then transferred abroad or sold on the black market. This sizable stratum, thoroughly acculturated to American values of consumerism, constitutes a principal social base of right-wing opposition to the Popular Unity governing coalition. Women of this stratum and some of their domestic servants have engaged in militant demonstrations such as the December 1971 "march of the empty pots" protesting shortages of consumer goods (shortages were caused by Allende's economic policies, which increased the purchasing power of workers and therefore demand). Many middle- and upper-class people watch TV programs such as "I Spy" and "I Love Lucy," read *Selecciones del Reader's Digest,* and generally imitate American life styles.

Prominent Chileans go back and forth between politics and employment with foreign companies. Dragomir Tomic, brother of the Christian Democrats' 1970 presidential candidate, was one of Anaconda's lawyers defending its interests in the enormous Chuquicamata mine. Rodolfo Michells, an ex-senator from the Radical Party, became a Vice-President of Anaconda. Arturo Matte, from an oligarchic Chilean family associated with the Alessandri family (Alessandri is ex-President of Chile and opponent of Allende in the 1970 election), was identified in the Anderson "ITT-Chile" papers as a co-conspirator with ITT and the CIA to prevent Allende from taking office.

Important decisions shaping Chile's underdevelopment have increasingly been made in the board rooms of U.S. corporations and passed on through the informal linkages connecting foreign companies to the local ruling class, and from this class to the pre-Allende state. The use of the Chilean state by the dependent bourgeoisie and foreign capitalists to achieve their ends proceeded further under the Christian Democratic regime of Eduardo Frei (1964–70) than under any other government since the early days of penetration by nitrate and copper interests (1891 through the 1920s). In 1969 the Frei administration agreed that ITT's phone company be permitted an annual 10 per cent return on an overvalued investment, provided capital for expansion, and allowed special foreign-exchange arrangements. The extremely favorable terms awarded Dow Chemical for its 1967 investment have already been mentioned.

One of the most dramatic examples of the state's generosity to foreign investors was the Frei administration's "Chileanization" of the copper mines. The "Chileanization" began with government purchase of 51 per cent of El Teniente mine. Critics claimed that the value of the property was no more than the book value of $72 million. Nevertheless, President Frei accepted the appraisal by Kennecott of $160 million and paid $81 million for 51 per cent. The majority stock held by Chile did not mean very much, as management control and sales offices were retained by Kennecott. In essence, the program was meant to provide incentives to the copper companies to increase production substantially by giving them subsidies, tax advantages, guarantees—and an alternative to the Left's proposed nationalization. As noted in the next article on copper nationalization, none of the aims and production goals were even remotely achieved.

Chilean Nationalism vs. Corporate Internationalism

The government of Salvador Allende and the Popular Unity is determined to reclaim the pillars of the industrial economy from foreign control. In attempting to do so, the Chileans are directly confronting the greatest concentration of economic power the world has ever seen.

It is important to understand that the multinationals are not simply a series of unrelated business concerns that happen to be operating in a number of countries. The big ones are American (the term "multinational" is misleading), they enjoy the full support of the U. S. Government abroad as at home, and they tend to come together at the level of ownership and control.

What emerges from our research is a picture of a series of corporate interest groups—Rockefellers, First National City, Morgans, Mellons, and others—which also form a web of corporate power brought together by common interests, complementary activities in the international sphere, and a good deal of overlapping and interpenetration among the top officers of the multinationals.

The Rockefellers' world empire extends into Chile. The Rockefeller brothers have IBEC, which will no longer be able to take over Chilean firms. Their Standard Oil of New Jersey markets petroleum products and owns lubes-blending and plasticizer plants. The Allende government plans to create a state enterprise to distribute petroleum products, which will also affect other oil companies in which Rockefellers have a part interest. The Rockefellers are linked to many other U.S. firms operating in Chile through having their men on the boards of directors. Six of the twenty-four largest multinationals in Chile share directors with the Rockefellers' Chase Manhattan Bank and seven with the Chemical Bank of New York, also under Rockefeller influence.

First National City Bank's eight branches in Chile played an important role in the financial aspect of corporate expansion into Chile during the 1960s. This principal seat of economic power will be directly affected by Chile's economic nationalism. The Stillman-Rockefellers of First National City share control of Anaconda Copper with the Morgan interest group. Ten of the twenty-four top multinationals in Chile share directors with First National City Bank.

The Morgan interest groups has a strong presence in Chile through its ties to Kennecott Copper and other corporations present in the country. The Morgans also have an interest in Anaconda copper (as well as another major copper producer not in Chile, American Smelting and Refining) and control Coca-Cola International, which operates in Chile as everywhere. Kennecott in turn maintains ties to the Guggenheim family, founder of El Teniente copper mine in 1903, who owned the Anglo-Lautaro Nitrate Corporation, now nationalized, which exploited Chile's vast natural nitrate deposits since the 1920s. Kennecott is also associated with the fiftieth-largest U.S. industrial, also big in Chile: W. R. Grace & Co. Eight of the twenty-four largest multinationals in Chile have interlocking directors with Morgan Guaranty Trust and four with Bankers Trust, the Morgans' other financial control center.

Other principal corporate interest groups are also present in Chile, at least at the level of sharing top personnel with a number of the twenty-four multinationals there. The Mellon family firm, Koppers Company, has a cement plant and an engineering and construction firm. Three of the twenty-four multinationals present in Chile have top corporate personnel from the Mellon interest group.

Presumably "independent" corporations such as ITT and Dow Chemical, which are not within the sphere of control of any of these groups, nevertheless have high-level personnel in close interrelationship with one or more of the established corporate interest groups and other "independent" multinationals. Eugene Black, for example, a director of ITT, is also associated with the Rockefellers' Chase Manhattan Bank, as well as with Equitable

Life Assurance and American Express Company, in which Rockefellers have a strong interest. Eugene Black came to the Board of ITT after fifteen years as President of the World Bank. The World Bank, together with U.S. creditors, pushed Chile hard on its 1972 renegotiation of the huge debt that Allende inherited from previous regimes. ITT also maintains interlocking directorates with the Rockefeller-influenced Chemical Bank of New York and Morgan Guaranty Trust.

In general, half of the twenty-four corporate giants in Chile share three or more interlocking directorates with each other, and every one of them is linked through the sharing of a director of some third corporation.

We cite the apparent existence of distinct "interest groups" that emerge from our data, because there seem to be some important differences among them with respect to modes of foreign expansion and ways in which they seek to utilize U. S. Government power in furthering corporate goals abroad. Of course, many of the indicated cases of interlocking directorates among the principal multinational industrials and banks serve mainly to facilitate business transactions and an easygoing, monopolistic competition on a world scale. We indicate the interlocking nature of the multinationals as a whole in order to emphasize the communications links among them at the policy level and the essential commonality of interest that unites them as the world center of economic and political power.

It remains in the next chapter to show how this web of economic power that Chile is in the process of confronting relates to the formation of the foreign policy of the United States Government.[7]

[7] The empirical parts of this research have been greatly facilitated by the North American Congress on Latin America's painstaking compilation of data on foreign investment in Chile, NACLA (ed.), New Chile. This excellent volume contains selec-

CHILE'S NATIONALIZATION OF COPPER*

CHILE RESEARCH GROUP, RUTGERS UNIVERSITY

On July 16, 1971, the Chilean Congress unanimously approved an amendment to the nation's Constitution making the country's vast resources of copper the property of Chile. The government assumed formal public ownership of all minerals in the nation's subsoil, and operational control of the Anaconda, Kennecott, and Cerro mines.

The constitutional amendment stipulated compensation for the value of the installations and authorized the government to make certain reasonable deductions from the book value of the properties to arrive at their true worth. In October 1971 the Controller General of Chile ruled that after appropriate deductions from the book value, no compensation for the nationalized properties was due Anaconda and Kennecott and that Anaconda owed Chile $68 million and Kennecott owed $310 million. This occurred after Chilean authorities deter-

tions of Chilean materials and is available from NACLA at P. O. Box 226, Berkeley, Calif. 94701. We have also relied on a major study by Victor Wallis, "Foreign Investment and Chilean Politics" (Columbia University Ph.D. dissertation, 1970) as well as numerous Chilean sources (see selections in Chapters 5, 21, and 24). Some of the ideas and facts herein were previously incorporated in Dale L. Johnson, John Pollock, and Jane Sweeney, "ITT and the CIA: The Making of a Foreign Policy," *The Progressive*, May 1972.

* An original article for this volume. Members of the Chile Research Group who contributed to this article are James Cockcroft, David Eisenhower, Henry Frundt, Dale Johnson, John Pollock, and Jane Sweeney.

mined that the two copper giants had repatriated $774 million in excess profits (computed on the basis of 12 per cent as a "fair return") between 1955 and 1970, and after other adjustments were made for faulty equipment, disrepair of the works, etc. On the other hand, Chile will probably assume debts of the local subsidiaries of Anaconda and Kennecott that amount to the approximate book value of the corporations' installations. Cerro Corporation, which began mining copper in a joint venture with the Chilean state in 1967, will be paid $33 million plus $3 million in interest for its investment. Cerro will be compensated in full because, unlike Anaconda and Kennecott, the smaller corporation had not repatriated excessive profits or engaged in other activities injurious to the mines or the national interest of Chile.

This article examines the operations of the foreign-owned copper corporations in relation to Chile's underdevelopment and the benefits that Chile may derive from nationalization of its principal natural resource. The analysis is based on a rather exhaustive review of materials on copper published in Chile, as well as on U. S. Government documents, statements by Anaconda and Kennecott, and studies by American researchers.

Copper, Chile's Wages of Toil

Copper has been Chile's principal export since the collapse of the world market for natural nitrates after the First World War. The benefits that accrue to Chile have been largely in the form of foreign exchange and tax revenues. Seventy-five per cent of Chile's foreign exchange and a fluctuating but substantial proportion of government revenues derive from copper exports. The enormous size of the operations—in recent years the mines have exported over six hundred thousand tons of copper annually—also involves large local expenditures for operating supplies. The mines employ about eighteen thousand workers, who, after long and bloody labor struggles, are relatively well paid. Kennecott Copper Corp. has pointed out some of the benefits from their Chilean operations:

The El Teniente mine, in its 67 years of operation, employed more than 100,000 people with economic, social and educational benefits to Chile. Chileans were trained to fill managerial, professional and technical positions throughout the Braden organization, in line with the Company policy to develop Chileans for every available position. (At the time of expropriation in 1971, out of a total of 10,000 employees, only two were U.S. citizens.)

Braden assisted in developing through its education and financing program a broad spectrum of independent Chilean entrepreneurial enterprises which provided materials and services to El Teniente and others throughout Chile.

For the employees who operated the mine at Sewell, high in the Andes, housing was constructed and maintained by the Company and provided at minimum rent. Streets, mostly stairways, were built; power and telephone lines were installed, and shops, churches, social clubs, schools, a gymnasium, a theater, and a highly efficient hospital were provided. Similar facilities were built in the towns of Caletones and Coya. The Company's investment in housing for its employees totaled over $45 million.[1]

Nevertheless, all these benefits are small in comparison to those derived by the American copper corporations.

[1] "Expropriation of the El Teniente Copper Mine by the Chilean Government," Kennecott Copper Corp., 1971, pp. 3–4.

Since their establishment in the early part of this century, Kennecott and Anaconda have, in our judgment, operated in the worst tradition of corporate imperialism:

1) The copper corporations have taken out billions of dollars in profits, with minimal reinvestment of earnings to the benefit of the Chilean economy.

Foreign capital began extracting copper in Chile early in the century with an investment of $3.5 million. Since that time, most of the profits—several billions of dollars —from the exploitation of Chile's principal natural resource have been transferred to the home offices of the U.S. corporations. Enough profits have been retained and reinvested to bring the present value of the mines, together with other investment capital, to about $600 million. Still, the basic truth is that foreign capital has appropriated the wealth of Chile, while reinvestments or new investments by the corporations have been a fraction of total profits. According to the U. S. Department of Commerce, in the period between 1953 and 1968 U.S. mining and smelting operations in Chile (about 90 per cent copper) earned $1,036 million, while new investments and reinvestment of profits together totaled only $71 million. The "Chileanization" agreements reached with the previous government called for new investments and required the companies to double production between 1966 and 1972. But the only increase was in corporate profits, which totaled $426 million for Anaconda and $198 million for Kennecott between 1965 and 1971. In 1967 and 1968 the return on U.S. investments in Chilean copper was 27 per cent and 26 per cent respectively. In 1969 Anaconda had profits on investments of 39.5 per cent and Kennecott 24.1 per cent.[2]

---

[2] Unless otherwise noted, the statistics cited are from Chilean sources. Facts cited in the literature on copper are sometimes inconsistent and we have tried to use our best judgment to resolve such inconsistencies. Two sources of fairly reliable data and inter-

The profits involved in copper assume great importance because the Chilean Government contends, referring back to Law No. 11,828 of 1955, that Chile has a right to define a fair rate of return on the investments of foreign capital that can be repatriated as profits. Considering a 12 per cent annual return on investments as fair, the Allende government has determined that Anaconda and Kennecott took out $774 million in excess profits between 1955 and 1970. This capital is generated by the exploitation of Chile's natural resources; it is logical that Chileans feel strongly that these huge sums should be utilized for national development rather than lining the pockets of wealthy stockholders, enabling the copper corporations to expand copper production elsewhere in the world to create competition for Chilean exports, or investing in the corporations' copper-fabricating activities located in the United States.

2) The corporations have exported partially refined copper to markets in the United States and Europe, resisted refining copper within Chile, and made no attempt to initiate the fabrication of copper products in Chile.

During the 1950s the Chilean Government insisted on smelting the ore and refining the copper in Chile. Up to 85 per cent of exports then were refined copper. By the 1960s only 40–45 per cent of exports were refined copper. The Chileans estimate that this cost them over $100 million a year during this period. In this, as in other instances, the U. S. Government backed corporate interests by imposing a tariff on the import of refined copper, with even higher duties on copper products. No duties are

pretation consistent with our own are North American Congress on Latin America, "They Took the Copper and Left Us the Holes," *NACLA Newsletter* V, September 1971, pp. 8–32, and André Gunder Frank and Gladys Díaz, "Los ladrones quieren indemnización," *Punto Final* No. 135, July 20, 1971.

levied on the kind of copper imported by Anaconda and
Kennecott for their fabricating plants located in the
United States. In its loss of the complete refining process,
Chile has also lost the industries developed from copper
processing, such as sulfuric acid, as well as valuable by-
products such as molybdenite, gold, and silver. This costs
Chile additional millions each year.

In general, the copper monopolies seek to realize profits
on all facets of production. Their Chilean subsidiaries
mine and concentrate ore, smelt and refine part of it in
Chile, and complete the refining in the United States,
and then sell in European markets or to American subsidiaries such as Kennecott's Chase Brass & Copper Co.
and Anaconda's American Brass Company or Anaconda
Wire & Cable Co. Anaconda manufactures copper products in seventeen different plants in the United States.
There is very little manufacturing activity using copper in
Chile, and none by Anaconda or Kennecott.

3) The copper corporations have controlled and manipulated the price of copper to the detriment of Chile.

Until the nationalization, Chile had no effective control
over the marketing of copper. It was sold to the corporations' subsidiaries or to established clients in Europe. The
price at which Chilean copper was sold, export taxes com-
puted, and foreign exchange earned was a "producer's
price," set by the corporations. This price was consistently
lower during the 1960s than the price quoted on the London Metals Exchange, which roughly reflects world supply and demand for the metal. The difference between
the producer's price and what Chile could have gotten for
some of its copper in the best world markets has cost the
Chilean economy very dearly. The U. S. Government has
also acted to deprive Chile of its rightful earnings from
copper. In 1966, for example, when the Vietnam build-up
was well under way, the United States persuaded Chile
to sell ninety thousand tons of copper for the government's

strategic reserves at a price of $.36 per pound when the producer's price was $.42 and the world market price was $.60 per pound. Such generosity on the part of Chile's Christian Democratic government was rewarded with an AID loan. The U. S. Government also stockpiles copper and sells it in times of supply shortages to keep prices from rising. A rise of one cent in copper prices means anywhere from $9 to $15 million for Chile. During World War II and the Korean War, the U. S. Government fixed the price of copper at artificially low rates. This hit Chile hard, but the American copper corporations were much less affected, since what they lost in lower metal prices they gained back in reduced raw-material cost for their fabricating operations.

4) The companies have subverted every effort by successive Chilean governments to gain reasonable advantages from the foreign exploitation of national resources.

During 1952–55 Chile tried to gain greater benefits by requiring more refining in Chile, by widening markets, by imposing customs duties on imports used in mining operations, by maintaining special exchange rates to gain more dollars from local operations of the corporations, and by increasing taxes on copper exports. The response of the copper monopolies to this was to hold back production in Chile and to increase their activities in other countries. As a consequence, Chile's share in the world production of the metal dropped from 21 per cent in 1948 to 11.6 per cent by 1953–54.

In 1955, "New Deal" copper legislation was enacted, which attempted to stimulate the corporations to increase production by lowering taxes and by authorizing a more favorable dollar exchange rate for *pesos*. Production did increase, but the benefits to Chile did not.

By 1964 an entirely new approach to copper was the principal issue in the presidential election, which pitted Salvador Allende, candidate of the socialist Left advocating nationalization of the mines, against Eduardo Frei, the Christian Democratic candidate with a program of "Chileanization." After Frei's victory, several mines were Chileanized through purchase of 51 per cent of Kennecott's El Teniente, 25 per cent of Anaconda's new La Exótica mine, and 25 per cent of Cerro's Rio Blanco mine. Anaconda at first refused to sell shares to its Chilean subsidiaries. *Business Week* magazine tells why: ". . . [Anaconda] refused to sell an interest in the Chuquicamata and El Salvador mines. The reason was obvious: A former Anaconda employee says that production costs at these mines amounted to about 18¢ per lb. for copper that was bringing 60¢ on the London Metal Exchange. In the U.S., copper costing 30¢ per lb. to produce sold at that time for 35¢."[3] In 1969—after wide recognition of the lack of benefits from Chileanization, Anaconda's failure to increase production as agreed and other activities of the corporation—the Frei government made a last, desperate attempt to remedy the situation through purchase of 51 per cent of Anaconda's Chuquicamata and El Salvador mines.

The principal aim of Chileanization was to increase benefits to Chile by increasing production. The companies were to double production by 1972 in return for decreased taxation and other advantages to the companies and new investment capital provided by Chilean stock purchases, government loans, and government-guaranteed loans negotiated with the Export-Import Bank and other U.S. financial institutions.

Incredible as it may seem, a new, $579-million investment of borrowed capital between 1966 and 1970 failed to increase production significantly. The corporations accumulated $632 million in debts without investing any of their own capital, in spite of the fact that Anaconda's and

[3] "An Ex-Banker Treats Copper's Sickest Giant," *Business Week*, February 19, 1972, p. 54.

Kennecott's profits were increased substantially by Chileanization and rising copper prices.

President Allende has indicated that Chile will probably assume the debts incurred by the companies in the expansion program. Chile made the first installment, of $5.8 million, on a total of $92.7 million in notes to Kennecott. This occurred after Kennecott obtained a court order in New York blocking the bank accounts of fourteen Chilean agencies in the United States and after the Chilean Government discounted about $8 million of the total debt on the grounds that this amount was not "usefully invested" by Kennecott. Payments on the other debts incurred by the subsidiaries of Anaconda and Kennecott may depend upon whether the United States continues to exercise economic pressures against Chile. There is also increased questioning of the justice of assuming the debts in Chile as the full implications of the bad deal given to the country by the corporations are realized. The Controller General of Chile has also determined that Anaconda and Kennecott owe Chile $388.5 million, which the government will be unable to collect unless it refuses to assume the corporations' foreign debt obligations. Moreover, the suspension of U.S. aid and dollar credits, as well as the drastic decline in copper prices since 1970, may make it difficult if not impossible to repay these debts under the existing terms.

5) The mines have been left in a condition of general disrepair, creating production problems and the need for large expenditures to get the mines in shape.

In 1971 a team of ten engineers from a French technical consulting firm carefully surveyed the mines and prepared a report on their condition. The report, corroborated by a team of Soviet engineers, spelled out in detail an appalling picture of neglect, mismanagement, and corporate irresponsibility. The mines, especially Anaconda's Chuquicamata, exhibited glaring deficiencies. These

include poor construction of new plants, involving use of
inferior materials, badly planned roads, and failure to
provide for adequate water; negligent installation and
maintenance of equipment; widespread unsafe and un-
hygienic working conditions; sabotage of future production caused by such practices as bulldozing earth on top
of deposits yet to be mined; and inferior or non-existent
training of Chilean technicians.

Historic Justice and the Vested Interests

The five points indicated above are not a complete in-
ventory of the means by which the copper monopolies,
acting as imperialist corporations and enjoying the support
of the U. S. Government,[4] have essentially sacked the
national wealth of Chile for sixty years. Nevertheless the
facts cited seem sufficient to justify nationalization of the
mines. It is a matter of historic justice for a poor country
long exploited and manipulated by monopolistic giants.

Moreover, no compensation is due. In fact the finding
of the Controller General that the copper corporations
owe Chile $388.5 million seems to be of reasonable mag-
nitude in view of the facts of the case.

It is important for American readers to understand that
both the nationalization and the absence of compensation
by the Allende government were extremely popular acts
among the Chilean people, including many who sharply
opposed other policies of the nationalist and socialist
government. The method of compensation proposed by
Allende was modified and approved before incorporation
into the constitutional amendment by opposition political
forces traditionally friendly to the copper companies and

[4] The generous government support of these private corporations
continues: the Internal Revenue Service has authorized Anaconda
to write off its Chilean properties as an "extra-ordinary loss."
Business Week noted that ". . . the company will not be paying
U.S. income taxes for up to ten years." (Feb. 19, 1972, p. 53)

the United States. Moreover, the Allende government was extremely careful to follow Chilean law and legal procedure to the letter. The nationalization also conformed to the United Nations' resolution on the "inalienable right of all countries to exercise permanent sovereignty over their natural resources in the interest of their national development." This resolution of the 21st Session of the General Assembly also "confirms that the exploitation of natural resources in each country shall always be conducted in accordance with its national laws and regulations."

Nevertheless the copper corporations and the U. S. Government both demand that Chile conform to the only international law that private business and our government seem to recognize, namely, that "prompt, adequate, and effective" compensation be made for expropriated properties. This demand ignores the clear intent of the United Nations resolution on nationalizations and implies that the value of properties held abroad by American corporations is what the corporations say they are worth. Anaconda Copper stated, "In a clear violation of international law, the new Marxist government of Chile has stolen $1.2 billion worth of mines and properties from the Anaconda Company."[5] (The book value of Anaconda's mines was $415 million, according to the company; other sources indicate $200 million. The $1.2 billion cited includes unexploited mineral deposits.) A "white paper" issued by Kennecott used more moderate language: "The right of a sovereign nation, in accordance with accepted principles of international law, to expropriate private property, is beyond dispute. However, the same principles which secure the right of a nation to expropriate, obligate it to make prompt, adequate and effective compensation for the property."[6] However, Ken-

[5] "Confiscation of Anaconda Properties by the Chilean Government," Anaconda Company, 1971, p. 1.

[6] Kennecott, op. cit., p. 8.

necott had the audacity to claim that minerals of the subsoil of Chile belong to foreign corporations and to state that Chile's claim to sovereignty over these unexploited mineral deposits is in violation of international law:

> The Chilean Constitution now specifically authorizes compensation for the related facilities of El Teniente.
> While compensation for these facilities could be substantial, the maximum amount which might be paid for them cannot make up for the expropriation of the mineral resources of El Teniente, compensation for which is not authorized.
> It is clear, therefore, that the expropriation contravenes accepted principles of international law.[7]

It is understandable, of course, that the corporations are upset. For many decades they have extracted enormous profits from their Chilean operations. Anaconda was particularly hard-hit, as the corporation had about 17 per cent of its total investment there and derived about 80 per cent of its profits from Chilean mines (1969 figures). The Rockefeller interests sent in one of their top men from Chase Manhattan Bank in an effort to put the corporation, which also had problems with its U.S. operations and management, back on firmer footing. Even more serious to the copper giants than the loss of their properties and future profits from Chilean mines is the threat of economic nationalism to the prevailing structure of the world copper industry. The industry is made up of about ten firms, mainly U.S. based, and has a highly integrated structure. What this means is that each corporation, in a sector where a handful of giants monopolize world markets, has a complex set of interrelated operations: different divisions of the same company mine and con-

[7] Kennecott, op. cit., p. 8.

centrate ore, smelt, refine, fabricate, and sell. The structure is highly monopolistic; of the ten multinationals in copper, half that number produce most of the copper, fabricate the bulk of copper products, and control the markets. Moreover, four (possibly others) of the giants of the industry are controlled by two corporate interest groups. Anaconda is under the wing of the Stillman-Rockefellers, of the First National City Bank group. The other wing of the Rockefeller family, working out of the Chase Manhattan Bank, seems to have some influence over Anaconda, as the new chief officer of Anaconda is from Chase Manhattan. The First National City interest group also influences Kennecott, which is more directly in the domain of the Morgans. The Morgans own a large bloc of stock in two more of the copper giants, Phelps Dodge and American Smelting & Refining.[8] Cerro Corporation was founded by J. P. Morgan in 1902.

The reaction of the U. S. Government to the Chilean nationalizations has been to back the corporations by word and deed. President Nixon issued a "tough" policy statement on nationalizations of corporate properties abroad, and severe economic sanctions—credit cutoffs and aid suspensions—have been employed against Chile (see our subsequent article on U.S. policy). Since such sanctions contravene United Nations and Organization of American States principles of non-intervention, it is the United States that stands in violation of international law. Such violations, of course, are nothing new for the United States, which has consistently flaunted practically every international law on the books for many years with unilateral international monetary and trade policies and

8 The Corporate Information Center of the National Council of Churches has provided an informative study of Kennecott: Curt Danforth and Bob Huie, "A Preliminary Profile on Kennecott, Inc.," Corporate Information Center, 1971.

economic pressures and military interventions throughout Latin America and Southeast Asia.

Foreign Dependence and National Development

Corporation executives, government officials, and many other Americans believe that foreign investment is indispensable for development in Third World countries. The nationalization of foreign enterprise is consequently viewed as an irrational political act that will have adverse economic effects. Although this is no more than a rationalization for the promotion of the interest of private foreign capital, it is adhered to as a rigid dogma.

Nationalists in Chile and other underdeveloped countries, on the other hand, contend that development requires national control of both natural resources and the decisions as to how and for whose benefit those resources are to be exploited. Proceeds from the exploitation of resources, they argue, should be retained within the economy and used to reduce the excessive dependence upon primary exports that historically has been the key structural element in the development of underdevelopment. These arguments bear considerable merit.

In the history of Chilean underdevelopment, copper has made the economy dependent upon primary production and has structurally thwarted development of other sectors of the economy. By controlling its own resources, Chile will be able to retain the substantial profits from copper production within the country for investment in other sectors, which will produce goods and services to meet the needs of the Chilean people.

The Chilean economy had been essentially stagnant for seventeen years preceding the assumption of power by the Popular Unity government. The nationalization of copper is certainly no guarantee of economic development, but it is a necessary condition for development. Controlling its prime national resource, Chile will have the opportunity to create additional economic activity, increase employment, and earn greater foreign exchange by fabricating and exporting copper bars, wire, and other products rather than semi-refined copper. Moreover, Chile will be able to market its copper wherever the best price is offered.

All these benefits to Chile assume, of course, that the multinational copper monopolies are not able to squeeze Chile out of world markets. Certainly Chilean copper will no longer find its way to U.S. markets. American corporations will probably now expand production and open new mines in areas "secure" from the threats of economic nationalism.[9] World production of copper already exceeds demand, and markets will not expand very fast over the next few years, so if production is increased sufficiently in secure areas, the corporations may be able to win back their Western European customers, which Chile assumed from Anaconda and Kennecott upon take-over of sales operations. Ominous words have already been sounded in the innermost sanctuary of American corporate power, the Council on Foreign Relations. The following frank comment in the organization's closed meeting of December 14, 1970, was recorded in the minutes and attributed to William E. Butler of Chase Manhattan Bank: "Mr. Butler took exception to the example of Chile's copper obviating a boycott by the United States. He said that Chile will soon become a residual supplier of copper."[10]

[9] Considered "secure areas" are the United States, Canada, Australia, Puerto Rico, and perhaps Mexico. However, U.S. interests are pursuing "technical discussions" with the governments of the U.S.S.R. and Eastern European countries with respect to joint operations with U.S. investors.

[10] "Liberated Documents: New Imperial Strategy for Latin America," NACLA's Latin America and Empire Report VII, November 1971, p. 15. The Council on Foreign Relations, made up mainly of top corporate officers, high government officials, and

We interpret Mr. Butler's statement to mean that the strategy of Rockefeller and/or other copper interests may be to deprive Chile of its copper markets. This strategy appears to fit Harvard economist Theodore Moran's theory of the behavior of oligopolistic producers of primary materials when they are faced with economic nationalism. Moran notes:

> One can predict, then, how multinational corporations will react when faced by the growing wave of economic nationalism. The corporations will try to shift the bulk of the profits generated within the system to a stage over which they still have firm control (processing, fabricating), and they will try to shift the burden of the uncertainties and risk in the industry onto the new "independents."[11]

Moran comments specifically on copper:

> As the international copper oligopoly becomes more diluted, more and more of the "regular" sales or long-term arrangements will be covered between the large corporate producers and their major fabricators or industrial consumers while the nationalists' share will be treated as a spill-over market—subject to great fluctuations in volume and price. Onto the nationalistic independents will be shifted the burden of risk and instability for the international industry as a whole.[12]

---

academic experts is highly influential in the formation of U.S. foreign policy. The significance of the CFR is treated in our article "The Low Profile Swings a Big Stick," in Chapter 2.

[11] Theodore H. Moran, "New Deal or Raw Deal in Raw Materials," *Foreign Policy,* Winter 1971–72, p. 126.

[12] Ibid., pp. 131–32.

But the Chileans see their copper as a key element in overcoming underdevelopment, and they are resolutely determined to protect and promote their markets. The needs and aspirations of the Chilean people, as of the peoples in all of Latin America, have long been denied and thwarted by their inability to break out of the structure of foreign dependence and underdevelopment and by their inability to make their own development decisions. In Chile these decisions will no longer be made in the board rooms of corporations based in the United States. They will now be made by people who know what underdevelopment means because they experience it, by Chileans with a vision of a better future, by Chileans who are determined to develop along lines of their own choosing.

CHAPTER 2

U. S. Policy in the Making:
Chile, to Accommodate or Crush

THE LOW PROFILE SWINGS A BIG STICK*

DAVID EISENHOWER WITH DALE L. JOHNSON

United States relations with Chile since the assumption of power by the Popular Unity government provide a convenient opportunity to analyze the content and institutional forces behind the proclaimed "low profile" approach which the Nixon administration has adopted as the main component of U.S.-Latin American policy.

United States policy toward Chile since September 1970 has developed through three distinct stages. From September 1970 to July 1971 the government officially pursued a "wait and see" approach. A second stage, from roughly July 1971 to December 1971, consisted of a gradual tightening of the economic screws in an effort to coerce Chile and create economic difficulties for the country. The third stage, the "big stick," still prevails and was symbolized by President Nixon's "no nonsense" policy on nationalization of properties of U.S. corporations operating abroad, proclaimed in January 1972 and concretized with stiff economic sanctions against Chile.

All three stages are consistent with the Nixon adminis-

* An original article for this volume based upon work by the Chile Research Group of Rutgers University. David Eisenhower is a graduate student in sociology at Rutgers University.

tration's general "low profile" approach to U.S.-Latin American relations. The low profile is based on a conception of a "mature partnership" between the United States and its southern good neighbors, a limited tolerance for Latin American nationalism, a shifting of some of the panoply of coercive powers underlying international relations from the U. S. Government to international institutions, and an avoidance of the military interventions that the United States has historically relied on to impose its will upon Latin American dependencies. Our analysis of Chilean-U.S. relations from September 1970 to May 1972 leads us to conclude that the "low profile" in the end is based on a "big stick" exercised through economic and diplomatic sanctions and covert subversive operations against nations that pursue their economic independence. In the case of Chile, the Nixon administration and the constellation of corporate interests behind U.S. policy have adopted a course of action that may have the short-run consequence of creating grave economic difficulties and political turmoil within Chile. The ultimate consequence of this policy may be to precipitate civil war in Chile.

The first "wait and see" stage actually had two thrusts. At the level of official government policy, a cool but "correct" diplomacy prevailed, with the exception of a few veiled threats and diplomatic affronts apparently meant to show disapproval of the direction of the new government and to warn Chile that relations could go downhill if the country did not behave properly in the eyes of the United States. The veiled threats consisted of Nixon's denunciation of Chile's early diplomatic recognition of Cuba as a "challenge to the Inter-American System" and the government's Export-Import Bank classification of Chile as a "poor risk." The diplomatic affronts consisted of such measures as Nixon's failure to send Allende the customary congratulatory message upon his election and Henry Kissinger's cancellation of a scheduled visit to Valparaíso by the nuclear carrier *Enterprise*.

A second thrust to the low profile, however, developed immediately upon receiving news of Salvador Allende's plurality in the September 4, 1970, election. This consisted of covert activities by the CIA and behind-the-scenes efforts by one U.S. corporation, ITT, to pressure the U. S. Government and other American corporations operating in Chile to prevent Allende from taking office on November 3, 1970. There is evidence that the CIA was in contact with elements within the Chilean right wing and Armed Forces who evolved plans to maneuver Allende out of this electoral victory, even to plunge the country into economic chaos and create a situation propitious for a military intervention. The weight of the evidence indicates that the State Department, Henry Kissinger, and President Nixon politely listened to ITT's concerns but were somewhat resistant to the corporation's pressures for immediate strong action. Nevertheless the CIA continued its operations, and the State Department has not denied sending September 17, 1970, instructions to Ambassador Korry "to do all possible—short of a Dominican Republic-type action—to keep Allende from taking power."

The second stage, consisting of suspension of economic aid and credits, was anticipated as early as March 1971 with the cutoff of shipments of foodstuffs under the previous aid program and the holding up of credits for "review," while officially denying that Chile's loan requests had been disapproved. The economic pressures became serious, however, after Chile nationalized the Anaconda and Kennecott copper mines, in July 1971. Shortly thereafter the Export-Import Bank held up credits to Chile to purchase three Boeing commercial jets "pending a clarification in policies toward foreign investment." No credits have since been granted, or are likely to be granted, by the Export-Import Bank to Chile to finance imports of U.S. goods. With measures applied subsequently by the U. S. Government, private banks, and international lenders, this amounts to a *de facto* embargo on the import of U.S. goods. (Chile's industrial economy is highly dependent upon U.S. technology and replacement parts.)

During this period, economic sanctions included such measures as the closure of credit from private U.S. banks and the blocking of loans for petrochemical and agricultural development, as well as the denial of a $50-million request for earthquake aid, by the Inter-American Development Bank. By October 1971 all U.S. aid programs (except military), which had previously been held up for review, were officially suspended. Also in October the newly appointed ambassador, Nathaniel Davis, arrived in Santiago. Davis is ex-ambassador to Guatemala, where he oversaw all forms of assistance to Guatemala's repressive, right-wing regime. One suspects that the appointment of an ambassador with experience in dealing with and strengthening counterrevolutionary regimes is one indication of what the Nixon administration anticipates for Chile.

By the end of 1971 a state of virtual economic warfare existed between the United States and Chile. Chile is determined to gain economic independence and maintain its national sovereignty, while the strategy of the United States is to attempt to paralyze the Chilean economy through external pressures. Apparently the government believes that the economic difficulties in Chile will become so overwhelming that the Allende government will be overthrown. In December 1971 presidential aides Robert Finch and Herbert Klein returned from a tour of

Latin America to comment that "Allende won't last long."

As long as the Allende government remains in power we can anticipate a close co-ordination between the U. S. Government, private corporate interests, and the World Bank, International Monetary Fund, and Inter-American Development Bank to effect a policy of the "big stick." Minimally, this will involve application of constant diplomatic pressures and maximum feasible economic sanctions, such as efforts, already in motion, to undermine Chile's position as a leading world producer of copper (see our previous analysis of copper nationalization).

This paper will examine the development of U.S.-Chilean policy through these three stages in terms of the institutional means, which we term "official conspiracies," by which "multinational" corporations shape the working assumptions and give concrete direction to U.S. foreign policy. Throughout each stage of the "low profile" there have been two general policy lines pursued by different actors in the political drama. On the one hand, a "hard line" has been consistently pushed by certain corporations with immediate vested interests at stake such as ITT, and certain government agencies, specifically the CIA and the Department of the Treasury. On the other hand, a "softer line" has been pushed by corporate interests with a broader vision (IBEC, for example), the U.S. press, and the Department of State. The policies actively pursued during the first two stages seemed to be a compromise between these two positions. In the process of consensus formation among the concerned parties, the third stage of U.S.-Chile policy evolved to represent a commitment closer to the hard-line position. The emergent policy can only be considered "low profile" in that an embargo or a blockade has not been mandated or troops dispatched.

We begin with an analysis of the reactions to Chilean nationalism and socialism by U.S. corporations with substantial investments in the country.

Corporate Reaction

The "ITT-Chile papers," staff memos[1] that escaped the busy teeth of International Telephone & Telegraph paper shredders to find their way into the syndicated column of Jack Anderson, reveal the details of abortive plans to prevent the Marxist government of Salvador Allende from taking office in Chile. The principals involved in the scheming were ITT, the CIA, the American ambassador, and rightist elements of the Chilean upper class and the Army, with Eduardo Frei, ex-President of Chile, and White House and State Department people also implicated.

—That the CIA plotted with "select members of the Chilean Armed Forces in an attempt to have them lead some sort of uprising"[2] is not in itself very shocking, since the CIA with past operations in Cuba, the Congo, Indonesia, Guatemala, Laos, and Brazil, among other places, is commonly known, or justifiably suspected, to be involved in such clandestine activities.

—That the American ambassador, Edward Korry, received a message from the State Department giving him a "green light," that is, "maximum authority to do all possible—short of a Dominican Republic-type action—to

[1] The papers obtained from ITT confidential files and released by Jack Anderson are available in their entirety from the North American Congress on Latin America (NACLA): "Secret Memos from ITT," *NACLA's Latin America and Empire Report*, VI, April 1972. ITT board and executive committee member John McCone, former director of the CIA, has substantiated the authenticity of the memos in question, calling them routine "staff" memos (*Business Week*, April 1, 1972, p. 23).

[2] Memo dated October 9, 1970, from William Merriam, ITT vice-president, to John McCone; See NACLA, op. cit.

keep Allende from taking power,"[3] does make one pause,
but mainly to ask why the military solution to troublesome
situations (Lebanon, Vietnam, Cambodia, Laos, Dominican Republic, etc.) was ruled out.

—That ITT personnel were so actively engaged in attempts to both influence U.S. policy and shape Chilean
events, however, is a different matter, raising some serious
and far-reaching questions about the nature of corporate
influence on policy in general which, in the process of
being raised, immediately cast doubt on the officially held
distinction between the private and public sectors.

As the following examples of ITT's activities demonstrate, both the questions and the doubt are well founded.
ITT:

> 1) contacted Henry Kissinger's staff to convey "deep
> concern" about the developing situation in Chile "not
> only from the standpoint of our [ITT] heavy invest-
> ment but also because of the threat to the entire hemi-
> sphere";
> 2) sent a letter to Henry Kissinger advising him that
> after "serious consideration" of the implications of
> events in Chile, particularly their potential impact on
> foreign investment, it was ITT's conviction that "the
> present moment [represented] a most expedient time
> to *reappraise* and *strengthen* U.S. policy in Latin
> America";
> 3) made direct contact with clandestine CIA opera-
> tives in Chile concerning the Agency's plans to pre-
> vent Allende from taking office;
> 4) made it known that the company was "prepared

[3] Memo dated September 17, 1970, to ITT vice-president E. J.
Gerrity from two ITT operatives in Santiago. The substance of
this memo has not been denied by the State Department (New
York *Times,* March 24, 1972, p. 7).

to assist financially in sums up to seven figures" in any plan the government might have to deal with the Chilean situation;

5) tried to "get other American companies aroused over the fate of their investments and join [ITT] in pre-election efforts"—efforts that included attempts to persuade "American business to cooperate in some way to bring on economic chaos" in Chile, producing the conditions that would then trigger the military coup the CIA was apparently working on;

6) presented the company's case to "friends in Congress" and directly to President Nixon and Secretary of State Rogers to arouse their sympathy and support for a "tough" response.

Thanks to Jack Anderson and his informant(s), then, we not only have a suggestion of what initial U.S. reaction and intentions were vis à vis Chile's nationalism and incipient socialism, but we also have a rare peek at the behind-the-scenes maneuverings of a powerful corporate interest. This certainly lends substance to the thesis that U.S. private enterprise with government support engages in what the Washington *Post,* after reviewing the ITT-Chile papers, conceded to be "aggressive economic imperialism abroad. . . ."

The ITT-Chile papers also reveal that consensus and concerted action among the different corporations concerned and government agencies was not entirely present. ITT did not work from behind a united front of U.S. investors in 1970. GM, Ford, Bank of America, and other U.S. corporations apparently refused at the time to go along with ITT's plan to induce "economic chaos" in Chile. Not that ITT was alone in acting. Anaconda is said to have helped finance a pre-election "campaign of terror" and undertook, with Kennecott, actions amounting to sabotage in the copper mines. Both Anaconda and Kennecott issued sternly worded "white papers" stating their positions on nationalization. Ralston Purina sharply cut back production at its plant, and the U.S. firm NIBSA shut down its operation the day preceding Allende's inauguration. A representative of NIBCO, parent company of NIBSA, was accused of suggesting an "Indonesian solution" (killing of all Communists) for Chile. Ford shut down in May 1972, throwing six hundred workers off the job until the state intervened to reopen the plant. A consulting firm for business information/intelligence, World Wide Information Service, prepared a report on Chile for its clients in early 1971. The report gave accurate information on the Allende government's progress, then concluded that Chile was on its way toward becoming a Communist state that would experience great problems.[4]

Just as among the various corporate interests, there was dissension among elements of government officialdom concerning the appropriate official response. Assistant Secretary of State for Latin American Affairs Charles Meyer and National Security Adviser to the President Henry Kissinger were officially cool to ITT-CIA maneuvers, while Treasury Secretary Connolly was said to be pushing for an immediate hard-line response.

Nevertheless, by the end of 1971 a consensus among private corporate interests had apparently been reached and the U. S. Government had shifted its official policy from "wait and see" to the "big stick." To understand what lies behind this achieved consensus and policy shift it is necessary to understand established interconnections between private interests and public policy. Analysis of

[4] World Wide Information Service, Inc., *Chile 1971* (660 First Ave., New York); for more details on the activities of other U.S. firms, see Chapter 5.

the content and sponsors of policy can proceed fruitfully by focusing on "official conspiracies," that is, on the formal, open, routine, institutionalized arrangements linking business to government.

Such arrangements have been found to proceed from organizational forums within which various policy alternatives and directions are debated, developed, and disseminated to concerned parties in business and government. The result is that a semblance of policy consensus among the nominally competing corporate interests has an opportunity to emerge, with the further result that united actions may then be undertaken.

Official Conspiracies

"Official conspiracies" are those institutionalized ways in which corporate interests shape and guide policies of the U. S. Government. They exist to formulate and disseminate general definitions of policy; that is, they deal with the underlying concepts, which have in the past given birth to such programs and institutions as the Marshall Plan, the World Bank, foreign-aid programs, international banking and monetary policy, "containment" policy, and more recently the "low profile" approach to Latin American policy. Stated yet another way, they furnish the ideological background that in turn provides those *directly* in the actual policy-making apparatus (the National Security Council, the Council on International Economic Policy, the Departments of State, Treasury, and Commerce, etc.) with the critical assumptions that help guide major as well as day-to-day decisions.

The main apparatus of official conspiracies consists of organizations controlled by members of the corporate elite class that sponsor research, commission studies, publish influential journals, issue reports, engage in formal and informal dialogues with government officials, formulate policy guidelines, see that their men are appointed to key government posts, etc.[5] Such organizations dealing with foreign policy include:

——Corporate-controlled research-planning, advising, and report-issuing *public affairs groups:* the Council on Foreign Relations (CFR), the Committee for Economic Development (CED), and the National Planning Association (NPA).

——*Businessmen's organizations:* the Chamber of Commerce (both domestic and international), the Council of the Americas, the National Foreign Trade Council (NFTC), the Emergency Committee for American Trade (ECAT), the Agribusiness Council, Inc., the International Economic Policy Association (IEPA).

——*Executively commissioned task forces, committees, and missions:* Recent ones include the Commerce Committee for the Alliance for Progress (The Grace Report, 1963; Chairman, W. R. Grace); The Task Force on International Development (Peterson Report, 1970, chaired by former President of Bank of America); the Committee to Strengthen the Security of the Free World (Clay Report, 1963); the Advisory Committee on Private Enterprise in Foreign Aid (the Watson Report, 1965, chaired by Chairman of IBM); the Commission on International Trade and Investment Policy (Williams Report, 1971, chaired by head of the Finance Committee, IBM); and the U. S. Presidential Mission for the Western Hemisphere (Rockefeller Report, 1969).

——*Citizen* (read business) *advisory councils and*

[5] See William Domhoff's two works *The Higher Circles* (New York: Vintage Books, 1970) and *Who Rules America?* (Englewood Cliffs, N.J.: Prentice-Hall, 1967), and David Horowitz (ed.), *Corporations and the Cold War* (New York: Monthly Review Press, 1969).

committees: Those are associated with such agencies as the Export-Import Bank, the Agency for International Development, the Overseas Private Investment Corp., the Inter-American Development Bank, Treasury, State, Commerce, etc.

——*U.S. Representatives to U.N.-sponsored panels:* the 1969 panel on Foreign Investment in Developing Countries, which included Emilio Collado (Standard Oil), David Rockefeller (Chase Manhattan), and David Meads (IBEC).

——*Research Institutes:* the RAND Corporation, the Twentieth Century Fund, the Brookings Institution, the Hudson Institute, and various university "think tanks" at places such as Harvard, MIT, Stanford, and Columbia.

——*Foundations:* Ford, Rockefeller, Carnegie, and others.

"Official conspiracies" are taken for granted. That is, they appear to be very natural phenomena. And in fact, what could be more natural than a chairman, president, or vice-president from a large corporation or partner from a corporate law firm taking some time off from his business duties to perform his "civic duty." In the context of American society nothing is more natural. However, the upshot of such a common practice is that almost all official conspiracies are engaged in by men who share essentially the same "life-space" and "world view," the former generally restricted to corporate structures (multinational corporate structures especially) and the latter restricted to the ideology of corporate private enterprise. Hence the perspective brought into their civic duties is overwhelmingly one that consciously or unconsciously considers the world in dire need and desirous (except where there are "irrational" strains of nationalism) of American corporate investment and technology. Their frame of reference allows them to assume that their own private interests are the national interest.

The impact of official conspiracies can be illustrated by examining the composition and influence of a recent presidentially appointed commission, the Task Force on International Development (the Peterson Report).[6]

The Task Force was appointed by President Nixon in 1969 and submitted its report and policy recommendations in March 1970. Rudolf Peterson, former President of the Bank of America, chaired the Task Force. He was joined by top corporate officials such as David Rockefeller of Chase Manhattan Bank (who is also an official of a host of other corporations and policy-making organizations); presidents or board chairmen of corporations such as H. J. Heinz, Levi Strauss, Deere & Company, and Encyclopaedia Britannica; and partners in key corporate law firms. The Task Force was filled in by such persons as Terence Cardinal Cooke, Archbishop of New York; a past president of the American Bar Association; a retired general now with Research Analysis Corporation; and two experts on foreign affairs from Harvard University.

The major themes of the Peterson Report revolved around the "depoliticization" and "multilateralization" of foreign assistance. It recommended the establishment of quasi-public agencies similar in structure to the Overseas Private Investment Corporation (OPIC was established in early 1970 at the bidding of big business' Senator Jacob Javits in order to promote and insure U.S. private foreign investment). These agencies are to replace the Agency for International Development's machinery, over which Congress exercised some control. The idea behind

[6] *U. S. International Economic Policy in an Interdependent World.* Report to the President by the Commission on International Trade and Investment Policy (Washington D.C.: Government Printing Office, July 1971).

the quasi-public agencies advocated—the International Development Bank, the International Development Institute, OPIC—is that their businesslike operations, which would include corporate-dominated boards of directors and advisory councils, would make them relatively autonomous and outside the purview of Congress, thus supposedly depoliticizing foreign assistance. Regarding the "multilateralization" of aid, the report urged that steps be taken calculated to lessen the identification of assistance exclusively with the United States, thus lowering its profile, and to spread the risk, costs, and responsibility for aid, which is so often political in nature, lessening in the process the chances of the United States being charged with intervention. Intervention, of course, would still take place, but now behind the multilateral coloration of international agencies. In reality, this multilateralization does not alter U.S. hegemony over the direction and intent of aid (as this paper will demonstrate); it simply gives the appearance of doing so.[7]

Departures from particular policies normally involve studies and discussion among corporate officials in different policy organizations over a period of several years. This was the case in the shift on foreign-aid policies recommended by the Peterson Report. In the Preface, Peterson gratefully acknowledged the influence of reports dealing with aid issued by other corporate-elite missions and organizations: the Rockefeller Mission on the Americas, the Perkins Committee, the Committee for Economic Development, and the National Planning Association reports.

Policy recommendations contained in such reports normally end up as U.S. policy. President Nixon said of the Peterson Task Force:

[7] See also Michael Hudson, "The Political Economy of Foreign Aid," in Hudson and Dennis Goulet, *The Myth of Aid* (New York: IDOC, 1971).

The Task Force on International Development . . .
undertook a comprehensive assessment of the conditions affecting our foreign assistance program and proposed new and creative approaches for the years
ahead. Its report provides the basis for proposals which
I am making today.[8]

While Congress did not implement the Administration's
aid program in 1971, it will again be pushed and implemented unless Congress takes the nearly unprecedented
step of resisting corporate programs strongly backed by
the Executive. Aid programs are unusual in the foreign-
relations field in that Congress usually has little or no say
in foreign affairs. Normally policies proceed from corporate policy organizations directly to the highest levels of
the Executive branch, where corporate interests have their
carefully selected agents. Henry Kissinger was groomed
for his present job as national security adviser, for example, by the Rockefeller family and through active
membership in a principal corporate policy organization,
the Council on Foreign Relations; Secretary of State
Rogers has a long history of involvement with corporate
policy organizations; Charles Meyer came to his present
job as Assistant Secretary of State for Latin American Affairs from Sears Roebuck, United Fruit Company, and
other multinational corporations with extensive Latin
American operations.

The new corporate strategy on aid bears on U.S.-Chil-
ean relations in two interrelated ways. The Task Force
recommendations on multilateralizing aid fit into the "low
profile" strategy, while U.S. aid and control of international sources of financing are the principal means by
which the big stick is brought down on Chile's head. For

[8] "Foreign Assistance Act of 1971," *Weekly Compilation of
Presidential Documents* (Washington, D.C.: U. S. Government
Printing Office, February 9, 1972).

Chile and Latin America generally, the low profile in fact is an effort to make the big stick heavier, at least in matters that do not require a military solution. This is to be accomplished by transferring the power inherent in control of credit and dollar flows from the U. S. Government to international agencies controlled by U.S. corporations and their European business allies.

Multilateralizing aid is one aspect of an attempt by U.S. corporations to maneuver the government into a posture in which it is not so readily apparent that U.S. foreign relations are a direct function of corporate desires for a "free world" (e.g., a world safe from the forces of nationalism and socialism), in which the corporations can expand their operations. The virtue of this is that the U.S. business interests that control the international institutions charged with funneling aid and credits to Third World nations on a businesslike basis would have tighter control of American taxpayers' money than ever before and could use it to pursue their ends as they define them, while the American government would be freer of charges of paternalism, attaching "political strings" to offers of aid, and using foreign assistance to bully other nations.

Chile became fully enmeshed in this multilateralization of credit and aid just as the new pattern was emerging. The Popular Unity government inherited a debt contracted by previous governments (part of it to finance U.S. investments there) of about $3 billion, divided between loans from the U. S. Agency for International Development, Export-Import Bank and other U.S. public and private lenders, the Inter-American Development Bank, and international agencies such as the World Bank and the International Monetary Fund, as well as European creditors.

This huge foreign debt, one of the highest on a percapita basis in the world, came about as a consequence of two interrelated factors: 1) United States willingness to

extend loans year after year because aid finances exports
of U.S. goods, facilitates U.S. private overseas investment,
provides economic and political support for a friendly
government, and gives the United States a certain leverage
over the international and internal policies of another nation; 2) the inability of previous Chilean governments to
finance imports and development projects in any other
way, due in turn to their inability or unwillingness to make
the necessary structural changes to raise the level of internal investment. A 1966 U. S. Senate study of aid to
Chile reported that "in recent years foreign credit has
financed as much as 40% of official investment."[9] Service
on the gradually accumulating foreign debt had already
become unmanageable when Eduardo Frei was elected
President in 1964. Frei renegotiated the debt in order to
avoid paying 40 per cent of foreign-exchange earnings
from copper exports for debt service, and then proceeded
to borrow even more heavily. Repayment of the debt
necessarily came out of state investment funds, and the
state therefore had to borrow still more investment capital
abroad in the vain hope that additional resources would
be generated through development to eventually pay off
the debt. In 1965–66, AID was financing 14 per cent of
the entire Chilean budget. Throughout the years of the
Frei regime, a substantial proportion of Chilean investment was from foreign loans, and up to 30 per cent of
available foreign exchange went to servicing the debt.
Foreign aid turned out to be a vicious cycle of dependency. The Alessandri and Frei governments mortgaged
the nation's future to foreign creditors, and Chileans today must pay the consequences.

[9] U. S. Senate, Committee on Government Operations, Sub-
committee on Foreign Aid Expenditures, Report by Sen. Ernest
Gruening, *United States Foreign Aid in Action: A Case Study*
(Washington, D.C.: U. S. Government Printing Office, 1966),
p. 2.

A substantial piece of Chile's debt falls due during 1972–74, so the Allende government, faced with dwindling foreign exchange from declining copper prices and an ambitious investment program, asked for a three-year moratorium and rescheduling of the debt. Facing the power of the bankers composing the "Paris Club" of creditors, the compromise finally reached was agreed upon with an implicit understanding that if the creditors pushed too hard, Chile's only recourse might be default. Part of the agreement extracted from Chile a "stand-by" arrangement that would permit International Monetary Fund "surveillance of Chilean economic measures."[10] At the present time, all U.S. aid and credits are suspended, and Chile finds new international credits extremely scarce. The point seems very clear: governments that pursue policies of reclaiming their national resources from foreign control and adopt policies of fomenting economic independence will have to depend upon internal resources or credits from the socialist countries.

The Peterson Task Force's warm endorsement of the Overseas Private Investment Corporation also bears directly on the Chilean case. OPIC insures American investment against losses due to expropriation, revolution, or currency inconvertibility and provides loans and pre-investment information to American corporations. OPIC now insists upon multinational participation in its underwriting activities. "This will tell the world," Bradford Mills, President of OPIC, says, "that seizure of U.S. property won't affect only the U.S., it will damage the expropriator's credit worthiness worldwide."[11]

OPIC holds the insurance for $631.8 million in U.S. investments in Chile, including Kennecott, Ford, ITT, and others. (OPIC rejected Anaconda's insurance claim for

[10] New York *Times,* April 20, 1972.
[11] *Forbes Magazine,* March 1, 1972, p. 59.

$159 million on the grounds that the company failed to keep up its premiums.) This insurance was taken out during the Frei regime, when Chile's economy experienced a rapid process of de-Chileanization; $452.8 million in insurance was issued to U.S. corporations in Chile during 1968. OPIC has insufficient reserves to meet its claims from Chilean nationalizations and has turned to Congress, asking for authorization to increase its reserves from taxpayers' money. This insurance automatically makes any dispute over the amount of compensation for nationalized investment a conflict between an agency of the U. S. Government and the government of another country. This opens the possibility for the government to use its power to act as a collection agency for those investors who believe they have been unjustly compensated by their former hosts.

This situation also makes it possible for corporations to use their insurance to strengthen their bargaining position. This was precisely the tactic of ITT when Chile indicated its interest in transforming the Chile Telephone Company into a public enterprise by purchasing ITT's 70 per cent share of the company.

In March and April of 1971, ITT representatives met with President Allende to discuss the transfer and Chile's offer to create a joint venture with ITT's Standard Electric Co., in which the government of Chile would own 51 per cent of the shares.

Negotiations took a turn for the worse in June 1971, when ITT asked for payment according to the book value of the company. Chilean negotiators pointed out that the book value was highly overstated, citing the value of telephone lines in Chile in relation to averages in other countries (in Chile the value of a line was placed at twice the world average) and other data. Chile asked that international experts, appointed with the consent of both parties, undertake an assessment of the properties of the Chile Telephone Company. ITT refused. The value of its property in Chile was highly overstated by ITT due to the corporation's privilege, accorded by previous Chilean governments, of repatriating a 10 per cent return on its investment. During the negotiations, ITT insisted that Chile accept all the corporation's conditions, repeatedly pointing out "the problem" that would be created for Chile if ITT were to collect from OPIC insurance of $108.5 million contracted for its Chile Telephone Company investment.

In September 1971 the Chilean Government appointed an "intervenor" to the telephone company, which meant that the state took over management while recognizing the property rights of ITT. Negotiations to purchase continued until the March 1972 sensational disclosures of ITT's interference in Chile's internal affairs caused President Allende to send a nationalization bill to Congress.

The Rockefeller Mission and the "Low Profile"

The low-profile policy of the Nixon administration on U.S.-Latin American relations also has its origin in the recommendations of another presidential commission, the Rockefeller Mission to Latin America of 1969.

Nelson Rockefeller, Governor of New York and founder of the Latin America-based International Basic Economy Corp. (IBEC), headed the mission. He was joined by such businessmen as William Butler (vice-president of the Rockefellers' Chase Manhattan Bank), Augustine Marusi (chairman, the Borden Company), Arthur K. Watson (chairman, IBM), and George Woods (consultant, First Boston Corp. and former president of the World Bank).

Following their rather turbulent tour of Latin America, the mission issued the *Rockefeller Report on the Ameri-*

cas, which contained a number of findings and policy guidelines. The mission reported that:

> The forces of nationalization are creating increasing pressures against foreign private investment. The impetus for independence from the U.S. is leading toward rising pressures for nationalization of U.S. industry, local control, or participation with U.S. firms. . . .
>
> Thus the rising drive for self-identification is naturally and inevitably leading many nations to seek greater independence from U.S. influence and power. . . .

However, the mission suggested that:

> The U.S. cannot allow disagreement with the forces of the domestic policies of other American governments to jeopardize its basic objective of working with and for their people to our mutual benefit.

Thus the President should issue a policy statement enumerating

> the principle that the U.S. national interest must supersede those of any domestic special-interest group in the conduct of Western relations.

In addition, the statement should

> convey a new character and style to our western hemisphere relations—one based on partnership, not dominance.[12]

The Rockefeller report is not, however, without teeth. Significantly it strongly recommends increased U.S. mili-

[12] *The Rockefeller Report on the Americas* (Chicago: Quadrangle Books, 1969), pp. 29, 59, 144, and 61, respectively.

tary and police aid. The underlying idea here is to strengthen forces resistant to the pressures for change, thus shifting some of the burden of the policeman's role from the United States to internal forces of law and order (see Chapter 5).

In October 1969 Nixon acknowledged before the annual meeting of the Inter-American Press Association that the "new approaches" that made up the emerging "mature partnership" between the United States and Latin America had "been substantially shaped by the report of Governor Rockefeller."[13]

The most novel of the "new approaches," as spelled out later in a statement on foreign policy to Congress, dealt with the appropriate U.S. policy in light of the mission's findings on the trend toward rising nationalism. The statement reads:

> And we shall avoid actions which foster or reinforce anti-U.S. nationalism.[14]

This is also the same sentiment expressed at a March 1971 Council on Foreign Relations Latin America strategy session by academic expert John Plank of the corporate-controlled Brookings Institution, who acknowledged it also to be the current thinking of Henry Kissinger. Plank told the discussion group:

> that direct confrontations with Latin American governments are to be avoided . . . that such confrontations would serve the interests of those fanatically

[13] *Public Papers of President Richard Nixon, 1969* (Washington, D.C.: U. S. Government Printing Office, October 31, 1969), p. 424. "Mature partnership" was defined as dealing "realistically with governments in the inter-American system as they were."

[14] *U. S. Foreign Policy Report to Congress* (Washington, D.C.: U. S. Government Printing Office, February 25, 1971).

ideological, or cynically opposed to the U.S., more than they would serve our interests, and that the cost to us, domestic and international, of such confrontation would far outweigh any conceivable benefits.[15]

Indeed, so widely held was this new-found sensitivity to nationalistic feelings that even conservative ideologue William Buckley sided with liberal academicians and the establishment press to counsel that any belligerent act on the part of the United States directed at Chile's new socialist regime would only "serve the purposes of the Allende government which can count on Chilean nationalism above all things."[16]

Thus, one of the basic assumptions growing out of the Rockefeller report, subsequently elaborated on in elite-controlled "public affairs" groups, publicized in the press, and incorporated into policy, was the notion that the United States must eschew blatant retaliation in defense of particular "special-interest groups," since such would only heighten "anti-American nationalism." It is such a notion that helps explain both ITT's inability to rally the support needed "to stop Allende" and at least the *appearance* of the "correct" approach the United States assumed toward Chile in the first months of the Allende government. In fact this is precisely the explanation that was put forward in an October 1970 ITT memo. To wit:

In retrospect Meyer [Assistant Secretary of State] may . . . be the victim of the new Latin area straight jacket called the "low profile of the U.S. in Latin America," which when applied to Chile today could

---

[15] "Liberated Documents: New Imperial Strategy for Latin America," *NACLA's Latin America and Empire Report*, VII, November 1971, p. 20.

[16] Los Angeles *Times*, February 16, 1971, editorial page.

be a salient reason why the United States failed even to head off in 1970 that which it so successfully and energetically aided Chileans to avoid in 1964—the emergence of a Marxist president.[17]

Emerging Reality of U.S. Chilean Policy

Reconciling the sentiments underlying a U.S.-to-Latin America low profile with the vested interests of particular U.S. corporations abroad and a spirited defense of international capitalism increasingly became the concern of the American corporate-elite class as nationalism built up in Chile and to a lesser extent in Peru, Bolivia, Ecuador, and Colombia. Events made it clear that Salvador Allende was really serious about making good on his campaign pledges "to socialize the heart of the Chilean economy" and to "liberate Chile from her subordination to foreign capital," and the official low profile was gradually revealed to be covert conspiracy and stiff economic sanctions against Chile.

Essentially what transpired was that in the process of nationalizing the "heart" of the Chilean economy, the very core of American corporate power was touched, affecting not only the immediate interests involved but an entire network of U.S. interests maintained through a series of close corporate interconnections.

As was pointed out in Chapter 1, Chile's economic nationalism strikes directly at the established corporate-interest groups, the Rockefeller empire, the Morgan and Grace interests, and an array of who's who among multinational giants: Ford, GM, ITT, Dow, Du Pont—in total,

[17] October 30, 1970, memo from Hendrix to Gerrity, NACLA, op. cit., note 1. The 1964 reference is to the financial and other forms of support given to Eduardo Frei and the Christian Democrats to help defeat Allende in the election of that year.

twenty-four of the top thirty U.S.-based multinationals.

A low profile based on a certain tolerance for national-ism, or shifting some responsibility to international in-stitutions, and on the "soft" policy responses by the U. S. Government recommended by the Rockefeller Report and implied in the Peterson Report and other guide-lines of corporate-controlled policy organizations can be adopted only in cases in which one or a few multinational interests are adversely affected (as in Peru and Ecuador). When economic nationalism proceeds beyond this point, the *class interests* of the multinational complex as a whole are affected. In the case of Chile these class interests in-clude:

> The potential loss to the United States of Chile's mineral resources;
>
> The loss of sizable investments in industry and, more seriously, the closure of opportunity for con-tinued multinational investment in the most dynamic sectors of Chile's economy;
>
> The potential for "ideological infection"—Chile's notions of socialism possibly permeating the conscious-ness of its neighbors, thus affecting the "climate for private investment" elsewhere;
>
> The potential "demonstration effect" of Chile's na-tionalization; that is, if Chile "gets away" with its "expropriations," other countries might follow the pattern, conceivably endangering U.S. investment throughout the region if not the world.[18]

And finally, the potential threat to the survival of

[18] Businessmen are very worried about the "demonstration effect"; see the comments, by Alphonso de Rosso of Standard Oil at the December 1970 CFR meeting, in NACLA, "Liberated Documents . . . ," p. 11, and the October 21, 1970, ITT memo in NACLA, op. cit., note 1.

American-dominated world capitalism posed by the combination of the above—since an increasing percentage of earnings are derived from foreign operations and since the greatest potential for growth and absorption of surplus lies abroad.[19]

Throughout 1971, then, different tendencies, "hard" and "soft," "vested interests" and "enlightened interests," among different corporations were coming together under the impact and implications of nationalizations. In the process a consensus among the various corporate interests was produced, thereby insuring their relatively active support for and participation in a policy designed to protect their threatened class interest. This consensus formation and its dissemination were provided by such groups as the Council of the Americas (which regularly holds "meetings with State, AID, IBRD, IDB, CIAP and other government agencies whose work may affect U.S. business interests in Latin America"[20]); the International Economic Policy Association (whose Latin American Committee met early on in the Chilean situation to see what pressures it could "drum up to make the State Department stiffen its attitude"[21]); and the Council on Foreign Relations (which offers both a "confidential" environment for frank and open discussion and easy access to govern-

[19] Solid theoretical works on the forces pushing corporate expansionism are Paul Baran and Paul Sweezy, *Monopoly Capital* (New York: Monthly Review Press, 1966) and Harry Magdoff, *The Age of Imperialism* (New York: Monthly Review Press, 1969).

[20] Membership of the Council of the Americas represents 90 per cent of the U.S. investors in the region. The quote is from Jerome Levinson and Juan de Onis, *The Alliance That Lost Its Way* (Chicago: Quadrangle, 1970), pp. 159–60.

[21] October 22, 1970, ITT memo from Merriam to Gerrity, NACLA, op. cit., note 1.

mental officials[22]). Each helped to forge a framework within which a consensually arrived-at policy regarding Chile could emerge.

Next, all that was required was some sort of pretext that would guarantee a semblance of public support for the policy that was soon to surface.

This was provided in late September 1971, by the refusal on the part of Chile to compensate Anaconda and Kennecott for their mining interests on the basis that the two copper companies had reaped profits in excess of that permitted by Chilean law. "Serious departure from accepted standards of international law" became the official U.S. reaction. It was a response clearly calculated to legitimate the actions the United States had taken, was taking, and would take against Chile.

In October 1971, shortly before executives from Anaconda, ITT, First National City Bank, Bank of America, Ford, and Ralston Purina met with Secretary of State Rogers to discuss the "possible response by the government" and presumably the respective role each of the companies could play in that response,[23] Murray Rossant, director of the Twentieth Century Fund, outlined a policy that he understood as appropriate but "not ruthless retaliation." Rossant rationalized the appropriate strategy as one that "would consist of encouraging Congressional sanctions, withholding all aid and assistance to Chile and exerting maximum leverage in international lending agencies . . . to follow suit." Assessing the impact of such an approach, Rossant went on to write, "If further private and governmental credit is cut off by a combination of American sanctions and pressures on international

[22] See NACLA, op. cit., note 1, and Domhoff, op. cit., for analysis of CFR influence.

[23] *Wall Street Journal*, October 25, 1971. Kennecott was not at the meeting. Their executives were busy courting Eduardo Frei, Chile's opposition leader, at a New York luncheon.

sources, commercial banks and corporations, the Allende government would be paralyzed."[24]

It is impossible to be unaware that a policy intent on producing paralysis, if successful, would provoke internal crisis, possibly civil war within Chile, given the intense divisions there. Therefore the only adequate explanation for such a policy is one that assumes that it was (and is) the intention of U.S. business and government to try to create sufficient pressures for internal opposition forces to bring down the Allende regime.

This explanation is similar to the one offered by James Petras and Robert La Porte in their analysis of "U.S. Response to Economic Nationalism in Chile":

> The overall purpose of U.S. policy is to create economic disorder and provide a domestic social crisis that could lead to . . . the overthrow of the Allende government by a civil-military coalition made up of the Army, the Christian Democrats and the extreme right-wing National Party.[25]

With the big stick turned economic, policy "formation" and execution tended to shift from the Department of State to the Treasury Department. Secretary Connolly is notoriously "tough" in promotion of corporate interests. There the secretary chairs the National Advisory Council on International Monetary and Trade Policy, which is responsible for co-ordinating the policies and operations of the representatives of the United States to the International Monetary Fund, International Development Bank, Inter-American Development Bank, Asia Development

[24] Murray Rossant, "The Big Stick Is Now Economic," New York *Times,* October 10, 1971.

[25] James Petras and Robert La Porte, "U. S. Responses to Economic Nationalism in Chile" (unpublished, Penn State University, 1972), p. 14.

Bank, Export-Import Bank, and any other agency of the government that participates in making foreign loans or engages in foreign monetary transactions. As chairman of this council, the secretary easily co-ordinates the sanctions, both bilateral and multilateral, imposed against "wayward" nations. In addition, the secretary is in a good position to influence world markets, say of copper, if he were ever so inclined. Aiding the secretary in formulating instructions going to the various U.S. representatives to multilateral institutions are a number of business advisory groups, for example the Treasury Liaison Committee of the Business Council, whose 1970 members included such notables as the chairman of Morgan Guaranty Trust, Deere & Co., and American Express, former chairmen of Mobil Oil and Burlington Industries, the presidents of Kennecott Copper and Eli Lilly, and the inevitable David Rockefeller, chairman of the Chase Manhattan Bank.

The essence of Rossant's article, in which he rationalized the policy the Secretary of the Treasury had been unofficially following with increasing hardness throughout 1971, became official in February 1972, when the "economic big stick" was officially certified. This was accomplished in a presidential statement on the protection of U.S. private investment overseas, delivered in a report to Congress. Nixon said:

> Henceforth, should an American firm be expropriated without reasonable steps to provide prompt, adequate and effective compensation, there is a presumption that the expropriating country would receive no new bilateral economic benefits. . . . Similarly we would withhold our support for loans to that country in multilateral development institutions . . . and, because expropriation is a concern of many countries, we are placing greater emphasis on the use of multilateral mechanisms for dealing with this problem.

Later on, with specific reference to Chile, Nixon declared:

> We and other public and private sources of development investment will take account of whether or not the Chilean government meets its international obligations.[26]

Thus did the low profile come to swing the big stick in the case of Chile.

THE NEW COLD WAR IN LATIN AMERICA: THE U. S. PRESS AND CHILE*

JOHN C. POLLOCK
WITH DAVID EISENHOWER

The press performs an important political role when it structures issues for public discussion. It is especially potent in shaping opinions on foreign policy, for citizens have few alternative sources of information on foreign affairs. The role of the press has been especially noticeable in reports on the programs and aims of the Allende government in Chile, for U.S. newspapers clearly reflect the hostility manifested by the U. S. Government and some U.S. corporations toward the first elected socialist government in our hemisphere, a phenomenon evident in certain key "themes" emphasized by the press. This analysis identifies and documents these "hostile" themes, evaluates their accuracy, and suggests which explanations best account for their presence. Specifically, we examine the way

[26] *U. S. Foreign Policy for the 1970s,* pp. 70 and 96.

* An original article for this volume by members of the Chile Research Group. The authors wish to thank Henry Frundt for his invaluable assistance on an earlier draft of this paper.

the Allende government's actions and intentions are covered in several U.S. newspapers: the *Christian Science Monitor* (CSM), the *Wall Street Journal* (WSJ), the New York *Times* (NYT), the Washington *Post* (WP), the Miami *Herald* (MH), and the Los Angeles *Times* (LAT). Our analysis will cover the period beginning just before the September 1970 election of Dr. Salvador Allende as President of Chile to January 1972.[1]

A. FIVE THEMES

Imbedded in U.S. press coverage of Chilean politics are five themes, which, although they do not necessarily dominate such coverage at all times, reappear frequently and form patterns that merit attention. They are evident in every newspaper in varying degrees, not only in editorials and opinion columns but also in news reports from the papers' own journalists and Associated Press and United Press International reporters. The themes are the following: (1) Allende is isolated from the vast majority of Chileans in his actions and goals; (2) almost all threats to political stability and continuity are leftist in origin; (3) the middle and upper classes are the chief repositories of political wisdom and virtue; (4) resentment of U.S. multinational corporations operating in Chile is essentially irrational (and their nationalization is bound to engender production difficulties as key technical personnel leave); and (5) Allende's political and economic problems are of "crisis" proportions, his successes being rarely if ever mentioned. The use of each of these themes can be documented.

[1] News clippings on Chile and other Latin American countries are available from *Information Service on Latin America,* which provides photocopies of news on Latin America printed in the mentioned newspapers. It is located at P. O. Box 4267, Berkeley, California 94704.

1. Chile's socialist President is isolated.

U.S. press coverage suggests that Allende is isolated in at least two ways. First, acts are attributed to Allende alone that are actually acts of the Chilean Congress as well as the Executive branch. For example, the nationalization of copper companies and other U.S.-based multinational corporations is often attributed to Allende's implacable zeal for expropriation.

A second way Allende is given an isolated image is through the use of language suggesting that he is not to be taken seriously; that he is a "clever" fox deceiving everyone, and like a "light-tripping fox" must eventually be trapped (Sulzberger, NYT, July 2, 1971). Metaphors such as "acrobat" and "adroit juggler" (Sulzberger, ibid.) are ripe with the suggestion that the acrobat must one day fall and that the juggler will one day slip up. All these innuendos convey, if not in substance, then in tone, that Allende is: a) an individual performer without a team act or audience support; b) somehow deceiving everyone with his "tricks" and therefore certain to be unmasked or ordered to stop his deception; and c) by extension, a historical aberration, a side show or bad turn in Chile's political history, bearing little relation to long-term political trends there and not to be taken seriously by those who have the patience to wait until the show is over. The "plump little doctor" (*Newsweek,* January 31, 1972, p. 33), a "former county coroner" (MH, December 16, 1970), is considered an amusement.

2. Threats to the political system come exclusively from the Left.

Evident in the U.S. press in early reporting on Allende's victory after September 1970, especially since U.S. copper companies began protesting Chile's compensation terms in September 1971 and notably again during Cuban Prime Minister Castro's visit to Chile in November 1971, is a flagrant pandering to Cold War stereotypes. Socialism and democracy have been treated as mutually exclusive. For example, "the Chileans voted themselves into the state of affairs which now *threatens* [emphasis added] their free institutions and by the nature of things it is going to be largely up to them to work their way out of it" (WP, October 26, 1970).

To its almost reflexive Cold War caricatures of the Allende regime the press has added exhaustive studies of a left-wing group, the Left Revolutionary Movement (Movimiento de la Izquierda Revolucionaria, or MIR). This group is given considerable attention by means of interviews of prominent right-wing and right-of-center politicians and businessmen, who offer opinions about the ideological debates and activities of the MIR. Almost nowhere is there to be found mention, much less investigative study, of the right-wing groups active in Chile.

A third example of the news media's preoccupation with threats from the Left is found in efforts to depict Allende's legal position as essentially "manipulative." Allende's widely publicized devotion to legal methods has earned him adjectives such as "calculated," "relentless" (MH, February 19, 1971), someone who is obviously trying to "debilitate" opponents through legal methods.

3. The middle and upper classes are repositories of political wisdom.

Almost all the reporting on citizen reaction to the Allende regime is based on interviews with national business leaders (e.g. MH, January 21, 1971) or owners of small and medium-sized firms (NYT *Magazine,* October 17, 1971). Such people and such interviews are presented as typical of Chilean popular reaction to Allende, and almost all those interviewed by the U.S. press are reported opposed to Allende in varying degrees. By contrast, almost no interviews are reported with organized labor, and virtually never with unorganized labor, the underemployed, the unemployed, or farmers on small and medium-sized plots of land. Those groups the U.S. press fails to interview comprise about three quarters of the Chilean population.

4. Chile's effort to diminish foreign corporate influence is irrational.

The U.S. press often portrays nationalization measures as basically irrational, in that a major source of capital is ousted, future investment is clouded, and key foreign engineers and technicians leave. Also evident in the U.S. press, especially in reports by Juan de Onis in the New York *Times,* is a diversion of public attention from recent evidence suggesting that ITT and the CIA plotted to prevent Allende from taking office. Reporting in the *Times* has generally focused not on the veracity of the "ITT-Chile papers" or on the appropriateness of corporate intervention in Chilean politics, but rather on whether the conspiracy documents have helped Allende, and on the way Chile's Popular Unity government has "irrationally" employed the documents to draw attention to a right-wing threat (*cf.* NYT, March 24, March 26 [editorial], and April 2, 1972).

5. The metaphor of crisis.

Reports about both political and economic issues are replete with dark hints of impending disaster for Chile's incumbent government. Tales of food shortages, unemployment, the flight abroad of key technicians, agricultural turmoil, inflation, and the scarcity of foreign exchange are all reported as though economic ruin were just around the corner. These Cassandralike accounts often imply, either directly or through juxtaposition of a "happy" past and the "dismal" present, that Chile's troubles began essentially *after* it a) elected a socialist government; b) began nationalizing foreign multinational corporations (thus "irrationally" prompting technicians to leave); and c) endangered the subhemisphere by raising the possibility of a "ripple effect" (the latest of domino theories, evoked especially for Latin America), which threatens, through Chile's example, to promote socialism south of Panama.

B. AVAILABLE EVIDENCE CONTRADICTS THE THEMES

If these five themes were viewed as the best possible estimate of the political situation in Chile, then reports about the Allende government in the U.S. press could not be considered hostile. But the themes contradict a substantial body of information available on events in Chile, as informed study of foreign newspapers and even our own press reveals. To note that the U.S. press provides evidence contradicting the themes is not to suggest that the press denies its own point of emphasis. Contradictory information is given less space or attention than information substantiating the themes, and when mentioned, is often put in contexts that minimize, or encourage skepticism about, its significance.

To imply that Allende's nationalization policies are not popular is to ignore both the constitutional amendment authorizing nationalization of copper, which passed a Congress controlled by opposition Christian Democrats by a unanimous vote and the fact that both Allende and Christian Democratic candidate Tomic, who together received about two thirds of the presidential vote in 1970, made the nationalization of copper and other U.S. companies central issues in their presidential campaigns. Although 1972 elections for two deputies, one senator, and the President of the National University in Santiago all resulted in narrow defeats for pro-Allende candidates, those defeated won between 41 and 48 per cent of the vote, better than Allende's presidential plurality of 36 per cent of the popular vote in 1970. These results do not necessarily reflect sentiment in the nation as a whole, but even were they considered as such, it is clear that Allende has a substantial amount of support, perhaps the most support of any coalition led by a single man. When some U.S. papers imply that Allende is isolated on the Left, they ignore both his considerable following and what several reputable foreign newspapers regard as his role as mediator or middleman between forces on both the Left and the Right.

It is also essential to understand that Allende is a serious politician whose entire career has been anything but a charade. The President, a founder of the Socialist Party in Chile, has long championed working-class and women's rights, a broader distribution of medical services and housing, and nationalization of key industries, as well as various measures to redistribute a larger share of national income to Chile's working classes. He ran for the presidency as a Socialist four times over a period of eighteen years, giving the voters substantial opportunity to evaluate his position on issues. To insist, therefore, that Allende is some sort of cunning magician who duped the Chilean people to support him against its own interests is to make charges that are historically spurious.

With regard to the threat from the extreme Left emphasized in the U.S. press, little effort is made to give readers a sense of the spectrum of political opinion in Chile. The Left is analyzed in some detail, typically by means of interviews with members of the upper and upper-middle classes, citizens who almost invariably voted against Allende. The Left is never asked how it views the Right, nor does the U.S. press even mention or seriously speculate about the role of the right wing in Chile. Yet rightists have engaged in a variety of disruptions, especially in efforts to prevent President-elect Allende's ratification by the Chilean Congress, in the period September–October 1970, during which General René Schneider, Commander of Chile's army, who vowed to uphold Allende's election, was assassinated.

A good example of this unwillingness to mention right-wing activities is found in reporting on the "March of the Empty Pots," in December 1971, in which about five thousand women from the upper-middle and upper classes (see CSM, December 8, 1971; *Le Monde,* December 3, 1971) marched through downtown Santiago protesting food shortages. Highly respected foreign newspapers such as the French *Le Monde* and the Mexican equivalent of the New York *Times, Excelsior,* reported the event as a right-wing attack on President Allende (he, Prime Minister Castro, and the presidential palace were stoned) in which rightist and racist placards were openly carried by the marching women.

Le Monde and *Excelsior* both described the massive demonstration as a right-wing riot and reported it broken up by the police when the President and his palace were stoned. (Refer to issues of December 26 in each.) Both *Le Monde* and *Excelsior* mentioned in passing some confrontation between the women (and the helmeted, club-carrying men marching with them) and left-wing counter-protestors, but this incident was given little importance.

The U.S. press, by contrast, chose to present the women's march as "peaceful" and disrupted not by the police but by "hard-hatted brigades of leftist youths" (LAT, December 1, 1971; MH, December 3, 1971) who "threw stones at the women" (MH, December 3, 1971; LAT, December 2, 1971). Such militant terms were not used to describe the *rightist* men marching with the women. They were described as a "group" (rather than a brigade) of about eighty men with "safety helmets" (rather than hard hats) "escorting and guarding the women." (See, for example, the LAT, December 2, 1971; NYT, December 2, 1971.)

The U.S. press also presents upper and upper-middle class opinion as representative of Chile's popular will. While *Le Monde* and *Excelsior* stated that the marching women were clearly from the upper classes and elegant sections of Santiago, the U.S. press presented the march as a protest against the Allende government by a cross section of *all* Chilean women. The U.S. press, in addition, curiously dodged all mention of the social origin of the women (with the exception of the *Christian Science Monitor,* December 8, 1971, which agreed that the women were clearly from the wealthier sections of Santiago). Juan de Onis of the New York *Times* even hinted in one article that "there appeared to be a significant number of women from working-class neighborhoods" (NYT, December 2, 1971). Such selective exclusion of information, especially in reporting by De Onis, has been misleading. In these and similar ways the U.S. press has presented protests by a few as harbingers of ominous polarization, volatility, and political collapse in Chile.

The assumption that Chile is irrational in wishing to minimize U.S. control of corporate activity there is contradicted in a variety of evidence contexts, especially in reports available on the performance of the U.S. copper companies.[2] But the assumption can be challenged without a wealth of illustrative examples. As foreign investment in Chile grew, decision making in both the economic and the political realms increasingly passed out of the purview of Chilean nationals. That some Chileans have participated in foreign ventures has not diminished the export of decision making to more-industrialized countries, notably those which influence industrial as well as

[2] See Chapter 1, and Victor Edward Wallis, "Foreign Investment and Chilean Politics" (Ph.D. dissertation, Columbia University, 1970).

copper markets. If development is defined as an increase in a nation's ability to make decisions that govern its destiny, then development has clearly been hindered in the Chilean case. The U.S. press contains countless examples of sympathy for the desire for more autonomous decision making on the part of former European colonies in Africa and South Asia. Yet a similar desire for development is not awarded similar sympathy when the region involved is one where the United States has more substantial investments: Latin America.

Like the other themes, that of political and economic crisis in Chile is also vastly overblown. The *Christian Science Monitor* and the *Wall Street Journal,* contrary to other newspapers, have reported on two occasions each that Chile is having no special difficulty replacing technicians in nationalized industries (WSJ: March 15, July 19, 1971; CSM: July 16, 17, 1971). The *Journal* and the *Monitor* also mention that the major problem confronting the mines is replacing worn-out equipment with new, indirectly noting that the U.S. companies left the mines' machines in a condition of disrepair.

Also contrary to U.S. reports, there is considerable evidence that Allende's economic performance is superior to that of his predecessor, President Frei. In his first year in office Allende reduced the rise in consumer prices by one half, contrary to U.S. press reports picturing Allende as a unique source of inflation, and unemployment was also halved. What food shortages do exist are due not so much to any food austerity policy of the Allende government, but to the increased purchasing power of Chile's working classes. Scarce foodstuffs are now equitably distributed under Allende. The upper classes are not protesting a shortage of food per se, but rather its more equitable distribution, and hence its relatively reduced availability for the upper sectors.

In fact, agricultural production increased by 5.2 per

cent in 1971, Allende's first year in office, almost doubling the growth rate of the Frei government. And total consumption has predictably increased. Although upper-class women were protesting "meatless days," something not uncommon under the previous president, beef consumption increased 15 per cent. The Inter-American Committee on the Alliance for Progress released a twelve-page document showing that the rate of growth of Chile's GNP during 1971 was the second highest in Latin America, 8.5 per cent. There were substantial increases in industrial production (14.6 per cent) and housing (12.2 per cent). Unemployment was down from 8.3 per cent in 1970 to 3.8 per cent in 1971, the lowest rate ever recorded in Chile. Medical and educational services rose sharply.[3]

C. CONCLUSIONS

In reporting political events in Chile, several themes emphasized by the press have skewed reader perception through two significant failures:

1. *The failure to place events in historical context.* The press has often attributed economic and political problems arising in Chile since Allende's incumbency almost entirely to the mismanagement of the new President. The press has also suggested that unless these issues (e.g., inflation, unemployment) are resolved, the government is headed for disaster. A less hostile press would compare Allende's problems and performance with those of his predecessors and might even mention his successes, something the U.S. press rarely does.

2. *The failure to place events in comparative context.* The Allende government should not be expected to topple

[3] A review of the performance of the Chilean economy is also available from the Oficina de Planificación Nacional, "Analysis of the Economy in 1971" (Santiago: ODEPLAN, April 1972, Document #4).

if it fails to solve problems that other Latin American countries have been largely unable to solve. Chile does not have the highest rate of inflation in Latin America or necessarily the greatest "brain drain" of skilled professionals migrating elsewhere. Chile is also unlike two of the largest countries in Latin America, Brazil and Argentina, both military dictatorships, from which reports on the torture of political prisoners emanate frequently. Yet Chile is painted with the brush of crisis, said to be "hanging by a thread for months as an incipient dictatorship" (MH, December 28, 1971). A less hostile press might compare Chile's record as one of Latin America's most stable and flexible political systems with the performance records of other countries in the southern hemisphere.[4]

What accounts for the failure to place events in historical and comparative context? What accounts for the hostility manifested in reports on the Allende government? Is the press endeavoring to confirm what the Nixon government wants to see? Is it perhaps the presence of historically determined cultural blinders that prevents the press from witnessing Allende's successes or noticing that his performance compares favorably with his predecessors'? Or is the press structuring issues and events in ways that satisfy U.S. multinational corporate interests?

The newspapers have not necessarily followed President Nixon's lead and have differed sharply with his tactics when he refused to send diplomatically routine congratulations upon Allende's election, encouraged the postponement of an Export-Import Bank loan requested by Chile to purchase U.S. commercial Boeing jets, and refused to allow a Navy-authorized stopover of the U.S.

[4] For a more considered account of the progress and problems of the Allende government, refer to Eric Hobsbawm, "Chile: Year One," *The New York Review of Books,* 17:4 (September 1971), pp. 22–33.

aircraft carrier *Enterprise* in Chile. These exhibitions and "get tough" statements by Secretary Rogers and White House adviser Klein have met with the following critical press responses: "Boorish rebuff to Chile" (NYT, March 2, 1971), "Fat-headed diplomacy" (MH, March 2, 1971), "High Noon showdown not diplomacy" (MH, August 14, 1971), "Bullying Chile" (WP, September 14, 1971), and "U. S. Big Stick Boomerangs" (MH, September 16, 1971).

Nor are cultural blinders wholly adequate in accounting for changes in the way the press structures reporting in Chile at different points in time. Cold War stereotypes are pervasive, but their use varies markedly. Reporting *has* changed its emphasis several times since Allende's election in September 1970, but cultural assumptions fail to explain such changes. Although cultural assumptions may explain relatively stable, enduring perceptions, they account less well for dynamic ones.

How, then, do we explain variations in reporting? There is considerable evidence that shifts in reporting correlate with related shifts in U.S. corporate fortunes and policies. All the papers agreed initially, after Allende's election in September 1970, that his government would pose some sort of "problem" for the United States. The press abounded with scare stories about "Marxist Allende" putting Chile on the "Road to Socialism" until July 1971, when Congress passed Allende's constitutional amendment authorizing nationalization by a unanimous vote. That amendment, along with Allende's scrupulously legal behavior, belied most predictions of imminent dictatorship and political chaos touted in the U.S. press, and Cold War reporting gave way to a major debate over the best means to deal with the "problem." Rough-edged snubs such as those practiced by President Nixon were criticized as too flagrant and really unnecessary. Besides, the newspapers counseled (with some justification, as publicity of the

ITT-Chile papers later demonstrated), a policy of "provocation" has a tendency to boomerang and rally support
around Allende. From January through September 1971
the papers suggested, in effect, that flagrant provocation
only endangered the other myriad investments in Chile
solely in order to prevent the nationalization of a few.

After a period of considerable debate in the U.S. press,
the news media decided to view as a viable course of action a low-profile policy of economic reprisals.[5] But the
process of co-operating with corporate interests did not
stop with the articulation of a program of economic
strangulation for Chile. In late September 1971 the press
set about reporting events as though the strangulation
policy were being successfully implemented, and renewed
its themes of political crisis and perfidious socialism. Renewed alarmism was evident especially at the time
Messrs. Finch, Klein, and Rogers criticized Chile and
cast doubts on the government's ability to survive during
Prime Minister Castro's visit to Chile in November 1971
and during the "March of the Empty Pots" in early
December 1971. The press has continued to exhibit those
themes up to the present writing.

This chronology of shifts in U.S. press reports on Chile
suggests that certain assumptions pervade those reports
which parallel the goals or decisions of major U.S. multinational corporations. The language and themes of the
Cold War are prominent when U.S. businesses consider
themselves threatened (during Allende's election and
after nationalization negotiations stalemated). The themes
are still evident, yet less prominent, during periods when
U.S. multinationals are engaged in negotiations (e.g.,
January through August 1971). The five themes can be
considered "cultural assumptions," because they are per-

---

[5] The clearest statement is by Murray Rossant of the Twentieth
Century Fund, "The Big Stick Is Now Economic," New York
Times, October 1, 1971.

sistent over time and homogeneously present across a wide range of news sources. Yet the extent to which the assumptions are displayed and the extent of press coverage given Chilean politics generally has paralleled the variations in attention given Chile by U.S. corporate interests.

Perhaps the suggestion that cultural assumptions and favoritism toward corporate interests are divergent explanations for U.S. press reports is a spurious distinction. The charge of favoritism toward business clearly raises a variety of questions for further research: Which multinationals and corporate spinoff groups have close links with the major sources of news? How closely do multinationals and the press co-operate? What are the consequences of corporation/news-media co-operation for the formation of U.S. foreign policy? But whatever the answers to any of these questions, it is important to notice that effective co-operation between U.S. corporations and the press requires no "conspiracy," no series of interlocking directorates, no careful recruitment of "acceptable" journalists for top positions. There is some evidence that these mechanisms of control exist, and their use merits documentation. But the basis for co-operation may rest less on formal control mechanisms than on a culturally derived perception of common interests, especially the widely shared, historical U.S. assumption that private property is sacrosanct.

As the United States became more inextricably involved in the war in Southeast Asia in the early 1960s, the U.S. press generally reported the war "dutifully," accepting the government's thesis that U.S. interests were endangered there. Perhaps when the U. S. Government and corporate interests declare themselves endangered, the press considers itself endangered, too. If someone raises the heresy of "socialism," and U.S. corporate interests are involved, the press seems likely to take up the cudgel to do holy battle with the infidels. In this respect the press acts not as a watchdog of the activities of big government and big business, but rather as their agreeable colleague, functioning as a "voluntary arm of established power."[6]

This tendency and the assumptions described in this analysis are indicators of the way the press structures the formation of "climates" of opinion on specific issues. It is important to explore this process of climate formation if we are to learn more about the role of the press in our political system.

[6] The record of co-operation between the government and the press (especially the New York *Times*) in foreign affairs has been documented by former *Times* correspondent James Aronson in *The Cold War and the Press* (New York: Bobbs-Merrill, 1970). Of special interest are descriptions of the treatment by the New York *Times* of the Russian Revolution in 1917 and the Bay of Pigs invasion.

CHAPTER 3

The Coincidence of Internal and External Counterrevolutionary Forces

CHILE AND THE FORCES OF COUNTERREVOLUTION*

DALE L. JOHNSON

The internal and international opposition to Chilean socialism pursues two options. One is to box in Allende and the Popular Unity so that little can be accomplished, while the economic and political difficulties of the regime increase to the point where accommodation is the government's only viable course. The practical end of this would be that the process of socialist transformation would end, the Chilean business community would consolidate and strengthen itself, and U.S. corporate interests would reassert their presence in Chile. In 1976 ex-President Eduardo Frei, now undisputed leader of the combined opposition forces, would then step back in to further consolidate and rationalize a state capitalist regime closely linked to U.S. "multinational" investors. The other option is to instigate a counterrevolution which would bring the Popular Unity government down by force.

These are not mutually exclusive options. In fact, both are simultaneously pursued by opposition forces within the country and by U.S. corporations and government agencies. Moderate Christian Democrats, the more "en-

* An original article for this volume.

lightened" U.S. corporate interests, perhaps the State Department, would prefer the option of boxing in and forcing accommodation. Reactionary sectors within Chile, the CIA, ITT, and other hard-line multinationals, and perhaps Henry Kissinger and Richard Nixon, would rather bring about a counterrevolution. Regardless of the strategic objectives of the different forces, the opposition as a whole coalesces around tactical considerations. These tactics are: 1) to undermine the economy and make political capital of any economic problems created, 2) progressively to restrict the political means of effecting further socialist changes, and 3) to bring the middle strata of society all the way over to the right and to mobilize politically this substantial sector.

Undermining the Economy

The attempt to undermine the economy occurs at both the internal and the international levels. Landowners slaughter animals and fail to plant and cultivate crops, strategic consumption items (shoes or school uniforms, for example) mysteriously disappear from the market, women of the *barrio alto* buy up meat and other scarce consumer items for their freezers and then march banging their empty pots in protest of shortages, investments in the private sector are withheld, capital is transferred out of the country, etc. Meanwhile U.S. corporations and Government tighten the economic screws: private and U. S. Government credits are cut off, economic aid is suspended, Chilean assets here are frozen unless Chile pays off the copper corporations, Chile's U.S. and international creditors push hard on debt renegotiations, copper prices are kept down and the country's foreign exchange reserves dwindle, and the interests that control the major copper corporations maneuver to make Chile "a residual supplier of copper."

These policies have not as yet been notably successful,

however. Chilean economic policy in 1971, under the skilled direction of Pedro Vuskovic, has been very successful in redistributing income to salaried and wage workers and thereby increasing effective demand on the part of consumers, in holding back inflation, in decreasing unemployment, and in creating a minor economic boom. While the 1972 economic scene does not appear as bright as 1971, socialization of basic industries in a number of key sectors has brought more of the economic life of the country under control of the state, thereby giving the Popular Unity a considerable basis of economic power and ability to plan production. The economic sanctions employed against Chile by the United States have as yet not been sufficient to undermine the economic viability of the regime. The net political effect of the aggressive and hostile policies pursued by the United States which encourage and feed the internal opposition, has probably been to strengthen sentiments of nationalism by self-respecting Chilean citizens of different political tendencies and thereby the nationalist policies of the Allende government.

Political Opposition

The general situation in Chile is one of increasing polarization. Polarization of political forces developed within the first year of the Allende government. Eduardo Frei moved rapidly to the right, taking the main body of the Christian Democratic Party with him. This means that the Christian Democrats and the right-wing National Party work in close alliance. This caused the split of the genuine reform elements from the Christian Democratic Party to join forces with the now organized and significant Christian Left movement, which supports the government. At the social level, polarization means that the dominant class interests, previously divided between intransigent conservatives and reformists, have come together to undertake an aggressive fight to hold back the Left and to recuperate their lost power. At the same time, the astute politics of President Allende and the Communist and Socialist parties have gained the Left greater organizational and popular support. Meanwhile the Movement of the Revolutionary Left (MIR, a well-organized and militant revolutionary party on the PU's left) serves as the revolutionary conscience of the traditional Marxist parties and mobilizes grass-roots revolutionary pressures.

Strategically, however, the Popular Unity is not in the best of situations to achieve fully its democratic socialist program. In having the presidency, there is an opening—no more. The opposition is firmly entrenched in all institutions, although the Left has made significant inroads in the economic sphere, the church, the media, and education. The Left controls only part of the apparatus of the state—the Executive branch of government. The Congress and the courts serve the opposition. The Armed Forces and the national police, nominally under control of the government, nevertheless remain institutions created and manned by previous regimes to protect the bourgeois state and capitalist institutions. The armed organs of state power are not necessarily dependable in situations that may well arise. The Chilean Left puts it this way: "The Popular Unity is in the government, but not in power."

The principal ends of the opposition in the sphere of day-to-day politics are to impede the advance toward socialism through the constitutional means that the Allende regime is careful to follow and to force the government into the role of suppressing the very revolutionary process that brought it to power. Opposition control of Congress has placed great obstacles in the way of accomplishing the PU program wherever Allende could not move legally through executive action. The only significant exception to this was the nationalization of copper, which enjoyed such wide popular support that no party could politically afford not to support it. At the same time, the opposition parties and the media controlled by the Right exert enormous pressure upon the government to repress forcefully the pressures from peasants, slum dwellers, and Left forces operating at the grass-roots level.

An illustration of this tactic is the censure and constitutional removal from office of José Toha, Allende's Minister of Interior, in January 1972. This had its origin in the opposition's attempt to divide the PU from the MIR and other sectors of the revolutionary Left. The demand is that the government repress the MIR and use force against "illegal" land invasions and other militant grass-roots pressures (see Chapter 18). The opposition also attempted to remove Pedro Vuskovic, the Minister of Economy, from office toward the end of 1971. Vuskovic is the principal architect of the PU's economic policy, which has been remarkably successful. Nevertheless, the opposition charged Vuskovic with creating "shortages" and economic chaos. There are in fact shortages, though not economic chaos. As noted previously, their origin is in the success of the economic policy in stimulating demand, and not in its failure (see Chapters 22 and 25).

By March 1972 the Congressional opposition was trying to push through legislation to make it legally impossible to move on with socialization of the economy.

In general, opposition at the political level has been much more successful than the policy of trying to undermine the economy.

The Popular Unity has nevertheless achieved a tactical offensive by moving emphatically against the economic oligarchy, which was caught off balance by the election and subsequent events, by adroit moves in the sphere of promoting economic nationalism and national sover-

eignty, by capitalizing on the errors of the Right, and by
involving the Armed Forces in the process of change
(for a critical view of the last tactic see Chapter 15).
For the rest, political tactics are dictated by the maneuvers of the opposition. The PU is forced to try to
neutralize the middle strata through economic and social
policies that do not overly restrict their privileges and
through strict adherence to the democratic rules of the
game institutionalized within Chile's political culture. The
rules of the game, of course, have been devised to guide
and limit change *within* an existing social order; they
do not lend themselves to facilitating revolution, or
even basic changes not necessarily revolutionary. These
are probably the only viable tactics open to the PU for
the time being.

The Struggle for the Middle Strata

It is precisely in the Right's attempt to win over and
politically mobilize the rather substantial medium and
petty-bourgeois sectors and white-collar strata that the
threat of violent counterrevolution and fascism emerges.

In his Farewell Speech to Chileans, at the National
Stadium, Fidel Castro analyzed the danger and potential
of fascist reaction with brilliance and passion (see Chapter 17). At one point Fidel stated:

> You're going through a period that is very special,
> albeit not a new one, in the matter of class struggle.
> . . . You're going through that period in the process
> in which the fascists—to call them by their right name
> —are trying to beat you to the streets, are trying to
> beat you out of the middle strata of the population.
> The fascists . . . stop at nothing. . . . They'll try to
> sow terror and unrest among the middle strata, by
> telling the most terrible lies. . . . They'll appeal to
> the basest sensibilities. . . . They will try to arouse

feelings of chauvinism, arouse the lowest passions, arouse the most groundless terror.

The fascist potential is built into the social structure of Chile just as in other Latin American countries, such as Brazil and Guatemala, which are already well advanced on this most barbarous stage of capitalist development. It is the last defense of the dominant classes, and they play upon the petty privileges, status insecurities, and social pathologies of the social strata that class societies generate.

Countries such as Brazil and Guatemala (perhaps the Dominican Republic and Bolivia could also qualify) are not fascist in the classic Italian or German sense. They are in fact "colonial-fascist," to mention just one salient difference from European models. The dominant bourgeoisie of these countries, including Chile, are not aggressive imperialist classes, but *comprador* bourgeoisies, locked into dependent subservient relationships with foreign capital. Even the lesser bourgeoisie and sectors of the salaried middle strata are situated in structural patterns of dependence. They owe their jobs and social privilege directly or indirectly to the operations of multinational corporations and the cultural apparatus of world capitalism. They are thoroughly acculturated to the imported values of consumerism. The women of these strata in Chile were the ones who took to the streets of Santiago in December 1971 banging their empty pots, accompanied by fascist goon squads who went on a violent rampage against government supporters and offices of leftist organizations.

Having failed in their attempt to provoke a military coup in October 1970, rightist elements within Chile, the CIA, and corporate interests such as ITT may very well be working covertly to create a fascist reaction to the socialism of the Popular Unity. Moreover, the open political opposition of the parties within Chile and the official policy of the "big stick" on the part of the Nixon administration have objective implications similar to the behind-the-scenes operations of conspiratorial groups: the creation of a strong vested-interest reaction on the part of the middle strata, which are then mobilized to bring the threat of socialism to an end.

Fidel said in his Farewell Speech to the Chilean people:

> What do the exploiters do when their own institutions no longer guarantee their domination? . . . They simply go ahead and destroy them. . . .
>
> And we have been able to verify the manifestations of that law of history in which the reactionaries and the exploiters, in their desperation—and mainly supported from the outside—generate that political phenomenon, that reactionary current, fascism.

But Chile of 1972 is not Brazil of 1964 or Bolivia of 1971, and the violently repressive counterrevolutions of these countries cannot so easily be brought down in Chile. The Chilean Left and the Chilean people have great strength and resources. They have in fact some advantages in this struggle, because the Right and the United States often overplay their hands. While the opposition constantly raises the specter of the Popular Unity threat to cherished democratic traditions, the opposition itself uses its freedom to promote violence and sedition. The Right murders generals and conspires with foreign interests to provoke a military coup. The Right engages in sabotage and organizes private armies. The Left respects the best of Chile's political tradition and disavows violence. The United States swings its big stick again and again, and with each blow ten thousand more Chileans stand up to support their government, which shoulders each blow with firmness and dignity.

The strategy of Chilean reactionaries and their U.S. allies may very well fail, as it has up to now; even if they are successful in mobilizing a fascist groundswell and even if more and stronger pressures from U.S. business and Government are applied, the resultant civil war could very well create the conditions for America's second socialist revolution.

No one in his right mind wants socialism to emerge from fratricidal war and imperialist aggression. Only men like David Rockefeller, John McCone of the CIA-ITT complex, Richard Nixon, and their counterparts among the Chilean oligarchy shrug their shoulders when blood must run in the streets. Unfortunately the terms of the struggle are always dictated by the counterrevolutionary forces. That is an objective fact that we have to deal with. And it is the obligation of those of us situated here, within the world's center of imperialism, to work with total commitment and all the energy we can muster to constrain the capabilities of United States aggression, and finally, like other Chilean brothers and sisters, move onward toward the creation of a society free from the threat of fascism and the evils of militarism, a society of justice, equality, and social well-being, a nation that respects and lives in peace with other nations.

PART II

UNDERDEVELOPMENT
AND DEPENDENCE:

A View from Chile

CHAPTER 4

Copper: Chile's Wages of Toil

The Copper *Cueca**

by Evaristo López Almuna

Friends and comrades,
here I begin to sing
the national joy
because now the copper is Chilean,
friends and comrades.

It's all Chilean yes,
everybody's content.
The *gringos* robbed us
of our sustent.

Our sustent yes,
with arrogance
they took the copper
for their company.

For their company yes,
pocketing
the sweat
of the exploited miner.

Exploited yes,
for a century,
fattening the evil
blond guys.

* From *Puro Chile,* July 11, 1971. The *cueca* is a folkloric
Chilean rhythm and dance.

Bad guys yes,
drinking whiskey,
they left us the holes
taking out the blister.

They took out the blister yes,
Chuquicamata,
the Chilean is valiant,
never balking.

Never balking yes,
in El Teniente,
the copper has been won
for the people.

For the people yes,
of all Chile,
firmly carrying on
our *compañero*.

Our *compañero* yes,
in the Presidency,
with all its wealth
Chile remains.

Chile remains yes,
absolute owner,
the Yankees got
laid to rest.

Laid to rest yes,
El Salvador,
will fulfill its quota
of production.

Production yes,
as never before,
the corporations
got their due.

Got their due yes,
right on,

Anaconda, Kennecott
and Andina too.

And Andina yes,
copper so fine,
it's your strength and life
Chilean worker.

Chilean worker yes,
exporter
making a true
revolution.

Now the copper is Chilean,
putas, que güeno.

THE DECISIONS ON CHILE'S RESOURCES ARE MADE IN NEW YORK*

The working of Chilean copper mines by U.S. companies constitutes in fact a truly colonial hold on our country and on the Chilean economy. Chile is prevented from taking sovereign decisions regarding all basic aspects of this industry which forms the heart of our economic life. An exceptional system for the repatriation of the foreign currency has been imposed on Chile by the sale of the metal; modes of amortization have been fixed which involve a truly usurious process; our rate of exchange has been hurt by constant and periodic price rises, which explain to a large extent the chronic inflation that we suffer; the markets to which the metal must be sold have been designated and the prices at which it is to be sold. That is to say, the Chilean State cannot make any decision with regard to its basic natural resources: such decisions are made in New York.

* From an advertisement placed by the Chile Copper Corporation in the New York *Times,* January 25, 1971

The firms that have been working the copper mines in Chile are part of the financial groups that also own the processing companies. Hence, they are interested in taking the copper from our country at the lowest possible price. For this reason, they fixed the price of copper at 8 U.S. cents/lb in 1931 and lowered it to 5.5 cents in 1932. During World War II, they established it at 11.5 cents in spite of the fact that the world market price was considerably higher, resulting in a loss for our country of $500-million. During the Korean War, the U. S. Office of Economic Mobilization, jointly with Anaconda and Kennecott, determined unilaterally, without taking into account the public opinion in our country, the copper price at 24.5 cents. Morally speaking, Chile appeared to be financing a part of that war. In 1966, during the Vietnam war, they compelled us once again to sell 90,000 tons to the U.S. strategic reserve, at a price of 36 cents. In those years, copper was being quoted in the London market at 60 U.S. cents per lb.

For Chile, obviously, it is advantageous to get high prices for her raw materials. For the monopolies it is preferable to have low prices in order to reduce the cost of their processing plants. For Chile, it is advantageous to have more processing done in the country in order to enable her to integrate her national economy, to have more jobs, more industrial processing, more salaried positions, more taxes, more sales in the country, and more foreign currency. The foreign monopolies are not interested in industrializing Chile; their objective is to leave in their home country the great worth that adds the processing costs to the price of the metal and produces great industrial and commercial activity and high salaries. Chile is interested in safeguarding her reserves and in obtaining from them the maximum advantage, as the need arises. The foreign companies are interested in taking out the maximum amount of copper at the lowest price and within the shortest possible time. Chile is interested in doing business with all countries of the world and in such manner that our copper can contribute to a better life for all men. The monopolies are interested in keeping us restricted to their captive markets that totally serve their commercial convenience.

Large American companies have made fabulous, almost incredible profits with minimum investments in Chile. The original investment by U.S. companies in the copper industry represented only $3.5-million. All the rest was derived from the operation of that same industry.

A similar situation exists in the iron and nitrate industries. The four big U.S. companies that have been working these natural resources in Chile collected earnings of $10.8-billion in the course of the past 60 years.

This figure is of tremendous significance for Chile if one compares it with the fact that the G.N.P. achieved throughout the entire existence of the country, that is, approximately 400 years, amounts to $10.5-billion. The conclusion is clear: in a little over half a century these U.S. companies took out from our country an amount greater than that created by Chileans in terms of industries, highways, cities, ports, schools, hospitals, trade, etc., during our country's entire history.

This is the basic cause of our underdevelopment, the basic cause of our meager industrial growth, of our primitive agriculture, unemployment, low wages, our very low standard of life, the high rate of infant mortality, and it is the cause of our poverty and backwardness.

Worldwide Consensus

In point of fact, the United Nations, during its Seventeenth Session, formulated a declaration of principles, as follows:

"The right of peoples and nations to permanent sovereignty over their natural riches and resources is the one to

be exercised by them in the interest of national development and the well-being of the people or the State, respectively.

"The exploration, the development and the making
available of these resources, as well as the importation of
foreign capital to carry them into effect must be in conformity with the rules and conditions which these peoples
and nations deem necessary and desirable of their own
free will for authorizing or prohibiting such activities.

"The free and advantageous exercise of the sovereignty
of the peoples and nations regarding their natural resources must be developed through mutual respect among
States on the basis of sovereign equality.

"The international cooperation in the economic development of the developing countries, the investment
of public or private capital, exchange of goods and services, technical assistance or exchange of scientific information, shall be of such a nature as to promote the interests of the independent national development of those
countries and shall be based on the respect of their sovereignty over their natural riches and resources.

"The violation of the sovereign rights of the peoples
and nations over their national riches and resources is
contrary to the spirit and the principles of the Charter of
the United Nations and obstructs the development of international cooperation and the maintenance of peace."

In turn, the Encyclicals of Pope John XXIII and Paul
VI, "Pacem in Terris" and "Populorum Progressio," respectively, do, besides recognizing it, establish the obligation of the States to expropriate those activities that constitute an impediment to the progress of the peoples and
the needs of organized communities.

All of Chile in Favor of Nationalization

On the other hand, it is indicated to recall that the
nationalization of the copper industry constituted a part

of the electoral platform announced by the candidates of the Popular Unity Party (Unidad Popular) as well as by the Christian Democrats. Even the candidate of the right, Mr. Alessandri and notable members of that wing had considered the need for carrying out drastic reform measures in the mining field and, to that end, had submitted various drafts on nationalization in the past.

Finally it must be pointed out that the Draft of the Constitutional Reform affects neither directly nor indirectly the essential elements inherent in a Constitutional State, such as the basic freedoms of the human being: of free thought, belief, and expression in any form, nor those that govern the free functioning of the democratic and representative institutional system.

NATURAL RESOURCES AND DEVELOPMENT*

FIDEL CASTRO

To have an idea of the work done by the Chilean copper workers all one needs is to look at this amphitheater nearly 1200 feet deep. This gives us an idea of how much sweat, how much effort, how much sacrifice, how much work—year after year, month after month, day after day —was required to extract an incalculable amount of copper from the deposits which nature so generously bestowed on the people of Chile.

And yet, there is a new circumstance which makes this effort a much more noble effort, which makes this work much more honorable, which makes the shedding of every drop of sweat infinitely more satisfactory. And this circum-

* Excerpts from a speech given by Fidel Castro before the copper miners of Chuquicamata, Chile, on November 14, 1971. Translation by the Cuban Government.

stance is that today this copper belongs to the Chilean nation.

These machines, these installations—whose cost was infinitely less than the vast quantities of copper which were obtained through the sweat of the Chilean workers and taken out of the country decade after decade—now belong to Chile.

And everything that is conceived and developed in this mining center from now on will be placed at the service of Chile.

Considering the production of this mine, one day lost in this mine means one million dollars less in foreign exchange for the Chilean economy. Each day's production in this mine means one million dollars for the Chilean economy. Ten tons less in 360 days means a difference of 3.6 million dollars less; 100 tons less means 36 million dollars less. Now, you can imagine how much a country can do with 36 million dollars in foreign exchange, no matter where they are invested.

Suffice it say, for example, that our country has a program for building high schools. . . . We expect to build, from now to 1980, around 1000 junior high schools in the countryside; excellent schools. These schools will have laboratories for the study of physics, chemistry and biology so the students will be given a top-flight education. The laboratories for these schools, with their film projectors, etc. will cost 15,000 dollars.

Now then, the laboratories for these 1000 schools with a capacity for half a million students, will cost us 15 million dollars. This means that 100 tons less produced here in a year's time—to mention one example—would mean the loss of the resources with which you could purchase the laboratories for approximately 2500 high schools; the technological equipment needed to give 1,250,000 young people a top-flight education. This will give you an idea.

In terms of cattle—to cite an example—36 million in

foreign exchange would make it possible for you to acquire high-quality cows, capable of producing 15 quarts
of milk a day, paying 360 dollars each in foreign exchange
—they can be obtained for less—and bring them to the
pasturelands in the valleys. . . . You could buy 100,000
cows with 36 million in foreign exchange. With 70,000 or
75,000 of these in production you could get one million
quarts of milk per day out of the cows you can purchase
with 36 million in foreign exchange. This would mean
half a quart of milk a day for two million children. That's
what the cows purchased with 36 million in foreign exchange—a difference of 100 tons a day—would produce.

By the time we got to the concentrate plant today,
things were getting rough—you know what I mean?
Turning a corner, I saw three workers holding bottles of
milk in their hands. I didn't know it was milk then; all I
saw was these white bottles and I asked, "What is it?"
Well, right away, I found myself with one of those bottles
in my hand, and I was so thirsty and a little hungry from
all the driving around the pampa and all the altitude, that
I had that bottle of milk for lunch. Good milk, too, but
imported. How many millions do you spend on milk?

Now, wouldn't it be wonderful if it were possible to
give two million workers every day—every day, mind
you!—a bottle of milk like that which was offered us;
like the ones those workers were drinking, with their noon
or midnight snack?

That is why I was trying to explain to you what a difference of 100 tons in the production of copper can mean
to the people of Chile. And, quite often, if we want to
really understand the value of things we have to speak in
terms of schools and hospitals. And this is only the difference in one year. I'm speaking of one year's time. If it
were a case of 10 years, just multiply all these figures by
10. In terms of schools, it is no longer a matter of 2500
schools but rather 25,000 schools; no longer a matter of

laboratories for five and a half million young people but rather for 25 million young people. It's no longer the case of 100,000 cows but rather of one million cows plus their daughters and granddaughters.

The nation needs many industrial plants. This is true of all of our countries. I'm telling you about the problems we also have and how we analyze these things. You have development programs now. These development programs weren't designed to enrich anyone in particular. These programs were designed to enrich the Chilean nation; to boost employment, to create wealth for the good of all Chileans.

Our peoples have nowhere near provided for all their needs. We still need many schools, school equipment and supplies, just to cite one example. We still need many hospitals, hospital equipment, medicines and pharmaceutical factories. Our peoples need housing by the hundreds of thousands if not by the millions. They need roads, irrigation systems and dams to boost food production and raise their standard of living. Our peoples need everything—all kinds of factories, synthetic goods factories, modern factories—in order to keep up with civilization and achieve the ideal for which they have sacrificed and struggled all through the generations: a better destiny for the human being.

I have mentioned all these things, all these viewpoints, because you are the principal producers of foreign exchange for the Chilean economy. You play a decisive role in Chile's economy. You play a decisive role in the future of Chile. What you produce, the product you turn out, is vital to the people of Chile. And we are convinced that the more the workers in this center realize its importance the greater effort they will put forth; that the more aware they become of the problem the harder they will work to consolidate their country's independence.

The former owners of these installations tried—for

their own benefit, of course—to maintain a top-flight organization in the flow of production. They tried to obtain top-flight discipline. And they got it through various means: by paying higher wages, by putting on pressure, sometimes by using psychology, that is, by giving prizes, etc.—in other words, by employing all kinds of resources to obtain organization and discipline.

When the nation takes over for the foreign owners, when these mines and these resources pass into the hands of the nation, everything that is effective in organization must be maintained. The equipment must be maintained. Discipline must be maintained. Because if there was discipline in the past—not to benefit Chile, not to benefit the Chilean workers, nor for the well-being of the Chilean people but, instead, for the benefit of the outside—then all the more reason for the workers, aware of their duty, to maintain their discipline and improve their organization to maintain and increase work discipline.

If, in the past, all these things were done without any benefit to the country or the people, then all the more reason to make a great effort now, when all this copper is placed at the service of the Chilean people, of the Chilean nation.

We have always spoken in these terms to our compatriots. Always. And we've told them the following: it is easier to change the structure than to change the consciousness of man. Social structures are changed. Sometimes this takes a lot of work. But if it takes a lot of work to change structures, it often takes a lot of work, too, to change habits. A change, a new situation, comes about as a result of long years of struggle, of a conflict between the interests of the homeland and the interests of those abroad; a conflict between the interests of the working class and the interests of those who exploited the workers.

When the circumstances change, when this conflict disappears, when the interests of the nation and of the working class are the same as the interests of the workers of this center, the same as the interests of production and of the functioning of this work center, an effort must be made to see that these interests will always be the same.

We have infinite confidence in the workers. We know how they always come through; how they always take hold and do what they have to. Because, gentlemen, a worker is a worker!

And this worker, who knows what work is, who knows what sacrifice is, always responds to the interests of his homeland; always responds to the interests of his people, and he is always in the vanguard when his country needs him, when his class needs him!

CHAPTER 5

The United States Presence in Chile

By the time Salvador Allende was elected President of Chile, United States influence throughout the Chilean economy and society was extremely pervasive. Mining and significant sectors of the industrial economy were under U.S. control; the country was heavily in debt to U.S. financial institutions (or international institutions under U.S. control) and thereby subject to the "strings" attached to U.S. aid; military and police forces were equipped and trained by U.S. assistance programs, and the national culture had been undermined (especially among the middle strata and upper classes) by a very strong North American cultural presence propagated through penetration of the Chilean communications media. The selections in this chapter document some aspects and consequences of U.S. corporate presence in industry and the mass media, Chile's technological dependence, and the U.S. build-up of a contingent of the Carabineer Corps (The "Mobile Group" tactical squad) as a reactionary and repressive force.

Wall Street Behind the Plot Against Chile*

One billion dollars—which produce a yearly profit of $500 million from return on investments, interest, amortization of investments, and payments for technical services—is the sum of American capital invested in Chile. This billion dollars converts Chile into a big business for

* Abridged from *Punto Final* No. 119, December 8, 1970. The author is unidentified except by the pseudonym "Observador."

the imperialists. Different governments, such as the Christian Democratic, have endeavored to protect these investments to such an extent (as occurred with El Salvador Copper Mine in March 1966) that the state preferred to assassinate Chilean workers rather than endanger the interests of the North American companies.

After the triumph of the Popular Unity in September, imperialism embarked upon a rightist conspiracy that culminated in the murder of General René Schneider. In the meantime, measures were taken to withdraw certain projects installed in Chile, such as "meteorological" observation centers, and to reduce the large Yankee military and police missions. Parallel to this, private American firms such as NIBSA, a foundry employing 280 workers, and Alimentos Purina de Chile, S.A. started output reductions that almost resulted in total shutdowns.

NIBSA, a subsidiary of the conglomerate NIBCO, which controls over 50 per cent of the shares (25 per cent are owned by ADELA, an international financial corporation, and the rest by the Chilean firm SGM), adopted a belligerent attitude toward the new government. NIBCO sent David Hyams to Chile, and the manager proceeded to close down the factory on November 2 (Allende was inaugurated on November 3, 1970). Simultaneously, unacceptable communications were exchanged between NIBCO and their representative in Chile. One in particular referred to the anti-Communist blood bath occurring in Indonesia as a good remedy against the revolutionary process in Chile. This revealed the line of thought of the American investors.

President Allende's government ordered state intervention of both these companies. The workers began to produce under optimum conditions. In Purina (a plant producing balanced poultry and pig feed near Limache, a farm producing six hundred thousand chickens per year, and a plant processing three hundred thousand chickens per month in Nogales), the workers raised production by 50 per cent. They have requested the government to definitely expropriate the industry so that this may form part of a state-owned feed enterprise. . . .

The Purina Ties

Like all North American consortiums, Purina is a link in a vast financial complex with ramifications buried in political terrain. The firm intervened by the government is an affiliate of Ralston Purina, whose capital is valued at $676 million. At the same time, Ralston Purina is an active participant in the Latin American Agricultural Development Program (LAAD), headed by the Bank of America, whose tentacles within the Chilean banking system will shortly be cut off.

In February 1970 the Bank of America announced the formation of LAAD, with the participation of the Atlantic Development Corporation for Latin America (ADELA), a private investment corporation, and ten other large, multinational corporations. Among these are Caterpillar Tractor Co., Deere & Co., Gerber Products Co., Monsanto, Standard Fruit, Borden Co., Cargill, Inc., CPC International, Ralston Purina, and Dow Chemical. The Bank of America (which has eight branch banks in Chile) slipped into Chile under the Christian Democratic administration of Frei. The same happened with Dow Chemical, which took over our petrochemical industry. . . .

Alimentos Purina de Chile, S.A., had handed over 20 per cent of its shares to the influential owner of the *El Mercurio* newspaper, Agustín Edwards, who is presently in self-imposed "exile" in the United States. Edwards, through his influence, acted as an agent to obtain —without too much difficulty—what Ralston Purina wanted from Frei's government.

Ralston Purina, which owns four plants in the Peruvian

fish-meal industry, was fortunately not able to penetrate into the Chilean fishing industry, where there are already other foreign interests. The strategy of Ralston Purina in Latin America includes three stages: 1. The establishment of a marketing organization to collect, process, and distribute chickens produced by the numerous small breeders, who in general are badly organized. 2. Once this network is established, Ralston Purina sets up plants to produce feeds and organizes supplies to provision breeders. 3. Once the breeders become dependent upon Purina for their feeds, sale of birds, etc., they are faced with the situation of increasing exploitation and are more and more subject to any crisis in the industry, such as the recent shutdown of Purina. This is what motivated the government intervention.

A multinational corporation such as Ralston Purina can, as it did in Chile, suspend its operations in any country without seriously affecting its margin of total profit. The Chilean "partner"—in this case, Agustín Edwards—also does not suffer as a result of the closure of the plant. Those really affected are the Chilean poultry producers and consumers.

It is worth noting that Ralston Purina, established throughout Latin America, has already achieved the first stage of its strategy in Colombia, Brazil, Peru, Nicaragua, El Salvador, and Jamaica. It has also made firm progress in Venezuela, Argentina, Guatemala, and Mexico. Nor is this mechanism peculiar to Latin America. Their strategy is in advanced stages in countries such as Australia, where the effects upon the producers and the deterioration of their standard of living has become a political issue.

The Bank of America

The alliance established by the Bank of America with the largest multinational corporations operating in agriculture means that the influx of foreign monopoly capital (represented in the agricultural sphere in Chile by Petrodow and Ralston Purina) will be difficult to control. Through the Bank of America the financial alliance reached with LAAD has a direct influence on the North American "aid" program. The President of the Bank of America, Rudolf Petersen, was chosen by Nixon to head a committee to study and make recommendations redefining North American "aid."

The strategy of the Bank of America is to obtain control of Chilean agriculture. Agriculture is the specialty of the bank. In the past five years it has managed to establish forty-five branches in Latin America. In 1968, the president of the bank made the following statement regarding its interests in the agricultural fields: ". . . [we] have profound roots in agriculture. We are the largest agricultural lenders in the world. . . . Our total commitments in agriculture are approximately three billion dollars. We have been in agriculture for a long time and it is our aim to remain [in this field] for an even longer period. In a very real sense of the word, agriculture is our business."

Due to the fact that further exploitation is somewhat difficult in the United States, the Bank of America has extended its operations abroad since 1968. Within Latin America it has shown special interest in Chile, where it has the largest number of branches.

The danger that is presented separately by Ralston Purina, Petrodow, and the Bank of America is multiplied even more by the joint strategy of these corporations through LAAD.

Foreign Control of the Chilean Economy

The real magnitude of foreign control in the national economy, accentuated during the Frei administration in manufacturing, has not been estimated or analyzed by many of the Left's analysts. . . . Foreign capital tries to control the industrial sector and, within it, the more advanced and dynamic technological sector. Due to the insufficiency of data, it is difficult to make a detailed examination of the process. However, as a result of a recent publication made by ODEPLAN,[1] it has been possible to appreciate more exactly how foreign capital has penetrated and exploited those sectors of commerce and manufacturing where expansion and profits are possible.

The statistics indicate that foreign investments grew rapidly from 1966 and that the remittances abroad started to rise sharply as of 1967. In the fields of rubber, chemical products, petroleum, and coal the investments started to diminish in 1966, whereas the profit remitted abroad rose spectacularly after 1967. If it can be considered that this trend has continued, it might well be shown that in 1969 and 1970 the foreign capital investments were slowly being illicitly withdrawn. If other sectors are examined (apart from commerce and construction), where investments have grown rapidly, it can be shown that foreign influence was already well advanced by 1968. Some experts calculate that in manufacturing the proportion of the total assets controlled by foreigners was thirty per cent, as against the 17 per cent estimate indicated by Pedro Vuskovic, present Minister of Economy. . . .

The notorious movement of investments toward manufacturing makes it necessary for nationalization to be introduced in this field also. It is possible that the industrial field, which has replaced the Yankee interest in mining, will be where the most serious confrontations with imperialism will take place. The same will occur in banking, insurance, and shipping, where the influence of North American capital is tremendous. The nationalization of the financial and insurance sectors will no doubt

[1] National Planning Office.

produce an important reactivation of the conspiracy governed and financed from the United States with a view to destroying the national economy. . . .

THE HIDDEN INVASION*

JOSÉ CAYUELA

Technological dependence is one of the most complex problems confronting today's Latin American governments. In simple terms, the question is, how much does it cost the Chilean economy to assemble in Chile the cars we use? How much does each Chilean pay for the privilege of wearing a prestigious American-label shirt made here in Chile, by Chileans, with Chilean materials? More importantly, how can we replace foreign technology with our own?

The International Research Institute of the University of Chile is currently working on a study project that shows that most technological innovations currently in use in Chile have been imported from abroad. This process of technological importation, while probably as old as our industrialization process itself, was accelerated in the fifties to reach an incredible level during the Frei administration.

What has been called the "denationalization" of Chilean industry is part of a world-wide trend. While grave, the Chilean case is less alarming than that of Argentina or Brazil. Yet this is a difference in degree, not in kind. Moreover, did not our governments in the past two decades claim to hold to a much more independent international road than those adopted in Buenos Aires or Brasilia? Yet a close examination of patent

* From *Ahora* No. 5, March 5, 1971.

registration yields these disturbing facts: in 1965, 87 per cent of the registered patents were of foreign origin. In 1969, as a result of the acceleration of the "denationalization" process, the proportion of foreign patents reached 94.5 per cent. . . . In 1969, forty-seven foreign firms, most of them North American, controlled 53.7 per cent of all patents registered in Chile.

The Price of Dependence

This situation is grave for two reasons. First, it is economically costly. In 1968, for instance, we paid foreign corporations $4,670,000 for patent rights. In the sector of food, beverage, and tobacco production alone, we paid $1,713,000—quite a price to pay for the privilege of producing Coca-Cola, Viceroy cigarettes, and Nestlé's powdered milk. . . . Much graver still is the political dimension of this denationalization. Foreign corporate giants not only seek to curb our technological creativity, but also attempt to determine our collective needs and aspirations, making sure that our privileged classes will keep up with the Joneses. . . .

Our technicians in the copper industry are now acutely aware of the political dimension of technological dependence. In the old days, when our mineral resources were foreign controlled, technical problems were easily solved. A telex message was simply rushed to the United States and a new part promptly flown in. Now, of course, the replacement of broken parts is not so easily resolved. . . .

Technocrats have always preferred to "solve" such problems by merely paying the political and economic costs of technological invasion. Under the Christian Democrats, our markets were literally flooded with American-brand products, and our economy was turned over to American corporate giants. The present government must face the problems of technological dependence with courage in order to curb its economic costs and, more importantly, protect our political independence.

FOOD PROGRAM FOR CHILE WILL BE ENDED*

The U. S. government will not renew its government-to-government food for peace program with Chile, according to a U.S. embassy statement.

The elimination of the program, valued at $4,320,000 in 1970, comes at a time when Chile is experiencing serious problems in agricultural production.

News was communicated to the government of President Salvador Allende by Charles Mathias, head of the U.S. economic mission.

The decision could also foreshadow the refusal of a $12,000,000 project request made by Chile to the U.N. World Food Program for nutritional assistance to hospitals, university hostels and disadvantaged children.

Allende is carrying out at present a national plan to supply free milk to all children up to 15 years old and to pregnant and nursing women. To fulfill this, it has been necessary to import whole milk from Belgium.

During the present year, the government has contracted commitments for $21,000,000 with the object of assuring the supply of 105,600,000 lbs. of free milk to Chilean children. The proposals for 1972 are reported to be for the supply of 132,000,000 lbs. of milk.

To meet these goals, the country has to supply a good proportion through its own milk production. This presupposes that agricultural activities are normal with preferential treatment for dairies. These last two requirements are not being fulfilled.

Agrarian reform has been, in the last three months,

* From *Times of the Americas,* March 31, 1971.

tremendously disturbed by the seizures of lands and strikes. To these have been added adverse climatic conditions all of which indicate a decrease in national farm production.

U.S. GIVES CHILE CREDITS
FOR MILITARY PURCHASES*

The United States has granted Chile $5 million in credits for purchase of military equipment here in the first such gesture by Washington toward the socialist government of President Salvador Allende Gossens.

YANKEE TELEVISION CONTROL†

MÁXIMO HUMBERT

During the past ten years, television has become the world's most important means of information and communication. The North American imperialists have well understood that it could be utilized as an essential tool of political propaganda, as a vital instrument with which to shape societal values and aspirations. . . .

In the United States, three powerful networks compete in the field of television: the American Broadcasting Co. (ABC), the Columbia Broadcasting System (CBS), and the National Broadcasting Co. (NBC).

Unable to compete within the United States with the two giants (CBS and NBC), ABC was the first to extend itself into international markets. Its international subsidiary, Worldvision, controls an extensive chain of com-

* From the New York *Times,* June 30, 1971
† From *Punto Final* No. 87, September 9, 1969.

mercial stations throughout the world. In 1965 ABC and ITT proposed to merge. Had the merger been completed, it would not only have permitted ABC to consolidate the precarious state of its internal finances but would also have provided it with the international "contacts" of ITT, the giant of international communications systems. As one of the five corporations authorized by the Federal Communications Commission to lease transmission channels from COMSAT (the Communications Satellite Corporation), ITT would have found in ABC an ideal client. ABC of course would also have become an ideal outlet for ITT's manufactured telecommunications systems. Alas, both corporations were forced to scrap their idyllic plans. The Justice Department, in the name of the anti-trust law, denied them the merger, which the Federal Communications Commission had already authorized. In spite of such adversity, ABC continued to expand. In 1968, ABC controlled sixty-seven television stations in twenty-seven countries. Twenty-seven of those stations are located in Latin America, reaching twenty million households, or roughly eighty million spectators. ABC expanded abroad in a typical imperialist fashion. Counting on the technological dependence of underdeveloped nations, ABC starts by supplying the elected station with technological know-how. Financial aid soon follows, with technical and administrative services and personnel-training programs. Most important, however, for the consolidation of its empire, ABC supplies the station with its prepackaged programs while it also becomes the station's sales representative.

As part of the business agreement, the station must surrender to ABC the power to choose both programs and sponsors for its peak hours. ABC, for instance, may sell "Batman" to a particular corporation and impose both the program and the sponsor's commercial "spots" upon any of its affiliated stations. Thus ABC is more than a gigantic publicity agency, for it directly controls the buyers and distributors of its products. ABC has thus constituted itself into a worldwide centralized network able to supply the prospective sponsor with whatever market he may wish to penetrate in any region or country of his choice.

ABC's expansion tactics and organizational structure illustrate the mode by which a communications medium, especially television, can be utilized to insure the penetration and domination of foreign economies. No sooner was the so-called Central American common market created than ABC invested $250,000 in each of the five member countries.

Through its television stations, ABC is promoting a style of consumerism that in the majority of the so-called Third World nations should in no way have precedence over public education needs, national health, and basic economic development. Such real development needs are of course totally opposed to the economic interests of international monopoly capital. Not satisfied with only CATVN, its Central American television network, ABC now plans a similar chain, LATINO (International Organization of Latin American Television), which would service Venezuela, Ecuador, Uruguay, Argentina, Chile, and Mexico. ABC's Chilean subsidiary station goes under the name of PROTAB.

The two giants of North American television, CBS and NBC, have not of course left their "small" competitor alone on the international gravy train. They have not, however, thrown themselves into the international field with the zest and ardor of ABC, for they enjoy within the United States exceptional financial strength. Their profits climb higher every year. NBC is itself a subsidiary of RCA, which also owns publishing houses, a rent-a-car company, various manufacturers of electronic equipment, etc. CBS's vast empire also includes publishing houses, film-production industries, toy companies, even the New York Yankees professional baseball team. Although much smaller than ABC's, CBS's and NBC's foreign investments tend to be placed in highly strategic locations. CBS, for instance, owns film-production companies in Buenos Aires, Caracas, and Lima. NBC is established in Mexico, Caracas, Saigon, and the Middle East. NBC specializes in the fields of programing and service contracts rather than in direct investments in television stations. Its subsidiary, NBC International, does business with eighty-two countries, selling programs and "administrative services."

The purpose of these "management services" becomes clearer as one encounters NBC insisting on a specific type of programing with respect to certain "priorities." NBC has declared that its objective for Latin America is not the control of television stations but rather the sale of RCA's television equipment.

As for CBS, it has concentrated its foreign investments in Latin America. CBS owns subsidiaries in almost every Latin American capital: PEOARTEL in Buenos Aires, PROVENTEL in Caracas, PANTEL in Lima, the Trinidad-Tobago TV Company, Telegramas Latinoamericanos de Panamá. The imperial octopus has not left a single region untouched. . . .

Meanwhile, no matter how violent or objectionable, certain programs keep on rising in the weekly ratings. These ratings are what determine a series' sale value. If it rates low in the United States, it disappears and the producer loses most of his investment. Not all of it, though: there is still the back yard, Latin America, where it can be peddled along with a high-rating program. Series are sold in "packages." The chain of distributors and intermediaries is endless, with sizable chunks for everyone involved. There are agents, for instance, who buy the distribution rights for all of Latin America or for a particular country and promptly resell these rights to specific stations. In Chile, there is PROTAB, a subsidiary of ABC whose objective is to resell television programs made in the United States. The price of each canned idiocy is determined in the United States and is directly proportionate to the number of prospective viewers and advertising benefits. . . . In order to lower these sometimes astronomical costs, the station is forced to buy whole "packages," which may well include particularly bad movies. All of this Yankee production aims at the moronization of the masses and strives to keep the people content inhabitants of the capitalist universe, to transform them into mindless consumers. All the "bad" men in American television have either Russian or Chinese names. As for the heroes, they are prototypical American marines.

The mind-rape occurs at all levels. The advertisers impose tremendous distortions of contemporary history. All television stations in the capitalist world must obtain their information through international news services. Most are North American, English, or French. To top this, the United States Government, through USIS, supplies free of charge the information any medium might request. We have all heard and seen in movie houses as well as on television the sinister apologies of the endless virtues of the Alliance for Progress.

Communication via satellite now provides imperialism with the greatest means of ideological subversion ever known to man. While the imperialists reap stupendous profits, mesmerized Latin America can see through the magic box what is happening on the moon—the planting of the American flag on lunar soil; President Nixon's chat with the astronauts—and listen to the United States national anthem transmitted directly from the moon. It can also see that Coca-Cola is better, that Ford is superior, etc.

U.S.A. MANIPULATED THE "MOBILE GROUP"*

P.D.G.

When the *guanacos* (high-pressure water trucks), which formed the attack vanguard of the Mobile Group, appeared in the neighborhoods of Santiago to comply with their peaceful mission of watering plants in the outskirts of the city, something must have collapsed in the Office of Public Safety Assistance (OPSA) of the United States. There, the expectations and calculations, as well as the high expense of maintenance in dollars, form part of a strong and protective tower of police assistance for all the organizations of repression that function in the countries of the Third World. The objectives are very different from the social task that is being carried out today by the former Mobile Group of the police.

North American imperialism attacks with its programs of foreign aid and investments by monopolies for the purpose of obtaining from the underdeveloped countries a very slow economic growth and, consequently, easy and abundant profits. In this environment, even the smallest manifestation of insecurity and rebellion becomes the main enemy to be combated. In this environment, unattractive for investments, OPSA put into practice a remedy that mixed the democratic concept of "law and order" with North American experience. The experience had been gathered by local police forces and compiled by the Office of Crime Control and Riot Security together with "counterinsurgency" measures and lessons drawn from the study of repression of urban subversives.

* From *Punto Final* No. 119, December 8, 1970.

The axioms for these programs stemmed from such elemental premises as: "The maintenance of law and order, including internal security, is one of the fundamental responsibilities of a government," and "In order to maintain the social, economic, and political progress of a country, it is first necessary to develop an ample program of police function."

The Mobile Group of the Carabineers was one of the favorites of OPSA. There were important considerations: its financing was lower than that of the military forces and its pay-off was greater effectiveness. Airplanes, tanks, and artillery cost more than water-throwing trucks, tear gas, laxative gas, shotguns, etc. At least that was the argument used to obtain backing from President John Kennedy and his brother Robert, Attorney General in 1962, for a substantial expansion of the Internal Security Program, which afterward centered all the activities of North American Police Assistance in the Office of Public Safety Assistance. These same two Kennedys also enthusiastically backed the creation of the Inter-American Police Academy in the Panama Canal Zone, which was later moved to Washington and reorganized as the International Police Academy.

It was here that Vicente Huerta Celis attended special courses. He later attained the rank of general of the Carabineers and became Director General of the Mobile Group. Under the command of Huerta, the Mobile Group grew enormously, until it became one of the most experienced repressive forces of Latin America. With the acquiescence of the former administration, North American "internal security" advisers proliferated. They gave complete courses not only to the personnel selected for the Mobile Group, but also to rank-and-file policemen and line officers. Many officers of the Carabineers followed the same road taken by the pioneer Huerta, thus converting the Carabineers into one of the favorites of the International Police Academy. This favoritism was concretized with light armaments, ammunition, radio equipment, patrol cars, jeeps, chemical munitions, and various other equipment, which were delivered with such generosity that it even created unpleasant difficulties with the Armed Forces.

The International Police Academy sent many of their personnel to other Latin American countries, and by the middle of 1970 they had no less than ninety internal-security advisers in about fifteen countries of this hemisphere. In addition, the Academy trained in its Washington headquarters about two thousand officers of Latin American police forces. Total spending by OPSA by July 1, 1970, was estimated at approximately $39 million. North American expenditures for police assistance for each country ranged from $2 million in Bolivia, Costa Rica, El Salvador, Guyana, Honduras, Uruguay, and Venezuela, to $3 to $4 million in Colombia, the Dominican Republic, Ecuador, and Panama. Chile occupied the second place with $5 million, while the gorilla military regimes of Brazil and Argentina were at the top of the list with $7 million. . . . The efficiency of these services has been proved quite well and to the liking of the United States if we measure the degree of repression that exists in the Brazilian regime. This regime holds the sad record of being one of the countries "where torture and police brutality have attained such a degree of perversion that it is repulsive to human nature," as denounced by international organizations and by Pope Paul VI himself. (Over one hundred thousand Brazilian police have been trained through U.S. aid.)

Thanks to the help and loyal service of Huerta, the Carabineer Corps not only gained the efficiency of its regular police, but also started to include in its organization paramilitary forces, distorting its old mission of guarding the security of citizens into that of a sort of praetorian guard. At one time, its chief—fortunately today former chief—intended to use the guard against the constitution of the republic. This plan of the former Director General of Carabineers has come to light before the military court hearing the case of the murder of General Schneider.

Converted into a sort of "Frankenstein," the former functions of the Carabineers became distorted, and the corps evolved into an organization for the detection and identification of subversive individuals or organizations, for the neutralization of "subversive" activities, and for the control of demonstrations and revolts. The objective of OPSA in Chile had thus been attained. The Mobile Group was a power that acted rapidly, vigorously, and effectively against any popular expression. Attesting to this are the many students, workers, and slum dwellers who faced the Mobile Group and became victims of their actions.

The OPSA must indeed be in mourning for this sudden change in the function of the Mobile Group of Chile in compliance with point 37 of the first forty measures to be taken by the government of the people. The reorganization of this section of the uniformed police, so that it may not be used again as an organization of repression against the people, has now become a reality.

However, within the Carabineer Corps—in spite of Allende's instructions that they should not shoot against the people—there are still provocateurs at the service of the parties of the Right. One incident occurred on November 26, 1970, at the "Lo Prado Abajo" estate of Las Barrancas. A group of Carabineers under orders of Captain Conrado Pacheco Cárdenas, who has a fearful history, fired upon a group of peasants and severely wounded seventeen-year-old Juan Félix Leiva Riquelme. The estate, property of José Guzmán Riesco, was intervened by "CORA" (Agrarian Reform Corporation).

The landowner, who did not farm even 10 per cent of his land, asked the Carabineers to attack the peasants, a task that Captain Pacheco accomplished with pleasure. The government ordered a thorough investigation, and sanctions were announced. Cases like this reveal that the reactionary seed sown by Huerta and the North Americans in the Carabineers grew vigorously and that it will be hard to remove it by its roots. However, this is a task that must be done without hesitation, because the threats that proceed from that quarter are obvious.

CHAPTER 6

The Search for National Independence

Chile's search for national independence involves much more than taking control of the nation's natural resources from foreign capital; it is a process of transferring many large private business enterprises, foreign and domestic, into the sphere of social property in order to direct all available resources toward national development. Selections for this chapter therefore include a statement of the economic policies of the Popular Unity government together with a case history, the intervention of Ford Motor Co., to illustrate one means by which socialization of industry is carried out. Also included are a summary of the PU's foreign policy, a poetic statement by Pablo Neruda on the renegotiation of Chile's foreign debt, and a news story on economic aid from the Communist countries.

ECONOMIC DEVELOPMENT PROGRAM OF THE POPULAR UNITY*

The united popular forces seek as the central objective of their policy to replace the present economic structure, putting an end to the power of national and foreign monopolistic capital and of latifundism in order to begin the construction of socialism.

In the new economy, planning will play an extremely important role. The central planning organizations will

* From the electoral program of the Popular Unity.

be at the highest administrative level and their democratically generated decisions will have an executive
character.

Area of Social Property

The process of transforming our economy will begin
with a policy destined to make up a dominant state
area formed by the enterprises that the state presently
possesses along with the enterprises that will be expropriated. The first step will be to nationalize those basic
sources of wealth such as the large mining companies of
copper, iron, nitrate and others which are controlled by
foreign capital and internal monopolies. Into this area of
nationalized activities will be integrated the following
sectors:

1) the large mining companies of copper, nitrate,
iodine, iron and coal;

2) the country's financial system, especially private
banks and insurance companies;

3) foreign trade;

4) the great distribution enterprises and monopolies;

5) the strategic industrial monopolies;

6) in general all those activities which determine
the country's economic and social development such
as the production and distribution of electrical energy;
rail, air and maritime transportation; communications;
the production, refining and distribution of petroleum
and its derivatives—including bottled gas; iron and
steel production; cement, petrochemicals and heavy
chemicals; cellulose and paper.

All these expropriations will be carried out with complete respect for the interest of the small shareholder.

Area of Private Property

This area includes all those sectors of industry, mining, agriculture and services in which the private ownership of the means of production remains in effect.

In numbers these enterprises will be the majority. For example, in 1967, of the 30,500 industries (including craft industries), only some 150 controlled the markets monopolistically, monopolizing state aid and bank credit and exploiting the other industrial enterprises of the country by selling raw materials to them at a high price and buying their products at a low price.

The enterprises that make up this sector will be aided by the general planning of the national economy. The state will provide the necessary financial and technical assistance to the enterprises of this area so that they can fulfill the important role they play in the national economy, paying heed to the number of persons who work for them as well as the volume of production they generate.

In addition the systems of patents, customs duties, taxes and tributes will be simplified for these enterprises and they will be assured of an adequate and just commercialization of their products.

In these enterprises the rights of workers and employees to just salaries and working conditions should be guaranteed. The respect of these rights will be guarded by the state and the workers of the respective enterprise.

Mixed Area

This sector is called mixed because it will be made up of enterprises that combine state and private capital.

The loans or credits granted by the development agencies to the enterprises of this area will be made as contributions so that the state will be a partner and not a creditor. The same will be valid for those cases in which these enterprises obtain credits with the endorsement or guarantee of the state or its institutions.

Policy of Economic Development

The state's economic policy will be carried forward through the national system of economic planning and the mechanisms of control, orientations, production credit, technical assistance, tax policy and foreign trade policy as well as through the state's administration of the economy. Its objectives will be:

1. To resolve the immediate problems of the great majority. For this the country's productive capacity will be turned from superfluous and expensive articles that satisfy the high income groups toward the production of articles of popular use that are cheap and of good quality.

2. To guarantee employment with adequate remuneration to all Chileans of working age. This means designing a policy that will generate employment by planning the adequate use of the country's resources and by adapting the correct technology to demands of national development.

3. To liberate Chile from her subordination to foreign capital. This means the expropriation of imperialistic capital, the realization of a policy of ever-increasing self-financing of our activities, the fixing of conditions on which foreign capital will operate in this country if it is not to be expropriated, the achievement of greater independence in technology, in foreign transport and others.

4. To assure rapid and decentralized economic growth which tends to develop our productive forces to the maximum and to produce the optimal utilization of human, natural, financial and technical resources available for the purpose of increasing work productivity and satisfying both the demands of the independent develop-

ment of the economy as well as the necessities and aspirations of the working population that are compatible with a dignified human life.

5. To execute a foreign trade policy that tends to develop and diversify our exports to open new markets, to achieve a growing technical and financial independence and to avoid the scandalous devaluations of our currency.

6. To take all measures that will lead to monetary stability. The fight against inflation will be decided essentially on the stated structural changes. Monetary policy should also include measures that adapt the flow of circulating money to the real necessities of the market, that control and redistribute credit and avoid usury in the money business. There should be measures to rationalize distribution and commerce, stabilize prices, and to prevent the structure of demand that comes from high incomes to drive up prices.

The guarantee of the fulfillment of these objectives lies in the control by the organized people of political and economic power that is expressed in the state area of the economy and in the economy's general planning. It is this popular power that assures the fulfillment of the outlined tasks.

THE GOVERNMENT AND THE WORKERS
TAKE CONTROL OF FORD MOTOR COMPANY*

Having exhausted all possibilities of conversations with executives of Ford Motor, the government proceeded to requisition the installations that this company has in the country. These are the plant at Casablanca and the administrative offices and warehouses in Santiago. Jorge Fabra, Secretary of the Automotive Commission of the

* From the government newspaper *La Nación*, May 28, 1971.

Development Corporation, acted as representative and was named legal intervenor. . . .

"Today we have won a decisive battle of great importance. Here we have a demonstration that the popular government is a government of the workers and for the workers," said the president of the union of Ford employees when the requisition was known. The workers, in publicizing their feelings about the requisition, sang the national anthem in the presence of the Under-Secretary of Economy, Oscar Garretón, and other parliamentary representatives. The battle of the Ford workers ended after several days of struggle. The industry, disregarding Chilean legislation, had decided to terminate its activities in Chile and proceeded to dismiss the 604 workers at the plant.

In view of this completely illegal attitude, the workers proceeded to take over the Casablanca plant and demanded payment of their legal benefits. The Ministry of Economy immediately started talks with the executives of Ford regarding this matter.

"Ford is well aware of the efforts made by the government to solve the problems that the paralyzation of the industry has caused," said Garretón. The Under-Secretary indicated that various meetings had been held with Ford executives, including Vice-President Robert Stevens and Vice-President for Latin America and the Orient Edward Molina.

All these meetings had no result. The government logically asked as a first measure that the 604 dismissed workers be reinstated in their jobs. Ford did not accept. Until 8:00 P.M. on Wednesday, May 26, the Under-Secretary of Economy held telephone conversations with Ford's executives in Buenos Aires. Not receiving favorable replies, the Minister of Industries proceeded to sign the resolution requisitioning the Casablanca plant and other Ford installations in Chile. Garretón immediately contacted the U.S. ambassador, Edward Korry, and notified him of the government's decision. "The measure we have taken is not against the United States, but affects a private firm that has violated Chilean law," Garretón said. After his meeting with Korry, Garretón traveled to Casablanca to communicate the decision to the workers, who were in assembly with congressmen. "This measure in no way puts an end to conversations with Ford executives. We are prepared to continue our talks about the situation," he said.

The requisition signifies that the government now has legal use of the installations and offices that belonged to Ford in Chile. Garretón stated that while negotiations were in progress, the government would be responsible for paying the workers. The funds for this commitment would come from the sale of spare parts presently held by the industry.

The thirty-two Ford distributors throughout the country have indicated their wish to participate in the process of production at the plant and have guaranteed the availability of Ford spare parts.

POPULAR GOVERNMENT'S INTERNATIONAL POLICY OBJECTIVES*

The international policy of the popular government will be directed toward affirming the complete political and economic autonomy of Chile.

There will be diplomatic relations with all the countries of the world irrespective of their ideological and political position on the basis of respect for self-determination and the interests of the people of Chile.

Ties of friendship and solidarity with independent or

* From the electoral program of the Popular Unity.

colonized people will be established, especially with those who are developing their struggles of liberation and independence.

A strong Latin American and anti-imperialist sense will be promoted through an international policy of peoples rather than chancellories.

The decided defense of self-determination of peoples will be stimulated by the new government as a basic condition of international life. As a consequence its policy will be vigilant and active in defending the principle of non-intervention in rejecting every attempt at discrimination, pressure, invasion, or blockade on the part of imperialist countries.

Diplomatic relations, interchange, and friendship with the socialist countries will be reinforced.[1]

More National Independence

The position of active defense of Chilean independence implies denouncing the present OAS as an instrument and agency of North American imperialism and struggling against all forms of Pan-Americanism implicit in this organization. The popular government will opt for the creation of an organism that is truly representative of Latin American countries.

It is considered indispensable to revise, denounce, or forget about, according to individual cases, the treaties or agreements that limit our sovereignty, specifically the treaties of reciprocal assistance, the mutual-assistance pacts, and other pacts that Chile has signed with the United States.

Foreign aid and loans conditioned on political agreements or which imply the imposition of realizing in-

[1] Chile re-established diplomatic relations with Cuba on November 12, 1970, and with Communist China on January 5. On February 26, the government announced it would sell copper directly to Communist China.

vestments which derive from these loans on conditions that made our national sovereignty vulnerable and which are against the interests of the people will be rejected and denounced by the government. At the same time, all types of foreign impositions with respect to Latin American raw materials such as copper and with respect to the obstacles placed on free trade that have long been translated into the impossibility of establishing commercial relations with all the countries of the world, will be rejected.

International Solidarity

The struggles that people are unleashing for their liberation and for the construction of socialism will receive the effective and militant solidarity of the popular government.

Every type of colonialism or neocolonialism will be condemned and the right to rebellion of the people subjected to these systems will be recognized. The same treatment will be reserved for every type of economic, political, and/or military aggression provoked by the imperialist powers. Chilean international policy should maintain a position of condemnation of the North American aggression in Vietnam and recognition and active solidarity with the heroic struggle of the Vietnamese people.

In the same way, the policy will solidify itself effectively with the Cuban revolution and with the advances of revolution and the construction of socialism on the Latin American continent.

The anti-imperialistic struggle of the peoples of the Middle East will also receive the solidarity of the popular government, which will support the search for a specific solution that is based on the interests of the Arab and Jewish peoples.

All reactionary regimes that promote or practice racial segregation and anti-Semitism will be condemned.

Latin American Policy

The popular government will defend an international policy of affirmation of the Latin American personality on the world scene.

Latin American economic integration should be constructed on the basis of economies that have liberated themselves from all imperialistic forms of dependence and exploitation. Nevertheless, an active policy of bilateral agreements on those materials that are of interest to Chilean development will be maintained.

The popular government will act to resolve pending frontier problems through negotiations that prevent the intrigues of imperialism and the reactionaries and will keep present the interest of Chile and of the peoples in the neighboring countries.

Chilean international policy and its diplomatic expression should break all forms of bureaucracy and immobility. It should get along with peoples with the double purpose of learning from their struggles the lessons to aid in the construction of our socialism and to offer them our own experiences in such a way that in practice the international solidarity we defend is constructed.

PABLO NERUDA SPEAKS ON CHILE'S DEBT RENEGOTIATION*

In the course of my roving life, I have attended quite a number of strange meetings. Only a few days ago, however, I was present at what seems to me to be the most mysterious of all the meetings in which I have ever

* Address by Pablo Neruda, Chile's ambassador to France and winner of a 1971 Nobel prize for his poetry, before the fiftieth-anniversary celebration of the American Center of P.E.N., April 10, 1972.

taken part. I was seated there with a handful of my fellow countrymen. In front of us, in what looked like a vast circle to my eyes, sat the representatives of banks and treasuries and high finance, the delegates of numerous countries to which—so it would seem—my country owes a very great deal of money. We, the Chileans, were few in numbers, and our eminent creditors—almost entirely from the major countries—were very many: perhaps fifty or sixty of them. The business in hand was the renegotiation of our Public Debt, of our External Debt, built up in the course of half a century by former governments.

In this same half century, men have reached the moon complete with penicillin and with television. In the field of warfare, napalm has been invented to render democratic by means of its purifying fire the ashes of a number of the inhabitants of our planet. During these same fifty years, this American Center of the P.E.N. Club has worked nobly for the cause of reason and understanding. But, as I could see at that relentless meeting, Chile was nonetheless under the menace of an updated version of the garrote, namely the Stand-By. In spite of half a century of intellectual understanding, the relations between rich and poor—between nations which lend some crumbs of comfort and others which go hungry—continue to be a complex mixture of anguish and pride, injustice, and the right to live. . . .

For my part, I, who am now nearing seventy, discovered Walt Whitman when I was just fifteen, and I hold him to be my greatest creditor. I stand before you, feeling that I bear with me always this great and wonderful debt which has helped me to exist.

To "renegotiate" this debt, I must start by recognizing its existence, and acknowledging myself to be the humble servant of a poet who strode the earth with long, slow paces, pausing everywhere to love, to examine, to learn, to teach, and to admire. The fact of the matter is that this great man, this lyric moralist, chose a hard path for himself: he was both a torrential and a didactic singer —qualities which appear opposed, seemingly also more appropriate to a leader than to a writer. But what really counts is that Walt Whitman was not afraid to teach— which means to learn at the hands of life and undertake the responsibility of passing on the lesson! To speak frankly: he had no fear of either moralizing or immoralizing, nor did he seek to separate the fields of pure and impure poetry. He was the first totalitarian poet: his intention was not just to sing, but to impose on others his own total and wide-ranging vision of the relationships of men and nations. In this sense, his patent nationalism forms part of a total and organic universal vision: he held himself to be the debtor of happiness and sorrow alike, and also of both the advanced cultures and more primitive societies.

There are many kinds of greatness, but let me say (though I be a poet of the Spanish tongue) that Walt Whitman has taught me more than Spain's Cervantes: in Walt Whitman's work one never finds the ignorant being humbled, nor is the human condition ever found offended.

We continue to live in a Whitmanesque age, seeing how new men and new societies rise and grow despite their birth pangs. The Bard complained of the all-powerful influence of Europe, from which the literature of his age continued to draw sustenance. In truth he, Walt Whitman, was the protagonist of a truly geographical personality: the first man in history to speak with a truly continental American voice, to bear a truly American name. The colonies of the most brilliant countries have left a legacy of centuries of silence: colonialism seems to slay fertility and stultify the power of creation. One has only to look at the Spanish empire, where I can assure you that three centuries of Spanish dominion produced not more than two or three writers worthy of praise in all America.

The proliferation of our republics gave birth to more than merely flags and nationalities, universities, small heroic armies, or melancholy love songs. Books started to proliferate as well, yet they too often formed an impenetrable thicket, bearing many a flower but little fruit. With time, however, and especially in our own days, the Spanish language has at last started to shine out in the works of American writers who—from Rio Grande to Patagonia—have filled a whole dark continent (struggling toward a new independence) with magical stories, and with poems now tender, now desperate.

In this age, we see how other new nations, other new literatures and new flags, are coming into being with what one hopes is the total extinction of colonialism in Africa and Asia. Almost overnight, the capitals of the world are seen studded with the banners of peoples we had never heard of, seeking self-expression with the unpolished and pain-laden voice of birth. Black writers of both Africa and America begin to give us the true pulse of the luckless races which had hitherto been silent. Political battles have always been inseparable from poetry. Man's liberation may often require bloodshed, but it always requires song—and the song of mankind grows richer day by day, in this age of sufferings and liberation.

I ask your pardon, humbly, in advance, for going back to the subject of my country's troubles. As all the world knows, Chile is in the course of carrying out a revolutionary transformation of its social structure with true dignity, and within the strict framework of our legal constitution. This is something which annoys and offends many people! Why on earth, they ask, don't these pesky Chileans imprison anyone, close down newspapers, or shoot any citizen who contradicts them?

As a nation, we chose our path for ourselves, and for that very reason we are resolved to pursue it to the end. But secret opponents use every kind of weapon to turn our destiny aside. As cannon seem to have gone out of fashion in this kind of war, they use a whole arsenal of arms both old and new. Dollars and darts, telephone and telegraph services: each seems to serve! It looks as though anything at all will do, when it comes to defending ancient and unreasonable privileges. That is why, when I was sitting in that meeting in which Chile's External Debt was being renegotiated in Paris, I could not help thinking of *The Ancient Mariner*.

Samuel Taylor Coleridge drew upon an episode which took place in the extreme South of my country for the basis of his desolate poem.

In Chile's cold seas we have every kind and species of albatross: wandering, gigantic, gray, and stormy, and supremely splendid in its flight!

That is, perhaps, the reason why my country has the shape of a great albatross with wings outspread!

And in that unforgettable meeting, in which we were striving to renegotiate our External Debt in a just fashion, many of those who appeared so implacable seemed to be taking aim in order to bring Chile tumbling down, so that the albatross should fly no more!

To mention this may be the indiscretion of a poet who has only been an ambassador for a year, but it looked to me as though it was perhaps the representative of United States finance who concealed an arrow underneath his business papers—ready to aim it at the albatross's heart! Nevertheless, this financier has a pleasant name (one which would sound well at a banquet's end): he is called Mr. Hennessy.

And if he would take the trouble to reread the poets of former times, he might learn from *The Ancient Mariner* that the sailor who perpetrated such a crime was doomed to carry the heavy corpse of the slain albatross hanging from his neck—to all eternity.

SOCIALIST COUNTRIES OFFER THEIR TECHNOLOGY AND OPEN THEIR MARKETS*

The Chilean technical mission returned from its two-and-a-half-month tour of eight European socialist countries with what may well be the most important key to our technological and economic independence: free advanced technology.

Hugo Cubillos, who presided over the technical mission that established contracts with the European socialist governments, announced the good news yesterday. The mission succeeded in finding support for 90 per cent of the projects that had been elaborated by the popular government's National Development Plan.

Not only did the Chilean mission obtain almost free technological aid from the socialist countries, but it also received $135 million in loans to contribute to the $300 million necessary for the financing of the projects that were agreed upon during the tours.

Hugo Cubillos pointed out the extraordinary interest in the popular government that he found in these countries. He remarked that the technical mission had been everywhere received with the greatest of cordiality. Cubillos remarked, "The socialist countries were especially interested in hearing about our first months in office. They showed their support for the popular government

* From the Communist newspaper *El Siglo,* August 7, 1971.

and they approved of every measure that has been taken in our road to socialism."

The director of the mission reviewed the diverse agreements that had been reached in each of the countries visited.

The Soviet Union agreed to establish a lubricating-oil plant and a plant for the making of sulfuric acid, and to prepare a project for an industry of prefabricated housing components. A vaccine production plant will also be created to serve the agricultural sector.

The Czechoslovakian Government has agreed to collaborate in planning a heavy-machinery plant, as well as a plant for machinery and tools. A plant for the fabrication of nitrate fertilizer will also be erected.

The Polish Government will participate in the extension of ASMAR (naval dockyards and shipbuilding), which will permit the construction of 30,000-ton vessels. Projects for the treatment of gold minerals as well as for a partnership in the construction of copper and copper-alloy products were agreed to.

The Yugoslavs have agreed to join the government in an engineering design that will produce industrial projects. Also planned are plants for copper reactors, prefabricated panels manufactured in Punta Arenas and in Magallanes, a meat-packing and -processing industry, and a commercial plant for the drying of meat and agricultural products.

The Hungarians have agreed to contribute to the installation of a factory for railroad-engine frames and railway cars. They will also help in the creation of a pharmaceutical industry. The Hungarians have agreed to build an aluminum production plant coupled with a hydroelectric plant that will cost fifty million dollars. Furthermore, a plant for the processing of fruits and production of fruit jams and preserves will be created.

The Romanians have agreed to provide their technology

almost free for the building of a national chemical plant and have opened their markets for the commercial sales of the products.

Bulgaria will help in the construction of a plant for mining machinery and spare parts. They will also help in the construction of a plant to treat copper residues to obtain electrolytic copper. The Bulgarians will also contribute to the planning and construction of an onion-dehydration plant so as to help us meet the demand for this product.

The East German Government will contribute to copper mining, agriculture, and the food industry. They will also contribute their geological and scientific expertise for the treatment and commercialization of production in the salt plains of Atacama. To top this, plans are in the making for a mixed industry which will manufacture finished copper products to supply the East European COMECON.

The Chilean technicians pointed to the fact that previous government missions did not seek technology abroad but merely equipment. "Chile wants its economic and technological independence. To achieve this, the experts will transmit to us their experience and it will remain in Chile. We did not go out to acquire complete plants but rather these will be built here so as to incorporate socialist technology that stays here." The technicians added that this will avoid the payment of royalties and other problems that are created with Western countries.

PART III

POPULAR UNITY:

Program, Ideology, and
Political Allies

CHAPTER 7

Popular Unity: Direction and Leadership

Salvador Allende's speeches are invariably meaty, pointed, and straightforward. In his inaugural address President Allende attributed Chile's underdevelopment to a system, capitalism, that counterposes the rich minority to the needy majority internally and the powerful nations to the poor nations internationally. The victory of the Popular Unity is a consequence of the contradictions and inhumanity of this system. The poor and exploited masses have their first president. The government of the Popular Unity is the government of the people, and its program is the road to real human liberty and a new economy for the benefit of all the people. If violence is to come, Allende suggests, it will be because "the powerful were always the ones who unleashed the violence, shed the blood of Chileans, and blocked the progress of the country."

A more appropriate title for the second article, "A South American Mao Emerges in Chile," might be *"El Compañero Presidente."* Salvador Allende bears little resemblance to Chairman Mao in personal or political style, but to many Chileans he is *Compañero,* Brother, Comrade Allende, a man to be loved and admired but not worshiped. To most of his political enemies he is President Allende, a man to be respected for his integrity and patriotism. Nevertheless there are still those who hate and fear, and attempts have been made upon the President's life.

Firmness and a direct approach to fundamental problems are Allende's outstanding characteristics. This is also true of the government Allende heads. Although the Popular Unity is composed of distinct and often conflicting political forces, the government has moved with considerable firmness and political agility to accomplish its carefully prescribed program of socialist transition. The forty measures indicated at the end of this chapter were energetically acted upon almost immediately upon assumption of the government by the Popular Unity.

CHILE BEGINS ITS MARCH TOWARD SOCIALISM*

SALVADOR ALLENDE

We will win, and we have won, so, comrades, here we are today to celebrate the start of our victory. . . .

This victory belongs to the workers, to those who suffered and endured for more than a century and a half, under the name of independence, the exploitation of a ruling class which was unable to provide progress and wasn't even concerned about it.

We all know the truth, that the backwardness, ignorance and hunger of our people and of all the peoples of the Third World exist and persist because a few privileged people profit from them.

But the day has finally come to say enough—enough of economic exploitation, enough of social inequality, enough of political oppression.

Today, inspired by the heroes of our country, we gather here to celebrate our victory—Chile's victory— and to mark the start of the liberation of the people, who are at last in power and are taking over control of their national destiny.

* Speech after becoming President of Chile at National Stadium in Santiago, November 5, 1970. Translation by Prensa Latina.

One of the Great Tasks Facing the Revolution Is That of Breaking Out of the Encirclement of Deceit

But what kind of a Chile are we inheriting?

Excuse me, comrades, that, on this happy day and before the delegations from so many countries that are honoring us with their presence, I should have to discuss such an unfortunate subject. It is our right and duty to denounce age-old sufferings, as Peruvian President Velasco Alvarado has said.

One of the great tasks facing the revolution is that of breaking out of the encirclement of deceit which has made all of us live with our faces turned away from reality.

We must say that we, the underdeveloped peoples, have failed in history.

We were colonies in the agrarian-mercantile civilization. We are barely neocolonial nations in the urban-industrial civilization, and, in the new civilization which threatens to continue our dependency, we have been the exploited peoples—those who existed not for themselves, but rather to contribute to the prosperity of others.

And what is the reason for our backwardness? Who is responsible for our underdevelopment?

After many deformations and deceptions, the people have understood. We know from our own experience that the real reasons for our backwardness are to be found in the system, in this capitalist-dependent system which counterposes the rich minority to the needy majority internally and the powerful nations to the poor nations externally, a system in which the many make possible the prosperity of the few.

We have received a society torn by social inequality; a society divided into antagonistic classes of the exploited and exploiting; a society in which violence is a part of the institutions themselves, which condemn man to a never-satisfied greed, the most inhuman form of cruelty and indifference in the face of the suffering of others.

We have inherited a society wracked by unemployment, which throws growing numbers of the citizenry into a situation of forced idleness and poverty. These masses are not, as some say, the result of overpopulation; rather, with their tragic destiny, they are living witnesses to the inability of the regime to guarantee everyone the elementary right to work.

We have received an economy plagued by inflation—which, month after month, eats up the miserable wages of the workers, leaving them with next to nothing to live on in the last years of their lives, when they reach the end of an existence of privation.

The working people of Chile are bleeding through this wound, and it will be difficult to heal. But we are confident we will be able to heal it, because the economic policy of the Government will, from now on, be aimed at serving the interests of the people.

We have received a dependent society, one whose basic sources of income were alienated by the internal allies of the great international firms. We are dependent in the economic, cultural, technological and political fields.

We have inherited a society which has seen its most deeply felt desire of independent development frustrated, a divided society in which the majority of families are denied the right to work, education, health care, recreation and even the hope of a better future.

The Only Way We Can Overcome Underdevelopment Is by Putting All Our Shoulders to the Wheel

The people of Chile have risen up against all these forms of existence. Our victory was the result of their crystallized conviction that only a genuinely revolutionary government could stand up to the power of the ruling classes and at the same time mobilize all Chileans to build a republic of the working people.

This is the great task which history has given us. To carry it out, I call on you, workers of Chile, today. The only way we who love this country and believe in it can overcome underdevelopment and build a new society is by putting all our shoulders to the wheel.

We are living at a historic time, that of a great transformation of the political institutions of Chile, a time in which the parties and movements which represent the most neglected social sectors are assuming power by a majority vote.

Let us stop and think a moment and cast a glance back over our history. The people of Chile are proud of having made the political road prevail over the violent one. This is a noble tradition, a lasting achievement. Throughout our permanent battle for liberation, the slow and hard struggle for justice and equality, we have always preferred solving social conflicts by means of persuasion and political action.

From the bottom of our hearts, we Chileans reject fratricidal struggle—but without ever giving up the defense of the rights of the people. Our coat of arms says "By reason or force," but it puts reason first.

This civic peace, this continuation of the political process, is no accident. It is the result of our socioeconomic structure, of a particular relationship of social forces which our country has been building in keeping with the reality of our development.

In our first steps as a sovereign country, the determination of the men of Chile and the ability of its leaders helped us to avoid civil war.

In 1845, Francisco Antonio Pinto wrote to General San Martin, "I think we will solve the problem of being republicans while continuing to speak Spanish."

The Few Breaks with Institutionalism Were Always
Caused by the Ruling Classes

From that moment on, the continuity and institutional stability of this country was one of the greatest in Europe and America.

This republican and democratic tradition thus became a part of our identity and the collective conscience of all Chileans.

Respect for others, tolerance for others, is one of the most important sources of our cultural wealth.

And when, amidst this institutional continuity and within the basic political norms, the class antagonisms and contradictions come forth, they do so in a political way. Our people have never broken this historical pattern; the few breaks with institutionalism were always caused by the ruling classes. The powerful were always the ones who unleashed the violence, shed the blood of Chileans and blocked the normal progress of the country. This was what happened when Balmaceda, aware of his duties and a defender of national interests, acted with a dignity and patriotism that posterity has since recognized.

The persecution of trade unions, students, intellectuals and workers' parties is the violent reply of those who are defending their privileges. However, the ceaseless struggle of the organized popular classes has, little by little, succeeded in its demands for recognition for civil, social, public and individual liberties.

This particular evolution of institutions in the context of our structures has made possible this historic moment, in which the people are taking political control of the country.

The masses, in their struggle to overcome the capitalist system, which exploits them, are arriving at the Presidency of the Republic, united in People's Unity and in what constitutes the most extraordinary demonstration in our history: respect for and validity of democratic values, a recognition of the will of the majority.

Without renouncing their revolutionary goals, the popular forces have adjusted their tactics to the concrete reality of Chilean structures, viewing victories and setbacks not as definitive victories or defeats but rather as stepping stones on the long, hard road to emancipation.

Chile has just provided an indication of its political development, which is completely unprecedented anywhere in the world, making it possible for an anticapitalist movement to take power by virtue of the free exercise of the rights of all citizens. It takes power to guide the country toward a new, more humane society, one whose final goals are the rationalization of economic activity, the progressive socialization of the means of production and the end of class divisions.

Chile Is Beginning Its March Toward Socialism

As Socialists, from the theoretical and doctrinal points of view we are well aware of what the forces and agents of historical change are. And I know very well, to quote Engels, that "We can conceive of peaceful evolution from the old society to the new in countries where the popular forces hold all power; where, in keeping with the Constitution, it is possible to do everything one wants from the moment there is majority support."

And that is the case of Chile. Here what Engels wrote is at last a reality.

However, we must point out that, in the 60 days that have followed the elections of September 4, the democratic vitality of our country has been put to the strongest test it has ever had to face. After a dramatic series of events, our dominant trait has once again prevailed: confrontation of differences through political channels. The Christian Democratic Party has recognized this historical moment and its duty toward the nation, and it is but right that we declare this here today.

Chile is beginning its march toward socialism without having had to undergo the tragic experience of a fratricidal war. And this fact, in all its grandeur, has an influence on the way in which this government will undertake the tasks of transformation.

The will of the people gives us legitimacy in our tasks. My administration will respond to this confidence, making the democratic traditions of our country real and concrete. But, in these 60 decisive days through which we have just passed, Chile and the rest of the world have witnessed admitted attempts to fraudulently alter the spirit of our Constitution; mock the will of the people; attack the economy of the country; and, above all, effect cowardly acts of desperation designed to provoke a bloody clash between our citizens.

The Law Will Be Implacable with Them

Personally, I am convinced that the heroic sacrifice of a soldier, General René Schneider[1] the Commander in Chief of the Army, was an unforeseen event that saved our homeland from civil war. Permit me, on this solemn occasion, by honoring him, to voice our people's thanks to the Armed Forces and to the Carabineer Corps, which abide by the Constitution and the rule of law. This amazing episode, which lasted barely a day and will go down in history as a civil war in the embryonic stage, has once more demonstrated the criminal insanity of those who know that their cause is lost.

They are the representatives, the mercenaries of the minorities who, ever since the time of Spanish rule, have borne the unenviable responsibility for having exploited

[1] General Schneider, Commander of the Armed Forces, was assassinated in a right-wing conspiracy to prevent Allende from taking office.

our people for the sake of their own selfish benefit and for having handed our wealth over to foreign interests. These are the minorities who, in their wanton desire to perpetuate their own privileges, did not hesitate in 1891 and have not hesitated in 1970 to create a tragic situation for the nation.

But the law will be implacable with them and provide just punishment for them. They failed in their unpatriotic designs. They failed when they came up against the strength of the democratic institutions and the firmness of the will of the people, who were determined to confront and disarm them in order to secure tranquillity, the nation's confidence and peace from now on, under the responsibility of people's power.

Power to the People

What is people's power?

People's power means that we will do away with the pillars on which the minorities have found support— those minorities that always condemned our nation to underdevelopment. We will do away with the monopolies, through which a handful of families control the economy. We will put an end to a fiscal system that serves those who seek lucre, a system which has always borne down hard on the people and touched but lightly on the rich, a system which has concentrated the nation's savings in the hands of the bankers in their greed for amassing greater riches. We will nationalize money lending and place it at the service of the prosperity of Chile and the people.

We will put an end to the latifundia, which condemn thousands of peasants to subjugation and poverty and keep the nation from getting from the land all the food-stuffs we need. A true agrarian reform will make it possible to do just what we are saying—feed the people. We will call a halt to the ever more massive process of denationalization of our industries and sources of work, a process which subjects us to foreign exploitation. We will reclaim Chile's basic wealth. We are going to reclaim the large copper, coal, iron and nitrate mines for the people.

It is in our power—the power of those who earn their living by their work and who hold power today—to do these things. The rest of the world may sit back and observe the changes that are wrought in our country, but we Chileans cannot be satisfied with such a role for ourselves; we must play the leading role in the transformation of our society. Everyone must be fully aware of our common responsibility. It is the essential task of the people's government—that is, of every one of us—to create a new, just state, one that can offer a maximum of opportunities to all of us who live in this land.

You, All of Us, Form Part of the People's Government

I know that the connotation of the word "state" causes a certain apprehension. The word has been much abused, and it is often used to discredit a just social system.

Don't fear the word "state," because you, all of us, form part of the state, of the people's government. Working together, we should improve it and make it efficient, modern and revolutionary. But I wish to be understood correctly when I say "just," and this is precisely what I want to emphasize.

Much has been said about the people's participation, and this is the time to put it into practice. All Chileans, of any age, have a task to fulfill. In that task personal interest will merge with the generous conduct of collective work. No state in the world is rich enough to satisfy all the aspirations of all its citizens if these do not first wake up to the realization that rights go hand in hand with duties and that success has more merit when it stems from one's own efforts and sacrifice.

*The Time Has Come for All Young People to
Participate in the Action*

The full development of the people's awareness will
result in spontaneous voluntary work, which has already
been proposed by the young people.

Those who wrote on the walls of Paris that the revolution had to be made first in the people and later in
things were right.

Precisely on this solemn occasion I wish to speak to
the young people, to those standing on the lawn, who
have sung their songs for us.

A rebellious student in the past, I will not criticize
their impatience, but it is my duty to ask them to think
calmly.

Young people, yours is that beautiful age during
which physical and mental vigor enable you to undertake practically any endeavor. For that reason you are
duty-bound to help us advance. Turn your eagerness into
more work, your hopes into more effort and your im-
pulsiveness into concrete accomplishments. Use your
drive and energy to be better—the best—students and
workers.

Thousands upon thousands of young people have demanded a place in the social struggle. Now they have
that place. The time has come for all young people to
participate in the action.

To those who have not yet taken part in this process,
I say, "Come on, there's a place for everyone in the
construction of our new society."

Escapism, decadence, superficiality and the use of
drugs are the last resort of young people who live in
countries which are notoriously opulent but are devoid
of any moral strength. That cannot be the case of the
young people of Chile.

I've Been Deeply Moved by the Sight of Portraits of the Immortal Che Guevara

Follow the best examples, the examples set by those who leave everything behind to build a better future. That is why I've been deeply moved by the sight of portraits of the immortal Che Guevara.

What will be our path, our Chilean way of action, to defeat underdevelopment?

Our path will be that built on the basis of our experience; the path legitimized by the people in the elections; the path contained in the program of Popular Unity; the path toward socialism through democracy, pluralism and freedom.

The basic conditions which, used with prudence and flexibility, will enable us to build a new society, based on a new economy, are now to be found in Chile.

Popular Unity adopts this watchword, not as a simple slogan but as its natural way.

Chile has the unique virtue of having the social and political institutions necessary for carrying out the transition from backwardness and dependence to development and autonomy along the socialist path.

Popular Unity is, constitutionally, the exponent of such a reality. Let no one be deceived; the theoreticians of Marxism have never pretended, nor has history shown, that a single party is a prerequisite in the process of transition toward socialism.

Social circumstances and political vicissitudes—both internal and international—may lead to this situation. Civil war, when imposed upon the people as the only way toward emancipation, leads to political rigorousness; foreign intervention, in its frenzy for maintaining domination at all costs, makes the exercise of power authoritarian; and poverty and generalized backwardness make it difficult for political institutions to act dynamically and the people's organizations to grow stronger.

To the extent that such situations do or do not arise in Chile, so will our country, on the basis of its traditions, organize and create the mechanism that, within the pluralism supported by the great majorities, will make possible the radical transformation of our political system.

This is the great legacy of our history. It is also a most generous promise for our future. It is up to us to see to it that it does, someday, become a reality.

This decisive fact is a challenge to all Chileans, regardless of their ideological orientation, to contribute to the autonomous development of our country. As President of the Republic, I can affirm, recalling all those who have preceded us in the struggle, face to face with the future that will be our judge, that every one of my actions will constitute another effort at fulfilling the aspirations of the people in keeping with our traditions.

The people's victory marked the maturity of the awareness of a vast sector of our population. It is necessary that that awareness develop even more. It must flourish among thousands upon thousands of Chileans who, even though they were not with us in a part of the process, are now determined to join the great task of building a new life with a new morality.

Together with this new morality, patriotism and revolutionary feeling will be present in the behavior of the government officials. From the outset, I must point out that our administration will be characterized by absolute responsibility—to such an extent that, far from being prisoners of controlling institutions, we will demand that they operate as a permanent conscience, in order to correct mistakes and denounce all those who carry on abuses either within or outside the government. To each one of my countrymen who shares a part of the task to be carried out, I say that I am adopting Fidel Castro's statement that "In this Government anybody may make mistakes, but nobody will ever be allowed to be on the take."

As President of Chile, I shall be unflagging in my watchfulness over the morality of the regime.

Our program of government, endorsed by the people, is founded on the fact that the best guarantee of our democracy is the people's participation in our activities. Our democracy will contribute to increasingly strengthen all human liberties, in accord with the greater participation of the people.

Ours Is the Road to Liberty

The people are taking over the executive power in a presidential regime in order to start the progressive construction of socialism, through conscientious, organized struggle in free parties, in free labor unions.

Our road, our path, is that of liberty—liberty for the expansion of our productive forces, breaking the chains that have smothered our development thus far; liberty for each citizen, according to his conscience and beliefs, to collaborate in the collective task ahead; and liberty for all Chileans who work for a living to gain social control over and ownership of their work centers.

Simón Bolívar forecast for our country, "If there is one republic that will stand for a long time in America, I am inclined to believe that it is Chile. The spirit of liberty has never been extinguished there."

Let us remember the Liberator at this hour of our homeland.

Our road, our Chilean way, will also be that of equality —equality to overcome, progressively, the division existing between Chilean exploiters and Chileans who are exploited; equality so that everyone shares a part of the collective wealth, according to his work and at a level to meet his personal requirements; and equality for reducing the enormous wage differences that exist between similar jobs.

Equality is a sine qua non for investing all individuals with the dignity and respect they are due.

Within these directives, true to these principles, we will march onward toward the construction of a new system.

The New Economy Which We Will Build Will Seek to Have the Resources of Chile Produce for the Benefit of the People of Chile

The new economy which we will build will seek to have the resources of Chile produce for the benefit of the people of Chile. The monopolies will be nationalized, because the interests of the nation require it, and, for the same reason, we will give full guarantees to the small and medium-sized firms, which will receive all possible assistance from the state to carry out their activities.

The people's government has already worked out laws which will make it possible for it to fulfill its program.

The workers, technicians, professionals and intellectuals will have economic and political control of the country.

For the first time in our history, four workers are a part of the government as ministers of state.

Only by advancing along this path of basic transformations in the political and economic fields will we be able to draw ever nearer to the ideals which are our objective:

To create a new society in which men can fulfill their material and spiritual needs without having to resort to the exploitation of other men.

To create a society which guarantees each family—every man, woman and child—rights, securities, freedom, hope and other basic guarantees. We aim to have all the people filled with a sense of their being called upon to build a new nation which will also mean the construction of more beautiful, more prosperous, more dignified and freer lives for all. And, repeating what I have always said in a regime of justice, our country will only have one privileged person: the Chilean child, the son of the people.

To create a new society capable of making continuous progress in the material, technical and scientific fields; capable of guaranteeing its artists and intellectuals the necessary conditions for reflecting a true cultural rebirth in their works.

To create a new society capable of getting along with all the other peoples, including those of the advanced nations, whose experience can help us greatly in our efforts toward self-improvement.

Every Nation Has the Right to Develop Freely,
Marching Along the Path It Has Chosen

A society capable of living together with all the other independent nations everywhere, to whom we wish to extend our fraternal solidarity.

Our international policy today is based, as it was yesterday, on respect for international commitments freely assumed, self-determination and nonintervention.

We will collaborate resolutely in the strengthening of peace and coexistence among nations. Every nation has the right to develop freely, marching along the path it has chosen.

However, we are well aware of the fact that, unfortunately—as Indira Gandhi stated in the UN, "The right of the peoples to choose their own form of government is accepted only on paper. In reality," Indira Gandhi affirmed, "there is considerable interference in the internal affairs of many countries. The powerful make their influence felt in a thousand different ways."

Chile, a country which respects self-determination and

practices nonintervention, has the legitimate right to demand that all countries treat her the same way. The people of Chile recognize only themselves as the controllers of their destiny.

And your Government, comrades, the Government of People's Unity, will firmly see to it that this right is respected.

Chile Extends the Hand of Friendship to All Those Gathered Here

I wish to extend a special greeting to all the official delegations which are honoring us with their presence.

I also wish to greet the nonofficial delegations from those countries with which we still do not have diplomatic relations. Chile will do them justice by recognizing their governments.

Gentlemen, representatives of governments, peoples and institutions, this mass rally is a fraternal and deepfelt tribute to you.

As a Latin American, I consider the common problems, aspirations and interests of all the people in the continent to be my own. That is why, at this moment, I send my greeting, as a Head of State, to our brothers in Latin America, hoping that one day the mandate of our process will be fulfilled and we will all have but one, great, single continental voice.

We also have here with us the representatives of workers' organizations from all over the world and intellectuals and artists of universal renown who wish to demonstrate their solidarity with the people of Chile and celebrate, together with us, a victory which, while ours, is considered as their own by all those who struggle for freedom and dignity.

To all those gathered here—ambassadors, artists, workers, intellectuals and soldiers—Chile extends the hand of friendship.

Distinguished guests, permit me to say that you are witnesses to the political maturity attained by Chile.

To you, who have seen with your own eyes the poverty in which many of our compatriots live; to you, who have visited our marginal towns, the *callampas,* and have seen to what depths of subhuman existence men can be sunk in a fertile land brimming with potential resources and who must have recalled Lincoln's words when he said of his country, as I say of mine, "This Nation cannot endure permanently half slave and half free": to you, who have been informed of the way People's Unity will carry through the program supported by our people— to you I wish to make a petition:

Take back to your respective countries this image of the Chile that is and of the Chile that will be.

Tell your people that here history will take a new course, that here the people have succeeded in taking the helm of their destiny to embark on a democratic course toward socialism.

This Chile in the process of renovation, this Chile in the springtime and an atmosphere of festivity wants, as one of its greatest aspirations, every man in the world to know that we are his brothers.

A SOUTH AMERICAN MAO EMERGES IN CHILE*

FULVIO HURTADO R.

The Mao myth, originally formed in the biggest country of the world in response to vital internal necessities, is now spontaneously appearing in Chile in a less refined form.

After Salvador Allende's tenacious electioneering

* From *Brecha* No. 4, June 1, 1971.

through four presidential campaigns over the past twenty years, his followers, as well as many who were not, have come more and more to admire him. This admiration has been steadily growing through only 180 days in the hard exercise of governing.

To paraphrase a current slogan advertising a Chilean wine, it is said, "Don't vote for Allende . . . you might get to like him." In this case, the "liking" has become so contagious that it now forms a majority opinion among the blocs that divide the country.

During the past thirty-three years, seven Presidents have come to office. Six of them presented "revolutionary" programs. The greatest anxiety for each President on assuming office has been *how to get around complying with* his electoral program. These Presidents have "reigned" in Chile, but effective command has been exercised by those who had decision-making power within the system of agrarian, industrial, financial, and commercial feudalism. President Allende has opened profound breaches in these structures.

Past Presidents have declared themselves "prisoners of the law" and sometimes, after leaving office, have embarked on bitter campaigns against the "political habits" that impeded their governing. The truth is that they never denounced the hidden economic interests that they did not want to confront. Practically without exception they systematically expropriated consumers' wages and salaries by means of inflationary assaults that ranged between 18 per cent and forty-five per cent per year. . . .

Now, this habitual *game* of circulating Presidents is ended. Finally, "things are going to happen in Chile."

A Dynamic President

If we had to describe President Allende in two words, these would be that he is an "anti-President." At the same time, he is the first really dynamic President of this century. From him came the decision to fulfill without interruption the program that the electorate decided was best. In this respect, he has shown a firmness and will notoriously superior to the team that backs him up.

In dialogue with any group wanting to hear him, in direct human contact, he has shown himself to be a politician of firm hand, ready to confront both visible and unseen obstacles. He also possesses a quality not previously recognized: he is an authentic teacher with a global vision (though with sharp and opportune perception of detail) of the enormous task that it is his historic mission to realize. Allende has shown that in this country there is only one mastermind and that, at least for the time being, no one can be found to fill his shoes. At a recent meeting with three hundred journalists, Allende said, "Even though it does not involve me personally, I think it is useful and necessary to suggest that you must struggle to modify the law of the College of Journalists." Five days previously he had sent a proposal to Congress modifying this law. This is the way in which he steadily mobilizes the population, sector by sector, class by class. And thus he elevates his supporters to dedicated admirers.

This admiration which Allende has provoked is not destined to create fame without purpose. The respect, profusely reiterated, is in the voices of his party *compañeros,* but it is also expressed by Communists, Radicals, and others and, even more significantly, by independents of the most widely differing cultural, political, and professional backgrounds. Among them all there is a new realization that until now they *did not know the real Allende*. They knew nothing of his abilities, his ideas, and most of all, his formidable capacity to carry things out.

Thus, as we have said, the "Maoization" of Salvador Allende is gradually forming itself in Chile and Latin America, *spontaneously,* even against his will, without any recourse to the techniques of mounting a personality cult—which are alien to Allende's deep democratic convictions, the spirit of the Popular Unity, and the idiosyncrasies of our people. It is true, however, that the word *Allende* published in any newspaper in the world means *Chile.* He is now the second person in Latin America to be fully recognized by one and all for his great personality.

Chile needed an Allende. Chile needed a conscientious politician with a determination to carry things out. Now Chile has one. The rest is a matter of time.

When speaking of "Maoization," we are referring to the mystique that Allende is forming in the country. We believe that a measure of mystique around a worthy person is highly beneficial to the country after so many decades of disappointments and indecorous electoral postures that have not even corresponded to declared intentions. This mystique is just what is needed to awaken the people from the lethargy and frustration in which they have been submerged.

To the degree that the President continues his policy of integral development of Chile and its people, his name will increasingly be identified with the virtues of justice and revolution that so many have promised and failed to deliver.

THE FORTY MEASURES*

—Suppression of fabulous salaries
—More experts? No!
—Administrative honesty
—No more pleasure trips abroad
—No more state cars for private use
—The state will not make new rich people
—Just pensions, no millionaires
—Just and timely leisure
—Insurance for everyone
—Immediate and full payment to the pensioned and retired
—Family protection
—Equality in family allowances
—The child is born to be happy
—Better nourishment for children
—Milk for every Chilean child
—Maternity and pediatric clinics in every settlement
—Real vacations for all students
—Alcoholism control
—Housing, electricity, and water for all
—No more house-payment increases
—Rent ceilings
—Barren lands no! Settlements yes!
—Payments only for good homes
—A real agrarian reform
—Free medical care without bureaucracy
—Free medicine in hospitals
—No more swindles in the price of drugs
—Scholarships for students
—Physical education and tourism for the people
—A new economy to end inflation
—No more ties with the International Monetary Fund
—No more taxes on food
—An end to sales taxes
—An end to speculation
—An end to unemployment
—Work for everyone
—Disbandment of the Mobile Group
—An end to class injustice
—Legal-aid offices in settlements
—Creation of a National Institute of Art and Culture

* "The Forty Measures" was put to music by the Grupo Lonqui, Chilean folk singers.

CHAPTER 8

The Popular Unity Coalition

This chapter reproduces documents that reflect the political position of the main parties of the Popular Unity: the Socialist, Communist, and Radical (documents from MAPU, the other principal organization within the PU coalition are included in Chapter 10).

"The Political Position of the Socialist Party" is the resolution adopted in the Congress of the Socialist Party held in La Serena a few months after Allende was elected President. During this Congress, a Central Committee of forty-five members was elected. Senator Carlos Altamirano was designated as the Secretary General of the Party. Altamirano represents the left wing of a party that contains diverse tendencies, from moderate, middle-class social democrats, barely distinguishable from the non-Marxist state employees and professionals who make up the Radical Party, to militant Marxist-Leninist revolutionaries who are very close to the militants of the Movement of the Revolutionary Left (MIR). The Socialist Party markedly increased its voting strength in the important municipal elections of April 1971. The Party, together with the better organized, more ideologically homogeneous, and more conservative Communist Party, has deep roots in the Chilean working class.

"Work Without Rest to Win the Battle of Production" reflects the more pragmatic, less ideological line of the Communist Party during the first year of the Allende government. In general, the CP seems to be in favor of consolidation of the gains made by the Allende government and emphasizes the hard work and discipline that are necessary to strengthen the economic and political basis of Chilean socialism. The Socialist Party, on the other hand, is pushing toward an acceleration of the process of socialist transition.

The third document is a report of the outcome of the Radical Party Convention in August 1971, in which the Party declared itself Marxist and lost some of its more middle-of-the-road supporters. Alejandro Ríos Valdivia, Minister of National Defense in the Allende government, rightly points out that the Party has never been Marxist, nor is it a party of the workers. (Chapter 13 reproduces part of President Allende's speech to the same Convention appraising the role of the Radical Party with its middle-class constituency in the construction of Chilean socialism.)

THE POLITICAL POSITION OF
THE SOCIALIST PARTY*

1. The electoral triumph and the subsequent installation of the government, after inflicting a serious defeat on the bourgeoisie and on imperialism, have presented new and favorable conditions to the working class and to the Chilean masses for an effective conquest of power which makes it possible to initiate the construction of socialism in the country. To their organization, degree of consciousness, and combative experience, the workers now add a correlation of favorable forces and control of a fundamental part of the governmental apparatus.

Nevertheless, the ownership classes hold on to practically all the elements to continue exercising their class domination. In these conditions, the popular government develops its action hindered by bourgeois institutionality

* Published in *Punto Final* No. 124, February 16, 1971.

and by the more and more active resistance unleashed on all levels by the national and foreign reactionary forces.

2. After the electoral triumph, the Popular Unity encountered different political reactions of the bourgeoisie, each one similarly embracing the same counterrevolutionary objective: to prevent the ascent of the workers to the state apparatus. Some tried to create economic panic and chaos; others looked toward a *coup* by fascist forces and saw their intentions frustrated by the assassination of General Schneider, which provoked a national repudiation; still others sought to gain time by blocking the attainment of the government's program and by immobilizing the popular government through demands for so-called "democratic guarantees."

At the present time, the bourgeoisie is regrouping around the Christian Democratic Party. The so-called "left wing of Christian Democracy," by indecisively remaining part of this party, is serving as the smoke screen for the right wing and for the reactionary sectors which are part of the great conspiracy against the government of *Compañero* Salvador Allende and against the workers.[1] Only a policy of profound transformations and growing acceleration of the revolutionary process will oblige the groups of Christian Democratic workers to define themselves.

3. Among the working mass, the victory of the Popular Unity has led to the surpassing of the influence of Christian Democratic bourgeois reformism over some sectors. This victory, in spite of the immobilization of the

[1] Significant sectors of the left wing of the Christian Democratic Party broke with the Party to support the government in mid-year 1971.

people after November 4, has served to stimulate new popular strata which now openly set forth their aspirations and contribute to enlarging and fortifying the mass movement. The total of the measures taken and initiated by the government objectively reinforce the revolutionary potential of the situation and sharpen the polarization of classes.

The contradiction between the growing force of the masses and the power of the bourgeoisie defines this stage as an essentially transitory period. Our objective, therefore, must be to support the government, to accelerate the actions taken by the masses, to smash the resistance of the enemies, and to convert the present process into an irreversible march toward socialism.

4. We recognize as a form of self-criticism that some of the actions of the workers have gone beyond the political directions of the Popular Unity and are in fact putting into the forefront the question of power. We recognize also with satisfaction that the *compañero* President of the Republic has been in the vanguard in taking initiatives for the fulfillment of the program.

The General Congress of the Socialist Party, along with recognizing and fully supporting the actions taken by *Compañero* Salvador Allende as President, affirms that the vanguard of the Chilean revolutionary process must be constituted by the parties of the working class as the motor force of the social struggle. It is the responsibility of these parties to rejoin the struggle of the masses, helping to go beyond the economist character which still predominates in many of its sectors, and to orient it in the direction of revolutionary politics.

5. The General Congress of the Socialist Party recognizes that political confirmation of the Popular Unity re-

flects a multiclass composition whose nature is expressed in the government, where worker, petty-bourgeois, and bourgeois tendencies come together.

These class contradictions which exist in the Popular Unity will be surpassed by the revolutionary dynamic of the working masses led by their class parties. The consequent application of the program of the Popular Unity and the ideological struggle that must take place within it and among the masses will contribute to the resolution of these contradictions.

In this sense, in agreement with the programmatic bases of the Popular Unity which permit each party to maintain its own political profiles, the Socialist Party reaffirms its class program and the necessity for the leadership of the working class in conducting the struggle for economic and social liberation, which free the working masses and the rest of the exploited and oppressed sectors, against the national bourgeoisie and imperialism. It postulates the independence of the working class confronting the Chilean bourgeoisie, which, as the class that sustains the existing order, constitutes along with imperialism an irreversibly counterrevolutionary force. The alliances and permanent agreements with the national bourgeoisie have only brought defeats and delays for the exploited.

Concomitant with this policy of the workers' front and as a concrete necessity in the tasks that confront the popular movement, there is the necessity of strengthening Socialist Party-Communist Party unity, whose differences must be overcome in action and through ideological discussion. Similarly, the relations of the Socialist and Communist parties with other Marxist movements must be defined in action, with the establishment of whatever political alliances are necessary in light of the process of the Chilean revolution.

6. The presence of workers in the government cannot signify dependence of the mass movement on the governmental apparatus. The Socialist Party maintains its criterion that the unions and popular organizations ought to develop their own character. Moreover, organized workers must prepare themselves and begin incorporating themselves into the real exercise of power, through the direct management of the institutions and organisms of the state. The Socialist Party will fight to revitalize the committees of the Popular Unity and to convert them into instruments of political power for the working masses in the new popular state.

The committees of the Popular Unity should integrate themselves actively in the tasks that must be completed by the class and mass organs, such as unions, neighborhood committees, and others, which should serve as natural vehicles for the expression of the economic and social struggles which must be raised to an increasingly political level. In this area, the Central Única de Trabajadores (Central Union Organization) should broaden, strengthen, and give agility to its organization, in order to be in tune with the decisive circumstances the Chilean social movement is living through.

7. The special ways in which the Popular Unity has arrived at governmental power, which obligate it now to participate limitedly in a bourgeois state, should not constitute a pretext for making the government play the role of arbitrator in the class struggle. On the contrary, in the conflicts that are stirred up, the government must place itself resolutely on the side of the workers.

8. Consequently, the Socialist Party will struggle to convert itself into the revolutionary vanguard of this stage, developing a policy that tends toward accelerating the

conditions for changing, during the office of this government, the capitalist character of the dominant system in order to transform it into a socialist regime. Thus, the content of the Party program will be determined according to the essential propositions of the Popular Unity's program, which intends to eliminate the national and foreign monopolies and the power of the landed oligarchy. The Party program will also initiate the construction of socialism through the united and combative action of the working masses as the fundamental protagonists.

In addition to attending to the most urgent necessities of the masses, especially its poorest sectors, broadening the social base of support of the government, and politically strengthening the mass movement, the Socialist Party gives special priority to those programmatic measures that undermine capitalist power and connect the democratic-bourgeois tasks with socialist tasks in the same uninterrupted process.

In this sense the following measures are especially urgent.

a) Nationalization of the imperialist firms, the banks, and the insurance companies, expropriation of the large monopolies and public utility firms, and bringing foreign commerce under state control.

b) Drastic agrarian reform supported by the mobilization of the peasants.

c) Equal minimum wages and family subsidies for workers, peasants, and white-collar workers, a mobile scale for wages and salaries, and rapid absorption of unemployment.

d) Incorporation of the workers to the full exercise of power, developing workers' management in the nationalized firms and workers' control when necessary, and constructing from the base a new political structure which culminates in the People's Assembly.

9) Within these perspectives we need a Socialist Party invigorated by strict application of democratic centralism, which develops primarily among the working class, recognizes the legitimacy and the necessity of ideological struggle to educate its membership, and emphatically rejects any bureaucratic and *caudillista* [personalist leadership] tendencies.

Only by acting on these measures will the Socialist Party be able to prepare itself and the masses for the decisive confrontation with the bourgeoisie and with imperialism. We recognize that this confrontation forms part of the general picture of the revolutionary struggle in Latin America and in the whole world, and our line of action will be in accord with these general perspectives. The Socialist Party will move toward the extension and consolidation of concrete ties with all the revolutionary movements and organizations of the world.

WORK WITHOUT REST TO
WIN THE BATTLE OF PRODUCTION*

"The essential task of the moment is that stated by the Central Committee of the Communist Party during its plenary meeting in July: to win the battle of production. It is not only an economic battle, but also political and ideological," said *Compañero* Mario Zamorano, leader of the Central Committee of the Party, yesterday afternoon in the National Assembly of Company Committees.

This National Assembly began on Saturday with the participation of 160 delegates from the company committees of the Party, from Arica to Magallanes. The

* From the Communist daily *El Siglo,* July 26, 1971.

workers talked from their vast experience with regard to the development of production.

In his summary speech, Mario Zamorano reaffirmed that in the creation of the new bodies operating in the management of state enterprises, "the norms of democratic formation must be respected, in particular in forming the Production Committees."

With respect to the multiple forms that the workers' new attitude toward their plants, production, and work discipline must take, *Compañero* Zamorano recommended a broad and creative spirit to promote production. A concrete way to do this is "through the spirit of emulation that can be manifested a thousand ways."

With respect to voluntary work, Zamorano said that "it has to be encouraged through dialogue, persuasion, and intense propaganda." Voluntary work that gives greater dividends, in every sense, "is that performed within the worker's own company or service."

It was also stated that the Popular Unity must function, since it is the most efficient way to co-ordinate and unite with other popular forces. By no means should the Popular Unity replace worker organizations (trade unions, commissions, and delegate councils).

Help for the Countryside

The report pointed out that agricultural production is fundamental and that the worker/peasant alliance acquires new importance at this stage of the process that the country is undergoing. Therefore "the assembly recommends posing to all workers' organizations that they relate to the countryside, especially to the settlements. The most tangible form this aid should acquire," the report stated, "is the sponsorship by trade unions of determined agrarian developments or settlements. The most specific task should be the designation of activities with union support."

Valuable Experiences

During the meeting, leaders of various production committees spoke. The experiences related made it clear that the battle of production can be won, but that it is not an easy task. The essential thing is to develop the consciousness of the workers, to attain a change in their mentality in order to assume these new responsibilities that the conquest of power implies.

The experiences of the coal-mine workers were of extraordinary value. "We took over a company on the verge of chaos and now it finances itself and exceeds all the goals we set," said the delegate of the company committee, giving concrete figures. Each one of the leaders of company committees also made known how they have succeeded in surpassing their goals and the role that the Party has performed. In particular, the *compañeros* praised voluntary work, the symbol of the new stage we are now living in.

The workers from El Salvador copper mine told how they have exceeded their production goals. The *compañeros* of Andina [beverages] attained a productivity superior to the capacity of machines and they are now studying the method they should follow. Encouraging examples were also given by the leaders of the workers from the textile sector, showing with legitimate pride the overattainment of the established goals. The delegates from state enterprises such as ENDESA, ENAP, ENAMI, and Chilectra pointed out specific examples of voluntary work that contributed to exceeding production goals.

RADICALISM IS NOT AND CANNOT BE
MARXIST*

"I am not with those who stay, and I dislike the attitude of those who left the Party, because my method has
always been to fight within parties until I was thrown out."
This thought was categorically expressed by Alejandro
Ríos Valdivia, Minister of National Defense, when con-
sulted about his impression of the political situation in
Chile at the present moment. . . .

Journalists at the Moneda (presidential palace) surrounded Minister Ríos to ask him to detail his own position on the division created during the Radical Party's
last convention. The Professor and Minister belongs to
the Radical Party. He did not shun the questions, expressing thus his vision of the political moment: "I dislike
very much what is happening in my party."

A journalist asked him what faction of radicalism he
was with, to which he replied, "I have always been with
the left and no one can doubt it, because I was even expelled in 1964 for having maintained that position. But
at this moment I do not identify with any faction: I am
with the Party, I am in the Party. Naturally because I am
Minister of Defense, I took no part in the convention.
But my position is that I, personally, did not like the way
in which things were led in the Convention. Moreover,
I do not agree with the ideas established in the Declaration of Principles. . . .

"The Party has gone too far, in my opinion, in the Declaration of Principles. The position of wanting to appear
as if we were a genuine Marxist party of workers is un-
true. Within the Popular Unity we have a mission that

* From *El Mercurio*, August 5, 1971.

corresponds to the Radical Party: to attract the middle sectors, employees, small industrialists, businessmen, and farmers toward the task of the Popular Unity. We want, within the democratic concept, to march toward socialism."

Alejandro Ríos Valdivia said in answer to another question that he would not resign from the Radical Party, and if people wanted him out of it they would have to expel him. He also defined himself as legitimately radical and said, "I do not like the political vote approved in the recent Convention, but as I am a member I have to conform to it." He said that he did not blame the Radical Party's leadership for the vote, as it was unanimously approved, and regretted that he had not been able to attend when it was discussed in committee.

He finished by saying that "the Radical Party is not and cannot be a Marxist party, because in Chile there is no room for another party with these same principles."

CHAPTER 9

Christian Left and Revolutionary Left

For years, the Christian Democrats have wrestled with the question of what kind of society the Party should work toward in Chile. Sincere Christian Democrats were critical of capitalism and the social and political liberalism of the Chilean ruling class, but they were also fearful of the statism and authoritarianism believed to be inherent in Marxian socialism. Thus, they sought a middle ground in advocating a "communitarian" society, neither capitalist nor socialist, neither liberal nor statist. During the six years of the Frei Christian Democratic government, however, Chile failed to move significantly away from capitalism and liberalism, in spite of important social reforms accomplished. This failure occasioned a 1970 split in the Party in which sectors of the Party formed the Movement of Popular Unity Action (MAPU) to support the Popular Unity. Moreover, in declaring Rodomiro Tomic as presidential candidate in the election of 1970, the Party moved to the left. Finally, significant sectors of the Party, unhappy with the intransigent opposition of the Frei faction to the Popular Unity and the Party's rapid move to the right during 1971, formed a movement of the Christian Left. The Christian Left, though not officially a part of the Popular Unity, supports the government and works energetically at the grass-roots level to promote revolutionary consciousness among the masses, particularly among the peasants.

The articles by Pedro Felipe Ramírez present the key concepts of Christian Democracy which make a Christian Left movement ideologically compatible with the socialism of the Popular Unity. Rava, a socialist, is skeptical of the concept of "communitary socialism," but points to the class contradictions within the CDP which have, in fact, propelled the bourgeois sectors of the party into an opposition coalition with the right-wing National Party and the popular sectors toward the Christian Left.

Apart from the election of Allende and the consolidation of a genuine Christian Left, perhaps the most significant political development in Chile in recent years is the activity and growing strength of the Movement of the Revolutionary Left (MIR). The MIR, which is not part of the government coalition, has deep roots among three significant sectors of the population: students, peasants, and the masses within marginal settlements. In addition, the MIR is well organized and has outstanding leadership, disciplined militants, an intelligence apparatus, an uncompromising revolutionary ideology, and arms. The interview with Sergio Zorrilla, an MIR leader, reveals the level and the style of MIR activities and its attitude toward the Popular Unity.

SOCIALISM AND COMMUNITARISM*

PEDRO FELIPE RAMÍREZ

The most novel event of the recent meeting of the plenary council of the Christian Democratic Party (CDP), held at Cartagena, was the use for the first time of the words "communitary socialism" as an official definition of the type of socialism the CDP wants for the country. For years, the leaders of the Party have been discussing this matter. The more traditional members in-

* From the theoretical organ of the Christian Democratic Party, *Política y Espíritu* No. 322, April 6, 1971.

sisted on the need to utilize the word "communitarism" in order to affirm something in itself: on the philosophical level, something different from liberalism or Marxism, and in the social-economic sphere, distinct from capitalism or socialism. Others, however, recognized that a third, generically distinct model that was a species of neither capitalism nor socialism does not exist. Thus, to speak simply of "communitarism" was a way to avoid a definition and, at the same time, to run the risk of converting it into a new form of capitalism. This risk was not a theoretical question but something that arose from the orientation of the Frei government.

In the 1966 CDP Congress, the traditionalists held the upper hand under the leadership of the theoretician Jaime Castillo. There were three pressing reasons for the Christian Democrats not to wait for the next Party congress to abandon the word "communitarism" and adopt the term "communitary socialism." The vote on the matter was seventy-three for the motion and five against.

The first of these reasons was the presidential campaign of Tomic, whose program had a definite socialist orientation with a deep penetration of thought particularly among the militants of the Party. On the other hand, there were the socialist expressions and trends adopted in certain ecclesiastical sectors. Lastly, there was the rise to power of the Popular Unity, which led the Chilean people to believe that the elimination of capitalism and the introduction of socialism were irreversible facts.

In defining itself in favor of communitary socialism, the CDP tried to express its basic accord with the construction of a socialist society in Chile and, at the same time, to participate with their own ideas in the debate over what form of socialism should be introduced. . . . They wished to oppose "state" socialism with "communitary" socialism.

The CDP sums up their ideas with the slogan, "The

changes must be for the benefit of the people and not the state." This phrase is a double-edged sword.

On the one hand, it would certainly be negative to try to create an economy in Chile in which all the means of production belong to the state and are administered by a hierarchical bureaucracy generated by our "representative democracy." The creative capacity of Chileans would be limited if we were to be rigidly submitted to orders imparted by governing bodies. Our creative capacity is the greatest potential available to defeat underdevelopment. We do not sincerely believe that the Popular Unity is thinking of an absolute statism, but undoubtedly Christian Democracy can contribute much to the design of forms of organization of a socialist economy that incorporates the creative initiative of the men and women of our country.

The dangerous side of this slogan is the peril of placing the people before the government, giving a favorable image to reactionary propaganda. . . . The state must not be weakened but must be fortified. Socialism assumes the real supremacy of the common good over individual interest, and for this the people must count on an effective instrument with sufficient power to make this supremacy possible. That instrument is the state, a state genuinely representative of the people. . . . The state should not be confused with the government in power at any given time, as in the present case of the Popular Unity. If the actual structure of the state permits "excesses" on the part of governments, the solution is not to take power from the state but to radically democratize the structure.

The adjective "communitary" must, therefore, be interpreted as the necessity to gather the creative capacity of each Chilean and to give the state a character truly representative of the people. The reduction of the state's power in favor of multiple "production communities" working in free competition and oriented toward profits is inappropriate. Surreptitiously, this would be giving way to a capitalist communitarism.

THE CHRISTIAN DEMOCRATS AND
THEIR IDEOLOGICAL CRISIS*

RAVA

The Christian Democrats have brought to light an ideological offensive that they had kept buried for the past six years. During the Frei administration, the ideological principals were silenced instead of sustaining the action of the government. Now, entrenching themselves in an attitude of jealous opposition, they have again unfurled their banners; they have started to think again.

With its ideology, Christian Democracy pretends to affirm positions that will permit it to have a determining influence over the orientation of the political process now taking place in our country, undermining the policy of the popular government based upon a program for which the people have pronounced themselves in a clear and unmistakable manner.

In the conclusions reached by the plenary of the CDP held in Cartagena May 8 and 9, a new slogan has been launched: "communitary socialism." The slogan does not go beyond being a synonym of the vague concept of "communitarism" which presumably determined the political action of this Party. The strategic objective behind the actions of the CDP is, specifically, the actual process of socialization of the economy being carried out by the popular government. They want to impede our efforts to rationalize and plan production in our country on a national scale.

* From the socialist journal *Indo-America* No. 3, June 1971.

The CDP opposes the method of socialization voted for by the people with a reactionary formula consisting of the acquisition of industries for the benefit only of those who work in each factory or industry. These new private owners would engage in self-management and independently direct the firm, thus remaining isolated and outside of a general production plan.

The objective of this deformed capitalism, if it were possible to introduce it, would mean the moderation of the class struggle in that the workers would be identified with their particular industry and each group of workers would devour the other in an endless struggle. Fortunately this form of neofeudalism is inapplicable today. . . .

There are marked differences between a capitalist economy and a socialist economy. The determining objective under a capitalist system of production is *profit;* on the other hand, the aim of a socialist system is *the satisfaction of human needs*. This necessarily implies that a socialist economy, in order to be such, needs to plan the economic process.

Planning at a national level of basic investments and of the distribution of the national income and, in general, the harmonious growth of the entire economy, would not be possible in the neofeudal economy proposed by the CDP. Groups of divided workers producing essential goods and services independently of what other workers are doing in their same sector of production and independently of our country's needs is a system that is governed solely by the thin thread of supply and demand. . . .

Christian Democrats linked to the agrarian reform and the policy of supply of agricultural products can testify about the anarchy existent among the co-operative farms established during the Frei administration. Each one produced, without any centralized planning, whatever it thought to be the most convenient product that would yield the highest profits. Presently, ways and means are being introduced to correct this error. . . .

The insurmountable fear of the CDP is statism. For six years the Christian Democrats held the powers that the state implies in their hands and did not know what to do with it. Now they are afraid of it, because they know the monster from within. This monster is the bourgeois state. We must socialize our economy, and this implies, unfortunately for some, statism and centralization. To be truthful, we must point out that in no case can the old state system be capable of regulating an economy when it is destined to serve the interests of the bourgeoisie and to act as their instrument of enrichment and repression. We must implant a new type of state, democratic and popular, in which all the workers are genuinely represented and democratically concur in its direction.

The contradictions in the ideology of the CDP reflect the struggle within the Party. On the one hand they talk about socialism and on the other they abhor a centralized and planned society. On the one hand, the CDP defines itself in opposition to the government and on the other hand it demands a place in the battle against the monopolies and in the construction of the new society. The coincidences between the programs of Allende and Tomic are well known and both differ very clearly from the political attitude sustained by the Frei government.

The popular government has broken many traditions. One of these is the classical "opposition vs. the government." In actual fact it must be rather embarrassing for some sectors of the CDP to declare themselves in opposition to the government when their ideals are those being put forward by the government. The weak imputation of sectarianism made by the more reactionary levels of the CDP against the government are deflected by the public attitude of numerous Christian Democrats who work elbow to elbow with the Popular Unity on many fronts in the formation of a new Chile. Actually, the true opposition comes from those bourgeois sectors who are against changes by nature, represented by the Nationals, the Radical Democrats, and the right wing of the Christian Democrats.

In spite of the official arguments by the CDP on the differentiation between the Christian Left and *freísmo* claiming that the Party is united, we must point out the multiclass character of the Party. There are people of many classes who are Party militants. This naturally implies that within the CDP there is a class struggle, implacable and insistent as in any class struggle. On the one hand we have the bourgeoisie, who have used their Party to reach for the highest positions of the economic power and to share with the old "clans" positions on various boards of directors in banking, commerce, industry, the press, etc. . . . On the other hand we have the deceived peasant or worker who loves and trusts his Party and who, after six years of the Frei administration, still does not realize that he was used by the monopolistic bourgeoisie and Yankee imperialism which derived so much benefit from a government that he, in good faith, helped elect.

This class struggle within the CDP explains how the two antagonistic forces annul each other and give rise to a frozen and dead policy that has no practical application. This same class struggle was the motor impulse behind some changes that classified the last administration as "reformist." These were superstructural changes such as the Agrarian Reform Law, the law concerning agricultural unionization, and the law governing community organizations. On the other hand, this reformism implied, among other things, that the doors were opened wide to imperialist penetration, especially in light industry.

These antagonistic contradictions within the CDP will

be overcome only when the bourgeois sectors unite and identify themselves with the right-wing parties and when the popular sectors unite and identify themselves with the popular government; in other words, once the Christian Democratic Party culminates its division.

A NEW INSTITUTIONALITY*

PEDRO FELIPE RAMÍREZ

First question: What is the present situation?

Chile is presently going through a stage of construction of a new institutionality which will govern our behavior as as a nation in the future. This is a result of an inherited institutionality that no longer responds effectively to the needs of our present society. This institutionality was introduced at a time when the needs and possibilities were of a different nature. For several years diverse sectors of the national community have been aware of this fact. One of these sectors is constituted by the Marxist groups, who were without a doubt one of the first to denounce it, but they did so more on the basis of ideological concepts in accord with the experiences of other countries than on a full comprehension of our own process. After them came the secular groups who fought against the paternalistic forms of an aristocratic society affirmed by a paternalistic and aristocratic Church. They, however, concentrated on the social and religious aspects without understanding fully that the institutional crisis invaded all sectors of social organization. Later, there were the groups of Christian extraction, daring in their fight against Catholic orthodoxy but fearful of taking their denunciation too far.

For years this consciousness of need for a change was

* From *Política y Espíritu* No. 322, April 6, 1971.

cultivated in the country, and its first effective maturation was expressed in the presidential campaign of 1964.

President Frei's government signified for Chile a new stage of maturity. Facts and values until then self-evident stopped being so and were questioned. Many taboos were eliminated, expectations grew, and vast sectors of the population became conscious of their new rights. The national debate was amplified and radicalized. In this situation, large sectors of public opinion attempted to get a clear picture of the moment. The image that change must involve all aspects of national life and that, in order to succeed, the acceptance must be total became clearer, the more so in view of the peculiar exigencies of the country. During these years all the political parties, without exception, suffered a series of internal crises motivated by ideological conceptions or diverse strategies generated from within. Not only the political parties suffered crises, but also nearly all our institutions: the State, the Church, the Armed Forces, unions, and the universities. In the middle of this critical maturation came the presidential election of last year.

Allende's government has the virtue of grasping this fact and conducting it along a clear course. This course, in my opinion, has three characteristics that are decisive. First, it implies a total change that questions (without losing sight of the positive values) the whole of our old institutionality. This sets aside the danger of frustration, which was certainly one of the failings in Frei. Second, it is a course that is acceptable to the national community and therefore capable of sustaining itself. This is due to the fact that it recognizes that Chileans place a positive value on such matters as pluralism, political democracy, legal justice, and individual, family, and social liberty. Third, it is a course that points toward a general image of a new society, socialism, which allows national debate to be ordered and positions to be taken.

If the first characteristic is lost, there will be frustration. If the second is lost, there will be violence. And if the third is lost, there will be chaos. If all three are maintained, the country will be able to reach the imperative need of substituting a new institutionality for the old one, which will be an expression of majority sentiment within the national community.

Second question: Where is this situation leading us?

We are moving toward the creation of a new institutionality which will orientate our social existence of the future. This will be an institutionality generically socialist, but of authentically Chilean form. In order that it may succeed, it is imperative that the characteristics I have mentioned be upheld.

It is not enough to question only parts of our social organization. During these months, the changes have operated mainly within the sphere of our economic organization, but very little in our political, social, and cultural sectors. For example, the structure of the state in our country leads us nowhere. The President of the Republic himself has recognized this in his message to the Congress of May 21. The structures of the Executive branch, the Congress, and the Judiciary are anachronistic. If it is true that they have legal legitimacy, they have certainly, and dangerously, lost their social legitimacy. It is essential not to commit the error of identifying the state with those in power at any given moment. The fact that many sectors now have confidence in the government as never before does not signify that they trust the Executive power. On the other hand, the fact that many do not feel represented by the government in power does not signify that there is lack of confidence in the state as a regent of the common good. To postpone these transformations for very long could prove fatal, as could the postponement of changes that must affect our social and cultural organization.

It could also be fatal if the process did not incorporate the characteristics peculiar to our people and their sense of values that were gained during previous epochs. It is not enough to obtain the unwilling acceptance of those sectors who must, for the sake of strategic and tactical positions, join in as imitators. It is necessary to incorporate these sectors and values to the process, and these must form pivots of the new institutionality.

Here we have the question of pluralism. I sometimes feel that this is limited to the possibility that there be opponents of change; but this is not what is important and has nothing constructive to offer. The constructive effect is when pluralism pervades the task of constructing the new society. It is only in this manner that all the indispensable social energies can be generated to move ahead toward the new society that will reflect the feelings of the great majority of the people, which is the only way to make it lasting.

If this is not understood, little by little it will be discovered that the country does not respond to the hard demands that the process requires, and it will be extremely difficult to assure the irreversibility of change. Without a doubt, it is difficult for those sectors that are in favor of the change to fit our pluralist ideas to socialist construction. There is mutual distrust. Some do not think that the others are really socialists, and they have many arguments in their favor. Others do not think that some truly believe in the permanent values of our nationality, and they also have sound arguments in their favor. But both sides must understand that the actual process matures people and institutions. We must work to gain mutual trust and avoid the risk of mistrust. . . . In this way there can be creative dialogue.

You have, for instance, the debate over the new economy. On one hand the government is accused of wanting a state-controlled economy. On the other hand, the Christian Democrats are accused of trying to set up communities of workers in a capitalist formation. I believe that neither group is correct in their accusations, and I am convinced that an unprejudiced discussion, born of trust and not distrust, would lead us to discover with surprise that what the Popular Unity wants and what the Christian Democrats want are not greatly different. . . . How much could the process benefit, and as a result the country, if both these forces worked together in trying to find answers to the problems that have been encountered and have not been solved by either group on their own? Instead of being against each other, why not be for each other?

Without a doubt, there would be discrepancies between forces, but these will present themselves in a true light and can be ironed out using the nation's mechanisms of decision making. There will also arise occasions of misuse of this mutual confidence, and this would be very harmful. But this damage cannot be greater than that caused by the fact that we start from a basis where no collaboration is possible.

Therefore, in my judgment, the success of the actual process depends on its ability to penetrate all aspects of our society, to incorporate into itself the permanent values of our people, and to move ahead without vacillation toward the construction of a new society, generically socialist.

BLOW AFTER BLOW: UNTIL FINAL VICTORY*

JULIO HUASI

A strong wind shook Chile that Sunday, March 15, 1970, when the young leader of MIR, Sergio Zorrilla, shot at civilian policemen who had accidentally come

* From the *Prensa Latina* Feature Service, ES-963/71.

across him in a Santiago street. The MIR leader was on his way to a top-level meeting of his armed underground organization, which had been created in 1965 and was called the Revolutionary Left Movement (MIR).

Two police bullets—one in the leg and the other in the arm—immobilized the third-year student who studied philosophy at the University of Chile. Zorrilla was born into a working-class family in the district of San Miguel on May 30, 1945. He still had not celebrated his twenty-fifth birthday when the represessive apparatus of the Frei government captured him as a prize specimen. Sergio Zorrilla—called "El Chico" by the students—stayed in jail until November 14.

He remembers that when he was eleven years old he participated in the struggle that led to the popular demonstrations of April 2, 1957, during which a mass of people were machine-gunned in the streets by the Army, leaving hundreds dead on the pavements. He remembers that he fought in the streets of San Miguel against the Army, side by side with his father, René Zorrilla Rojas, a Communist linotypist, while his mother, Marta Fuenzalida, had no idea where the third of her four children was.

"I felt good," remembers Zorrilla, "with my old man because he was very brave. The troops opened fire against some ten thousand people in San Miguel who were armed only with stones. The people were brave enough but our defeat was inevitable. Papa was right in front, unafraid. I was only eleven then and had joined the Communist Youth."

In that family of Communist workers, familiar with the written word because of the father's profession (one of Sergio's uncles, Américo Zorrilla, was also a linotypist and is now the Minister of Treasury of Chile), the news of the world was commented on daily. The entrance into Havana of the revolutionaries led by Fidel Castro left an indelible mark on the adolescent, who had been participating in the class struggle practically from the cradle.

"I remember those days of April 1957. It was an impressive sight when the entire population of *La Legua* went out into the streets, about eight o'clock at night, banging together the stones they carried in each hand, like the Mexicans in the movie "Viva Zapata," shouting against the reactionary government of General Ibáñez. The noise of the stones was tremendous. And when the now Socialist deputy Mario Palestro led the insurrection of workers of the *Mademsa* and *Madeco* [steel plants] in the attempt to seize the Twelfth Carabineer Commissary, I remember we were all attacked with machine guns."

Amid the percussion of the stones and the bursts of machine-gun fire, Sergio Zorrilla grew in courage and character.

In 1966 Sergio joined the MIR, and in the MIR Congress of 1967 he was elected member of the central committee and the national secretariat. His entrance into the strict clandestinity of the organization demanded a tense mobility, since he had to maintain his position as a student leader. His sudden appearances in a school—conveniently protected—when the political police were expecting him someplace else, made headlines, and the people began to laugh at the repressive forces.

What Role Did the MIR Play in the Latest Political Events in Chile?

"Some people said that the MIR played a negative role in the electoral process that brought Popular Unity into the government. We insisted that in order to obtain power, a class struggle had to be developed and revolutionary ideas had to be accepted by the masses. In this sense, the MIR played a radicalizing role by developing the struggle against the system in the student movement, in the homeless-settlers' movement, and in the peasant

movement. We believe that this helped to develop the
class struggle in the country, and, obviously, to persuade
a large number of people to vote for Allende, since our
work destroyed the image of the reactionary candidates
in the eyes of the voters. We are not concerned about obtaining recognition for our participation in Allende's victory. The people who fought in our organization know
about this participation. In spite of the fact—and we
have always said this—that the polls are not the highest
expression of the revolutionary struggle, we believe that
because of the exact circumstances of Chile, the election
has created the possibility of unmasking and breaking up
the pseudodemocratic game of the bourgeoisie and has
played a very decisive role. . . . In àny case, we made
our position known to the effect that the struggle for
power in the underdeveloped countries, and in those dependent on imperialism, must be waged through revolutionary instruments, explaining that confrontation with
the bourgeoisie must of necessity be an armed one.

"The bourgeoisie's scope of political action in the superstructure of domination will not allow us to obtain real
power. There must be a decisive confrontation, but the
bourgeoisie will resort to all methods to win, even a blood
bath, and therefore all revolutionaries should be prepared.
In the document we call 'MIR and the Elections,' published in August 1970,[1] we saw the possibility of an
electoral triumph for the Popular Unity coalition and we
reaffirmed our principles regarding the defense of the government, radicalization and deepening of the process, and
the need to prepare ourselves to confront bourgeois treason. Because the people expressed a desire for a popular
government and because the bourgeoisie was temporarily
divided, the MIR decided not to carry out a specifically

[1] Available in translation in Régis Debray, *Conversations with
Allende* (Pantheon Books, 1971).

electoral work, but to continue and accentuate the development of the mass struggle, with the obvious head-on combat with the classes that promoted bourgeois candidates. This is the period when the struggles of the homeless settlers and the students began, eroding the right wing and Frei's demagogy.

"Once the elections were won, it was impossible to show that the MIR had been wrong. It's not true that the MIR took votes away from the Popular Unity. On the contrary, in the mass fronts under our influence—unlike others—there were no people who voted for Alessandri or Tomic, since the MIR's political orientation and our methods of struggle permitted radicalization on a political and not purely economic level, which kept the masses from being deceived by the pseudoprogressive rhetoric used in the electoral campaigns by the candidates running against Salvador Allende.

"Proof of the MIR's work is that we won the student leaderships of the University of Concepción, the Southern University of Valdivia, and the regional centers of the University of Chile in Osorno and Talca. We are a very important force in the University of the North, in the regional center of the University of Chile in Arica, in the Catholic universities of Santiago and Valparaíso, and in other cities. Moreover, we lead the Secondary School Federations in the provinces of Concepción and Bío-Bío in the central zone. We organized nationally the Revolutionary Office of the Homeless Settlers, with twenty camps in Santiago, Valparaíso, Concepción, Los Ángeles, Chillán, and Antofagasta. And we should say that in those camps the leaders are democratically elected by the settlers themselves. A short time ago, in the 'Lenin' camp at Concepción, the MIR slate won by 6,300 votes over the 1,200 votes received by the coalition formed by the Communist Party, the Christian Democrats, and the MAPU.

"We organized and led the struggle of the Mapuche Indians in the South of Chile, a work that was begun in 1967 by MIR students who went off to live in the Indian communities. We organized the seizure of lands and the moving of fences before and after the elections of September 4, lands that have been taken away, with blood and fire, from the Mapuche Indians by the *latifundistas* [big landowners] throughout the history of Chile, leaving the original inhabitants of our country steeped in hunger and the most savage exploitation. The MIR organized and led the Mapuches in the provinces of Cautín, Bío-Bío, and Osorno. Our strength among peasants has grown and we have a strong influence in the most important peasant organizations, such as the Ránquil Confederation. Our strength has increased through the struggles we developed in Melipilla, before the elections, with the seizure of funds and the expropriation of milk then distributed by our commandos to the agricultural workers.

"And we are sure that those thousands and thousands of exploited Chileans who participated in all those struggles under our leadership, voted for Allende and not for Tomic or Alessandri, and so did other sectors of exploited people who participated in our other struggles. All those people voted for Allende, because they want a socialist future for our country.

"We increased our influence among the industrial working sectors and among the intellectual workers, the professionals, the professors, artists, small businessmen, and civil servants. Nobody any longer can describe us as a 'splinter group.' MIR's influence is growing among the masses, because we are applying a line that we consider correct for the revolutionary process in Chile. We are not a large or a mass party, but an armed revolutionary organization, with a growing popularity among the masses."

What Role Will MIR Play Now, After the Election of Popular Unity?

"After September 4, we reaffirmed our strategic positions in regard to the Chilean Revolution. We insisted that the conquest of real power would take place inevitably through an armed confrontation with the bourgeoisie and imperialism. In the first euphoric days after September 4, during which many people expressed hasty and simplistic opinions, as if everything had already been won, the MIR continued to work tirelessly to locate and dismantle the reactionary conspiracy, because nobody can deny that the bourgeoisie and U.S. imperialism will not renounce power peacefully. We aimed our work at strengthening and defending the triumph, alerting the people against treason, all at the risk of appearing aggressive.

"Although the electoral triumph does not in itself mean a socialist revolution, it damaged bourgeois interests. The fact of politically dominating the state means that the quota of capitalist profits diminishes, which forces the bourgeoisie to turn to conspiracy. Before Allende took office on November 3, we exhorted the people to organize committees to defend the triumph; we insisted on the need to mobilize the masses and radicalize the program, to radicalize and awaken the proletariat and prepare it to confront armed right-wing sedition. Very few people thought we were in other sectors; moreover, some even called us 'opportunists,' and said that we had climbed on the 'bandwagon.'

"Unfortunately, our adversaries began to act. Before the assassination of General Schneider, a day before October 21, we denounced the conspiracy in detail. The MIR, as part of its investigation of coup-ist activities, had patiently infiltrated these groups and later revealed the plan and the participation in it of elements from the right-wing Christian Democrats and figures in the highest government ranks at the time. Among other seditious individuals we uncovered were former Major Arturo Marshall, whose hide-out the MIR discovered and whom we even thought of arresting to obtain certain information. We communicated the whereabouts of Marshall, and all the other information we had, to responsible figures in the sectors affected by the reactionary plan. The quick work of some informed sectors led to the arrest of Marshall by the police of the Frei government, who concealed Marshall's confession from Popular Unity, which was that instead of assassinating Allende he had planned to assassinate General Schneider. If the confession had been made public, we could have prevented the assassination of Schneider. On the very day Schneider was shot, the affair was published in the 'Top Secret' section of the newspaper *La Segunda* of the Edwards clan, perhaps because they make up that page a day before. We knew that this information was in the hands of Jaspard da Fonseca, who was Frei's Director of Investigations and, therefore, in the hands of Frei himself and his most intimate collaborators, but they did nothing to prevent the assassination.

"In any case, MIR's denunciatons made it possible to dismantle the sedition. From that moment on, MIR has continued to unravel the threads of conspiracy. We have published much of the information, with names and addresses, and we declared, with all responsibility, that if it were not for a revolutionary policy of averting a coup, this sedition would have taken place against trade-union, peasant, student, and left-wing leaders.

"One of the most important ideologists of the reactionary sedition, who for the moment we shall call Mr. K., affirms to his followers that the conspiracy will attain its objective as long as the government limits itself to reforms, but it will be much more difficult and less businesslike for the bourgeoisie if the reactionaries have to confront an 'organized and armed people,' with 'implications of civil war and necessary foreign interventions,' which would isolate the bourgeoisie and galvanize the people around the government.

"This Mr. K. maintains that 'a rapprochement should be avoided between the MIR and the Popular Unity coalition, and especially between the MIR and the Communist Party. It should be avoided at all costs,' says Mr. K., 'since the rapprochement would create in the people an image of power and audacity.' An agreement between a mass party, the most important in the Popular Unity coalition, and an armed organization composed of young people, is an image that would be difficult to destroy. 'We must, through our press,' continues Mr. K., 'give the impression that Popular Unity is divided into two sectors, one democratic and the other totalitarian, and especially isolate the Communist Party. The CP press should accelerate this confrontation between the CP and the MIR.' So much for Mr. K., one of the ideologists of the right wing."

While Sergio Zorrilla and the present writer shared the invigorating bitterness of a *mate* (tea made with the *yerba mate*), Zorrilla made his final statements.

"More than ever, we believe in the need to mobilize the masses and to accelerate the application of the program. We must fill the streets with combative and alert multitudes in order to isolate the reactionary and seditious sectors and change the correlation of political forces. Only by directly informing the people about the dirty maneuvers of imperialism and the right wing, and a correct conduct on our part, will it be possible to confront the situation that is approaching, one of sharp class contradictions. In this situation the MIR will play a highly responsible role united to the revolutionary and Left forces. The unity of these forces should necessarily lead to the elimination of all types of sectarianism, which are very nega-

tive for the revolutionary process and for the formation of
militants. More than ever before, the different strategic
concepts of the process should be allowed to express
themselves politically, since they will help increase the
revolutionary awareness of the people. The MIR has
given proof of a conscientious and responsible conduct,
encouraging and carrying forward into practice mechanisms of unification in the mass sectors that it leads, and
in which it participates. The case of the FECH (Student
Federation of the University of Chile) is a good example.
There, we supported the Popular Unity candidates
against the danger of the bourgeoisie installing itself in
such an important political center. Months ago we insisted on the need for uniting the Left in order to confront the reactionaries. In the case of the FEC (Student
Federation of the University of Concepción), where the
MIR has been leading for years and has the biggest majority, we exhorted the Popular Unity comrades to support
our roster, but not everyone did this, and events later led
to the killing of an MIR militant, Arnoldo Ríos, a victim
of sectarianism.[2] The unification prospects that opened
up after his death are welcomed by us. The price of the
death of one of our comrades should not be a circumstantial unity, but a firm, solid, and combative unification
of all left-wing forces. We will make every effort necessary to achieve this unity, without the least prejudice or
sectarianism. In front of us, united by fear and by the defense of lost privileges, is U.S. imperialism and the reactionaries, ready to do anything, even to carry out a mas-
sacre such as the one in Indonesia. These are the people
we must fight, together, blow upon blow, until the final
victory of liberation and socialism, just as Che wanted."

[2] Ríos was killed in a fight between Communist and MIR
students.

the direction of the latter) grouped into economic clans and closely linked to the bourgeoisie of the imperialist countries. These capitalists are a very small minority of the bourgeoisie, but they are the owners of the most important sectors of the country, including factories, insurance companies, banks, and large commercial companies. Many of them are also large landowners, and all of them are closely dependent in their business operations on the foreign bourgeoisie, especially the North American, which is still the owner of the large-scale copper-mining enterprises and many important industries in our country. For this reason, the monopolistic bourgeoisie have absolutely no national Chilean interests, but instead their interests are those of the anti-national imperialist bourgeoisie; in order to deceive the proletariat, however, they have named the chief party to which they belong (which is not their only instrument) the "National Party." Together with imperialism, the monopolistic bourgeoisie is the chief enemy of the proletariat, the revolution, and the Chilean people, and the principal beneficiary of the capitalist regime still ruling our country. The Popular Unity has declared that the industries, banks, etc. of this bourgeoisie should pass into the hands of all Chileans through the people's state.

2. The Large Agrarian Bourgeoisie (Modern).

This sector of the bourgeoisie consists of agrarian capitalists who cultivate their farms intensively with the use of machinery and other modern means of production and pay cash salaries to their laborers. Their farms are highly profitable and generally well exploited. They also usually have urban industrial properties, and their interests coincide with those of the traditional landowners and the monopolistic bourgeoisie. The political expression of this sector tends to be the National Party or the Radical

Democrats, and it is also an enemy of the people to be expropriated by the people's government.

3. The Large Landowners (Traditional).

This is the oldest branch of the oligarchy, whose traditional political expression was the old Conservative Party and today is integrated with the Liberal Party (which at first included businessmen and bankers) in the National Party. They are the owners of the large estates that are being expropriated by the Ministry of Agriculture, directed by *Compañero* Chonchol. These landowners have always been characterized by their aristocratic delirium, which has led them to live a grand life of leisure in the cities while their estates were being run by administrators or foremen who worked the land by means of a pitiless exploitation of rural labor, to whom not money but a hut and a small piece of land were paid—with almost no capital investment. The program of the Popular Unity is directed to the total disappearance as a class of both the large agrarian bourgeoisie (modern) and the traditional landowners by means of the serious carrying out of agrarian reform. Together with the monopolistic bourgeoisie and imperialism, these classes constitute one of the three fundamental enemies of the Chilean people.

4. The Large Urban Non-monopolistic Bourgeoisie.

They are the owners of the large and/or modern industrial and commercial concerns that do not belong to the monopolistic sector and generally are located in the branches producing or distributing consumer items. This bourgeois sector has also borne the weight of the monopolies on its shoulders. Not infrequently, however, it joined up with them and with foreign capital, so that it would be difficult to ally this sector with the proletariat (although it could be neutralized by certain measures such as mixed enterprise, for example). . . . This sector is a potential if undeclared enemy of the proletariat, and it will be necessary to be on guard against it. Many of these capitalists express themselves politically through the Christian Democratic Right, the Radical Democrats, or the National Party.

5. The Small and Medium Urban Bourgeoisie.

These are the owners of small industrial and commercial concerns or industries of somewhat backward technology and low income return. This sector of the bourgeoisie is the one that bears the entire weight of the monopolies, being subordinate to and exploited by them, credit is not granted to them, they are heavily taxed, their production costs are high, their markets are restricted, and attempts are made to eliminate them from the bourgeois class. These medium and small capitalists thus have interests opposed to those of imperialism, the monopolistic bourgeoisie, the large agrarian bourgeoisie (modern) and the traditional landowners. They can therefore be allies of the proletariat in its struggle against the principal enemies, and the people's government should aid them by granting them credit, tax exemptions, production agreements, etc. Many of these industrialists express themselves politically in the Christian Democrats, Radicals, Radical Democrats, Social Democrats, and the Popular Independent Action Party. However, these small and middle-size concerns fundamentally depend on the monopolies in order to function, and the people's government will not be able to aid them effectively and thereby strengthen its alliance with them as long as it does not control monopolistic and large companies. In the current situation, it is known that these small and medium capitalists are the ones suffering the most anxieties within their class, reaching the border of bankruptcy, which seriously threatens their alliance with the proletariat and makes joint and rapid action against the monopolistic

bourgeoisie, imperialism, and the landowners an urgent
necessity.

6. The Middle and Small Agrarian Bourgeoisie.

These are owners of farms containing less than eighty
basic hectares, representing a sector that could be gained
by the proletariat as a tactical ally or at least neutralized.
Like the middle and small urban bourgeoisie, this division
is exploited by the large agrarian bourgeoisie, the landowners and fundamentally the monopolistic bourgeoisie,
on whom they depend for products, credit, and the marketing of their products.

THE PETTY BOURGEOISIE

The petty bourgeoisie is the social class consisting of all
owners of means directly or indirectly used in production
and who work independently. The petty bourgeoisie is
neither bourgeois nor proletarian, and it is very important not to confuse it with the small bourgeoisie. The latter, as has already been stated, are the capitalists pos-
sessing small companies in which outside labor power is
purchased and the capital is reproduced and increased,
so that they form part of the bourgeoisie. On the other
hand, the petty bourgeoisie does not possess its own capital; it is possible that some workers may contract to work
for a salary along with their families, but a value greater
than that invested in means of production, wages, and
their own consumption is not obtained thereby. Since it is
an intermediate class between the proletariat and the
bourgeoisie, the petty bourgeoisie has contradictory interests; on the one hand, it aspires to become wealthy
and thus acquire capital, making it possible to convert into
bourgeoisie, and on the other hand it finds itself constantly more oppressed and enslaved by the bourgeoisie,
which tries to convert it into the proletariat. The outlook

of the petty bourgeoisie thus fluctuates between capitalist and proletarian viewpoints, which can be decided in one direction or the other according to circumstances. The petty bourgeoisie is therefore always unstable, and it is never possible to entrust revolutionary leadership to it. The stability and strength of an alliance with the petty bourgeoisie depends on leadership by the proletariat. Nevertheless the proletariat should consider the petty bourgeoisie its principal and natural ally. Due to its inherent ambiguity, the petty bourgeoisie can be found in any party. At present, however, it is found mostly in the leftist parties. . . . This is not a fortuitous situation but instead demonstrates a phenomenon affecting it as a class: its enslavement by the bourgeoisie drives it more and more to proletarization. . . .

1. The Urban Petty Bourgeoisie.

These are the owners or tenants of small artisan industries, stores, or businesses that yield only what is necessary for life, and who themselves work with their families and friends or by contracting with a few workers or employees. . . . They constitute a mass of independent workers whose poorest strata frequently convert into semi-proletarians, since their very poor living conditions oblige them to work part time as salaried labor. They are an important ally, which the proletariat should attempt to win over completely.

2. The Agrarian Petty Bourgeoisie.

This consists of sharecroppers, tenant farmers, reservation Mapuche Indians, farmers of tiny plots, etc., who cultivate the land with their families or with some hired person. The petty agrarian bourgeoisie has been exploited by the landlords and the monopolistic bourgeoisie; its poorest strata are sometimes converted into semi-proletarians, since they work part time as laborers or sharecroppers on the large estates. . . .

3. The Professional Petty Bourgeoisie.

These are professionals, especially university graduates, who practice their professions "liberally" without being employees or salaried workers. These professionals are the owners of certain work instruments and offices which serve as direct or indirect means of production; they defend their property through trade organizations called "professional associations." They constitute a sector of the petty bourgeoisie, and they include most attorneys, some physicians and architects, a considerable sector of the engineers, artists, writers, etc.; in fact, a considerable portion of the intelligentsia. This section of the petty bourgeoisie is very important, since on the one hand it tends to coincide in values with the bourgeoisie due to its privileged status, and on the other hand the knowledge it possesses puts it in a better position to assimilate revolutionary theory and join the proletariat, some of its members even becoming leaders of proletarian parties. It should not be forgotten that Marx, Lenin, Mao Tse-tung, and many other proletarian leaders came from this sector of the petty bourgeoisie.

THE PROLETARIAT

The proletariat, or working class, is formed by all those exhibiting the following characteristics: a) They are not owners of anything used to produce anything else; i.e., they are not de facto owners, renters, or occupants of any means of production. b) For this reason, they are compelled to sell their physical of intellectual energy to others in exchange for a remuneration making it possible for them to live, i.e., they sell their labor power for money. c) They participate in some phase of the production process of the entire society either as direct producers (who convert a raw material into a product) or as indirect producers (who collaborate in the planning and organizing of work, in publicity, in the transportation and distribution of goods, in sales and purchases, in the communications necessary for production, in payments and loans of money, etc.).

Since it does not have means of production, the proletariat is always obliged to work for the bourgeoisie, and its class interests are therefore completely opposed to those of the bourgeoisie. At the same time, since it is the only social class that does not own any means of production, the proletariat is the only class that does not have any type of interests linking it to private property of the means of production and is therefore the only one in a position to direct a revolutionary process precisely oriented to the destruction of all private control over those means. The proletariat is therefore the only class capable of carrying out a revolution leading to the collective appropriation of the means of production on the part of all the workers. It is convenient to distinguish the following strata of the proletariat in Chile at this time.

1. The Workers in Large and Monopolistic Industries.

This is the oldest, best organized, and most class-conscious sector of the proletariat, at this time clearly constituting the vanguard of the class. The copper, sodium nitrate, coal, and dock workers' unions were the ones who began the struggle of the working class with the large-scale strikes at the end of the last century and the beginning of this one, and they had to endure the massacres ordered by the bourgeoisie one after the other. They predominated the most intense chapters of our class struggle, and for that reason they have the most developed knowledge, experience, and traditions of the working class; they consequently represent the vanguard. To this old historical trunk it is now necessary to add the workers in the new large monopolistic and state industries who have also succeeded in building up strong union organizations through hard struggles. Due to the characteristics cited, this sector of the proletariat, which makes up the fundamental nucleus of the Central Workers' Union, the Communist Party, and in part the Socialist Party, is in the best position to press forward on behalf of its interests and has therefore obtained salary levels higher than those of less organized workers. As the current vanguard of the proletariat, it has all the good qualities derived from its combative history, its class consciousness, and its organic solidity; however, if its political vanguard does not struggle against tendencies toward bureaucracy and the maintenance of certain privileges in comparison with the other manual laborers, serious distortions may occur in the future. It is the duty of MAPU to conquer positions in this sector of the proletariat.

2. *The Workers in Small and Medium Industries.*

This sector represents one of the largest divisions of the working class, including many more workers than those in the large industries. It consists of workers in medium and small industries, which have higher costs and where unions are relatively small or do not even exist; it is thus in a bad position for pressing struggles for better wages and working conditions. For the same reason, their work stability is not very great, reaching an extreme case in the construction field, where layoffs are a constant threat. Due to their lack of organization, these workers also have a low political-consciousness level, and their class consciousness is not very high. The bourgeoisie has made every effort to prevent this sector of the proletariat from acquiring strength; it has opposed the formation of unions by industry sector instead of by plant and has tried to place these unions in opposition to those of the large industries. This fraction of the proletariat has few ties with political parties, but recently the Socialist Party, MAPU, and some small groups have conquered positions there. In the present setup, the workers of this sector are those who suffer most from the production boycott imposed by the monopolies, which causes layoffs and social conflicts at the level of small and medium industries and sharpens the contradictions between the workers and their employers, putting difficulties in the way of the alliance possibilities put forward by the popular government. The basic situation has no apparent solution except for a rapid and frontal struggle against the monopolistic bourgeoisie. MAPU should pay particular attention to working with this faction of the proletariat, organizing it and raising its political and class consciousness.

3. Farm Workers.

They are the hired hands and other field workers hired for wages particularly to work the lands of the agrarian bourgeoisie. Until recently, they had almost no unions, and their living conditions were miserable in comparison with those in the city. The incentive for organizing farm workers and for agrarian reform started from the time of Frei's government and considerably changed matters. Agricultural unions are now multiplying, and many of these workers are finding political expression in the Christian Democratic Party, MAPU, the CP, the SP, and MIR. Since these farm workers have always been treated as workers, they are the ones most identified with the general interests of their class. Their struggle is not for private ownership of the land, and therefore they do not aspire to convert into agrarian petty bourgeoisie. For these reasons, they are the vanguard of the proletariat in the fields.

4. Sharecroppers.[1]

These workers receive only a part of their wages in money, the remainder consisting of products, certain privileges, and the possibility of using some piece of land. Due to these characteristics, and in spite of being the most exploited rural sector, sharecroppers feel themselves to be personally connected with the owners. When they acquire class consciousness and are not yet unionized, their struggle is not so much for the destruction of all private property of the means of production as for obtaining private ownership of some piece of land. The Christian Democrats, dedicated to developing a new bourgeoisie and agrarian petty bourgeoisie, skillfully exploit these class characteristics of the sharecroppers. The development of capitalism in the country has produced the transformation of many traditional landlords into modern agrarian capitalists and the progressive proletarization of the sharecroppers.

5. The White-Collar Proletariat.

These are the so-called "employees" who work in the administrative sector of private or state industries, in banks, stores, etc. Since they sell labor power that is more intellectual than manual, the bourgeoisie has attempted and in part succeeded in convincing them that they are a separate class superior to that of the workers, and has even brought about a legal difference between workers and employees. This is clearly a simple deception on the part of the bourgeoisie, whereby an attempt is made to divide the proletariat and turn some against others in the

[1] Sharecroppers formed as a class in the eighteenth century together with the traditional landlords. Until several decades ago, they did not have any organization, and the chief feature characterizing them was access to the use of a means of production (the land) through work for the landowner.

different sectors. The bourgeois ideology has succeeded in its aim to the extent that it has not only imbued attitudes of superiority in these employees, but certain manual laborers who until yesterday were "workers" have also attempted to change their designation in favor of being called "employees." The power of this deceit reaches such a degree that even some revolutionary parties have classified these employees as "petty bourgeoisie." The truth is that they are not petty bourgeoisie by any means, although in their way of life and thought they frequently appear to be assimilated to the petty bourgeoisie. They are proletarians; they are people who can live only by selling their intellectual power. This white-collar proletariat is at present enormously influenced by the bourgeois ideology and still tends to despise union organization and politics, but they too are gradually beginning to realize their actual class situation. Some have become active in the Christian Democratic, Radical, Socialist, Communist, and MAPU parties. It is the duty of the most advanced sectors of the proletariat and their political vanguards to assist the employees in this process of acquiring consciousness. Abolition of the legal discrimination between workers and employees would be a step forward in this direction.

6. The Professional Proletariat.

This group consists of salaried persons selling a relatively scarce labor power; i.e., they are highly qualified and are therefore in a position to obtain quite high remuneration. Examples include the engineers and technicians working as common employees (not as managers or highly placed supervisors) in major industry and private or state economic institutions, computer programmers, hospital nurses, teachers, etc. All these professionals have in common with the professional petty bourgeoisie the possession of certain special knowledge or abilities, but they differ in that they use this knowledge not as their own means of production but as an integral part of a qualified labor force selling it in exchange for a salary. Sectors are involved who "normally" would have belonged to the petty bourgeoisie but found themselves obliged to be converted into proletariat because the development of productive forces organizes offices and professions in constantly more socialized ways; this same development (including education) has caused them to be constantly less scarce and more competitive. Consequently, the "professional proletariat" tends to coincide ideologically with the petty bourgeoisie from which it comes or into which it cannot yet be incorporated. However, it is progressively becoming aware of its actual class position and is even organizing itself in unions, realizing the ineffectiveness of the professional associations. Since this is the most intellectualized stratum of the proletariat, it is the duty of the more advanced strata to help it acquire consciousness and win it over to the common struggle of the entire class. For this reason, it is necessary to take care in applying certain salary levels or consumer orientation standards which could arouse resistance in this sector of the proletariat. The professional proletariat today finds its political outlets mostly in the National Party, the Christian Democrats, and the Radical Party rather than in the Socialist, Communist, and MAPU parties; it is necessary to win this sector for Popular Unity.

7. The Subproletariat.

This is formed by the mass of people in the large cities and also in the country who are temporarily unemployed or semi-unemployed as a result of Chile's dependence on imperialist capital, which restricts and distorts the development of our productive force. They make up a large part of the so-called "settlers" of the marginal zones of

Santiago and other cities. They do not make stable contributions to production, since they have only occasional jobs. They are actually the "reserve army" of the proletariat, participating in production only when it attains a rapid growth rate. The sector is at the limit of what a social class is and is not. It is the duty of the proletarian vanguard to organize the subproletariat, offer it concrete and objective solutions for struggle, and prevent it from being won over by the bourgeoisie due to its instability.

SOCIAL STRATA THAT ARE NOT CLASSES

Social classes are groupings of people according to their relation to the means of production. There are some sectors of the population that do not participate in production directly or indirectly; i.e., they do not convert a certain raw material into a product or conduct other activities necessary for doing so. Among the social strata that are not classes, it is possible to distinguish the following in Chile.

1. The Upper Management Bureaucrats.

These are the high-category employees who carry out co-ordinating functions in the protection of the interests of the ruling class. Managers, high-level supervisors, in general the upper stratum of private business and state hierarchies, are involved. It is believed by some that the management bureaucrats could be classified as a proletarian stratum due to the fact that their income, although very high, is in the form of a salary, i.e., remuneration for work and not income from capital. In reality, however, such "workers" are quite special, since they contract precisely for rationally and efficiently organizing the exploitation of the other workers. They hold the delegated authority of capital, the mandate of the capitalists, over them. This gives them the power to decide the life and death of each exploited person, which no proletarian could have, by definition. They frequently play a technical part in production, for example by planning, controlling, co-ordinating, supervising, etc. However, it is their social function as "guardians" of capital that essentially defines them as a social layer whose interests are absolutely identified with the bourgeoisie even though they are not strictly bourgeois. Now that there is a popular government and the class nature of the state and consequently of the state enterprises begins to change, the features of the upper management bureaucrats also begin to change. The administrators of the state enterprises in fact no longer have a mandate from the capitalists but from the popular government and through it from the people itself. This mandate cannot be executed autocratically against the workers but should be executed with the workers, who collaborate with it and control it. The fact that the upper management bureaucrats constitute not a social class with its own interests but a social layer that can put itself at the service of one class or another makes it possible for some of its members, who used to serve the bourgeoisie, now to serve the proletariat. Everything depends on their adaptability, since by themselves they are not objectively connected to any class.

2. The High-ranking State Bureaucrats.

These are the highest-ranking employees, who direct the state apparatus. They include ministers and undersecretaries, department heads, magistrates in the higher courts, high commands of the Armed Forces, etc. This stratum, like the foregoing one, receives its mandate directly from the ruling class and is absolutely identified with its interests. They are extremely sensitive to the smallest incidents in the struggle for power. For example, the conflict among different divisions of the ruling class was traditionally reflected both in the almost permanent rotation of the high-ranking state bureaucrats and in the government changes. In a transition period such as presently exists in Chile, in which classes are openly struggling for hegemony, the contradictions are much more marked in the high-ranking state bureaucrats—for example, in conflict between the Executive and the Supreme Court.

3. *The State Civil Bureaucrats.*

These are employees in the public administration who maintain the state apparatus in its properly political functions without direct or indirect relation to production. The development of capitalism has required a constantly more extensive intervention in the productive expansion of the bourgeoisie up to the point that now the state apparatus units connected with production (trust funds, the Development Corporation, ministries of Economy, Agriculture, Public Works, etc.) are much more extensive than actual political units (Foreign Office, ministries of the Interior, Justice, Defense, etc.). In the former, the penetration of capitalism proletarianized the "functionaries," since it made them direct or indirect producers of capital (see white-collar proletariat). On the other hand, employees performing non-productive functions continue being a non-proletarian salaried stratum. By means of political influence in all parties, the bureaucrats have secured privileged positions in comparison with other workers, which generally tend to protect them from the extreme instability of the high-ranking state bureaucrats, e.g., non-removability in position, automatic promotion due to years of service, etc. Consequently, they can be allied with the proletariat or with the bourgeoisie according to which gives them the more security. In this sense, they have an ideology similar to that of the petty bourgeoisie, which has led some parties to classify them as a stratum of the petty bourgeoisie. The proletariat must consider this social stratum as an ally which should gradually be incorporated into the proletariat. It is therefore very important to make this sector understand that the destruction of the bourgeois state will not necessarily endanger its social situation. The state civil bureaucrats form the bulk of the Radical and Christian Democratic parties and part of the Socialist Party, although they are also represented in the National and the Communist parties.

4. The Armed Forces.

Soldiers were historically the first group to receive wages; the Spanish word *sueldo* (salary) comes precisely from this source. However, in spite of being salaried, the members of the Armed Forces are not proletarians. In fact, with few exceptions (traffic police, etc.), they do not participate in the productive process. The state does not purchase their labor power to obtain financial gain; rather it purchases from the Armed Forces their professional services. The Armed Forces do not sell their services to any private individual but to the ruling class as a whole, and their interests therefore tend to coincide with those of that ruling class; they are the material basis of the power of that class. In Chile's present critical political period, however, it is not clear which is the ruling class, or who will finally control the state. The Popular Unity parties have constitutionally attained Executive power, but they do not control Legislative or Judicial power. If we consider their interests only as a body, the Armed Forces should tend to coincide with the government, but on the other hand there are small groups of officers who could be inclined to defend the interests of the bourgeoisie, to which they are connected by family and social ties. In Chile, the troops, who have connections with the proletariat, have not had access to political discussion and do not even have the right to vote. This prevents them from actually participating in the national development process.

The right to vote is an important right to obtain for all soldiers, not only for the officers.

5. The Students.

Students do not belong to any social class, since they do not participate in production but are preparing for it. However, belonging to a class is one thing, and the class position adhered to, i.e., the class of ideological attachment, is another. Class position in this case depends on a) family connections, i.e., the class to which the family belongs; b) the activity or profession to be followed upon concluding studies, i.e., what class the graduate wants to join; and c) the ideological influence the proletariat and the bourgeoisie can exert through teachers, *compañeros,* etc.

If we limit ourselves to university students, we see that generally their connections are bourgeois, petty bourgeois, or belonging to the higher layers of the proletariat or bureaucracy. On the other hand, the professions they study for belong to the petty bourgeoisie and professional proletariat. It is therefore not strange that many students assume bourgeois and petty-bourgeois positions on finishing their studies. Others, however, identify with proletarian positions through their ideological development. These characteristics make students an unstable element when they have not been educated politically. It is the duty of the proletarian vanguard to win the students to their cause and to seek a contact between students and workers to facilitate their proletarization.

6. Domestic Servants.

These include cooks, nurses, companions, housekeepers, private chauffeurs, stewards, and other salaried personnel working in the houses of the bourgeoisie, the petty bourgeoisie, and even some well-off strata of the proletariat. These workers receive a salary in exchange for a service that directly contributes to the consumption of their employers and not any production phase. . . . It is a very different matter when, for example, a restaurant contracts for a cook; in this case, the labor power of the cook is used to produce a dish that is not to be eaten by the owner but sold at a good price, and the cook then becomes a proletarian. Domestic help tend to coincide ideologically with their employers, and they can therefore be used to defend the interests of the dominant classes, joining their "retinue." However, to the extent that domestic workers are exploited, the working class can find allies in this social stratum, particularly among those with family connections with the proletariat.

7. The Lumpenproletariat.

These are the permanent unemployed, who do not participate in production and therefore do not constitute a social class. A part of the lumpenproletariat live as "settlers" in the suburbs of the large cities, but habitual delinquents, prostitutes, vagabonds, beggars, etc. also belong to this marginal sector. In general, this entire social stratum is extremely unstable with respect to its ideological position; it can as easily be won over by the National Party, the MIR, the Christian Democrats, or by any demagogue. Everything depends on who is offering more means for satisfying their immediate needs.

A NOTE ON "PEASANTS" AND THE "MIDDLE CLASS"

In all the above, we have not referred to two groups frequently mentioned, the peasants (*campesinos*) and the middle class. The truth is that these groups are not social classes but rather various parts of classes. The peasants consist of sharecroppers, farm workers, the agrarian subproletariat, and the agrarian petty bourgeoisie, all of which, as we have seen, are quite different.

The "middle class," as the term is generally used today, would be formed by the middle and small urban bourgeoisie, the entire petty bourgeoisie, the professional proletariat, the white-collar proletariat, higher domestic help, the state civil bureaucrats, the Armed Forces, and the students. The expression "middle class" therefore basically does not mean anything; it is a hollow phrase, since it includes in its current use classes and strata with interests so different that they cannot be grouped under the same name. "Middle class" and "middle strata," as the terms are used today, are actually harmful concepts invented by the bourgeoisie and serving only to confuse the proletariat, making it believe that there is a "bridge," a way of passing from one class to the other. MAPU should struggle to destroy these myths and use a language of real content.

ALLIANCE OF CLASSES, POLITICAL FRONT, AND POPULAR UNITY

The task of taking power from the capitalist class to destroy its domination and begin the construction of socialism is in principle a task of the working class. This is in fact the only social class that does not have any means of production available, has nothing more than its bodies and its consumer goods, and therefore has no particular interest in maintaining private ownership over the means of production.

The working class is at the same time a product and a producer of capitalism. It sustains the latter with its work. Without its co-operation, purchased by the exploiters, capitalism could not subsist or develop; in this sense, it is possible to say that the life and death of capitalism depend on the productive work developed by the working class.

However, the development of capitalism within certain historical conditions has created other social strata and classes, including class segments that, since they are generally variations of the basic classes, become capable of developing autonomous policies and even policies contradictory to those of the basic class from which they are derived—for example, the middle and small bourgeoisie with respect to the large and monopolistic bourgeoisie, or the white-collar workers in comparison with the workers. This segmentation of the basic classes converts the struggle for power into a complex question that the working class should solve with intelligence and flexibility.

The first problem to arise clearly is that the conquest of power is a task the proletariat cannot fulfill by itself. To the extent that this task is to be accomplished, its vanguard should seek and permanently assure the co-operation of other social forces or classes until socialism is constructed.

This policy of alliances is oriented to obtaining essential objectives. The first task is to liberate worker strata with a lower level of class consciousness and with less proletarian political development—strata that can become powerful class allies—from the ideological influence of the adversary. The second task is to attract into combat against the chief enemies those factions of the dominant classes whose situation has deteriorated due to their actions.

A really proletarian political direction is measured, among other factors, by the capacity it has to add forces to its positions, systematically seeking the isolation of the enemy to make his defeat possible, or, similarly, preventing the systematic attempt by the enemy to isolate the working class from its potential allies.

STRATEGIC ALLIANCES

In military language, "strategy" relates to the rules for conducting warfare on the whole, and "tactics" to the laws regulating combat. This is the origin of the terms "strategy" and "tactics," used by extension in political language as well.

The proletariat has acquired considerable strategic and tactical experience in its many class wars and struggles with the bourgeoisie.

Lenin, the great leader of the Bolshevik Party, the October Revolution, and the first proletarian revolution of the world (USSR), is one of those who has contributed most to the scientific development of the strategy and tactics of the proletariat, i.e., the science of proletarian management of the class struggle.

In political language, strategy is concerned with the basic forces of the revolution and its chief and secondary allies. It changes when the revolution passes from one stage to another, but it remains basically unchanged with each of these stages.

Each historical stage of the struggle of the proletariat is characterized by the objectives it proposes. These objectives seek to isolate and destroy the principal enemies to create conditions for the advances of the following stage. These objectives are called strategic objectives, and the alliance of forces necessary to obtain them is called a strategic alliance.

Within the forces participating in the alliance it is necessary to distinguish the basic and the allied forces, and within the allied forces the chief forces and the secondary ones. The following pertain to the concrete case of the Popular Unity government of Chile.

Strategic Objectives:

1. To complete national independence (nationalization of foreign monopolies, truly independent foreign policy)

2. To deepen democracy (people's state, equal opportunities for all)

3. To prepare the material base for socialism (social-property area, planning system).

Fundamental Strategic Enemies:

   —the imperialist bourgeoisie
   —the large and monopolistic Chilean bourgeoisie (in-
     dustrial, agrarian, commercial, financial)
   —the landowners (traditional) and agrarian bour-
     geoisie (modern).

Strategic Alliance:

   All classes not connected with the chief enemies:
   —the proletariat
   —the petty bourgeoisie
   —the middle and small bourgeoisie.

Basic Force: the proletariat.

Principal Ally: the petty bourgeoisie (urban and rural).

Secondary Ally: the middle and small bourgeoisie.

TACTICAL ALLIANCES

Whereas the purpose of strategy is to win the "war,"
tactics pursue less essential objectives, since they are not
proposed to win the "war" taken as a whole but to win
this or that battle, to carry out successfully this or that
campaign or action corresponding to the concrete situation of the period in accordance with an exacerbation or
relaxation of the class struggle.

Starting from a given stage of the revolution, tactics
can change many times according to these ups and downs
and the different currents of the struggle. . . .

In a tactical situation, the objectives proposed by the
proletariat are partial and limited; the attempt is to strike
at an enemy but not to annihilate him, to win a battle but
not the war. The proletariat can find many allies for these
partial and limited objectives. Many of them can be unstable, transient, etc., but they serve to isolate and strike

at what in the given situation appears to be the chief enemy. These objectives are called tactical objectives and the corresponding alliances tactical alliances.

The more limited the tactical objective is, the more extensive (and therefore heterogeneous) the alliance can and should be. Tactical alliances therefore have a very broad multiclass base, since the basic classes attempt to exploit the most insignificant contradictions of the enemy forces and thus gain tactical allies in the opposing camp.

An example of a tactical alliance was the ratification of the election of Allende by the Plenary Congress. The tactical ally there was the Christian Democratic Party and the chief enemy the National Party (Alessandrism).

Another example of a tactical alliance was the negotiation of the copper-nationalization project. Principal tactical ally: the Christian Democratic Party; secondary tactical ally: the National Party; chief enemy: the copper companies and the U. S. Government.

Another example of a tactical alliance, in this case with the landowners, is the agrarian production plan for 1970–71. The landowners, who will not be expropriated during this year, will receive guarantees and facilities for producing the maximum. Similar tactical alliances are made with the monopolies not as yet expropriated or with those with which mixed companies are made. The main enemies in these cases are the landowners and monopolists who are expropriated in this phase. . . .

TACTICAL AND STRATEGIC ALLIANCES

Tactics is a part of strategy and is subordinate to and serves the latter.

Tactical direction is thus a part of strategic direction, to whose objectives and requirements it is subordinate.

If the tactical objective does not seek more than creating conditions for the strategic objective, this strict subordination of tactics to strategy is absolutely logical. From the standpoint of the proletariat, consequently, any tactical alliance is also subordinate to the strategic objective. It should approach it and not depart from it. It should strengthen the strategic alliance and not weaken it.

Without this condition, the policy of alliances gives way to opportunism and seriously retards the battle of the proletariat when the class objectives of the allies prevail over those proper to the proletariat. . . .

In a tactical alliance there are two components: the basic force, consisting of the strategic allies, and the allied force, which is in effect the tactical allies.

We distinguish in a tactical alliance a basic force, principal and secondary strategic allies, and principal and secondary tactical allies.

Let us return to the example of the agrarian production plan for 1970–71.

Basic Force: agricultural proletariat.

Principal Strategic Ally: agrarian petty bourgeoisie (small landowners, joint tenants, small farmers).

Secondary Strategic Ally: middle and small agrarian bourgeoisie (less than eighty basic hectares).

Tactical Ally: landowners not to be expropriated this year (in this case it is not possible to distinguish between principal and secondary tactical allies).

ALLIANCE AND PROGRAM

We have already seen that each type of alliance has its specific objectives, or, stated in another way, that each objective has a suitable alliance. Objectives and alliances should correspond perfectly.

The group of measures necessary to attain the objectives of an alliance is its program. The program can have a single point or many, may be written or not; in any case, there is never an alliance without a program.

The program of tactical alliances is also called the minimum program. For example, in the tactical alliance of the Popular Unity with the Christian Democratic Party for ratifying Allende in the Plenary Congress, the (minimum) program was the so-called "statute of democratic guarantees."

The program of strategic alliances is called the maximum program, since it gathers the objectives of an entire historical stage. For example, in the strategic alliance of the Popular Unity, the maximum program is the Popular Unity Basic Program.

The essential condition of every program is that of reflecting the interests and objectives of all the allied forces. A perfect coincidence between the program and the alliance should also exist in this sense. The consistency of the alliance depends to a great extent on the degree to which the program meets the demands of each component.

ALLIANCE FORMS

Alliances can have various ways of manifesting themselves politically. The most elementary is a simple coincidence between the allies. . . . Agreement on a series of actions or a number of objectives is a political pact. . . .

The most institutional form of alliance is a front. Here the allies draw up not only an explicit program but also a common hierarchy and structure that while respecting the autonomy of each ally, nevertheless makes it possible for the allies to make collective decisions and in general to have a permanent formal relation. An example of this is Popular Unity. . . .

Strategic alliances are not automatically and directly manifested in a front. On the contrary, the classes objectively called to a strategic alliance take a long time to develop themselves, accumulate fighting experience, and create their own parties; in their turn, these parties should pass through a long period of divisions, agreements, joint actions, and progressive regroupings before constituting a front. For example, the PU in Chile was preceded by a long history of the working class and the people, by the existence of three old parties (Socialist Party, thirty-eight years; Communist Party, forty-nine years; Radical Party more than a hundred), by the Popular Front, by a front including Communists and Socialists for fourteen years (FRAP, which also included social-democratic sectors), and recently by a process of joint actions with the RP and to a lesser extent with MAPU in the course of a prolonged rise of the mass struggle.

The more formal and more permanent an alliance is, the greater the importance of the program.

THE PRINCIPLE OF UNITY AND STRUGGLE

Alliances bring certain classes and class factions together in the struggle against other classes to obtain certain objectives. These classes and allied class factions have different and contradictory interests. . . .

From a proletarian standpoint, unity and struggle are equally important in the politics of alliances. Right opportunism tends to unity without struggle and ends in conciliation with the bourgeoisie. Left opportunism tends to struggle without unity and ends in sectarian isolation of the proletariat. Only unity with struggle makes an advance of the people and its proletarian direction possible at the same time.

ALLIANCE AND HEGEMONY

The existence of contradictions and struggle among the allies presents the problem of who orders whom in the alliance.

It is true that all the allies gain objectively from this

alliance. However, hegemony by definition belongs to some and not to all.

The quantitative force of a class can contribute to its hegemony but is never its chief determinant. More than the quantitative predominance, what is important is which class succeeds in imposing its interests and basic political positions within the alliance. . . . For example, in the cases of Chile and Vietnam, the chief force (quantitatively) was not the proletariat but the rural population, which did not prevent the proletariat from being the directing force. On the other hand, there have been alliances, as was generally the case with popular fronts, in which the proletariat was the chief force without being the directing force.

The political direction within an alliance is decided by the capacity each class shows at every moment to manifest, defend, and impose its basic interests.

The working class develops its controlling role if it is capable of creating a consensus around its positions. This objective is attained to the extent that it appreciates the deepest aspirations of its allies, expresses them in ways capable of involving the entire front, and works together with them on basic tasks corresponding to its own deepest class interests. . . .

PROLETARIAN POLITICAL DIRECTION

The united and class-conscious proletariat is nevertheless capable of completely exercising its directive function only when a proletarian political direction is given.

This management can exist in a single proletarian party or in several united by the common class imperative of developing proletarian positions in the front and making them dominant.

The important point is that this single- or multiparty political direction is actually capable of representing and historically achieving the cardinal objectives and interests of the proletariat. It must therefore be armed with proletarian theory, possess a revolutionary tactical and strategic line, and have an organization available capable of mobilizing the masses in the most varied critical situations in the struggle for power.

In Chile we have various workers' parties of different history, scope, limitations, and effectiveness (CP, SP, MAPU). We believe that the basic alliance is what unites these parties, since it restores proletarian unity at a political level. We also believe that this basic alliance can develop from the standpoint of a single party of the proletariat, a natural and necessary product for common combat. However, the present conditions, the state of development of the political forces representing the proletariat, the differences that still exist among them, the lack of experience and development of other proletarian detachments (ours, for example) do not permit the conversion of this basic objective into an immediate objective.

In order for this to be possible, it is necessary to strengthen the unity and joint practice of these parties.

This joint practice and unity will not be attained except on the basis of an intense ideological struggle among these detachments, making it possible to overcome the Right and Left deviations that frequently threaten the working-class movement and to develop a firm proletarian political line within these parties.

The strengthening of the working class, the increasing of the power of its union organizations, and the practical and theoretical uniting of its parties are the tasks we must undertake today to satisfy the objective of imparting a proletarian guidance to the alliance that will bring the people to the conquest of power. . . .

THE POPULAR UNITY

We have seen in an example at the beginning of this paper that the Popular Unity attempts to be a strategic alliance grouping the proletariat, the petty bourgeoisie and the middle and small bourgeoisie to confront imperialism, the monopolistic bourgeoisie, the landowners (traditional), and the agrarian bourgeoisie (modern) and to accomplish tasks that, while they begin a socialist transition, democratize the country and assure its independent development.

What we wish to underscore here is that the enemies of the people also attempt to develop a front to impart a mass character to their counterrevolutionary aims. In their attempt to overcome their minority character, the chief enemies of the Chilean people seek support in the middle bourgeoisie (urban and agrarian), in sectors of the wealthy small urban bourgeoisie, in sectors of the professional petty bourgeoisie, in the professional proletariat, in the white-collar proletariat, in the domestic help, in sectors of the state civil bureaucracy and the Armed Forces, and in a great part of the subproletariat and the lumpenproletariat. In addition, although with less success, they attempt to control the urban petty bourgeoisie and the agrarian petty bourgeoisie and even to deceive the proletariat of small and middle industry.

The battle to conquer the sectors cited is of decisive importance in the power struggle we are conducting in our country.

Consequently, when the Popular Unity declares itself the enemy only of imperialism, the monopolistic bourgeoisie, the landowners, and the large agrarian bourgeoisie at this stage, it is attempting to express the interests and objectives of all the rest of the classes and social strata as a political front.

The actual forces of the PU do not yet include all the proletariat, petty bourgeoisie, and small and middle bourgeoisie, so it is therefore a fundamental task for the program of the PU to be converted into the banner waved by the working class and effectively to gain as allies all the sectors and social strata whose common interests are expressed in the alliance.

CHAPTER 11

The Working Class: Principal Social Basis of Marxist Politics

For forty years the Communist and Socialist parties have championed the rights of the working people of Chile. Their constantly increasing strength over the decades has been tied to strong unionization and a growing class consciousness among workers in the mines and larger industries, and recently among farm workers and other strata of the working class. The force of organized and class-conscious workers with political parties to represent their interests has historically led to significant social reform, given substance to Chile's nearly unique democratic political culture, and finally resulted in a clear opening for the world's first socialist transformation through the ballot box.

James Petras demonstrates that Allende's 1970 election was due primarily to the fact that the overwhelming majority of Chilean workers support Allende and the Marxist parties behind him. Petras also counters theories that posit that well-paid, presumably "bourgeoisified" workers will not support revolutionary politics. This issue will be taken up in greater depth in the last section of the book.

THE WORKING CLASS
AND CHILEAN SOCIALISM*

JAMES PETRAS

For many years U.S. and Latin American sociologists circulated the notion that support for Marxist socialism was largely a product of the economic backwardness and "traditionalism" of Third World countries; that modern urban industrial cities served to "moderate" the outlook and behavior of the working class—especially the better paid industrial workers. Some sociologists who accepted this view began to speak of "integrated" sectors or classes (including urban industrial workers) and "marginal" classes. The notion of a "bourgeoisified" industrial proletarist even shaped the outlook of leftwing intellectuals who began to speak of a "labor aristocracy" and to look to the peasantry as the sole basis of hope for a revolutionary transformation. The idea that the working class could combine and act as a class in favor of a socialist society against capitalist exploitation and inequality seems to have eluded scores of U.S. investigators who claim to study the lower classes in Latin America. A careful analysis of the political behavior of the Chilean working class refutes the "integration" thesis.

From its formation in 1956, the Marxist Popular Action Front (FRAP) directed its political activity toward

* Reprinted with permission from *New Politics* VIII, No. 4, 1971, pp. 72–76. James Petras is Professor of Sociology at the State University of New York at Binghamton, a frequent visitor to Chile, and author of *Politics and Social Forces in Chilean Development* (Berkeley: University of California Press, 1969), as well as several articles on Chile.

gaining the support of the working class. In 1958, the FRAP candidate, Salvador Allende, lost by a margin of 35,000 votes out of a total of 1.3 million. In the 1964 elections, in a virtual two way race, Allende gathered 39% of the vote (about 45% of the male vote). In 1970, Allende, the candidate of the Marxist-led Popular Unity, won the election with 36.2% of the vote. The major base of support for this was the industrial proletariat located in the modern urban-industrial centers.

As Table I indicates, in 1964 FRAP obtained the support of the municipalities (*comunas*) which had the highest concentration of industrial workers. The higher the proportion of industrial workers, the higher the ratio of votes in favor of Allende. Obviously, the experience with a Christian Democratic government did not change the workers' political loyalty; on the contrary, the voting ratio of Allende to Alessandri, and Allende to Tomic, seems to have increased. The Presidential voting results suggest that the Christian Democratic "reform" government completely failed to win over the working class, as many of its supporters both in Chile and in the U.S. had hoped. The industrial workers chose to maintain their loyalty to the Marxist candidate and to reject the Christian Democratic alternative.

The Christian Democrats, proponents of a "third way" between socialism and capitalism, found little support among the class conscious Chilean working class for their program. No doubt the links between the Christian Democrats and U.S. and Chilean businessmen weakened their ability to pass social legislation and economic reforms which would have redistributed income and increased the participation of the working class in the industrial system. This suggests that the ability of the Unidad Popular to maintain itself in political power will depend on its capacity to meet the demands of the industrial working class

TABLE I

Relative Indices of Votes between Allende and Frei (1964), Allende and Alessandri (1970), Allende and Tomic (1970). Masculine votes in nine of the most important cities and towns of Chile.

(Percentages)

% of the Labor Force in manufacturing, mining & construction		City or Town	Nr. of Allende votes for each 100 votes for Frei (1964)	Nr. of Allende votes for each 100 votes for Aless. (1970)	Nr. of Allende votes for each 100 votes for Tomic (1970)
Under 30	20	Temuco	51 ⎫	78 ⎫	108 ⎫
	25	Chillán	113 ⎬ 80+	175 ⎬ 129	225 ⎬ 154
	28	Valparaíso	75 ⎭	135 ⎭	129 ⎭
30-35	30	Viña del Mar	71 ⎫	100 ⎫	130 ⎫
	30	Talca	112 ⎬ 100	193 ⎬ 151	194 ⎬ 182
	30	Antofagasta	116 ⎭	159 ⎭	222 ⎭
36-40	36	Valdivia	122 ⎫	173 ⎫	247 ⎫
	39	Concepción	95 ⎬ 117	153 ⎬ 208	170 ⎬ 204
	30	Talcahuano	134 ⎭	299 ⎭	196 ⎭

1 + average

for *radical anti-capitalist changes in the urban industrial centers.*

The non-working class municipalities continued to give their support to the Right (Alessandri) and to the Christian Democrats (see Table II). This suggests that the political support of the non-Marxist parties (Radicals, APT, Social Democrats and MAPU) were largely irrelevant in determining the size of the vote for Allende in the urban centers.[1] The size of Allende's vote in the urban industrial centers was largely the result of the traditional voting behavior of the industrial proletariat. Thus the non-Marxist parties are probably over-represented in the

[1] In *rural* Chile, MAPU played a very important role in mobilizing peasant support for Allende.

seats of government, in relationship to their contribution to the victory of Allende. Political agreements with the non-Marxist parties, while they may serve to bolster the image of a "multi-party government," could work against a coherent and profound reform program that could sustain the popular support of the Government. The imbalance between the homogeneous social base of the Allende

TABLE II

Relative Indices of Votes between Allende and Frei (1964), Allende and Alessandri (1970), Allende and Tomic (1970). Masculine Votes in the *Comunas* (Municipalities) of Gran Santiago Classified by the Relative Size of its Working Class.

(Percentages)

% of the Labor Force in manufacturing, mining & construction		Comuna or Municipality	Nr. of Allende votes for each 100 votes for Frei (1964)		Nr. of Allende votes for each 100 votes for Aless. (1970)		Nr. of Allende votes for each 100 votes for Tomic (1970)	
Less than 20	9	Calera de Tango	68		100		70	
	9	Lampa	89		112		117	
	13	Providencía	29	71	31	80	82	105
	16	Quilicura	79		108		152	
	19	Las Condes	42		47		103	
20-29	27	Nuñoa	59	59	86	86	142	142
30-39	31	Santiago	67		94		143	
	32	San Bernardo	92		146		155	
	35	La Florida	65	80	108	134	161	162
	36	Maipú	85		153		171	
	39	Conchalí	92		168		180	
40-49	43	Puente Alto	104		166		252	
	45	La Cisterna	90		164		188	
	46	Quinta Normal	96	103	168	188	191	203
	46	Renca	104		193		179	
	46	Barrancas	122		250		205	
50 or more	51	San Miguel	114	121.5	208	235	238	258
	52	La Granja	129		261		277	

victory (largely industrial working class socialists and communists) and the politically heterogeneous character of the party leadership could cause serious problems—depending on the constituency which Allende chooses to serve.

The second major basis of support for the Left was the mining sector, consistent supporters of Marxist political parties for several decades. Even among the highest paid sectors of the industrial proletariat (copper workers), Allende received over 2½ times the vote of Alessandri. And in the ultra-modern, technologically advanced Chuquicamata mine, Allende received 106 votes for every 100 votes for Alessandri. The notion of a "workers' aristocracy" hardly serves to explain the behavior of this highly paid sector of the labor force—which may have voted for the nationalization of the mines knowing full well that it might not improve its standard of living but serve Chilean economic development.

As Table III suggests, the mining workers, expressing a high degree of class solidarity, rejected the non-socialist alternatives and voted in overwhelming numbers for the socialist Allende. The political implications are clear: a social basis for an extensive program of nationalization of mines clearly exists in the sectors of the labor force most intimately involved. If Allende fails to carry out his program of nationalization, it cannot be blamed on the lack of political support.

The third major support for Allende's victory was urban working class women. Most observers have mistakenly generalized about the conservative voting behavior of Chilean women without taking account of the *class differences among women*. If we take all the municipalities in Greater Santiago which contain 40% or more industrial workers (see Table IV), we find that Allende received

TABLE III

Relative Indices of Vote between Allende and Alessandri and Allende and Tomic (1970). Masculine Votes in the Mining Centers.

(Percentages)

Copper Mining Zones	Nr. of Allende votes for each 100 votes for Alessandri	Nr. of Allende votes for each 100 votes for Tomic
Chuquicamata	106 ⎫	301 ⎫
Potrerillos	232 ⎬ 265	225 ⎬ 303
Sewell	406 ⎪ (average)	307 ⎪
El Salvador	319 ⎭	381 ⎭
Nitrate Mining Zones		
Iquique	194 ⎫	258 ⎫
Pozo Almonte	300 ⎪	289 ⎪
Lagunas	130 ⎬ 325	173 ⎬ 337
Toco	412 ⎪	541 ⎪
Padro de Valdivia·	591 ⎭	426 ⎭
Coal Mining Zone		
Coronel	640 ⎫	448 ⎫
Lota	916 ⎬ 794	658 ⎬ 571
Curanilahu	827 ⎭	608 ⎭

119 women's votes for every 100 for Alessandri and 147 for every 100 for Tomic.

If we consider the only two municipalities in the capital city of Santiago with an absolute majority of industrial workers (San Miguel and Granja), Allende received 130 women's votes for every 100 for Alessandri and 203 for every 100 for Tomic.

It appears that when modern industrial capitalist economic and social relations penetrate the Chilean household and when strong working class organizations emerge, they have the effect of breaking down the traditionalist beliefs of women, making them receptive to radical political movements. The social concentration of class conscious workers, in particular neighborhoods, appears to create a radical political culture which destroys the traditional paternalistic values that have customarily influenced women voters. In other social contexts, the lower proportion of women voting for the left is probably due to the fact that the women's vote is disproportionately influenced by such non-class factors as the mass media.

TABLE IV

Relative Indices of Votes between Allende and Alessandri and Allende and Tomic (1970). Female Votes in Seven Working Class Municipalities *(Comunas)* in Greater Santiago.

(Percentages)

% of Labor Force in Manufacturing, Mining & Construction	Municipalities *(Comunas)*	Nr. of Allende votes for each 100 votes for Alessandri	Nr. of Allende votes for each 100 votes for Tomic
40 or more	Puente Alto La Cisterna Quinta Normal Renca Barrancas San Miguel La Granja	119	147
50 or more	San Miguel La Granja	130	203

From a theoretical viewpoint, the social situation of work in a dependent capitalist society, the experiences that the workers acquire there, the conflicts engendered and the manner of resolving them are the central determinants of the working class vote.

The massive support of the Socialist and Communist

Parties resides in the working class and this provides, above all when they are politically allied, a cohesive and strategically situated social base that can be mobilized for social and political struggles and change. The Christian Democrats were not able to overcome the immobilism of the social situation in large part because its base was (and is) constituted by a heterogeneous mass of individuals with contradictory values and interests.

The radicalization of the industrial working class in Chile is largely the result of the failure of Chilean and U.S. capital to generate dynamic development. At the same time the radicalized workers, through their social struggles and political power, have provided the Marxist parties with an opportunity to develop Chilean society through socialist policies and institutions. The next few months or years will reveal whether the political leadership of the Chilean left is up to meeting its historical responsibility.

CHAPTER 12

New Social Forces: Peasants and Marginals

Two new types of political forces have emerged in Chile at the grass-roots level in recent years. One is a widespread movement in the countryside for unionization among farm workers and organized land seizures among peasants and Mapuche Indians. The other is a growing agitation among the poorest classes (or "marginal classes" in the sense of large numbers of people who are excluded from participating in the mainstream of society) and slum-settlement dwellers (not all of whom are poor) for housing and more control over the conditions of life that they are subjected to by Chile's underdeveloped capitalist structures. Neither the Allende government nor the parties of the Popular Unity have yet evolved a coherent strategy of how to relate the struggles and aspirations of *campesinos* and settlement dwellers to the building of a socialist Chile.

This chapter contains materials on peasant actions and on "marginal" peoples and settlements in urban areas. The leaflet reprinted was issued by a group of peasants in the South of Chile who seized a large, badly exploited farm from their landlord; the other article on rural actions is a description by a right-wing journalist of a land seizure by Mapuche Indians. These are included to try to portray the sense of rapid and dramatic movement that has characterized the countryside, especially in the South, in recent years. In contrast, "Political Significance of Neighborhood Committees in the Settlements of Santiago" is a highly sophisticated sociological and political analysis of social marginality, the stratification of settlement populations, and the implications of different styles of political penetration in relating to urban settlement populations. This article is included as a contribution toward the analysis of a problem of world-wide scope, as well as to provide an understanding of one of Chile's major problems of underdevelopment.

PEASANTS DENOUNCE THE INTRIGUES OF A MUMMY LANDOWNER*

The Workers of "Rucalán" to Public Opinion: The farm workers of the Arnoldo Ríos Camp at the Rucalán Farm, in view of the declarations made by Juan Landeretche and Manuel Valdés, inform:

1. That Landeretche did not acquire the farm with "his own sweat," as he declares, but by marrying the daughter of Manuel Maffiel, who, in addition to Rucalán, owns three other farms.

2. We took over the farm because it was abandoned and unworked while we starved on half a hectare for one family. We took over the farm at night with only a few sticks and a shotgun with no cartridges. It is not surprising that Sr. Landeretche in his fright mistook the sticks for machine guns, but it is odd, because he has a great knowledge of weapons and their makes. In the poverty that we suffer, we don't have enough to eat; where are we going to get money to buy the weapons that Landeretche imagined he saw?

3. We arrived at the farm and spoke to Landeretche and his sons. This was about 3:00 A.M. We told them they could leave in the morning and take with them whatever

* In February 1971, peasants at the *fundo* "Rucalán" seized the property and issued this leaflet, reprinted in *Punto Final* No. 124, February 16, 1971.

they wanted. He left at about 7:00 A.M. carrying all he could, saying he would come back later for the rest, but he didn't. At no time did we enter the boss's house, nor did we cause the damage of which we are accused. To this fact we have as witnesses the authorities that visited us during the take-over of the farm. Anybody can come and see for himself that the house has not been occupied since December 20. Since the arrival of the intervenor, Sr. Moritz Milies, we have been sleeping in the barns and warehouses despite the cold and dampness.

4. Landeretche says that his farm was well exploited. There were only two hundred cows here, belonging to the Esperanza farm, which he owns, in Puerto Saavedra. These are part of his breeding stock. Of these, only three have been milked since the beginning of December. The milk parlor of which he talks so much consists of six 30-liter tins, which are thrown in a shed somewhere. All the crops sown consist of forty hectares of wheat, twenty-five of rape, and three of grassland. The rest of the farm, 737 hectares, is very well planted with thorn and blackberry tangles, weeds, and thistle.

5. We, as workers, are clean people. Now we have had to work to get rid of the garbage accumulated in the warehouses, barns, yards, and other parts of the buildings. We have never seen so much filth, and we are ashamed to admit it.

6. The other "gentlemen" farmers say that Landeretche had no social conflicts with his workers. The truth is that the three workers whom he had on a permanent basis plus the tractor driver and the supervisor have joined us. The tractor driver is with us because, even after twenty-five years work, he still lives in a flea pit that cannot be called a house, together with his wife and eight children. He had to work thirteen to fourteen hours a day and was

never given a vacation. His Social Security was not up to date, and Landeretche never paid him the legal benefits to which he was entitled. He received a wage of E° 300.- per month. Landeretche had given him a cow for his insurance, but when he left he took the cow with him. He also took an ax from another worker. After retaking the farm with guns and the help of other mummies, he fired the tractor driver.

7. This gentleman says that he had no problems with his neighbors. He forgets that the Mapuche *compañeros* of the Huentemil Reservation had their land stolen from them. We are going to give it back as soon as the farm is expropriated.

8. Let the mummy Landeretche know, and all his friends, too, that we are going to show him how to work the land, together with intervenor Milies. We are going to make the farm produce, because it has always been the workers who, through the sweat of our brows, have made them rich. This exploitation is finished. We do not want any more injustice and we do not want to go on being treated like beasts. We are going to construct socialism even if everybody is against us. We will back up the government fully, as long as it defends us and is with the poor.

BREAD, LAND, AND SOCIALISM.
The Revolutionary Peasants' Movement.

ARAUCANIANS PROMOTE CIVIL WAR*

From the hilltop with war cries, raising their spears toward the skies while the sound of sinister musical instruments rends the air, half a hundred angry Mapuches

* From the conservative magazine *Portada,* February 18, 1971.

appear and descend in a threatening manner. Their faces and actions resurrect centuries as they prepare themselves again to open new pages in the hard history of their race.

We arrived at a modest 160-hectare farm near Quepe, occupied by the Mapuches a few days previously. We were accompanied by the owner of this land, a young widow with four children under ten years old. Naturally, neither the Intendant of the province nor the police, thirty kilometers away, had lifted a finger to help her.

Crossing the trenches dug in the road as obstacles, we stopped before a stockade behind which were waiting, with threatening faces and weapons, the present occupiers of the farm. After lengthy conversation, and with a spear held a few centimeters from the stomach, we were allowed to enter the premises. The Mapuches were eager to explain their attitude.

"I was born under those trees over there, because that's where my mother had her hut," an old woman said. "That is why this land is mine," she argued, laying claim to a piece of land lost more than sixty years ago. (The owner of the farm showed us the titles and deeds to the farm bought in a public auction by her father-in-law in 1905.)

This small farm, carefully worked and producing sugar beets, rape, wheat, and milk was taken over on December 30, 1970. "Why didn't you obey President Allende, who asked you to stop this land grabbing" I asked them. Another old woman—matriarchy is evident among the Mapuches—ignoring the vociferousness of the men, replied, "They are in agreement with the take-over, because approval was granted."

While we were talking outside the property, workers of the farm and friends of the owner stood by armed with cudgels and pruning hooks, waiting for a chance to move in and retake the property.

GUARANTEES FOR LAND GRABS

There were a total of fifty-two land occupations before December 20, a solemn date on which the President of the Republic visited Temuco and attended a meeting of the Congress of Mapuches. While guaranteeing that the occupiers would not be expelled by public forces, he asked the Mapuches not to continue taking over farms. The word of the day is "No more land grabs."

From December 20 to January 3, there were eighteen land occupations and boundary incidents, all carried out under the guarantees and protected against the eventual reaction of the dispossessed.

There is impunity for those involved, even when thefts, kidnapings, fistfights, threats, and shootings are involved. All these crimes go unpunished, and the guilty are immune even from the courts, whose enforcement arm, the police, has strict orders not to interfere in any way and not to carry out judicial orders of arrest or the return of the property to the legal owner.

On the other hand, the government has rigorously enforced the Law of Internal Security against those owners, now classified as seditious, who, deprived of their land by force and denied the help of the authorities, also recover by force their land and homes.

Cautín is a frontier zone populated by men of drive and effort, accustomed to difficult situations, hostile environments, loneliness, and isolation. They are sons and grandsons of the original pioneers who opened the land, crushed the Mapuche uprisings, and incorporated a vast territory into the national life and economy. Cautín and its men now live the tension of an encampment before battle, an encamptment awaiting an unwanted war that cannot be avoided if their homes and lands are to be taken away from them and their families exposed to danger.

No one intervenes. The police limit themselves to taking note of an aggression and reporting the fact to the Intendant. The Intendant, in turn, reports to the Minister of the Interior. And the latter, while assuring everybody that nothing serious is happening in Cautín, does nothing to stop the newspaper he managed for many years from printing the allegations that it is the right wing that is agitating and stirring up sedition in Cautín as it resists the Mapuche rebellion, which is recovering lands "stolen" by the landowners, who have generally bought them at public auctions during the past sixty or seventy years.

"LAND OR DEATH": THE MARXIST SLOGAN FOR THE MAPUCHE

In the majority of farms that have been occupied, especially in Lautaro and Carahué, the attitude of the Mapuche is belligerent and aggressive; they do not even claim hereditary rights over the land they have grabbed; they simply impose the fact of their occupation. "Land or Death" is the extremist slogan displayed on large placards implicitly demonstrating their Marxist affiliation.

In this area quasi-military camps exist. Armed guards, mounted groups, intensive indoctrination, and a bellicose exacerbation are driving forces not known until now among the Mapuche.

Not even the parliamentary commission was allowed to enter these occupied farms. They were forced to remain in one spot and were prohibited from seeing the damage to the houses and the open trenches dug for the sole purpose of resisting any type of intervention.

The Revolutionary Peasants' Movement, brainchild of

the MAPU and MIR,[1] does not cease its agitation and preparation for the revolt of all the Mapuches. They have the backing of the INDAP[2] and university students and the passive connivance of the authorities.

"Last year they came to teach us to read and write," said one Mapuche. "They spoke to us about Cuba, Fidel Castro, and Che Guevara." Of course the leaders deny that there are outsiders involved in land grabs.

CAUTÍN: PILOT PLAN OF THE POPULAR UNITY

At this moment the province of Cautín is the object of a pilot plan of the Popular Unity. From this has sprung the Mapuche uprising, the installation of Chonchol[3] as Minister of Agriculture, and the penal persecution of the landowners.

In no other province was the voting in favor of Allende so low or the sentiment against the intervention of Marxism so strong. Perhaps because of this, the strategists of the Marxist revolution have given the green light to the guerrilla and to the revolutionary way in this province.

Chonchol will expropriate, in conformity with the law, any farm larger than eighty hectares of basic irrigated area. MAPU-MIRista elements will take over the medium and small farms by inciting ancient resentments among the Mapuche. The peasants, caught between these two forces, will have to take the initiative and defend their properties, naturally at the margin of the law.

In a month's time, Cautín may be on fire with chaos, anarchy, and open fighting. And the government will impute it all to "rightist sedition."

[1] MAPU is Christian Left and MIR revolutionary Marxist Left.
[2] INDAP is a government agency concerned with agrarian reform and development.
[3] Jacques Chonchol was the principal architect of the agrarian reform under Frei and is hated by landowners and conservatives.

POLITICAL SIGNIFICANCE OF NEIGHBORHOOD COMMITTEES IN THE SETTLEMENTS OF SANTIAGO*

FRANZ VANDERSCHUEREN

The great majority of Chilean political parties or groups concerned with community organization, particularly among the popular sectors,[1] claim that their organizational efforts aim at social and structural changes. At the rhetorical level, there is a certain agreement among some representatives of "popular promotion"[2] and left-wing movements and parties.

However, organizational attempts appear in some cases as efforts to control or neutralize popular pressure, whereas in others they are attempts at real liberation that lead to popular mobilization.

We are interested in analyzing one type of community organization: grass-roots organizations in marginal settlements, especially neighborhood committees. Because of their aims and success during recent years in Chile, grass-roots organizations are more important than other functional organizations.

We do not intend here to draw general conclusions about neighborhood committees, but to focus upon some aspects that we consider important for understanding the

---

* Franz Vanderschueren is a political scientist at the Center for Urban and Regional Development (CIDU) of the Catholic University. The article is from *Revista Latinoamericana de Estudios Urbanos y Regionales* I, No. 2, June 1971.

[1] "Popular sectors," or "popular classes" refers to the poor and working class.

[2] "Popular promotion" refers to community organization efforts under the Christian Democratic government.

effects of the creation—or legalization—of grass-roots organizations in Chilean settlement areas. The study is based upon public-opinion polls carried out by the Center for Urban and Regional Development (CIDU) in 1969 in the Santiago area, and in Portes.

We are particularly interested in the political aspect of these effects. We go beyond the problems of the sociology of organization, because we think that it is more relevant to analyze settlements and their organizations in terms of class theory. There are fundamental questions raised by those who think seriously about structural changes: What is the real pressure that can arise from organized settlements? What are the obstacles, resulting from the impact of dominant culture through the political system, that hinder popular mobilization?

Popular mobilization implies fundamentally the cohesion of the dominated—in this case the settlers—around their true class interests, such that they see, through adequate praxis, the socioeconomic system as a source of exploitation. It is essentially a task of political education, the purpose of which is to make popular forces aware of their own power and to make them the basis of support for a power alternative in which the dominated of yesterday become the dominant.

To analyze concretely the effects of political penetration and to emphasize its mobilizing or demobilizing character, it is necessary to take two variables into account: first, the political intentions and manner of proceeding of the penetration agent. In our case the agents are the political system represented by the state (Christian Democratic government) and by left-wing political parties. The second variable to be considered is the subject of penetration: the settlers. The main factors that hinder cohesion must be pointed out. These factors, products of domination, generate the stratification that occupation and income standards reflect.

From these two central issues, the subjects of our work arise:

1. Analysis of the political meaning given by the state (Christian Democratic government) to the creation of the neighborhood committee. 2. Analysis of the policies of left-wing political parties, giving special emphasis to the position of the Communist Party, the only party of the official Left that has a defined policy and praxis. 3. Analysis of internal stratification in the settlements resulting from a system of domination and accentuated by marginality. 4. Analysis of the future possibilities offered by grass-roots organizations with respect to legislation, the relation among these organizations and trade unions, and the pattern suggested by the praxis of the Movement of the Revolutionary Left (MIR).

I

THE POLICY OF THE
CHRISTIAN DEMOCRATIC GOVERNMENT

In order to understand the political significance given by Christian Democracy to neighborhood committees, it is necessary to understand the meaning the government and Christian Democratic congressmen gave to the creation—or legalization—of neighborhood committees and other functional government organizations.

The Neighborhood Committees Act was unanimously passed by the Congress; all parties were in mutual agreement to legislate on grass-roots organizations.[3] There was nevertheless clear disagreement over the ways in which these organizations were to be used. On one hand, the government wanted these organizations to be under the tutelage of a state organization, the National Council for Popular Promotion. On the other hand, the parties of

[3] Act 16.880, passed by Congress on November 4, 1968.

the opposition, both right and left, conclusively rejected the creation of "popular promotion" and proposed that the grass-roots organizations be included within the municipal structure. In the end, the Act resulted in a compromise in which the National Council for Popular Promotion disappeared, leaving the state bureaucracy with the possibility of intervening in these organizations. In practice, the model of popular promotion was not completely abandoned by the Christian Democrats.

A. The Doctrine of Popular Promotion

Behind this disagreement on popular promotion there are ideological differences. On the government's side, the grass-roots-organization legislation corresponded to a certain theory of "marginality" propounded by DESAL.[4]

DESAL's concept of marginality leads directly to the creation of popular promotion "as overcoming marginality with the end of incorporation." Explaining the meaning of marginality, DESAL's director, Roger Vekemans, notes, "the term 'popular' refers exclusively to the 'marginal' sector of society, to that part of the population which is out of the mainstream, that does not belong—in the proper meaning of the word—to the global society."[5] Marginality implies only a formal belonging that "lacks its own content, which is the actualization of participation."

This lack of participation has two features. One is passive, that is, "Considering society as a source of resources and social benefits, participation becomes passive and receptive." There is lack of employment, education, social security, etc. This lack of participation is perfectly

[4] DESAL, Center for the Economic and Social Development of Latin America, is an applied-research institute supported by Church funds and directed by Father Roger Vekemans.

[5] Roger Vekemans, "La marginalidad en América Latina. Un ensayo de conceptualización" (DESAL, 1969).

measurable in statistical terms. If it were only this, we would have a statistical continuum, without break. But there exists a qualitative rupture due to the lack of active participation and active contribution to decision making. The latter is the cause of the former. "When we talk of resources or benefits, we are relating them in one way or another to the human being who chooses to act in relation to them. The privileged moment of action is decision."[6]

The cause of non-active participation for DESAL lies in the lack of cohesion and solidarity and the predominance of the principle of "multiplicity over that of unification" in "marginal" sectors.

Radicality, globality, and emergence are the features of marginality.

Radicality means that people are affected by marginality to such degree that "on their own, abandoned to themselves, they are unable to accomplish anything." There may be an analogy, but not an identity, between the Latin American marginal person and the European proletarian whose function was limited to the production of his "progeny." The marginal person is a "settler." In his human existence, as in his social action, he is reduced to only one significance: "to settle, in the existential sense Heidegger gave the word '*Dasein.*'"[7]

To overcome radicality there is "the necessity of a moving force that is not contained within the marginal group, but outside it."[8] The non-perception of this fact explains the failure of Latin American revolutions. It is utopian to believe, according to Vekemans, that marginal people will follow the movement of the working class, even though this movement may be organized. Therefore the only entity that can organize these marginal people is the state, "rector of the General Welfare." The party,

[6] Ibid.
[7] Ibid.
[8] Ibid.

in the Marxist sense of the word, could not play this part, because it is not an external agency of the working class, but intrinsic to it.

The second feature of marginality is *globality*. Marginality is not circumscribed to only one of the aspects of human life and social behavior. It is more than questions of economic, political, or cultural aspects. It comprises all aspects in their whole. Thus, "globality of the problem demands globality in its treatment." Therefore, at the level of Executive power, this globality demands intersectoriality. Globality leads to the determination of two characteristics of popular promotion. First, it demands a total engagement on the part of the nation, up to its state summit, formed by the Executive. Second, the engagement must be global, and therefore intersectorial or interministerial. Hence the initial project of the government was to create popular promotion as a body covering all ministerial sectors, directly dependent upon the President of the Republic.

The feature of *emergence* has two main characteristics: "the deepness of the problem, which actually summarizes the features analyzed before, and its scope."[9] The deepness is essentially due to the genesis of marginality, that is, to the superimposition of two cultures: the Spanish/Portuguese, and the native. Emergence demands priority treatment.

Functions of popular promotion important to this analysis are, internal integration by the organization of marginal people; participation in the form of collaboration between society and marginal people at a programmatic level (distribution of resources) and at an institutional level (creation of organisms that allow participation in decisions by marginals); and integration into the global society, which implies the reform of the various subsystems of society—judicial, educational, etc.

[9] Ibid.

B. Political Function of the Doctrine

Without wishing now to criticize in detail DESAL's work, it is nevertheless worthwhile to emphasize some hypotheses that, in our opinion, invalidate this "theory."

The very concept of "marginality," whose essential feature is, according to DESAL, non-active participation, does not explain anything. In fact, the absence of decision-making power and powerlessness in the generation of values and norms in the global society is also a characteristic of the working class as a whole—and not only in Latin America—and of a certain sector of the lower-middle class. This lack of participation leads to the impossibility of operationalizing the concept of marginality, except when it is reduced—which DESAL does in practice—to ecological "marginalization" (absence of participation in the prevailing standards in housing).

In the second place, supposing that the concept of "marginality" were somewhat precise, it seems to us to be a hypothesis distorting reality by the fact that it divides society into two distinct entities: the "marginal" universe on one hand and the "integrated" society on the other, without "osmosis" between them.

Marginality is nothing more than a form of domination, even though it has different features from the classic bourgeois exploitation of the proletariat. Therefore, it is a product of the "integration" of society. This domination is the result of the predominant mode of production that has effects in the different levels: social, cultural, ecological. It is also unrealistic to assume the existence of a unified entity in relation to a marginal universe. Antagonism, exploitation, and domination are also features of the global society, and raise questions about its integration.

In this sense the cause of "marginality," rooted in the economic level, cannot be looked for in the characteristics of marginal people, or in the supposed empirical foundations emphasized by DESAL: incapacity to organize, and cultural superimposition.

These two empiric foundations—never verified—seem to us rather the product of an ideology peculiar to the liberal philosophy that sees in society's division into classes the inevitable product of natural law.

The comparatively poor organization of the marginals or of the proletariat as a whole is the result of the dominant culture's repression, through its psychological impact, of a perception of society as modifiable, and its consequent suppression of all attempts at cohesion or organization. "Domination on the part of one class over another is not only exercised through political and economic power, but by perception of the possible and the impossible, of the future and the past, of the useful and the useless, of the rational and the irrational, of good and evil. . . . in other words, the possibilities, aspirations, and necessities that social relations exclude in the facts, are censured and repressed (in the Freudian, not the police, sense) at the specific level of its consciousness, by the deep conditioning it exercises on people, ideology, and the prevailing way of life."[10]

DESAL's doctrine consequently leads to ideologically clear political solutions, which we analyze now.

First, there is the concept of the state as a directing agency of the common welfare that organizes the marginal mass. In addition to legitimatizing the paternalist or populist state in practice, this concept does not reflect the reality of the state as an instrument of cohesion within a capitalist mode of production. An analysis of the state has meaning in relation to the existing class structure of a nation. It is utopian to suppose that the state, having all the contradictory characteristics of the capitalistic

[10] André Gorz, *Le Socialisme difficile*, (Paris: Seuil, 1967). p. 100.

state, can promote the cohesion of the dominated. The only thing that can be done is to channel the demands and aspirations of marginal peoples or of the working class in their favor, thus creating political palliatives by means of preventive measures in the face of the "emergence" of large sectors of the population that can constitute a threat in the long run to the established system.

What the DESAL theory provided was the ideological foundation (rationalization of interests of the established system) so that a non-Marxist party could efficiently penetrate the dominated classes and skillfully channel some of their demands without touching the essential problem of basic interests of the settlers, such as employment. In this sense, it hardly achieved a mediocre redistribution of income.

We touch here the second important point of DESAL's doctrine: the clear intention to remove the basic foundation of Marxist theory, starting from a "diagnosis" of marginality. That is, the doctrine denied the possibility that it has to be a party—in the Marxist sense—that penetrates the dominated classes in order to awaken their consciousness. . . .

Christian Democracy used DESAL's doctrine as an ideological foundation to implant popular promotion and to justify the neighborhood committees and the so-called "functional" organizations. For the government, it was a matter of creating a social structure parallel to the administrative and political structure. . . .

II

THE POSITION OF THE LEFT

A. Criticism of the Government

Two fundamental critiques were made of this ideological vision of marginality. On one hand, the idea of social structure established by law avoids the problem of the origin of this structure, which is essentially the consequence of existing productive relations. On the other hand, there was an implicit criticism of the notion of marginality: the people do not need a government to organize themselves, as the existence of neighborhood committees and other organizations previous to the existence of this law indicated. . . .

The second criticism was directed at Popular Promotion. The opposition parties saw a "fascist-directed" expression (Radical Party) or a product of ideological considerations of ecclesiastic origin—DESAL—(Socialist Party). All parties saw essentially an effort on the part of Christian Democracy to penetrate the settlements and to channel to their benefit the support and votes from the urban popular sector. Nevertheless, the Left did not clarify its concept of "marginality," being content to reject implicitly the theory that settlers are incapable of organizing themselves, and giving as evidence the existence —although in a lesser degree than at present—of organizations promoted by left-wing political parties, Christian Democrats, or the settlers themselves.

From these two critiques arises the position of the Left: the main effort of struggle for structural change will be manifested through the trade unions, while the territorial or functional organizations restrict themselves to solving problems of housing and to the improvement or the elemental organization of the settlement's collective services. In practice, there are no differences with the government's position—except in regard to the issue of popular promotion.

B. Left-Wing Penetration in the Settlements

. . . There are several possible explanations for the shallow penetration of the Left in the urban masses. The argument of the DESAL type, that marginal people are unaware of their condition and unable to organize themselves with political objectives, is very weak. Besides, it does not correspond to reality, since the marginal people, or "lumpen," of different countries in the world have been the bases of revolutionary actions.[11] It also does not seem realistic to underline the incapacity of left-wing leaders who seem, on the contrary, quite qualified in Chile.

Party leaders, however, have not developed political alternatives to government activities in relation to the masses of the urban periphery. The official Left parties seek support from the modern sector of economy, that is, the non-marginal group of settlers. Aníbal Pinto[12] relates this fact to the inflationary process. He emphasizes that the process is an agent of "disunion of the popular universe in the measure that it drives a wedge between groups that can follow the inflationary merry-go-round and those who, in the periphery, cannot even participate in the ring. . . ." These circumstances imply that in fact, and not by design, left-wing parties concentrate their action in a relatively restricted arena—the inflationary struggle—that is less an essential problem than a diversionist mechanism of political and economic strategy. This deviation provokes the electoralist deviation, since the problems of readjustments or solutions to strikes take place at a political level in Congress.

This situation also conditions the mode of penetration at the level of the Left's ideological thrust among the popular masses. The ideas developed by these parties are of two kinds. The economistic ideas are absorbed by readjustment problems and by bargaining concerns of trade unions. Secondly, the Left develops propaganda at

[11] The use of the "lumpen proletariat" sector in revolutionary actions was widespread in China, and it was also used in Santo Domingo (Colonel Caamaño).

[12] Aníbal Pinto, "Estructura social e implicaciones políticas," FLASCO-ELACP, No. 18, p. 19.

an ideological level that focuses only upon international problems such as anti-imperialism and the struggle against the war in Vietnam or Cambodia.

It is obvious that these international concerns—as legitimate as they may be—are beyond the concern and understanding of the popular masses, who have little political education. This creates the popular image of these parties: the people see them as defenders of wage readjustments, as opposed to monopoly profits, and as against the United States. But they do not know what long- or short-run national goals are represented by the left-wing parties. The valuable effort of a popular unity program is not enough, since it is perceived as an electoral instrument, except in so far as it becomes an instrument of permanent political education. . . .

C. The Communist Party's Present Position

However, it is worthwhile to consider the Chilean Communist Party's position. This has been expounded in a "National Housing Seminar" organized in 1969 by the Party. An analysis of the meetings and conclusions reveals some positive elements that show that the problem of organizing settlers for change has been at least partially perceived.

In fact, this party has a consciousness-raising praxis through support for the struggle of *"los sin casa,"*[13] though not accepting coexistence with the "homeless" group headed by the (very militant) leader of the "26 January" Settlement. The Communist Party organizes land occupations and sometimes ploys against the police forces. But the impact of these land occupations is diminished by the fact that some sectors of the Christian Democratic

[13] *"Los sin casa,"* the "homeless," who are organized to seize land and build shelter, are thousands and thousands who live in the makeshift housing at the periphery of Santiago and other cities.

Party promote them as well. Nevertheless, the positive side lies in the attempt to achieve an internal unity and union with all the "homeless" groups. The seminar assessed the high degree of organization and the homeless settlers' struggle, their heroism, and their confidence in their own strength to achieve their deepest longing: homes. . . .

It is true that the Communist Party sponsors participation in "tasks and in the generation of the policy lines of all neighborhood committees, mothers' associations, etc. . . ." The Party also states that "Communists must work within these bodies to convert them into bastions of popular struggle" and to stop them "from being transformed into bodies of reformist indoctrination under the leadership of the bourgeoisie." At the level of base operations, however, this has no further meaning than verbal propaganda and action limited to settlers' unity. . . .

It is likely that we will have to wait some time longer to see the effects of the Communist Party's penetration in political terms. But there is a consciousness, perhaps still in an obscure state, that has its expression in the perception of the necessity for cells in settlements. The Communist Party has gone further than the traditional Communist parties in the world, which have constituted cells at the work place; the inherent difficulty has been the impossibility of entering circles that are not the industrial proletariat. The success of this penetration is conditioned by the capacity to make the "marginal" sectors aware of their political possibilities and by breaking the stratification caused by the policy of the state in periphery settlements.

III

SOCIAL COMPOSITION OF
ECOLOGICALLY MARGINAL SETTLEMENTS

In addition to these limitations of the official Left, the absence of an analysis of marginality and the social formation of settlements needs to be emphasized. This analysis leads to a focus upon the stratification of the dominated classes living in "settlements" as conditioned by housing and organizational policy mechanisms. It is hardly realistic to analyze neighborhood committees as popular mobilization instruments without taking into account the relations between strata that exist in settlements.

We divide the settlement population into four groups:

The first group, the "lumpen proletariat," is formed by low-income workers on their own account. These can be lumpen who have never been incorporated into the working class, or former workers who have lost their jobs and work on their own for a low income.

The second group is composed of low-income laborers and the unemployed.

The third group, workers receiving comparatively high incomes, resembles what has been called "the worker aristocracy."

The fourth group, the "residual of the petty bourgeoisie," is formed by specialized or semi-specialized ex-workers who have become small entrepreneurs with personnel at their service, or white-collar employees in business or administration. All members of this group enjoy a comparatively high income, as do those belonging to the third group.

Thus stratification involves two main variables: income and occupation. Empirically this division is necessarily approximate, since it is difficult to define the limit that separates, for instance, the income of a "low"-income laborer from that of a "high"-income worker. However, they constitute "models" that allow one to see the internal divisions within the settlements.

A. The "Lumpen Proletariat" and the "Residual of the Petty Bourgeoisie"

The first of the four groups has traditionally been called the "lumpen proletariat." (We do not attach the derogatory sense the term sometimes has.) It is formed by workers not belonging to the working class—street sellers, cargo men, etc.—and receiving a very low income. To this group can be added ex-workers who fall back into the lumpen after sporadic incorporation into the productive force.

The features of the lumpen have been described in different ways.[14] Marx and Engels made an ethical judgment rather than a Marxist analysis of its role within society and ascribed to the lumpen a negative role in change—even though Marx recognized that "the lumpen is perfectly malleable, capable both of the most heroic feats and the most exalted sacrifices, as well as of the vilest brigandage, and dirtiest venality."[15] Lenin, Mao, and Fidel Castro have analyzed with greater insight from their own political experience the conduct of the lumpen. "These people lack constructive qualities and are given to destruction rather than construction; after joining the revolution, they become a source of roving-rebel and anarchist ideology in the revolutionary ranks. Therefore, we should know how to remold them and guard against their destructiveness."[16]

Analyzing this group's predisposition for actions of

[14] See Bruce Franklin, "Lumpen Proletariat and Revolutionary Youth Movement," *Monthly Review,* No. 72 (March 1970), pp. 10–25.

[15] Marx, "Class Struggle in France," cited in Franklin, *supra.*

[16] Mao Tse-tung, "Revolution in China and Chinese Communist Party," cited in Franklin.

"spontaneous and disorganized armed struggle," Lenin draws the following conclusion: "It is not actions which disorganize the movement, but the weakness of a party which is incapable of taking such actions under its control."[17]

Frantz Fanon summed up the experience of Marxism and projected it to the Third World, arguing that revolutionary movements cannot be successful without these people. Three reasons can be distilled from Fanon's work: "1) they are the most ready to fight; 2) they therefore provide the way by which revolutionary forces of the countryside enter the city; 3) if they are not fighting on the side of the revolution, they will be fighting against it."[18]

Thus the "lumpen proletariat" cannot be ignored. On the contrary, the real danger consists in depending upon their spontaneity.

The essential characteristics of this group can be summed up as follows:

1) They do not participate in productive work and therefore are not exploited by industry.

2) They do not retain any type of loyalty for their class of origin, whether working class or peasant. Therefore, different types of consciousness can be expected as conditioned by their class of origin and their present mode of living that put them in contact with various other classes. This makes it necessary to organize them into a movement that channels these tendencies, since the spontaneous behavior of this mass is unpredictable.

3) The lumpen class is found at the lowest level of stratification in periphery settlements. Relations of this group with other classes do not occur as much at the "occupational" level as at the "territorial" level. Consciousness of stratification plays a more important role in settle-

17 Lenin, "Guerrilla Warfare," cited in Franklin.
18 Franklin, p. 16.

ments than work relations, since occupations within this sector do not force people into a direct relation with the predominant sector, the working class. . . .[19]

Group four has a certain resemblance to group one. It is composed of heterogeneous subgroups: small entrepreneurs (owning a shop or having employees at their service), small employees in administration or commerce, and specialized workers who work on their own account. They all have two things in common, which allows us to place them in one category: they are not incorporated into productive forces and they have a comparatively high income.

One of these subgroups comes directly from a sector of the working class (group three) of highest prestige, income, and perhaps skill, whereas the former worker who has fallen into the lumpen comes from the working-class sector of lowest prestige and income (group two).

Group four is distinguished from the lumpen by its income and status, which bring it closer to the middle class. In the analysis of this major group it is important to emphasize the type of relations it has with other class sectors, in particular the working class.

In terms of the level of occupation, this group can enter into relations with another group either in its work, as in the case of the small merchant or entrepreneur, or through its occupational history, as with ex-workers who may maintain a certain working-class consciousness. At this level, given the heterogeneity of the group, considerable diversity may be expected.

At the territorial level, the prestige of this group, derived from its income—or in the case of employees in administration, from occupational status—makes it like the highest group of workers. In heterogeneous settlements

[19] Omitted from translation here are interesting data on consciousness and participation among lumpen sectors within Santiago settlements, from the author's empirical study. [Ed.]

its participation in the control of neighborhood organizations is highly probable. In fact, it comprises 20 per cent of the leaders within settlements studied, and in two of the six settlements shares the main posts of the neighborhood organizations with the worker group of highest prestige.

B. The Two Worker Sectors

Groups two and three comprise the whole of the wage-earning workers. We have divided this sphere into two groups, because we consider that a non-marginal worker sector exists which is employed in the most modern productive sector, with advanced technology and high productivity. This group is incorporated into the hegemonic productive sector, whereas the other worker group is incorporated into previous productive forms. In our judgment, "marginality" is precisely the concept that permits distinguishing one sector from the other.

The coexistence of the two productive forms characterizes the mode of capitalist production: archaic industry on the one hand and industry tied to the modern system and to the international centers of capitalist domination on the other. In relation to the modern sector, the surplus population plays the role not of "industrial reserve army," as at the beginning of European industrialization, but of a marginal mass. This mass in turn is only partially absorbed by an archaic sector that has maintained itself and constitutes a reserve of sources of employment. The role of workers incorporated into this latter sector is "marginal," since it forms a surplus population without a positive function with respect to the hegemonic industrial sector. It performs none of the functions of the "industrial reserve army." It does not intervene in the setting of wages. The weight of trade unions in Chile representing workers in the modern sector and the phenomenon of politically determined readjustments in Congress annul the effect that this available labor mass could have. Neither does it constitute available labor for periods of industrial boom, since these high-technology industries can grow without absorbing a new labor force, and even with diminishing labor utilization. We then term "marginal" all employed, underemployed, or unemployed workers not incorporated into the hegemonic productive form. . . .

The assumption of this classification is that the group-three workers (incorporated into the hegemonic productive form) constitute a higher income stratum in the labor world. They also have greater stability of employment. . . .

Another factor, the degree of unionization, could be important, since trade unions in Chile do in fact defend the interests of the non-marginal worker group, sometimes called the worker aristocracy. Two facts void this possibility, however. First, the degree of trade unionism is practically identical at each level: marginal, non-marginal, and unemployed. Secondly, unions intervene in the setting of wages at two levels: politically, where the Central Única de Trabajadores (Workers Central) defends the real interests of the labor aristocracy, and sectorially, where unions exist at the level of firms, for the defense of the workers' interests, be they marginal or not. Nevertheless, at this latter level, given the weakness of trade unionism and the political negotiation of wage readjustment, negotiation is very limited, especially in the marginal sector. . . .

An important variable, the type of political penetration, nevertheless intervenes. In fact, the tendency of left-wing parties, in particular the Communist Party, to recruit their leaders from the "labor aristocracy" is notorious. This occurs not by prejudice, but through the organization of this Party, which is based upon the cell within firms. The existence of cells within firms and their impact upon workers is directly dependent upon the degree of stability of the labor force. In fact, to establish stable political relations supposes an almost impossible permanent action in sectors such as construction, where relations are sporadic.

Christian Democracy's penetration in ecologically "marginal" settlements is based not upon occupation but upon territorial unity or the organization of the "homeless." This has naturally directed the efforts of this Party toward the higher strata of the working class, given its greater prestige.

We thus have a tendency to emphasize through political organization the stratification of the working class both by the left-wing parties and by Christian Democracy.

This politicization and the prestige correlating to stratification explain the higher participation in leadership of the working sector of greater stability and income.

Although it is true that group three forms the proletariat in the Marxist sense and, therefore, the agent of change, the existence of stratification and the tendency of the productive system to accentuate marginality leave the open questions: Is the present proletariat the basic force of all revolution? Could not the marginal group with its distinct characteristics form a new proletariat, a new motor force for structural change? The answers depend upon the real possibility of uniting marginals around a common objective.

Two important factors make this unification difficult: 1) The short-term social interests of the marginals, given their "non-participation" in the hegemonic mode of production and in the prevailing standards of consumption, are limited to survival in terms of nourishment, housing, and health. This mass is condemned to concentrate its efforts on the day-to-day struggle, making it more vulnerable to all "paternalistic" action on the part of governments. 2) There is an absence of a clearly perceived relation of domination. The traditional proletariat could clearly see its enemy in the industrial bourgeoisie, whereas the marginal mass, because of its heterogeneous nature, has various enemies. Perhaps the state as the political organ of the dominant classes could play this role. Nevertheless, the populist penetration of the state as a distributor of goods, such as housing, and as the agent of apparent cohesion (creation of neighborhood committees) makes this perception more difficult.

Hence, the only alternative, in our opinion, is the creation of a new class consciousness that unifies both the proletariat and the marginals around a common objective, structural change, while breaking the negative effects that originate in stratification and, above all, its manifestations on a territorial level. In the long run, it is evident that the logic of present development and its increasing tendency toward marginalization create a situation in which the essential objectives or class interests of the marginals and non-marginals are the same. Fundamentally, it is a matter of assuring marginals stable work and adequate pay, interests fully shared by the proletariat. Therefore, these long-term interests can form the basis of common action which tends to unite them around a central objective: the destruction of the system of domination. . . .

The consequences of this brief analysis of "marginality" and stratification of periphery settlements of Santiago at a political level are clear:

Parties working for change will have to take into account the diversity of the dominated classes and direct their action toward unification.

"Marginality" makes marginal groups vulnerable to "welfare" action on the part of the state because of their short-term interests. This makes permanent and unifying action around political objectives by whole settlements difficult.

Grass-roots organizations can nevertheless constitute centers of consciousness, providing that they surmount mere electoral party action. The constitution of cells by the Communist Party is a positive sign in this sense.

As we shall see further on, the work of the neighborhood committees must be co-ordinated with the tasks of other organizations such as trade unions, since these have an impact in the neighborhood committees.

Homogeneity in social composition of a settlement allows more profound action, given the internal cohesion of the group.

IV

FUTURE POSSIBILITIES OF
NEIGHBORHOOD COMMITTEES

A. Purpose and Use of the Neighborhood Committees Act

The purpose of neighborhood committees and other grass-roots organizations has been well defined by law. It is a question of providing organization to obtain housing and urban services. At the same time, it provides a degree of control over the sale of products of prime necessity. The creation of consumer co-operatives has also been suggested. Other objectives are related to the creation of functional organizations to promote the solidarity and human development of settlers. Contrary to the initial purpose formulated in some Christian Democratic publications, there is no allusion to structural change. . . .

One possibility lies in the progressive evolution of the functions of neighborhood committees. When the debate was started in the Senate, there was clear disagreement within the government party itself. An interpretation, in our opinion, in favor of the *status quo* was formulated by Senator P. Aylwin:

"Neighborhood committees cannot have any other objective than those indicated in Article 22, since

they are organisms of public law. And we all know
that in public law nothing can be done except what is
expressly indicated by law. Consequently, these neighborhood organizations cannot make statements on
general policies or on national or international problems, without in some way transgressing the area of
functions which are those that are related to the community and territorial jurisdiction in which the neighborhood committees reside."[20]

This interpretation is that of the present government
(Frei's), which wanted to determine a precise sentence in
the law that would force the committees to stipulate
definite objectives without any possibility of going further
than the law's contents. This juridical conservatism has
not been shared by some Christian Democrats nor, of
course, by the Left opposition. . . .

The Left opened the way for eventual evolution without specifying in which direction.

In spite of a practical agreement between Christian
Democrats and left-wing-party members. . . . actions
that tended to change the neighborhood committees into
instruments of political education (understood in the
sense of a greater cohesion and a genuine class consciousness) surged from the contact with "extremist"
movements. These initiatives arose in the "26 January"
Settlement, today transferred to the grounds of "La
Bandera" Settlement, in the "Lenin Camp" of Concepción, and in other settlements of the same type.

Our interest here is not to develop the conditions per-
mitting a political attitude of that type, but to show that
it constitutes in fact a praxis different from that suggested by the government and applied by the traditional

[20] Senator P. Aylwin, June 12, 1968, 3rd session, Senate
Diary, p. 208

Left. In fact, it seems important to us for actions that involve structural change to use the neighborhood committees—or any grass-roots organizations—or they will become another piece of the integrated bureaucracy that characterizes the Chilean system. In addition to accentuating the paternalistic vision of the state, this would tend to orient the settlers toward a "consensual" attitude and not give them the conviction that the modification of society is above all the result of pressures by those interested in change. . . .[21]

Alejandro Fortes suggests that "evidence goes directly against the theories of 'potential violence' by settlers. The data do not provide enough evidence to reject this theory. . . ."

This conclusion is correct to the degree that it is only the present consciousness of the settlers that is considered. This has been directly influenced by the actions of the state and, we add, in good part by parties of the traditional Left. In our opinion such conclusions do not make sense, because they assume that this is an immutable feature of settlers' mentality, when in fact it is the product of the dominant culture of the present political conjuncture.

It would, then, be a case of maximum possible class consciousness. This implies that the situation of settlers, when transformed, loses its essential social characteristics. We do not think that this is the case, but what should really be investigated is under what conditions and which conjuncture this attitudinal change can be made.

What is lacking, then, among neighborhood committees is a political praxis that modifies fundamentally the settlers' perception and their confidence in their own

[21] Not translated here are several paragraphs citing survey data that show that most settlers believe they "can change decisions of the government," and that many more believe they can do so by "peaceful" means than by "means of conflict." [*Ed.*]

strength as a pressure group capable of generating change. At this moment, only an intensive incorporating action by the government takes place along with verbal propaganda by parties of the traditional Left that in praxis goes no further than the proposed objectives of the government. At best, they compel the latter to greater agility.

In effect, the real problem is not to know what a group thinks today—this is useful information for future work—but to know which changes can take place in consciousness without any modification in the essential nature of the group. Considering the settlement inhabitants' social composition, we think that the only group that would see its prestige harmed by action for common change, that is, class struggle, would be workers incorporated within the modern system of production. But this sector of the proletariat is most strongly incorporated into trade unions or, more precisely, sees its interests better defended by trade unions. Therefore there is a necessary parallel between political action at the level of trade unions and at the level of local organizations. Only action that unifies the various organizations of the dominated classes and channels action in political terms toward radical change can be efficient. In this sense, political work in neighborhood organizations is essentially work among leaders. The fact that leaders arise mainly from the incorporated workers in the modern sector of production accentuates even more the need for co-ordinated work between neighborhood committees and trade unions.

B. Trade Unions and Neighborhood Committees

The composition of the leadership group in marginal settlements emphasizes the importance of group three, the incorporated workers.

The proportion of trade-union members, considering

all occupational categories, is 30 per cent of the participants in neighborhood committees.

A more political trade-union policy related to territorial organizations would have an impact on about one third of the committee's membership and therefore would impose itself upon these organizations.

A position identical to ours was developed in the Communist Party's seminar that we previously cited. However, the contents of the analysis were not considered in the conclusions and directives of that seminar.

In our opinion, the link between the various popular organizations, especially between trade unions and neighborhood committees, is fundamental, given the high participation of trade-union members in the committee and the greater importance that workers have within the leadership group.

C. Another Alternative: Campamentos

Another possible and very positive orientation has evolved through the activities of the MIR (Movement of the Revolutionary Left) in its settlement front based upon the experience of *campamentos*[22] such as "26 de Enero," "Ránquil," "26 de Julio," and "Elmo Catalán," in Santiago, and "Campamento Lenin" in Concepción. The contribution of these experiences has been to give an adequate ideological content through a corresponding praxis to all types of demands by the settlers. The occupation of lands is thus transformed into political education that goes much further than demands for housing. The settler has the opportunity to become conscious of his class interests through an experience of forming political cohesion.

It is useful briefly to consider here the lines of action

[22] *"Campamentos"* (literally, "camps") are often the result of land seizures by marginals in peripheral urban areas, where makeshift housing is constructed by the settlers themselves.

developed by these settlers. The Congress of the "Homeless" (*"sin casa"*), which synthesized its praxis, emphasized the diverse aspects of the misery to which the low-income sectors are subjected and gave it an adequate ideological content: "A clear definition of the objectives that must direct the workers' struggle is urgent and undeferrable. This must not end merely with obtaining land, but with the definitive destruction of the causes that produce, among others, the housing problem."[23]

The Congress pointed out the necessity of political education among the settlers: "Inside the *campamentos,* organization must be directed not only at the defense of settlers, but also at their consciousness and education."

They propose organizing the unity of all settlers, and in practice they act in solidarity with other settlements that find themselves in the same situation: "Today we have the opportunity to create a strong unity around the most urgent and concrete things that concern us all."

In fact, they use various methods of pressure, including the extensive use of mass media: "Mechanisms must be created that assure a rapid and effective access to mass media so that propaganda and diffusion of our demands can be secured, including the formation of popular militias."

We believe that, although it may be difficult to create identical situations, the unity of the different sectors of workers together with an adequate political education and the use of all means of available pressure will lead to popular mobilization that imposes change.

CONCLUSION

In the development of this work, we have emphasized some main points that we can restate as a conclusion.

Grass-roots organizations, specifically neighborhood

[23] Declaration of the Congress of the Homeless organized by the Población "26 de Enero."

committees widely diffused in settlements, constitute an instrument of penetration for the state which in itself is ambiguous.

Penetration was used by Christian Democracy as a neutralizing element emphasizing the welfare image of the state and thus diminishing the possibility of centering the settlers' struggle against the state, center of power of the dominating classes.

The action by parties of the official left, through its weak ideological penetration and lack of appropriate language, organization, and consciousness, tends to fortify this image, making neighborhood committees objects of electoral competition. Nevertheless, new styles of organization and new alternatives formulated by parties, leftist movements, or the settlers themselves indicate some predictable changes.

All popular mobilization efforts suppose an awareness of the diversity of strata fortified by increasing marginality and patterns of settlement. Thus a new consciousness is necessary to unify the different subgroups of settlers. The neighborhood committee can be an excellent instrument to clarify the central objective of changes and their real possibility. It seems fundamental to us that this action must be accompanied by parallel work at the trade-union level, since these organizations have an impact on the central core of settlement organizations, the worker groups, in particular the non-marginal workers, whose weight is greater within the leadership.

Moreover, the possibility offered by the law should permit the promotion of some initiatives, such as unions of the unemployed and pilot experiences in urban industrial settlements, whose function would be a unifying one and would concentrate the settlers' problem in one of their basic interests, employment. The latter would also create an image of feasible alternatives for the settlers through an experience of self-management.

CHAPTER 13

Equivocal Forces: The Middle Strata and Women

The Popular Unity posits the working class as the motor force of Chilean socialism. Their strategy, however, is to win over, or at least neutralize, other important social classes and strata of Chilean society, especially the professional and technical, white-collar, and petty-bourgeois sectors. Salvador Allende speaks to this point in his address, here produced in abridged form, to the 1971 Convention of the Radical Party, a political grouping within the PU coalition that has its political base among these key strata.

The opposition also has its sights set upon these social strata and since the end of 1971 has engaged in an energetic campaign to win them over and mobilize them to bring Chilean socialism to an end.

The Right has made women a special target of propaganda and agitation. Historically, many Chilean women have been resistant to the long-established leftward trend in Chilean politics. While the majority of working-class women now vote for leftist candidates, they do so in smaller proportion than male workers, while the overwhelming majority of non-working-class women tend to be less open to change, and vote for Christian Democratic and rightist candidates. This situation is not necessarily a permanent one, as Fidel Castro pointed out during his 1971 visit to Chile.

On several occasions, Fidel spoke to and about women in the revolutionary process, often generalizing from the importance women have assumed in the Cuban Revolution. Fidel's themes were several: the exploitation, degradation, and oppression of women in capitalist society; the fact that women suffer most in existing societies and have the most to gain from liberation; the strategy of the reactionaries, who, faced with a revolutionary process, try to sow fear, insecurity, and terror, especially among women; the necessity for women to incorporate themselves fully into the struggle for the new society.

RADICALISM AND BOURGEOIS SECTORS*

SALVADOR ALLENDE

The presence of the Radical Party in the broad and turbulent Chilean people's movement is not accidental, nor can it be expressed as a temporary or occasional event. Radicalism is born with material and ideological arms in hand inexorably to combat the oligarchic and reactionary sectors of our country. Its men, who have pointed out its road like visionaries, have not done more than be consistent with the doctrinal principles of this body, which, although it certainly represents essentially the petty and middle bourgeoisie, has been and shall be together with the workers in the great and definitive battle to attain full liberty for our country. . . .

Consistent with its tradition, radicalism headed the people's movement of 1938, the Popular Front, which marked a very important stage for Chile at that time. We live today in a different stage, in which it is also possible to appreciate the presence of the parties that essentially formed that front; but it should unquestionably be said once again that the Popular Front is not

* Abridged from President Allende's speech to the convention of the Radical Party, July 1971, from the text printed in *El Siglo*, July 31, 1971.

the Popular Unity of today. The Popular Front of yesterday was the decision of the people's parties to be the Left within the capitalist system. The task of the Popular Unity of today is that of effecting a revolutionary transformation of the capitalist regime, of opening the road to socialism.

There is no ruling party within the Popular Unity; all the parties have the same responsibility, and the growth of one also accentuates the influence of the others. And I say to some people of a conventional radical approach who for lack of experience could feel discouraged by the results of the elections of last April,[1] that your president does not measure the parties by their votes but by their revolutionary will and consciousness.

Consequently, in this country, whose economy is not of a rural character and in which we have reached a higher industrial expression than other countries that have characteristics of underdevelopment, the presence of the Radical Party is logical and will be permanent in the building of socialism. Socialism is advancement, it is progress, it is humanistic content. Socialism involves collectivizing the means of production; it is the definition of classes plus technology and expertise, and for this reason we require the presence of the sector represented by the Radical Party: that of the professionals, merchants, middlemen and small industrialists, small farm owners and peasants, technicians and scientists, because they are the great support that will make an efficient building of socialism possible. . . .

I ask you to think a little about the tasks accomplished so as to understand the unavoidable obligation that we have today and will have tomorrow. In our opinion, it is necessary to point out whom we are fighting, what we

[1] Votes for Radical Party candidates in the municipal elections of April 1971 fell, while the Socialist Party, to which Allende belongs, sharply increased its votes.

are struggling for, what social force we have to attract, and the means we consider indispensable to complete what we have achieved to date. No one can be deceived about whom we are fighting in this country; our struggle is against imperialism, the monopolies, and the oligarchy. Let no one call it deceit if, proceeding with responsibility, we advance at the rate we have established for ourselves. We considered this necessary. But you should know, and I so state due to my responsibility, that this struggle does not allow for truces; our enemies are and will be imperialism, the monopolistic bourgeoisie, and the monopolies.

We should also not forget that by nationalizing what has until now been retained by the power centers, the minority and privileged groups who have governed this country, we are strengthening the sectors of the middle and petty bourgeoisie. It is very important to remember this and not overlook it in order to oppose the mendacious campaign that attempts to distort our attitude. We shall not relinquish a single one of the programmed points. The Popular Unity Program is sufficiently clear so that all Chile can know what it is we are going to do, how we are going to do it, and how we shall accelerate this process, which is the responsibility not only of the government but of the people of Chile and their revolutionary consciousness.

I therefore wish to point out once again the higher responsibility of radicalism as the most qualified interpreter of the sectors of the petty and middle bourgeoisie, the employees, teachers, technicians, the small merchants, industrialists, and farmers. We require these social groups to understand that they have and shall have a decisive influence in the building of the new society. It is our obligation to understand and recognize the efforts of all Chilean professionals, technicians, and scientists so that their capacities and knowledge will be generously provided for in the great battle of Chile, the great road of the fatherland.

I want the people to know that our great concern is also that of securing the presence of the worker, the peasant, the student, and the woman in this struggle in which all must take part. I now call upon these sectors and even those which are not part of the Popular Unity, since our task is so great and has such historic content that we must understand that we cannot proceed with sectarianism or dogmatism and deny participation to those not in our ranks who want to be at our side in the great collective struggle. These sectors make up a part of the same social class; they are not owners of production property, but wage earners, and therefore they will have to understand that they too will be benefited in this emancipating and liberating struggle. Therefore, along with the essential tasks of carrying out the program, we have been concerned with pointing out that Chile must reduce the distance separating it from the scientific and cultural development processes of the metropolises of capitalism and the socialist countries. Thus, we have strengthened the Nuclear Power Commission; we vigorously support the presence of scientists and technicians in the Scientific Research Council; we are attempting to utilize all the human and technical value Chile has available, since the undertaking we are committed to requires this. . . .

Our road which has rightly been called the "Chilean Way," is unquestionably of profound significance beyond these frontiers, beyond even the Latin American continent. It is with satisfaction that I can say to you as partners representing the people's movements who have lent the prestige of your presence to the solidary support of your popular bodies: in this country, *compañeros,* there are no political prisoners; in this country, where the press sometimes goes beyond limits, not a single daily has been closed; in this country, we respect the social rights the people themselves have conquered. We should also understand that if we work for the workers and the peasants, we do so with the same passionate interest for the technicians, professionals, middlemen, and small merchants and industrialists. We do so, with passion, with tenderness, for youth, since it will live fully in the new society, and we shall fight without rest because the Chilean woman, the proletarian mother, the mother of the people understands that our struggle benefits her more than anyone else. And whenever I see, as in the case of Valparaíso, that in an occasional election, in an emotionally charged atmosphere, it is the woman who decides a battle against us, even though on a tiny scale, I want to appeal to the conscience of the members of the Popular Unity parties and their directors. Our great task, our great obligation is to make it possible for the Chilean woman, our sister, daughter, mother, and friend, to understand that we need her and will fight for her, because she is the seed of the future in the son of the people.

Every peasant, every employee, every man from our own class, whether or not he is a member of the Popular Unity, should understand that he is a friend and brother in this great combat. How good it is to point out this exemplary unity among parties of different doctrinal and philosophical concepts. There is plenty of room for an authentic Christian Left, which is a basic factor in this revolutionary task. I am sure that this sector, which incorporates the truth and doctrine of Christ, will join the Marxists and laymen to make the Popular Unity stronger and more powerful.

As a *compañero,* I propose to this radical convention a great campaign, a public campaign to reach the sectors I have named, whose presence the Popular Unity government considers essential for the building of socialism.

FIDEL CASTRO ON WOMEN
AND REVOLUTION*

Dear Chilean Comrades:

With your cooperation we can converse for a few minutes. In the first place, I would like to say something: we have been to many rallies in this country, we have been to many meetings, but with all frankness I can say that this is one of the most important of all, this is one of the most warmhearted, one of the most moving.

If I am to speak here, after the efforts you have made to organize this rally, I will try to talk of questions which in my opinion are essential.

In the first place, Chile is in the middle of a revolutionary process, and this has a special importance. Chile is not living through an ordinary moment of its history. Chile is living through a special moment of its history. This was indicated here in the words of Mireya and Maria Elena [Mireya Baltra and Maria Elena Carrera, deputy and senator of the People's Unity coalition, respectively]. They stated they were ready to defend this process and to resist any attempt to crush it. They said that the *"momios"* (mummies) shall not pass which is the same as saying that the reactionaries shall not pass, the same as saying that the fascists shall not pass.

In This Struggle Women Have a Decisive Role, a Very Decisive One!

Now, then, in this struggle women have a decisive role, a very decisive one! We should bear in mind the efforts of the reactionaries in this country to deceive

* Abridged version of Fidel Castro's speech to women gathered at Santa Laura Stadium, Santiago, November 29, 1971. Translation by the Cuban Government.

women, to confuse women. We should bear in mind all the tricks, the lies and the methods they have used to keep women from joining the revolutionary process. Why? Because they know that women are a force, a real and a potential force of the Revolution. They also know that revolutionary social change will most benefit, will most dignify, will most elevate the woman.

This has been the history of our country. . . .

If women are on the side of the Revolution, the "*momios*" shall not pass, the reactionaries shall not pass, the fascists shall not pass.

What role do women play in the old society?

(A WOMAN: "THAT OF A DOLL!")

A comrade gave the answer: that of a doll! In the old society what consideration and respect do women have? In the old society what does woman have as a woman, as a citizen, as a worker, as a mother? Nothing! The Revolution begins by giving woman the place she should have within human society.

In our own country—and in our country the Revolution has tremendous support from the women, the women are a decisive force—we explained things this way: we liberated women twice, as workers and as discriminated and mistreated members of society.

What do the exploiters do with women? What fate do they reserve for women? A role in society as a worker? No! A role in society as a mother? No! A role in society as a human being? No!

You have seen how the reactionaries hypocritically and pharisaically talk of human rights. But what role have they given women in society? For the reactionaries, the exploiters, the fascists, woman is simply an instrument of pleasure, a decoration, an object to abuse, to humiliate, to offend and many times to degrade.

We should not confuse the apparent respect given

to women. In no sense is it human respect, or social respect, or revolutionary respect.

What role do they reserve for working mothers, for peasant mothers, for poor mothers? What role do they reserve for their children? They are given the role of poverty, the role of ignorance, of disease, of misery and even the more painful role of corruption.

The reactionary capitalist society which never takes human values into account does not care about the morals of children, or the dignity of children; it does not care about the morals of women, or the dignity of women. The whole system is based on profit, on private interest, on exploitation.

If they can do business with a movie that is poisonous or harmful for children, they don't care, they throw it on the market. What they're interested in is to make money! If they can make money, they don't care if they prostitute women.

One of the most painful things in a capitalist society is the woman who has no work, the discriminated and humiliated woman who is many times driven to prostitution. We remember how in our country thousands and thousands of women went through these painful situations. If a mother had a child and was abandoned by the man, if she had to give food to her child and had no job or somebody to help her or a scholarship for her child, she had to take the horrible road of prostitution.

The Revolution Offers Women a Human Role

Social prejudices, discrimination of women, feudal concepts, led women to the worst roads; gave them the worst jobs—jobs in brothels, jobs in bars or casinos, jobs in amusement centers—with the most vulgar concept of mercantilism, with the most inhuman of concepts. And then the reactionaries speak of human rights!

Women were discriminated against in technical careers

and in terms of employment. Woman is the one who suffers most; as a mother, when there is no work, no job, when the children get sick, when there is exploitation. Woman suffers in silence and abnegation. Woman suffers the most from poverty.

In our societies women have historically played a subordinate role, a relegated role. And that is why we ask: what do the reactionaries offer women?

What does fascism offer women?

What does capitalism offer women?

Nothing! Nothing! Nothing!

The Revolution offers women a human role. It offers them all the possibilities of developing themselves; all the possibilities of their energy, their enthusiasm, their spirit, their most noble feelings. The Revolution dignifies women. The Revolution gives women genuine human treatment. The Revolution works for the future, works for the children, works for the youth; for a dignified and happier future.

The reactionary capitalist society corrupts not only women but also men, children and youth. It has no moral principles. Do you know what its moral—if we can use the word moral—principle is? Do you know what the principle of that society is? Interest, egoism, profit. You all know that, right?

Today We Have Struggle and Effort. A Revolution Is Made for the Future

We can never forget what they did at the beginning of our Revolution.

With what lack of scruples, with what cynicism did they launch and propagate one of the most shameless, the lowest and most infamous of lies. They thought up something diabolical. They started the stupid, absurd, ridiculous, inconceivable rumor that the Revolution was going to deprive mothers of their rights over their children. With what total absence of scruples did they appeal to maternal sentiment! And the worst thing that happened is that they succeeded in deceiving some women.

In our country some women began to send their children to the United States—possibly several thousand women sent their children to the United States because of that base rumor. You can imagine what fate awaited those children. In Cuba the young people, the children, study, work, develop themselves and develop a sense of duty, and a sense of morality. But what happened to those children who were sent to the United States? What happened to them when they fell into that monstrous, egotistical society? Many of them became drug addicts. Others became delinquents and gangsters. Many girls, still children, became prostitutes.

In our country the Revolution has devoted all its attention to the children, and what hurts the Revolution is that it still doesn't have enough resources, enough good schools for all of them. It will take us at least ten more years—listen well, ten more years—to build enough installations for all our children of primary and secondary school age.

In our country today all children have teachers. But many times the classes must be given in a straw-thatched hut or in a rundown building, which does not have all the conditions, all the resources, all the laboratories, all the teaching aids, all the recreational facilities necessary.

We can really say that the quality of our young people is impressive today. A Revolution is not made to give immediate results. No! Today we have struggle and effort. A Revolution is made for the future.

Our Revolution works to take care of the children and to give women facilities to join the labor force.

In our country today women are constantly asking for more schools, more day-care centers, more facilities for obtaining employment. In our country there is no drug addiction, there is no gambling. In our country there has been no prostitution for many years. In our country all those horrible things, those painful things of an exploiting society have disappeared.

In our country we protect mothers. In our country we protect children.

The Revolution has eradicated many diseases. For example, in our country every year hundreds of children died or were crippled from poliomyelitis. However, we have not had a single case of polio in Cuba for years. Hundreds of children used to die of tetanus because there were no preventive medical campaigns. However, we have implanted a program of vaccinations against tetanus and we have practically reduced the effects of this disease to a minimum. In our country thousands of children died of gastrointestinal diseases every year. The Revolution has reduced these diseases to minimum levels. We have wiped out typhus and malaria. Moreover, when the Revolution triumphed in our country we had dozens of tuberculosis hospitals, thousands of men, women and children who suffered from tuberculosis. Today we can say that happily our country has virtually wiped out tuberculosis and that we expect to eradicate it completely. Many tuberculosis hospitals are now being used as clinics and for other purposes.

We Think It Magnificent That the Leftist Women of Chile Are Uniting in One Organization

In our country the majority of women used to bear their children in their homes, without any medical attention. Many of them died, many of their infants died or contracted infections, problems of all types. Today almost 100 percent of the Cuban women bear their children in hospitals, in conditions of maximum security for themselves and their infants.

The job possibilities for women were minimal. Their

possibilities for a higher education were also minimal. Today, we can say that in the School of Medicine, for example, there are just as many women students as there are men students. The same is true in the School of Engineering and in many others.

The organized women in our country are participating more and more in the solution of social problems, of the problems of the Revolution. They are interested in everything that has to do with the family, with children, with everything that has to do with . . . in short: education, public health, the campaigns for hygiene, campaigns against diseases, in all aspects. That is why the women in our country are a great force of the Revolution.

We think it very correct, we think it magnificent that the leftist women of Chile are uniting in one organization, putting aside sectarianism, and organizing Chilean revolutionary women's committees.

In Cuba more than one million women belong to the Federation of Cuban Women. They have thousands and thousands of committees. They organize educational courses, courses to prepare women. Tens of thousands of young people have been taught in institutions and centers organized by the women. The Federation is an organization that is developing more and more; an organization that services numerous social institutions. The children's day-care centers are tended by women, the Institute of Child Care is tended by women. And women are participating more and more in the economic, social and political life of our country.

In this country we have come across great quality. You have chosen the road of change. This road is not easy. It is difficult, it is a hard road. You must organize. You must increase consciousness. You must call upon the women. You must win over the women of Chile to the cause of Revolution. You must wage an ideological battle, a political battle.

You must show up the demagogues, the liars, the deceivers, those who have been deceiving the women and attracting them with their little tricks, their little lies, their little favors. Tell them: we don't need favors. What we need is the liberation of women. What we need is the vindication of women.

We don't need charity!

We're not asking for alms!

They have to be told: what we need is dignity!

What we need is to be considered like human beings! What we need is our rightful place in society! What we need is the future of our children, the future of our children!

You must show up the lies, the tricks of the fascists and reactionaries. You must struggle, as Mireya and Maria Elena said. You must organize yourselves. You must develop an awareness. You must accumulate forces.

If the reactionaries think that the people are disunited or weak or ignorant, then they feel brave and daring; they will attack, organize and deceive. They will try to use all the difficulties; any difficulty. But the women should be firm. Never allow yourselves to be confused! Never allow yourselves to be deceived!

We are in the definitive stage, in the stage of attaining definitive independence, a just society, a human society. We will unite our flags in brotherhood! We will continue forward and will reach definitive freedom! And on this road we are certain that in Chile, as in Cuba, the women will take up their role; the women will contribute their energy, their strength and passion to the revolutionary cause; that in Chile, as in Cuba, the women, united, will also be in the first line of battle for the revolution.

PART V

Institutional Forces

CHAPTER 14

The Church

The Church, long a pillar of the status quo in Chile as in other Catholic countries, has lately begun to experience a profound transformation. Young priests have become revolutionaries, students at the Catholic University have deposed conservative rectors, and the latest current in religious thought is the theology of liberation. This does not mean that the Church has become transformed from an institution of domination to a vehicle for liberation from oppression, only that the deep divisions and social struggles of society have permeated this traditionally conservative institution.

THE CHRISTIANS AND THE TRIUMPH OF THE POPULAR UNITY*

ARTURO NAVARRO CEARDI

There are many reasons for Salvador Allende's victory in Chile. One of them is the special support he received this time from various Christian groups that had previously denied it to him during the presidential elections of 1952, 1958, and 1964. This support originates in the special attention the Church itself has paid to social problems ever since the Second Vatican Council and the meeting in Medellín, Colombia—a time when the major-

* From *Prensa Latina* Feature Service ES-857/70. Navarro Ceardi is with the Catholic University.

ity of priests no longer were satisfied with merely changing the liturgy from Latin into Spanish or discarding their
ecclesiastical robes.

This progressive movement within the Chilean Church
originally expressed itself when the Catholic bishops became the first to implement President Alessandri's "Mini"
Agrarian Reform on their own lands. Another sign was
the overwhelming victory won during the presidential
election of 1964 by the Christian Democratic candidate,
Eduardo Frei, with the slogan "Revolution with Liberty."
Frei is a faithful Catholic, studied law at the Catholic
University of Santiago, and was a leader of the Conservative Youth until he abandoned it to set up the
Falange Nacional.

Perhaps the frustration felt by many Christians with
the Christian Democratic Party—which, as Radomiro
Tomic (their candidate) acknowledged, "had accomplished a great deal but not the revolution"—accelerated
their radicalization. Yet this process also took place in
other Latin American countries: in Colombia with
Camilo Torres, the guerrilla-priest, and in Brazil with
Dom Hélder Cámara and his concepts of reform through
non-violence.

The crisis within the Church, however, kept growing,
especially among the young people, and in 1967 it ex-
ploded. On June 15, the students of the Catholic University of Valparaíso took over their university and attacked the chancellor, the Bishop of Valparaíso, and the
rector (his appointee), Arturo Zavala. Their example
was followed by the students of the Catholic University
of Santiago who, on August 11 of the same year, also
occupied their university and, with the explicit support of
the CD Party and the Cardinal Archbishop of Santiago,
managed to remove the rector, Monsignor Alfredo Silva
Santiago, and began a reform process that was more

easily won than the one in Valparaíso but that was equally important.

As if by coincidence, on August 11 of the following year the Metropolitan Cathedral of Santiago was taken over by a group of priests, nuns, and laymen who, under the name of Young Church, proclaimed their support of "a new society that will give dignity to the human person," where "love will be possible." Their Manifesto, after explaining why they were in the cathedral, stated their views:

"WE SAY

—No, to a Church that is a slave to structures of social compromise.

—Yes, to a free Church that serves mankind.

—No, to a Church that is committed to power and wealth.

—Yes, to a Church that risks poverty because of her faith in Jesus Christ and in man.

—No, to a hierarchical structure imposed on the Christian people.

—Yes, to pastors born from the people who search with the people.

—No, to a Church that is afraid of confronting history.

—Yes, to a Church that is brave and commits herself to fight for the real liberation of her people.

WE WANT A CHURCH THAT IS FAITHFUL TO THE TRUTH OF THE GOSPEL."

The sign that appeared in front of the metropolitan Cathedral summarized their feeling: FOR A CHURCH THAT STANDS WITH THE PEOPLE AND THEIR STRUGGLE.

After occupying the cathedral, the Young Church movement lived through an internal process which later expressed itself through religious and social action: it participated in the take-over of factories along with the workers, in the creation of workers' co-operatives, in the aid to homeless citizens, in Christmas street festivities, etc.

In 1969 the young intellectual and Catholic vanguard received political support when the Christian Democratic Party split into a new political group called Movimiento de la Acción Popular Unitaria—MAPU, which in the language of the Araucanian Indians means land—consisting largely of the young people of the Christian Democratic Party plus certain legislators and peasant and labor groups.

Together, the Young Church, the MAPU, and the reforms in the Catholic universities—movements that interconnected through people and ideology—sought, above all, co-operation with Marxists to change society and build the Kingdom of God on earth ("Thy Kingdom come . . .").

Presently, various Christians who own part of the mass media are contributing in various ways to a return to the essence of Christianity and, as a result, are sometimes harshly attacked by conservative elements within the Church. Catholic magazines such as *Mensaje* of the Company of Jesus, *Mundo 70* of the Missionaries of the Heart of Mary, the Capuchins' teaching-radio "Voice of the Coast," which offers cultural programs to the peasants in the South, plus the television channels of the Catholic universities of Santiago and Valparaíso, are also part of this crusade.

A study by the Office of Religious Sociology of the Jesuit Center also gives us an idea of the ideological position of Chilean priests. According to *Mensaje* (No. 193, October 1970), the largest percentage of young priests (78 per cent identify themselves with the Young Church, while the smallest per cent (18.7 per cent) with FIDUCIA (Chilean Society for the Defense of Tradition, Family, and Property). In other words, more than three fourths of the Chilean priests identify themselves with the Left.

Another interesting fact comes from the results registered in the School of Theology (the only one in the nation) of the Catholic University of Santiago during the October 1969 election of the Student Federation. The university's student body was given more or less the same alternatives the nation received last September: a list of Christian Democratic candidates; a list of apolitical right-wing candidates; and a list of the Leftist Front (consisting of candidates from the MAPU, the Revolutionary Left Movement, and other independent groups). Although in the entire university the Right won with a small margin over the Left (44 per cent over 43 per cent), the voting pattern within the School of Theology overwhelmingly favored the Left, with 64.5 per cent in their favor, 22.5 per cent in favor of the Right, and 13 per cent in favor of the Christian Democrats.

This sense of emergency among revolutionary Christians had inevitably to manifest itself during the presidential campaign of 1970. Certain priests publicly supported Salvador Allende: Father Dario Marcotti, the parish priest of a working-class neighborhood in Valparaíso, proclaimed that the only Christian way is to form part of the people "by being a worker, and the only way to be true to the gospel of liberation and justice is by turning it into action along with the working class. Christ always stood with his people and unmasked the oppressors. . . ." The "comrade-priest," as they call him in his parish and as Allende called him on TV, is the founder of the People's Church (Valparaíso equivalent of the Young Church), a movement with deep roots among the workers. This is not the only case, nor a mere electioneering trick (as in the case of the Allendista Catholic Movement of the 1964 campaign), but the result of the efforts of hundreds of priests in working-class neighborhoods, peasant settlements, and unions. These priests are convinced that the "light of the gospel is with the people and that one's love of God must be expressed through the love for our brothers who suffer exploitation, misery, and injustice."

Christian leftists incorporated themselves immediately into the Popular Unity: Rafael Tarud, an independent Senator and a Christian, is president of the PU's National Headquarters; and the MAPU was the movement that gave most support to Allende's campaign (without having the strength of the Radical, Communist, or Socialist party). All of this occurred in spite of the fact that the two other presidential candidates tried to use religious values in their favor. For example, the Christian Democrats geared a large part of their campaign toward differentiating the Christian Left from the exclusively Marxist Left; the Right used revered Catholic symbols such as the Virgin of Mount Carmel, the nation's Patron Saint, to "free us from communism." In connection with these supplications, one of the leaders of the Young Church commented, "If they organize a mass against Allende's election, we will respond with ten masses for the triumph of the popular government."

The rumor that the Catholic religion forbade praying for a non-Catholic candidate (the only one was Salvador Allende) was categorically denied by the moderate Christian magazine *Mundo 70*, which, in its August 1970 issue, answered the following question: "How should the Christian vote?" Answer: "The Christian has the absolute right to decide in favor of any one of the three alternatives. What matters is that his choice be the result of a serious and realistic appraisal responding to the following question: Which of the three alternatives is the most adequate so that Chile can become a more just, brotherly, and profoundly Christian society?"

Allende won. His majority was not overwhelming, and

we therefore cannot say that the support of the Christians was quantitative, but we can certainly affirm that its qualitative contribution was most important. . . .

Christian support for the people's cause is evidenced in the recognition of Allende's triumph given by the Bishop of Puerto Montt, the Catholic Action Worker Movement, the Young Catholic Worker, the Rural Catholic Action, the University Catholic Youth, and the rectors of the Catholic universities. Their position contrasts greatly with that of the Chilean bishops, who before the election declared they would only pay their respects to the candidate with an absolute majority; if no one obtained such a majority they would then postpone their visit until the candidate was ratified by the full Congress on October 24. The Conference of Bishops clarified their position in another statement: "The Bishops wish to cooperate with the changes and especially with those that favor the poor." They also appealed to the nation to keep calm during the uncertain situation right after the election, and urged Catholics to seek "together with the rest of the nation a just, original, and creative solution to the Chilean problem."

In summary, what the Left had not accomplished during previous elections—i.e., the legitimization of its program by the Christians—it accomplished qualitatively this time thanks to the reformist tendencies within the Catholic Church which are growing increasingly stronger.

Large groups of Christians took part in the three political groups during this election, and, as a result, we find Catholics who are committed to building Chilean socialism—something that for many only confirms Christ's message and represents real evidence that the "Kingdom of God" must be built here, in this world, and with everyone's participation.

It would be deceitful not to acknowledge that the majority of Christians were not followers of Allende. But the belief predominates that they will set aside personal disputes and will incorporate themselves to the difficult task of building a society where everyone is free and equal—a task which in Chile is just beginning.

CHAPTER 15

The Military

There is very little public information on the military in Chile. To my knowledge, there are only three studies of the Armed Forces that address themselves to the basic question of the role of the institution in the process of development and sociopolitical change of the country. Two of them are by non-Chileans: Alain Jaxe, *Las Fuerzas Armadas en el sistema político de Chile* (Santiago: Editorial Universitaria, 1970), and a Ph.D. dissertation by Roy Hansen (University of California, Berkeley, 1966). The third, reprinted here, is by Robinson Rojas, a Chilean socialist. It is a penetrating analysis, which raises extremely uncomfortable questions and was not well received by sectors of the Popular Unity. In a preface to the article the author states that Prensa Latinoamericana (Socialist Party press), which normally prints the magazine *Causa ML,* refused to take this issue, giving as a reason that "the *Causa ML* articles damage the left image of *Compañero* Allende." Robinson Rojas replies, ". . . we want to make clear that our principal enemies continue to be Yankee imperialism and the oligarchy of the city and countryside. Our differences with the government are precisely its political actions with respect to the basic enemies that we consider conciliatory and of grave consequence."

THE CHILEAN ARMED FORCES:
THE ROLE OF THE MILITARY IN THE
POPULAR UNITY GOVERNMENT*

ROBINSON ROJAS

Since September 4, the night of Salvador Allende's victory, one question has been foremost in all minds: what will the Armed Forces do?

During the month of October (including the moment of General Schneider's assassination) and afterward, there have been two kinds of simplistic answers to this question. These answers have been marginal to class struggle and its specific characteristics in Chile.

One simplistic and subjective answer has been given by oligarchic and imperialist sectors. They believe that the Armed Forces are a barrier against "Marxism" and will defend them and help them to effect a *coup d'état*.

Another simplistic and subjective reply has been given by wide sectors of the Popular Unity (I think that Allende should not be included among those who think this way). These have said that the Armed Forces will support us and are supporting us, because they are "democratic" and "professional" and "we have legitimately won the presidential elections."

Neither of these answers takes into account the class character of the Armed Forces. The first answer is based

---

* From *Causa ML*, No. 21, July-August 1971. This is the first of a three-part article. Part two, not included here, is an analysis of military thinking on key questions. The third part, also omitted here, is based upon a study by Roy Allen Hansen, "Military Culture and Organizational Decline: A Study of the Chilean Army" (Ph.D. dissertation, University of California, Berkeley, 1966).

on a false assumption that the Popular Unity is a Marxist government; it is also based on a feudal concept of the Chilean military, seeing them as mere servants, "until the last consequences," of the financial, landowning, and capitalist Chilean oligarchy and of the more archaic sectors of Yankee imperialism.

The second answer is also founded on false assumptions. It is false that "legality" is beyond classes. One legality serves the bourgeoisie and another legality serves the large majority of the people. The Armed Forces of the bourgeoisie constitute the main support of "formal democracy" and will always act in its defense. They are, therefore, "bourgeois professionals" and "democratic bourgeoisie." If a "popular legality" were implanted in Chile at this moment, the present Armed Forces would have to depart from "the Constitution and law" in order to make a *coup d'état* and re-establish a formal democracy. Therefore, when the Chilean Armed Forces support the government, as is now happening, it is because they believe that that government has not and will not abandon bourgeois channels. What this government is in fact doing is introducing decisive reforms (against some oligarchic and imperialist sectors) to reorganize and consolidate the system, adapting itself as well to imperialism's new strategy in Latin America.

Oligarchic Miscalculations

During the month of October (1970), Chile witnessed a wild race in pursuit of the "support" of the Armed Forces. On the one hand, Christian Democracy tried from the beginning to become the "political spokesman" for them, trying to get formal (constitutional) guarantees on the part of Allende. On the other hand, landowning sectors, the financial oligarchy, and Yankee Anaconda formed a conspiratorial structure, trying to attract the Armed Forces by raising the hollow specter of "communism" in the electoral victory. Finally, Salvador Allende personally began to explain to the Armed Forces the real scope of the program of the Popular Unity.

In this race, Allende bettered the Christian Democrats as "mediators." He left them behind and started a direct dialogue with the high command.

On October 1, 1970, in Allende's public reply to Christian Democracy's challenge of the "constitutional guarantees," the essential points of the conversation between the President-elect and the Armed Forces came to light.

Point one: agreement that the Armed Forces are the "spinal column" of the system, with Allende stating, "I have repeatedly pointed out the pure patriotic tradition, democratic and professional, of our Armed Forces and have stated my purpose of fulfilling the national obligation by facilitating their technical improvement and by respecting their specific function, so that their mission of guarding the sovereignty and territorial integrity of the country should be more effective."

Point two: agreement that the Armed Forces have to integrate themselves into the *direction* of key aspects of the national economy. This goes against classic oligarchic thought that they are organs of repression without a voice or vote. Allende promised them a voice and vote. His words were as follows: "I believe that a more modern concept of national security and of Chile's needs makes the integration and contribution of the Armed Forces advisable in some basic aspects of our development, without implying deviation from their professional function or distraction from their essential role in the defense of the sovereignty."

Point three: agreement that no politician, except for Allende, could interfere in the appointment of the high command. Allende put it this way: "I must express that I am an uncompromising defender of the prerogatives of the head of state. As Commander-in-Chief, I state that not even the Popular Unity will have the right of intervening in the appointment of the high command, because this is an exclusive attribute of the President of the Republic, and I will be a zealous guardian of my constitutional powers."

While Allende expressed ideas closely related to those of the majority within the Armed Forces, the oligarchs continued conspiring. They took advantage, of course, of one fact: within the military, as a reflection of class struggle, there was no unitary and tranquil attitude. There were minority sectors, frankly gorillas[1] (and there still are), a large undecided majority, and a majority of the high command in favor of the "modern line" of the armies in Latin America, where sparks of restricted nationalism (Peru) are blended with support for "structural" reforms in order to consolidate a Western regime or, in the military's own words, "to consolidate formal democracy and the solidarity of the Western bloc." This idea has much to do with the new global policy of Yankee imperialism with regard to the forms of domination in Latin America. The similarity to Chilean military thought is not strange. Since the 1950s the Chilean Armed Forces have depended in part upon Yankee material and have been totally dependent for training on adviser teams from the United States (military missions, special schools in Panama and the United States, and economic, social and military study materials).

During October 1970 contradictions and indecision were strong within the Armed Forces. Oligarchs and imperialist sectors counted on ex-General Viaux to form "a united front within the Army" against the Popular Unity. But they miscalculated. For reasons that someday

---

[1] "Gorilla" is the term applied in Latin America to military officers predisposed to establish military dictatorships of a right-wing nature.

will become known, they assassinated General Schneider.[2] This provoked unity of all the Armed Forces around the military "reformists." Even the Navy, traditionally gorilla mainly because of its British structure, closed ranks around the reformist leaders of the Army (Pablo Schaffhauser, Augusto Pinochet and Orlando Urbina). Thus, on the day of Schneider's assassination, Allende, for the first time since September 4, could be sure that he would become the President of Chile.

Entering the Government

The presence of the Armed Forces in the present government, no longer as "support" but as principal actors, is not an accident. It has a very clear historical development. Of course, within the framework of these articles, this historical development cannot be analyzed extensively, but a schema can be made.

At the end of the nineteenth century, Chile was governed by an oligarchy based on mining, trade, and large landed estates (*latifundia*) closely linked with British imperialism. In 1891, when British imperialism wanted to seize all Chilean saltpeter[3] against (then President) Balmaceda, the Navy assumed the pro-British leadership and overthrew Balmaceda. Thus, the domination of these sectors of the oligarchy was consolidated.

But at the beginning of the First World War, the crisis of saltpeter occurred. Forced by economic realities, the country started a stage of industrialization in order to manufacture substitutes for some previously imported products. Together with industrialization, the large, struggling proletarian masses appeared, to stagger the dominant class. The industrial bourgeoisie also appeared. The

[2] General Schneider, a constitutionalist, was then Commander of the Armed Forces.

[3] Saltpeter was mined from Chile's vast natural nitrate deposits and was then much more important as an export than copper.

military *coup* of 1924 took place, followed by other *coups* until 1932.

What was then the position of the Armed Forces? In the face of a stubborn oligarchy that no longer corresponded to the class reality in the country and that clung to its former privileges, the Armed Forces welcomed "social reforms" and "repression." They believed it was necessary to reform so that nothing should change, to save the ship, and to repress the working classes in order to prevent their organization.

The industrial bourgeoisie joined the dominant sectors of decadent landowners and the mining and trade oligarchy then supported by the Yankee imperialism that was beginning to take control of the economic structure (mining and commercial).

During the time of the Popular Front, in 1938, the Armed Forces preserved their class origin, located more and more in small-, middle-, and lower-bourgeois professionals, and did not oppose reformism or the consolidation of the state as the main industrializing agent. The oligarchy, of course, went on conspiring but did not find any support among the military's majority. The definitive decline of the class of large landowners began (a decline that will culminate this year, 1971), the industrial bourgeoisie grew, and the strength of the bureaucratic bourgeoisie was born under the shadow of the development of the state. They governed in collusion with oligarchic financial and commercial sectors, while imperialism's control, aided by the Second World War, became more general and solid. At the same time, contradictions between industrial bourgeois sectors and imperialist consortiums acting in Chile began to increase.

The state served these dominant classes and Yankee imperialism.

During this period, the state felt capable of repressing struggles of the urban and rural proletariat, cornering the Armed Forces in a useless role of internal decoration and consolidating the Carabineer Corps[4] as the real armed force of repression against the people. The Armed Forces, as an institution, felt themselves disintegrating and believed that they could recover their real role of upholding the bourgeois state only if they could get parity treatment with the politicians, who were seen as ineffective in controlling the surge of popular mobilization. . . .

In 1964, Frei's reformism appeared as the hope of saving the system for the dominant sectors. Frei transformed his government so that it was more of a lackey of the Americans than any other in our history. He opened the doors of Chilean industry to imperialism, he was unable to do away with the large-landed-estate system, and he continued the same policy of contempt toward the Armed Forces as his predecessors.

The crisis became violent in October 1969 with the *"tacnazo"* (General Viaux's abortive revolt). With the apparent purpose of demanding better arms and higher wages, the Armed Forces were claiming their true role within the bourgeoisie as coleaders of the reform process Chile required in order to continue as a bourgeois state: liquidation of the *latifundia,* corralling the financial oligarchy and part of the industrial and commercial bourgeoisie, and "rationalization" of imperialist domination by taking foreign capital out of conflictive areas such as copper, iron, and saltpeter and giving foreigners access to the dynamic sector of industry by means of mixed companies. All this occurred with greater "planning" on the part of the state ruled by a sector of the bourgeoisie.

The presidential election crisis came and, once more, the Armed Forces saved the system, although this time without resorting to overt repression. The Armed Forces

---

[4] The *Carabineros* are a national police force organized in a military fashion.

took over the leadership of the disconcerted bourgeoisie, which was disorganized in its historical incapacity in colonized countries to respond to the pressures of its own development and contradictions with imperialism. They confronted sectors of the oligarchy that had to be injured in order to settle with populist reformism, and they supported Allende, generally submitting to his programs on the one hand and establishing very definite limits of compliance with him on the other.

The institutional crisis was resolved for them (internal contradictions continuing, of course). They became the center of national political stability and retained the task of "supervising" reformism and the presence of imperialism in Chile, now somewhat distorted but still dominant in the total picture. This authority remains unchallenged, since the other world force of domination, Russian social imperialism, is in no position to dispute the supremacy of the United States in Latin America.

Allende's Steps

In the seven months of the present government, involvement of the Armed Forces in the economic and social life of our country has accelerated considerably. High-command members in active service have been appointed within the Development Corporation, the Steel Company of the Pacific, and the El Salvador and El Teniente mines. There have been agreements with the universities for postgraduate courses only for military personnel in such subjects as engineering, sociology, technology, and economics. Moreover, there are special scholarships in the Universidad Técnica del Estado for the sons of military men.

Allende has confessed in speeches that he holds meetings with the high command to deal with "the future of national institutions." He has met with them at least fourteen times during the seven months of his government, always to discuss highly important matters about the mass struggle.

The meeting with the generals that took place on February 10, 1971, is widely known. Two days later, the Minister of the Interior spoke on nationwide radio and television to make two important statements. The first was that "the only" bodies in charge of internal order were "the Armed Forces and the Carabineer Corps." This clearly indicated the realization of an old aspiration of the military: that the Carabineers remain in a secondary place, as an integrated part of the state system in which only the Armed Forces are the "spinal column." The second statement was that a bill would be sent to Congress to declare illegal the occupation of farms, precisely at a moment when the peasant struggle in Chile, centered in Malleco, Cautín, and Valdivia, was becoming stronger, employing its best fighting weapon, the occupation of lands.

On February 23, the Supreme Council for National Security held a meeting to give the General Staff for National Defense and the Carabineer Corps control of a projected plan for economic and social development in the frontier zones in the provinces of Malleco, Cautín, and Valdivia.

Finally, on the night of February 25, departing from Valparaíso, President Allende dined not with the regional heads of the Popular Unity parties, but with the regional heads of the three branches of the Armed Forces and the Carabineers.

The question is: where does this "integration" of the Armed Forces into the Popular Unity program lead, especially if the Armed Forces continue to have close ties to Yankee imperialism?

When I say "close ties" to Yankee imperialism, I do not refer only to the training, warfare technology, and war material for which the Chilean military depends upon the United States. I refer to something more than this: to the fact that our Armed Forces, in the confrontation between the socialist and capitalist worlds, are on the side of the capitalists; to the fact that, between the dictatorship of the proletariat and that of the bourgeoisie, they are on the side of the latter; to the fact that their reformist and nationalist character is framed within the frontiers of the capitalist world. In essence, no matter how many reforms they may support and no matter how many contradictions they may have with imperialism, their reformism is bourgeois and their relations with imperialism will be of a bourgeois nature, as is the case today in Peru.

In short, at the present moment in Chile, the Armed Forces are the referee (gun in hand) that imposes the rules of the reformist game embodied by the Popular Unity. When that referee judges that the rules of the game have been infringed, he will act so that they will be "respected."

In the face of this armed bourgeois referee, the proletariat has no other alternative than to oppose its own armed force, in order to be able to impose the rules of the proletarian game. This alternative, of course, is contemplated by bourgeois reformism, which tries by all means to curb proletarian organization. Allende says repeatedly, "The workers will achieve the revolution producing, . . . and the only armed organizations in our country will be the Army, the Navy, the Air Force, and the Carabineers."

In a word: work for the exploited, guns for the guardians of the bourgeoisie and the interests of imperialism.

This is the essence of the pact made between the civil government and the Chilean Armed Forces after September 4, 1970.

All this sometimes becomes dramatically evident when emotion pervades President Allende's words. For instance, on April 14, 1971, when decorating the new generals of the Chilean Armed Forces, Allende finished his brief address by saying, "You who attain the high command have, then, rights and duties and responsibilities, and I surrender to your responsibility, to your rights and your duties, the reiterated conviction of the people of Chile that the Armed Forces will continue being the root of Chile's history, ennobled in war and peace, and that you will continue to be those who, knowing the value of material force, are aware of spiritual force when it is expressed in the ballot boxes and written down in the Constitution of the homeland."

These words constitute a dramatic call to the bourgeois Armed Forces to allow Allende to govern "within the framework of the Constitution" and let him prove, at the same time, that he is a "new Marxist," capable of preventing the struggle of the people from definitively destroying imperialism, the financial oligarchy and monopolists and all their lackeys, thus smashing the bureaucratic-military apparatus of the bourgeois state.

It should not be forgotten that, from January 14 until May 25, 1971, the high command of the Army, Navy, and Air Force have been visited by an admiral and a vice-admiral from the U. S. Navy, a general from the Army, and another from the Air Force of the United States, all selected from the General Staff of the imperialist army responsible for the "Southern Command" (Latin America).

Neither should it be forgotten that *all* agreements on Chilean military training in American bases or American territory still function . . . and will continue to function. Finally, one must bear in mind as well that Yankee military supplies for the Chilean Air Force and Navy continue as before. . . .

This situation has pushed President Allende to state,

each time with greater clarity, what role the Armed Forces must play in his government.

On March 19, Allende stated, "What I have said is that the professional Armed Forces, who have had technical capacity and moral reliability throughout our history, must play an important role in all processes of economic development in Chile. They must be linked to the country's progress."

On May 1, before the workers at Plaza Bulnes in Santiago, Allende advanced one step further and said, "Only a disciplined, organized, and conscious people, together with the loyalty of the Armed Forces and the Carabineers, will be the best defense of the government of the Popular Unity and the future of the homeland."

Three weeks later, Allende's concept of the Armed Forces had undergone a remarkable process of refinement. On May 25, before foreign correspondents, he said, ". . . the Chilean Armed Forces are the guarantee of this process, . . . and what we also need is that these Armed Forces have, within reasonable limitations, the technical elements that guarantee their efficiency. . . ." He continued, "And if there is something that shows this government's attitude, it is precisely to incorporate the Armed Forces more and more into the process of economic development, with which we accord to them a wider perspective while strengthening them. The Armed Forces must know what should or should not happen in copper, iron, and saltpeter. . . . I have said, in the end, what are the Armed Forces? They are the people in uniform. . . ."

Speaking to the peasants of the town of Linares on May 28, the President said, "I have pointed out that this process of change is possible, because the Armed Forces and the Carabineers have a professional conscience. They respect the laws and the Constitution, which is not the case in the majority of Latin American countries, and this constitutes an exception in this and even in other continents."

In sum, and in the words of the leading sectors of the government coalition, the arbiter of the situation is the Armed Forces.

CHAPTER 16

Education

For several years prior to the election of President Allende, Chilean universities had been undergoing a profound, critical self-examination. Important reforms in higher education were well underway before antagonistic forces within universities, particularly the University of Chile, were again propelled into severe conflict. The sometimes violent confrontations in the University of Chile during 1971 were not based upon questions of whether or not the university should change—all parties agree that further reforms have to be imposed. The conflict has rather to do with what kind of changes the university should undergo. Immediately at issue are questions of who shall have power within the university and the role of the university in the socialist transformation of Chile. The candidate of the Right and the Christian Democrats won the 1972 elections for Rector of the University of Chile. "Three Patterns for University Reform" serves to clarify these fundamental issues.

THREE PATTERNS FOR UNIVERSITY REFORM*

TOMÁS AMADEO VASCONI

The notes and observations offered here are the result of several preoccupations which came about as a consequence of the events at the University of Chile after

* From *Panorama Económica* No. 243, August 1969. Tomás Avadeo Vasconi is an Argentine sociologist of many years' residence in Chile. He is presently with the United Nations' Economic Commission for Latin America.

the Memorandum of Agreement was signed (June 12, 1968) between the groups in conflict. The agreement "institutionalized" the conflict—violent up to then—by giving birth to a process that afterward developed into the constitution of reform committees and later into the Convention and Referendum. Through these committees, assemblies, etc. the demands of the reformist groups started to take shape.

We did not believe at that time—nor do we believe now—that consequences following from the decisions taken were very clear to those who acted in this process. Therefore, with a more settled vision due to the observation and study of the events that followed the signing of the memorandum, we are now publishing this article to establish the basis for a model of analysis that permits an evaluation of the final consequences of the process. Obviously we do not pretend to build a model in the strictly technical sense of the expression, but to formulate the basic propositions for its construction. . . .

During the process of conflict and in its subsequent "institutionalization," we found it possible to identify three different concepts whose content we would like to explain here: the "modernizing," the "democratizing," and the "revolutionary" concepts. . . .[1]

1. The Modernizing Concept

At this opportunity we cannot analyze the particular effects caused by industrialization—or more generically by "modernization"—in our countries; these, however, have already become evident for those who wish to see them, through the works of many authors. We center

[1] Omitted at this point in the translation is a critical analysis of the work of Clark Kerr *et al.*, *Industrialism and Industrial Man*, particularly as it relates to the "modernizing" concept of university reform.

our analysis on one specific problem: modernization of the university.

The "modernizing" concept particularly stresses "rationalization," "depoliticization," and "technification," and is primarily preoccupied with the attainment of greater institutional efficiency within the university.

Modernization appears as a process destined to attain greater efficiency in the university on one hand and, on the other hand, a closer correspondence between the university and the structures and organization supposed to be typical of the "modern" society.

In the "internal" functioning of the institution, the aspects that fit into modernizing considerations are several: renovation of teaching methods, making the content of instruction consonant with the development of science at an international level, the departmentalization of faculties, the optimum utilization of material and human resources, etc. Already at this level, in the concrete historical context of our societies, the first contradictory aspects between the "modernization" and "democratization" concepts appear. In order to attain high levels of efficiency and return, a rigorous selection of students is defended. This pattern will inevitably favor the dominant groups by limiting the number of students for the purpose of improving teaching, requiring full-time studies, etc. Under the present circumstances, such procedures deny every possible process of democratization of the university.

Even more fundamental is the thesis that a closer correspondence is needed between the university and the requirements of a modern society. . . . The university as an institution of "modern society" tends to satisfy its requirements—for example, preparing "human resources" demanded by the apparatus of production—by incorporating all its material and human resources to the "modern center or pole." By doing so, it becomes a subsidiary of its development and moves apart from the marginal sector (which comprises the greatest part of the society). Thus interpreted, the modernizing process—far from converting the university into a creative center that frees forces for effective social change—submits the destiny of the institution to the development of the "giant modern enterprise" and its requirements.

Moreover, to the degree to which the "modern pole" is increasingly dependent upon the dominant centers of world capitalism and subsidiary to its organization, development, technology, etc., the modernization process of the university implies also a process of growing dependence. Thus, the university becomes progressively converted into an organization for the reproduction and transmission of knowledge, techniques, etc., developed in the dominant international centers, which produce that knowledge in a defined historical social situation quite different from the one that can be considered typical of underdeveloped and dependent societies. The "modernizing" concept implies that the university constitutes a supranational institution. Thus, national universities become a steppingstone (naturally one of the lowest steps) on a professional, scientific, and cultural hierarchy, the highest point of which is represented by the universities and scientific centers of "international prestige."

2. The Democratizing Concept

The "democratizing" concept has as its ideological core the extension of participation within the university. This participation should be understood as very broad. It not only facilitates access to higher education for all social groups, but also brings the benefits of university activity to all sectors of the population.

The democratizing concept assumes university reform to be a political process. Therefore, seizure of power in the university appears at the center of its program. The groups that consider themselves genuine reformists, however (in the sense of directing reform as a process of substantive democratization) do not actually succeed in controlling the decision-making centers of the university. They barely escape into a process that appears more like "modernization" than reform.

Together with this seizure of power in which the students, as the most dynamic element of the community, must play the important role, democratization requires the conquest of effective autonomy within the university (although this aspect, as we shall see, is even more important in the "revolutionary concept").

In order to make this democratizing concept more precise, we distinguish three fundamental dimensions: a) the process of democratization "from within", b) the process of democratization "to the outside," and c) the process of democratization "from the outside."

A. The Process of Democratization from Within.

Within this process it is possible to distinguish several main aspects.

a) *Participation in power by different segments of the university community:* This participation must be effective to generate authority and to control decisions by the different sectors (professors, students, etc.) and by the various "strata" existing within them (the different ranks of professors, assistants, etc.). Student participation must be sufficiently broad to assure its "weight" in relation to the importance of this sector and give a dynamic, renovative character to the university.

b) *Periodic competitions to obtain teaching positions:* This avoids the generation of a university "oligarchy" implied by life tenure.

c) *Reform of the content of study programs:* This aspect is not always clearly defined in the democratizing concept. Sometimes democratization and the reduction of educational standards are identified (through a reduction of requirements, etc.) so that more people, it is supposed, can obtain a college degree (this approach appears more frequently among ideologists of populist style). Substantive democratization requires that the university find mechanisms to effectively incorporate the different social groups. This implies the need to structure varied organisms and opportunities. At the same time, the democratizing reformists have a commitment to development and to society to prepare people at the most advanced scientific and technical level.

d) *Research:* This decisive aspect is one in which "substantive democratization" tries to impose its criteria. The pretended "value neutrality" and "subjectivism" sustained by liberal ideology that leaves the selection of subjects and methods of research to the individual researcher's judgment and ideology are rejected. This research appears in the "democratizing conception" as *committed research* which tends to explain and clarify the mechanisms of underdevelopment and to scientifically point out the means of confronting it.

e) *Scheduling and provisions regarding work, class attendance, seminars, etc.:* The "democratizing concept" carefully points out that these provisions should not restrict those students who have to work in order to pay their tuition, etc. Another argument relates to the possibility of freedom in attending classes and to students' rejection of courses by certain professors.

B. The Process of Democratization to the Outside.

This dimension of the general process of democratization comprises a wide range of actions for the extension of university services to groups that are now excluded. Thus, democratization "to the outside" relates to access to the university and to the responsibility of the university to the whole society. There are a number of aspects.

a) *Free education:* This appears as a fundamental requisite. However, it is pointed out that, given the characteristics of the structure of these societies, this principle cannot be completely applied. In a stratified society, if free education is established at the university level unaccompanied by other social policies that compensate for the consequences, a regressive effect will take place. The groups that already had access to that level of education will be favored, and other groups will still not have access to free education. It is thus said that in the present social and economic conditions, it might be better to replace the general and simple concept of a free university with two standards of judgment. First, those who can, must pay for their higher education in proportion to their ability to do so. Second, a meaningful proportion of the university budget must be dedicated to the provision of full scholarships for those who otherwise could not go on with their studies.

b) *Revision of the system of selection and admittance:* This is to insure that the systems that will be adopted do not explicitly or implicitly discriminate among the candidates according to their economic and social positions.

c) *Creation of intermediate degrees:* This implies modification of the university structure itself, because these intermediate degrees must leave open the possibility that studies can be continued at a higher level. Professional careers could be set up that may comprise, through the years, alternate periods of study and professional work. This would naturally require not only reforms in university studies, but new provisions for professional practice.

d) *The creation of preuniversity and extra-university bodies:* These should depend upon the university. The creation of schools at an intermediate level (technical schools, etc.) must also respond to the general democratization process. Just as with the "intermediate degrees," they must not form closed entities, but the education given in them must be open to continuation at a higher level. These same objectives must dominate the regional policy of the University of Chile. Regional units must not go on being only ways of extending lower-level university programs. . . .

e) *Programs of university extension:* These programs include the diffusion of knowledge, and even art exhibits, which are generated and developed within the university in order to bring them closer to wider sectors of the population as well as activities . . . that allow access to the university by the new groups. . . .

C. The Democratization Process from the Outside.

Access to the university is conditioned by the degree of democratization of society. Although it is possible to take actions from the university that lead to increased access, many other changes will have to take place from society *toward* the university for "substantive democratization" actually to work. Immediately linked to university democratization would be a reform of the entire educational system at all levels. A process of democratization that makes possible the access and permanence of students until the end of their studies would have to be experienced at all levels prior to college. In this respect it is necessary to remember that in Chile during 1960–65, of each one hundred children enrolled in the first grade, sixty-one dropped out before completing the sixth grade. In the secondary level this attrition reached 74.1 per cent. It must be pointed out that all studies show an essential incidence of extraschool factors in attrition.

This last aspect constitutes the major limitation of the "democratizing concept."

D. Some Observations.

The democratizing position, except in its first expression as democratization from within, cannot be considered totally feasible except under the assumption of a progressive democratization of society. Only this will guarantee the possibility of the other two dimensions, democratization "to the outside" and democratization "from the outside." The historical experience of Latin American countries does not seem to correspond to such a process, but rather to a progressive concentration of income and power around the modernizing sector. Thus, a project of democratization appears insufficient when proceeding exclusively from the university. Going considerably further than this reform program is the "revolutionary concept" advocated by left-wing groups.

3. The Revolutionary Concept

The revolutionary idea seems to take into account what has been pointed out in the previous paragraph and assumes the perspective of the global society. It does not consider society in a general and abstract sense, but addresses itself to the specific historic situation of a country that is underdeveloped and dependent. Under these circumstances, to consider the main responsibility of the university that of preparing capable personnel ("human resources") for the efficient working of the system is viewed as reactionary.

Development of society is not perceived as a linear process which can be achieved through evolutionary progress or through "growth" within the present structure. Development implies a radical break from the prevailing structure (in this, the "revolutionary" is opposed to the "democratizing" concept). The reformed or "critical" university cannot be conceived as an institution responding efficiently to the requirements of the "establishment," but must place the entire institutional apparatus at the service of criticism of the status quo. The principal battle of the students—who form the most fundamental element of the process—must be fought in the name of the "great absentees," the exploited and pauperized people. The university constitutes a fundamental strategic and tactical center for the revolution. The university, today at the service of the dominant class, the national bourgeoisie, and of foreign capital, will have to abandon its function as part of the system (which means to stop producing ideologists, professionals, technicians, etc. who serve to consolidate the system) and pass on to the service of "workers and peasants." This is why the main subjects of this concept are the seizure of power within the university in order to place it in the struggle for social transformation, and the achievement of the greatest possible autonomy so that the institution may completely fulfill its critical and revolutionary role.

With regard to the seizure of power, those who hold the "revolutionary" position are clearly different from those who hold the "democratizing" positions in admitting that, because the university is part of the superstructure of bourgeois society, it will not be possible to institute in it a "revolutionary power." Moreover, "access to power" does not mean a compromise or coparticipation in the responsibilities of directing the institution, but a way to achieve a higher level of conflict.

Some subjects that are essential in the "modernizing" concept and have an important role in the "democratizing" concept are secondary in the "revolutionary" view. The revolutionaries do not attach great importance to measures related to administrative actions or the use of material and human resources, etc. When some of these aspects appear, such as the question of the organization of studies, they are always subordinated to the central question of revolution ("teaching must fulfill a consciousness-raising and politicizing role"; "research must be applied to the development of a revolutionary theory that allows the vanguard to accelerate the process of revolution"). . . .

Given the characteristics of this concept—which no longer applies exclusively to the university—struggle within the university must be intimately linked to the revolutionary struggle in society.

The most difficult aspect to define is the relationship that will be established between action within the university and the revolutionary process in society. An unequivocal concept about this aspect has not been formulated. This is why the "revolutionary process," though united in its essentials, is fragmented in terms of strategy and tactics (university as a "focus," only as "a moment of the process," etc.). Nevertheless, it seems that the main university function—if not in detail, at least in the general approach—consists of the formation, theoretically and ideologically, of cadres for the revolution.

PART VI

THE OPPOSITION

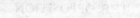

CHAPTER 17

The Reaction

By November 1971 the opposition forces within Chile were very much on the offensive against the Popular Unity government. During Fidel Castro's three-week stay in Chile, there were large demonstrations of middle- and upper-class women, "the March of the Empty Pots," protesting shortages of consumer goods and Fidel's presence, street fighting between Right and Left militants, bombings of offices of Popular Unity organizations, and martial law in Santiago. By January 1972 the government had suffered political reverses at the hands of the opposition in Congress and the voters in Congressional by-elections.

Fidel's final remarks in Chile, as usual with Fidel's didactic oratory, were pointed, lucid, and brilliant. He directed himself mainly to the questions of reaction, violence, counterrevolution, and revolution.

FIDEL CASTRO ON CHILEAN FASCISM AND REVOLUTION*

The President's words have made such an impact on us that we have to calm ourselves a bit. The President has said some very moving and courageous things, analyzing a number of current affairs. But in my case, although I have been a part of some of these events, I am a

---

* Fidel's farewell speech was delivered at the National Stadium in Santiago, December 2, 1971. The translation is by the Cuban Government.

visitor, and I must not concern myself with such events. We must and can speak of other things that are common to the interests of all our peoples. We must and can concern ourselves with other questions that are common to all revolutionary processes. . . .

We Have Visited Chile as Revolutionaries, as Friends, as Supporters of This Process and of This Country

We are interested, above all, in the human landscape, in the people, in you Chileans.

We have dedicated our lives to the human question, the social question, the revolutionary question. The thing that most stirs our interest is the struggle of the peoples and of mankind, the historic march of humanity, advancing from the man who lived in primitive hordes to the man of today. The thing that interests us the most is the living spectacle of a process in its critical moments.

We haven't come to Chile as tourists. We have visited Chile as revolutionaries, as friends, as supporters of this process and of this country. We would like to say in all frankness that we did come to learn.

But, let no one think that the libelers and seditious proponents of reactionary political theories were right when they said how fine it was that we had come to learn about elections, parliament, certain kinds of freedom of the press and the like. That's all very interesting, but we've already learned more than enough about it. We've learned a great deal during the past 50 years about those bourgeois, capitalist liberties; and we know only too well about their institutions. Now, we don't say they aren't good. Greek democracy was good, too, in its time. In its time the Roman republic, with its millions of slaves, its gladiator circuses and its Christians devoured by lions, also signified an extraordinary advance of human society. The medieval period was also considered an advance over primitive slavery, despite feudal servitude. The historic and famous French Revolution also signified an advance over medieval society and the absolute monarchs who enjoyed prestige in their times— and were also considered a step forward in the march of human progress. And there were even some so-called "illustrious despots."

But whoever claims that any society or social system and the superstructure that it represents are eternal is mistaken, because history has proved otherwise. One social form succeeds another—and is, in turn, succeeded by yet another, and so on, each new social form being superior to the old.

Even the bourgeoisie, in its epoch—before there was any such thing as a proletariat—was revolutionary, a revolutionary class, and led the people in struggle for a new social form, led the peasants who were serfs of the feudal lords, and led the artisans. And human society continued its march.

To claim that the form which emerged two centuries ago is eternal, to claim that it is the highest expression of human advancement, to claim that humanity's progress culminated with it, is simply ridiculous, from any historical or scientific point of view.

Moreover, all decadent social systems and societies have defended themselves when threatened with extinction. They have defended themselves with tremendous violence throughout history.

Truth, Reason and Ideas Constitute the Revolutionary's Arsenal

No social system resigns itself to disappearing from the face of the earth of its own free will. No social system resigns itself to revolution. As we said before, all those systems were once good. It is only today that they are condemned by history as decadent, as anachronistic. And anachronisms hang on just as long as they can. Anachronisms exist as long as the peoples lack the force to do away with them.

In our country, which has known the various forms of the state of exploitation, those instruments that served the exploiters to repress the exploited—their institutions— have been changed.

Very profound changes have taken place in our country! Very profound! It is a difficult thing to understand from a distance. It is very difficult to understand, especially through the prism of lies and calumnies, in which the reactionaries have specialized throughout their history. There is a difference between the revolutionary and the reactionary. The difference is that the revolutionary lives by inner convictions, by deep motivations. And the lie is a violation of character, the lie is a violation of man's innermost feelings. The lie is the weapon of those in the wrong. The lie is the weapon of those without argument. The lie is the weapon of those who disparage others and, above all, of those who disparage the people.

Truth, reason, ideas, thought, awareness and culture constitute the revolutionary's arsenal and the weapon of the contemporary revolutionary is the correct interpretation of the scientific laws that govern the march of human society.

We Have Come to See Something Extraordinary: A Unique Process Is Taking Place in Chile

We have come to learn about a living process. We have come to learn how the laws of human society operate. We have come to see something extraordinary— something extraordinary. A unique process is taking place in Chile. Something more than unique: unusual! unusual! It is the process of a change. It is a revolutionary process in which revolutionaries are trying to carry out changes peacefully. A unique process, practically the first in humanity's history—we won't even say in the history of contemporary societies. It is unique in the history of contemporary societies. It is unique in the history of humanity, trying to carry out a revolutionary process by legal and constitutional methods, using the very laws established by the society or by the reactionary system, the very mechanism, the very forms that the exploiters created to maintain their class domination.

And what has our attitude been? We, the revolutionaries who did nothing unique, nothing unusual. . . . The Cuban revolutionaries at least have the merit of having had the first Socialist Revolution in Latin America. But we don't have the merit of having made it in an unusual and unique form. But what has our attitude been? That of solidarity with this process. That of solidarity with the men who choose this road. Our understanding, our moral support, our curiosity, our interest.

Because, as we have said on other occasions, the revolutionaries are not the inventors of violence. It was the class society throughout history that created, developed and imposed its system, always through repression and violence. In every epoch, the inventors of violence have been the reactionaries.

And we observe, and the world observes with enormous interest, how this Chilean process is developing in today's world circumstances, and even within the present correlation of world forces.

For us, then, this constitutes an extraordinary event. We have been asked on several occasions—in an academic way—if we consider that a revolutionary process is taking place here. And we have said without the slightest hesitation: Yes! But when a revolutionary process is begun, or when the moment arrives in a country when what can be called a revolutionary crisis occurs, then the struggles and the battles become tremendously acute. The laws of history are in full force.

Anyone who has lived in this country three weeks,

anyone who has seen and analyzed the factors, the first measures taken by the People's Unity government— measures that hit strongly at powerful imperialist interests, measures that culminated in the recuperation of the basic wealth of the nation, measures characterized by the advancement of social sectors, measures characterized by the application of the law of agrarian reform— these measures, it can be said, have proven the great historic fact that a process of change generates a dynamism of struggle. The measures already carried out and which constitute the beginning of a process, have released social dynamics, the class struggle; have released the ire and resistance—as is true in all social processes of change —of the exploiters, the reactionaries.

Very well: the question quite obviously suggested—to a visitor observing this process—is whether or not the historic law of resistance and violence by the exploiters will be fulfilled. Because we have said that there is no case in history in which the reactionaries, the exploiters, the privileged members of a social system, resign themselves to change; resign themselves peacefully to changes.

Therefore, this is, in our opinion, a matter of vital importance, an aspect which has aroused our interest and which has taught us a great deal in the past few days. Yes, gentlemen—especially those who didn't want me to come here to learn—I have learned a great deal. I have learned how the social laws operate, how the revolutionary process operates, how each sector reacts and how the various forces struggle. We have gone through these experiences. And we've felt it in our own skin. Not because our skin was bruised by a rock or a bullet. I haven't even seen a rock—not even at a distance. As a visitor, as a friend, as a man in solidarity with you, I have felt another type of aggression, more than well-known to me—an aggression in the form of insults and campaigns.

We do not ignore the fact that our visit might very well make a number of problems even worse than they are. In fact, it might even constitute a source of stimulus to those who wanted to create difficulties for the government of People's Unity. At a time when, according to what is being said, there are here hundreds and hundreds of newsmen from all over the world covering our visit; at a time when people all over the world—in Europe, Asia, Africa and Latin America—are talking about this visit, about this meeting between Chileans and Cubans, between two processes which had such different beginnings; at a time when the image of Chile is in everyone's mind, it is obvious that this visit might cause some irritation, some feeling of discomfort, some exasperation which, in turn, might lead to the worsening of certain attitudes.

Unquestionably, the man visiting this country was not Benito Mussolini. The man visiting this country was not Adolf Hitler. The man visiting was not a fascist, or an instrument of the Yankee monopolies. The man visiting this country was not a friend of the powerful and the privileged. The man visiting this country was a friend of the humble people, a friend of the workers, a friend of the farmers, a friend of the students, a friend of the peoples!

This is why, when, after having been invited by the President, we spoke with Chilean comrades and they asked us what we would like to see on our visit here, we said we wanted to see the mines, the saltpeter, the copper, the iron, the coal, the work centers, the agricultural centers, the universities, the mass organizations, the parties of the left, everything and everybody, that we wanted to talk with the revolutionaries and even with those who, though they could not be considered revolutionaries, were decent people. We couldn't think of a better way to spend our visiting time.

And this is the way our visit was organized.

Why did we want it this way? Because we know where we can find our friends, among which social class. We know that wherever the workers, the farmers, the people of humble origin are, there we find our friends.

And that is why we got the kind of reception we got everywhere—in every town, university and agricultural area—the extraordinary reception we got in every work center without exception. In every one of them!

The Desperation of the Exploiters Today Tends Toward the Most Brutal, Most Savage Forms of Violence and Reaction

And—I repeat—we have learned something else. We have witnessed the verification of another law of history: we have seen fascism in action. We have been able to verify a contemporary principle: the desperation of the reactionaries, the desperation of the exploiters today tends toward the most brutal, most savage forms of violence and reaction.

You are all familiar with the story of fascism in many countries; in those countries that are the cradle of that movement. You are all familiar with the story of how the privileged, the exploiters, destroy the institutions they created once these institutions—the very institutions they invented to maintain their class domination: the laws, the constitution, the parliament—are no longer of any use to them. When I say they invent a constitution, I mean a bourgeois constitution, because the socialist revolutions establish their own constitutions and forms of democracy.

What do the exploiters do when their own institutions no longer guarantee their domination? How do they react when the mechanisms historically depended upon to maintain their domination fail them? They simply go ahead and destroy them. Nothing is more anticonstitutional, more illegal, more antiparliamentarian, more repressive and more criminal than fascism.

Fascism, in its violence, wipes out everything. It attacks, closes and crushes the universities. It attacks the intellectuals, represses them and persecutes them. It attacks the political parties and trade unions. It attacks all mass organizations and cultural organizations.

And we have been able to verify, in this unique process, the manifestations of that law of history in which the reactionaries and the exploiters, in their desperation—and mainly supported from the outside—generate that political phenomenon, that reactionary current, fascism.

We say this in all sincerity: we have had the opportunity to see fascism in action.

Of course, it is said that nothing can teach the people as much as a revolutionary process does. Every revolutionary process teaches the people things which, otherwise, it would take dozens of years to learn.

This involves a question: who will learn more and sooner? Who will develop more of an awareness faster? The exploiters or the exploited? Who will learn the faster from the lessons of this process? The people or the enemies of the people?

(EXCLAMATIONS OF "THE PEOPLE!")

Are you absolutely sure—you, the protagonists in this drama being written by your country—are you completely sure that you have learned more than your exploiters have?

(EXCLAMATIONS OF "YES!")

Then, allow me to say that I don't agree—not with the President, but with the mass.

Tomorrow there'll be a headline in some paper somewhere in the world, reading, "Castro disagrees with the masses." We disagree on one aspect of the appreciation of the situation.

In this sort of dialogue on scientific and historic matters, we can say that we are not completely sure that in this unique process the people, the humble people—which constitute the majority of the population—have learned more rapidly than the reactionaries, than the old exploiters.

And there's something else: the social systems which the revolutions are transforming have had many years of experience to their credit—many, many years of culture, technology and tricks of every kind to use against revolutionary processes. They face the people—who lack all that experience, know-how and technology—armed with the experience and technology accumulated through the years.

The Reactionaries and the Oligarchs Here Are Much Better Prepared than They Were in Cuba

Is it because the people lack qualities? Is it because the people of Chile lack patriotic virtues, character, courage, intelligence and firmness? No! We have been deeply impressed when we spoke with the farmers here, after having chatted with them for half an hour, we'd ask them how far they'd gone in school, and they'd answer, "We don't even know how to read or write."

We were deeply impressed by the Chileans' fiery character. Everywhere we went, at receptions, during our tours, we witnessed this courage, this determination; we saw how the men swarmed over our cars. And, what's more, very often we saw how the women, holding children in their arms, stood firmly across the road, with an impressive determination and courage.

We have seen, in the Chilean people, qualities which our people lacked in the early days of the Revolution: a higher level of culture, a higher level of political culture. Listen to this carefully!—a higher level of political culture, a much higher level of political culture! This is because the situation in our country was different than here. For example, an electoral victory for the Marxist parties—that is, the Communist Party and the Socialist Party—and other organizations which supported those parties.

In regard to political culture, you have started from a higher level than ours. Moreover, you start from a patriotic tradition which dates back 150 years. You start from a much higher level of patriotic awareness. A higher awareness of the problems in your country.

The imperialists' ideology had made deep inroads in our country. Our country had been invaded by the imperialist culture, by the way of life and the the habits of that society so close to us: U.S. society.

Therefore, in that sense, we were much weaker than you. You can see that there is a whole series of aspects which reveal that your people started from a much higher level than we did. From the economic standpoint, Chile has more economic resources than Cuba. Chile has an incomparably higher economic development than Cuba, based on a natural resource which it now owns. In other words, Chile is now the owner of its copper, where 30,000 workers produce close to 1000 million dollars in foreign exchange. It produces oil: almost two million tons. It has hydroelectric power resources, iron, coal, a food industry much more highly developed than Cuba's, a textile industry. In other words, you start from a technological and industrial level much higher than the one that existed in Cuba.

Therefore, all the human conditions, all the social conditions that make for advance exist in this country.

However, you are faced with something we didn't have to face. In our country, the oligarchs, the landowners, the reactionaries, didn't have the experience that their colleagues here have. Over there, the landowners and the oligarchs weren't in the least concerned about social changes. They said, "The Americans"—they called everybody from the United States Americans—"will take care of that problem. There can't be any revolutions here!" And they went to sleep on their laurels.

This is not the case in Chile, though!

The reactionaries and the oligarchs here are much better prepared than they were in Cuba. They are much better organized and better armed to resist changes, from the ideological standpoint. They have all the weapons they need to wage a battle on every field in the face of the process' advance. A battle on the economic field, on the political field and on the field of the masses—I repeat— on the field of the masses!

Now, then, we have beaten them everywhere. We beat them, first, on the ideological field; second, on the field of the masses; and, third, on the field of armed battle.

In our opinion, the problem of violence in these processes—including the Cuban process—once the revolution is in power, does not depend on the revolutionaries. It would be absurd, incomprehensible and illogical for revolutionaries to engage in violence when they have an opportunity to advance, to create, to work, to march toward the future. Therefore, it isn't the revolutionaries who promote violence in these circumstances. And, in case you didn't know this, you'll find out through experience.

That's the experience we went through when the Cuban revolutionary movement won.

Today, there's one revolutionary force in Cuba; the revolutionary force of the people of Cuba.

I have no idea how many people are here now. You may know more or less how many. But I can tell you that it takes 10 minutes to get as many people together in Cuba. And we can get together 10 times as many in a couple of hours! And, yet, the population of our capital is two thirds the population of Santiago!

Our country has reached a high level of unity, a high

level of revolutionary awareness. A very sound, really sound form of patriotism has been created, which makes our country a bulwark of the revolution and one trench among the nations of America which the imperialists will never be able to destroy.

We were simply amazed when we heard the President say that a very important newspaper in Washington—or New York—has published statements by a high-ranking government official who said that "The days of the popular government in Chile are numbered."

I would like to point out—regardless of the rudeness and intromission, the unheard-of prediction, the offense and insolence—that it's been many a year since some crazy U.S. official had the idea of saying that the days of the Cuban Revolution were numbered.

It would be logical, in view of a statement like that, not only to get angry, to protest the insult to one's dignity, to protest against the offense, but also to ask what makes them believe such a thing and why they feel so confident about it. What kind of calculations did they make? What computers did they put into operation to figure this out? This doesn't mean that Yankee computers don't make mistakes. They do, and we know it by experience. We have good evidence that they do make mistakes. In the case of Girón, the Pentagon's computers, the CIA's computers, the U. S. Government's computers, everybody's computers were wrong—a million times wrong.

Nevertheless, one must ask what are the grounds for such optimism, for such an assurance, and where does the encouragement come from. And you are the only ones who can supply the answer.

Or maybe you'd be interested in hearing the opinion of a visitor who is not a tourist? Do I have your permission to express it? (EXCLAMATIONS OF "YES!")

All those in favor, raise their hands.

(ALL HANDS GO UP)

Well, in view of the permission granted me in this sort of plebiscite—to express my opinion in matters of concept, I say that such confidence is based on the weakness of the very revolutionary process, on weaknesses in the ideological battle, on weaknesses in the mass struggle, on weakness in the face of the enemy! And the enemy outside, which supports the enemy at home, tries to take advantage of the slightest breach, of the slightest weakness.

You're Going Through a Period When the Fascists Are Trying to Beat You to the Streets

You're going through a period which is very special, albeit not a new one, in the matter of class struggle. There are countless examples of this. You're going through that period in the process in which the fascists—to call them by their right name—are trying to beat you to the streets, are trying to beat you out of the middle strata of the population. There is a specific moment in every revolutionary process when fascists and revolutionaries engage in a struggle for the support of the middle strata.

The revolutionaries are honest. They don't go around telling lies. They don't go around sowing terror and anguish or cooking up terrible schemes.

The fascists. . . . Well, the fascists stop at nothing. They'll try to find the weakest spot. They'll invent the most incredible lies. They'll try to sow terror and unrest among the middle strata by telling the most incredible lies. Their objective is to win over the middle strata. Moreover, they'll appeal to the basest sensibilities. They will try to arouse feelings of chauvinism.

If we weren't sincere, if we didn't believe in the truth, we wouldn't dare say what we just said. It might even sound as if we were saying something that the enemy could use to its advantage, to gain ground. No! The only way in which the enemy can gain ground is by deceit, by confusion, by ignorance, by the lack of an awareness about the problems!

If you want my opinion, the success or the failure of this unusual process will depend on the ideological battle and the mass struggle. It will also depend on the revolutionaries' ability to grow in numbers, to unite and to win over the middle strata of the population. This is because in our countries—countries of relatively little development—these middle strata are quite large and are susceptible to lies and deceit. However, in the ideological struggle, nobody is ever won over except through the truth, sound arguments and by right. There is no question about that.

I hope you will win. We want you to win. And we believe that you will win!

There was something which made a deep impression on us today, and that was the words of the President, especially when he reaffirmed his will to defend the cause of the people and the will of the people. Most especially when he said a history-making thing: that he was the President by the will of the people and that he would fulfill his duty until his term was over or until his body was taken out of the Palace. Those of us who know him know very well that the President is not a man of words but a man of deeds. All of us who know his character know that this is the way he is.

We saw how the people reacted to the President's words. . . .

When the chiefs, the leaders, are ready to lay down their lives for a cause, the men and the women of the people, too, are ready to lay down their lives!

The people are the makers of history. The people write their own history. The masses make history. No reactionary, no imperialist enemy can crush the people! And our country's recent history proves it!

How did we manage to resist and why? Because of the

unity of our people, because of the strength that such a unity generates.

We said that it would take two hours for us to get together 10 times as many people as there are here now. And we also say that we can have 600,000 men in arms within 24 hours!

A close, unbreakable unity between the people and the armed forces has been created in our country. This is why we say that we have a strong defense. . . .

What is it that gives our people this deep motivation in their defense against danger from outside? The fact that, when it comes to defending our homeland, that homeland is not divided into millionaires and paupers, wealthy landowners with all the privileges in the world and miserable peasants without land or work, living a life of poverty. The fact that our homeland is not divided into oppressors and oppressed, exploiters and exploited, ladies overloaded with jewelry and girls forced to lead a life of prostitution. Our homeland is not divided into privileged and dispossessed. . . .

No people, no armed force has more power to fulfill the sacred duty of defending the homeland than that where exploiters and exploited are a thing of the past. In other words, where the exploitation of man by man has disappeared.

It is not by accident that history taught us a lesson not too long ago.

In World War II, which brought about the collapse of a number of powerful armies, what was it that the fascists did to attack Europe, to invade France, Belgium, Holland and practically all of the western world? They sowed their fifth column, promoted division and morally disarmed the people. When the fascist hordes attacked with their armor, when their motorized divisions broke through, they made their greatest profit from the demoralization of the people.

But, when, one day, two years later—in June 1941—

four million experienced veterans of that same fascist army launched a surprise invasion on the Soviet Union, what did they find? They found a stiff resistance, from the very first moment, from the very first day, from the very first hours. They found a people ready to fight and to die, a people who lost 18 million lives, who accumulated the most extraordinary experience of war in recent times. . . .

We mentioned the French Revolution. You will recall that, when the bourgeoisie was a revolutionary class and led the people, the same thing happened: the country, invaded by a great number of nations, not only resisted but went on to defeat the aggressors. This is because, in the revolutions, the people become united when the age-old injustices disappear, and forces come forth which nobody and nothing can defeat.

Here we have a perfect lesson taught by history. Never before, notwithstanding the proverbial patriotism of that nation, had they put up such a heroic, determined resistance. This was because the society of the feudal lords and serfs, of the czars with their absolute power, no longer existed. The socialist state resisted even more. And what's really extraordinary is that this socialist state, made up practically of farmers became the powerful industrial power it is today and the country which has helped such small nations as Vietnam and Cuba to resist such great dangers as the imperialist danger. . . .

We Feel That We Are the Sons of a Whole Community, a Part of a World Much Larger than Cuba and Chile and That Is Latin America

The day will come when we'll all have the same citizenship, without losing one iota of our love for our homeland, for that corner of our hemisphere where we were born; for our flags, which will be sister flags; for our anthems, which will be sister anthems; for our traditions, which will be sister traditions; and for our cultures, which will be sister cultures. The day will come when our peoples will have the power to take an honored place in the world, when the powerful will no longer be able to insult us, when the empire, proud and arrogant, will no longer be able to threaten us with tragedy and defeat or make any other kind of threat. . . . Because it is not the same thing to threaten a small country as it is to threaten a union of sister nations that may become a large and powerful community in the world of tomorrow.

The day will come when reactionary ideology will be defeated, when all narrow-minded nationalism, the ridiculous chauvinism which the reactionaries and the imperialists utilize to maintain a situation of division and hostility among our peoples—peoples who speak the same language, who can understand one another as we understand each other now—will be defeated. Reactionary ideology makes for division.

For America to be united and become Our America, the America Marti spoke of, it will be necessary to eradicate the very last vestige of those reactionaries who want the peoples to be weak so they can hold them in oppression and submitted to foreign monopolies. After all, all that is but the expression of a reactionary philosophy, the philosophy of exploitation and oppression. . . .

We have met, and talked at length, with the workers, the students, the farmers and the people in general in our visit to so many places here. We have talked with newspapermen and intellectual workers and with economists and technicians, as those in ECLA. We have met and talked with deputies, with the leaders of the parties of People's Unity, with the leaders of the organizations of the left; with everybody.

(VOICE FROM THE AUDIENCE: "AND WITH THE WOMEN")

I'm not forgetting them. We have met with the worker's representatives. We have met with the women of Chile. We have met with the Cardinal of Chile. We have met with more than 100 progressive priests who make up quite an impressive movement. We have talked with members of the Army, the Navy and the Carabineers Corps. And we were met with affection and respect everywhere. And we have tried our very best to answer all the questions put to us.

Of all these meetings, those which were the source of the greatest irritation and criticism were the meeting with the Cardinal, the meeting with the progressive priests and the meeting with the members of the Army, the Navy, the Air Force and Carabineers Corps.

It is necessary, by all means, that we explain the essence of these meetings and the reason why they came about.

We had many things to talk about with the Christian left and with the Chilean priests, many, many things based on principles rather than on opportunism, on profound reasons, on convictions rather than on profiting; based on the possibility—and the need—of bringing together in this Latin-American community the Marxist revolutionaries and the Christians, the Marxist revolutionaries and the Christian revolutionaries.

We examined the many points of coincidence that may exist between the purest precepts of Christianity and the objectives of Marxism. There are many who have tried to use religion to defend exploitation, poverty and privilege; to transform people's life in this world into a hell, forgetting that Christianity was the religion of the humble, of the slaves of Rome, of the tens of thousands who were devoured by the lions at the circus and who had very definite ideas about human solidarity or human love and condemned greed, gluttony and selfishness.

That was a religion which, 2000 years ago, called the merchants and the Pharisees by their name, which con-

demned the rich and said virtually that they would not
enter the kingdom of heaven. That was the religion which
multiplied the loaves and the fishes—precisely what the
revolutionary man of today intends to do with technology, with his hands, with the rational, planned development of the economy.

When you search for the similarities between the objectives of Marxism and the most beautiful precepts of
Christianity, you will find many points of coincidence.
You will see why a humble priest who knows what
hunger means—because he is in close contact with it—
who knows what sickness and death and human pain
mean. . . . Or why some of those priests who practice
their religion among the miners or among humble peasant families become identified with them and fight shoulder to shoulder with them. You will see why there are
unselfish people who devote their whole life to the care of
people afflicted with the worst diseases.

When you find all those points of coincidence you will
see how much a thing as a strategic alliance between
Marxist revolutionaries and Christian revolutionaries is
possible.

The imperialists—and, of course, all the reactionaries—
don't want such an alliance to take place.

We also spoke at length with the military. And when we
say military we mean the men from every branch of the
armed forces of all the institutes. However, these talks
came about spontaneously. They were not planned. They
were the result of the official attentions given us, of the
extraordinary attentions with which the President, the
ministers and other government authorities showered us.
At the airports, everywhere, the men in uniform and
their representatives were there, too. Thus, a series of
conversations took place, spontaneously, at the receptions
and during our meetings with the authorities. It was ob-

vious that the men in uniform of Chile and our delegation had many things to talk about.

We have lived through the experience of having to organize combat units in the face of a real, great danger. We have had to develop powerful armed forces, create schools, learn how to handle modern armament, learn new combat techniques. We have studied the experience, the reports and the documents of the last World War.

Undoubtedly, from the technical point of view, from the professional point of view, there were many things which could have been the subject of talks. Interest in Cuba's experience, Cuba's process, and the natural curiosity about historic happenings that all men possess. In addition, there were subjects of a human nature, the competence, efficiency, traditions and history of each country, the present and the future. What will the future of our peoples be in the face of the technological gaps which are growing, in the face of the developed nation and those which have been left behind? What are the prospects of weapons, of the new systems of armaments?

That is, from both the professional and human points of view, as things which are related to the future of our peoples, there were plenty of broad themes of this kind, on which our talks developed.

We had the chance to meet many very talented, upright, efficient men, many worthy men, thanks to those talks. We had the chance to speak on matters related to our traditions. We have learned—all of us—many things.

Was this, then, a sin? Was this a conspiracy? Was this a crime? Was there anything that anyone could feel offended by? And why, since we talked with the priests, the Cardinal and the ECLA technicians, shouldn't we talk with the men in uniform of Chile? Why did they fear these talks so much? Whom have we offended with them?

*Advance with the People! Advance with Ideas! Advance
Uniting Forces! Advance Gathering Forces!*

Revolutionaries are moved by profound motivations,
by great ideas. They do not promote fear. No! Even
though they are familiar with the fate of crushed revolutions. To cite two examples: the revolution of the Roman
slaves, led by Spartacus, which was crushed by the oligarchs, and cost the lives of tens of thousands of men who
were nailed to crosses alongside the roads leading to
Rome; and, the revolution of the Paris Communards,
which was drowned in blood.

We could cite some more recent examples. Every time
a revolution gets under way, fascism makes its appearance with all its tricks and schemes, all its methods of
struggle, all its hypocrisy and pharisaism, all its tactics of
promoting fear and making use of lies and the most
criminal methods. But there's nothing to fear! Fight back
with arguments! Fight back with reasoning! Fight back
with the truth! Fight back with conviction! Fight back
without fear of the consequences of defeat! And remember the price the peoples must pay for their defeat!
Fight for an ideal! Fight for a just cause! Fight back
knowing that you're right! Fight back knowing that the
inexorable laws of history are on your side! Fight back
knowing that the future is yours! Advance with the
masses! Advance with the people! Advance with ideas!
Advance uniting forces! Advance gathering forces!

We have met and spoken at length with many Chileans.
The only ones we haven't spoken with—and will never
speak with—are the exploiters, the reactionaries, the oligarchs and the fascists.

We have never talked with the fascists, and we never
will!

As far as the rest of the Chileans are concerned, it has
been a great honor for us to have met them, to get to

know them, to have talked with them and to have exchanged views with them.

Beloved Comrade Salvadore Allende, we will be leaving this beautiful country very soon. We will soon be saying goodbye to this hospitable, magnificent, warm-hearted people. We are taking back with us a memento of our visit: the indelible memory of our stay here, of all the affection, all the attention, all the honors that you heaped on our delegation as the representatives of the people of Cuba and the Cuban Revolution.

All we want to say to you, beloved President, and to all the Chileans, is that you can count on Cuba. You can count on her unselfish, unconditional solidarity; on what that flag and that homeland really mean. Not the homeland of the exploited, but the homeland of free men! A homeland to which the Revolution gave equality and justice! A homeland where man has regained his dignity!

To those who attempt to deny the legitimacy of the Revolution, let them observe its force and then try to explain how it is possible for us to resist the powerful Yankee empire in the cultural field, in the political field and in the military field, if we don't have a conscientious, united people—a people who knows what dignity and freedom mean.

There's our country, firm and staunch! There's our flag, a flag which represents the dignity of Cuba, which represents the nation in the broadest sense of the word, which represents patriotism in its most fraternal sense, as sons of Cuba and sons of America!

These two symbols that today wave together here, also represent the closeness of our peoples, of our ideas, of our cause and of our motives.

And, being that today is December 2, allow me to end the way we do in Cuba.

Patria o Muerte!

Venceremos!

CHAPTER 18

Christian Democracy

The Christian Democratic Party is a loosely organized political grouping, the largest in Chile, with considerable support in all sectors of Chilean society, but particularly in the middle strata. As such, it reflects diverse and contradictory political tendencies from left-of-center to right. During Eduardo Frei's tenure in office (1964–70), the Christian Democratic government pursued, on the whole, modestly reformist policies. The Agrarian Reform Law, the major accomplishment of the regime, was a model of reform for a non-revolutionary government and was pursued with considerable vigor (the Allende government uses the same law, but applies it even more energetically). For the rest, however, reform was pursued largely at the rhetorical level or was used as a political instrument to pacify discontent or to bring sectors of the population under the political control of the government and the Party. Violent repression of opposition and protest assumed even greater significance than under the previous, conservative government of Alessandri. The Frei regime was considered by U.S. officials as a model Alliance for Progress government and was liberally rewarded with aid and political backing. (Allende was presented with one of the highest per-capita foreign debts in the world, $3 billion, when he assumed office.) U.S. multinational investors also found Chile under the Christian Democrats a good place to do business—and the Popular Unity government is now engaged in a struggle with powerful economic centers for control of the Chilean economy.

The seriousness and success with which Allende and

the PU have pursued their program have thrown all opposition forces into political alignment. In effect, Chile has become politically polarized. Eduardo Frei, taking the main body of the Christian Democratic Party with him (losing the Christian Left to the PU), has moved over to join the intransigent Right.

In this chapter, the Movement of the Revolutionary Left (MIR) analyzes Frei in office and in opposition. In doing so, MIR comments at length on its vision of correct strategy in view of the polarized situation, attacking the Communist Party in the process and thereby provoking the CP into a denunciation of the MIR for political error and ultraleftism. A principal tactic of the Christian Democratic and National Party opposition is to force divisions on the Left.

THE MIR ANSWERS FREI*

SECRETARIAT OF THE REVOLUTIONARY LEFT MOVEMENT

After the assassination of Edmundo Pérez Zujovic,[1] a new political situation was created in Chile, intensifying the social and political conflicts that had been crystallizing since the Popular Unity came to power. The dominant classes and their parties, the National Party, the Radical Democracy, and the Christian Democratic Party, became more aggressive in their struggle against the Left and the mass movement in order to regain their lost level of power. They managed to unite as a class, which they had been unable to do since the electoral victory of the PU,

* From *Punto Final* No. 134, July 6, 1971.

[1] Pérez, Minister of the Interior in the Frei government, was assassinated by a far-left underground group, the "VOP," in May 1971.

formulating new strategies and objectives and applying new tactics. They delivered the leadership of the reactionary counteroffensive to Eduardo Frei and publicly outlined their strategy in Frei's speech at the Caupolicán Theater.

The definitive swing to the right by the Christian Democratic Party and the beginning of a new reactionary counteroffensive are elements defining the new political situation. All this must lead the Left to evaluate what it has accomplished during recent months and to determine its next steps. This must be done by attacking and unmasking the political strategy of Freism and the Right. This is what we wish to analyze at this point without attempting to offer political lessons to anyone and without evading our own responsibilities in this area.

But there are also other reasons compelling us to state publicly what we think. During recent weeks, the Right and Freism through statements, speeches in Parliament, and the press have done their best to criticize and attack the MIR publicly. Sometimes they referred to what we have thought or said or done; at other times, and more frequently, they have ascribed evaluations and activities to us. They have used all methods to attempt to separate the MIR from the Popular Unity, to emphasize the differences between our organization and the PU, to induce us to attack the Communist Party or vice versa, etc.

Unfortunately, some sectors and representatives of the PU have allowed themselves to be carried away by this propaganda, and in the middle of this reactionary offensive they believed that the moment had come to start polemics within the left circles, "to require the MIR to define itself" or to "reflect."

Frei 1971: Hypocrisy as a Banner

Eduardo Frei takes the leadership of the counteroffensive by the dominant classes under precise conditions attempting to hide the real aim of their offensive, which is none other than that of arresting the progress of the workers, who threaten their interests, and defending the power and wealth they possess today. Frei thus appears as Chile's ex-President who returns from abroad after the death of his friend and "from a position above interests or sectors" he watches, "overwhelmed" by the situation of his country, and "offers a way."

His speech was addressed fundamentally to the urban middle classes and the officers of the Armed Forces who had been carefully "trained" by the Right and the Christian Democratic Party before and after the death of Pérez Zujovic; he seeks to frighten them with the Chile he describes in order to lead them in his struggle against the government. He presents the same two objectives the Christian Democrats had cunningly posed after Pérez Zujovic's death: the "dissolution of the armed groups," which is nothing other than a demand for repression of the MIR and pressure on the PU so that it may break with the revolutionary Left; and "that the campaign of insults and slander should cease," which is essentially a way of urging the government to tie its hands on one of the most important questions in the present process: the propaganda and agitation capable of being developed through the mass media, an important way of elevating the consciousness of the masses, pointing out their enemies and handing them banners.

This speech, which was intended as a call for struggle against the government, the Left, and the movement of the masses, hidden behind the banners of "peace, order, law, and security for all Chileans," is a masterpiece of impudence, cynicism, demagogy, and opportunism. It is the duty of the entire Left to unmask it to the people as seditious, reactionary, and hypocritical. Not that much time has elapsed nor are the people so stupid as to enable Frei and his party to erase their past and present themselves today dressed in the clothing they burned yesterday.

Frei and the Christian Democrats ask "as a first demand the re-establishment of peace, safety, and order for the citizens, the minimum harmony which is a condition of the democratic way." Nobody can wish anything else for Chile; but what "minimum harmony" did Frei and the Christian Democrats establish in Chile when from his desk he ordered that dozens of miners, settlers, employees, students, women, and children be killed at El Salvador, Puerto Montt, Puente Alto, Copiapó, San Miguel, etc? What "safety for the citizens" was there during his government when universities were trespassed against, when workers, journalists, members of parliament, and students were imprisoned, when country estates and settlements were evacuated, when university students and teachers were tortured and whipped? What peace was there in the streets of Chile, which were real battlefields, where tear-gas bombs, water tanks, beatings, chases, arrests, and sometimes bullets were the rule, as the result of his repressive policy against the people?

Frei, the council of the Christian Democratic Party, and the Christian Democrats in general today demand "respect for the law." It is not possible to demand "respect for the law" a few months after having instigated and assisted physical attacks intended to prevent the assumption of power by the PU.

Would they dare to deny that the September speech of Zaldívar on the economic situation, corrected in Frei's own handwriting, was aimed at creating a picture of economic chaos to justify the resignation of four of Frei's ministers, thus provoking a ministerial crisis and the formation of a military cabinet as a way of making a countercoup to prevent Allende from assuming governmental power? If the government knew that Viaux[2] and his gang

---

[2] Ex-Army officer involved in a 1969 military revolt and in the October 1970 assassination of the Commander of the Armed Forces, General Schneider.

were plotting, why were they not arrested before General Schneider was assassinated? The Minister of the Interior, Patricio Rojas, was informed by Vicente Huerta, one of the plotters; we ourselves denounced the plot on October 21, twenty-four hours before General Schneider's death, giving more than ten names of the plotters involved, and the plot was confessed to at the Central Police Station by an arrested person on the same day. The only thing Patricio Rojas did was to delete from the statement of the arrested person the paragraph implicating him. On the morning of October 22, General Schneider was assassinated by the same people known by the government to be plotting.

Eduardo Frei and the Christian Democrats state, "It is an essential condition for public peace that groups outside the law should be disarmed, that the nation be aware of their existence and that they are armed." What armed groups is Mr. Frei talking about? Does he refer to armed landowner groups that during his administration and with his knowledge were organized and armed to defend their wealth and privileges and that today murder peasants? Or does he refer to the right-wing group of plotters who assassinated Schneider and who during the last months of his government were sheltered by him, as he did not even investigate them, much less "dissolve" them while they were developing attempts against other people's lives, throwing bombs, etc.? Or is it a question of hired killers trained on the very premises of the Christian Democrats?

Frei's impudence does not stop there; he deplores the "climate of hatred and violence" created in Chile and demands its end. Frei forgets that he came to power supported by a campaign of terror, the most sinister Chile has known and to be compared only with the one of the Right in 1970 and with that of his party, the Christian Democrats, during the municipal elections.

Finally, with Pharisaean hypocrisy, Frei offers a novel and attractive road to Chileans: revolution in liberty, ". . . that as time goes by will acquire its true outline . . . ," because ". . . we are an option, we are an alternative, we are a way for Chile." What revolution in liberty is he talking about? The one that trespassed against universities? The one that stagnated the economic growth of the country? The one that surrendered copper to United States interests? The one that added two billion dollars more to Chile's foreign debt? The one that left behind more than three hundred thousand unemployed? The one that redistributed the national income in favor of the upper classes through a galloping inflation?

All this is what Chile and its people have to ask Frei. He, the Christian Democratic Party, the newspaper *La Prensa,* and Freism in general must be unmasked. Their hands are stained with blood, they are responsible for six years of government, and we cannot permit the hypocritical and unpunished to set themselves up as judges of situations they themselves created or as bearers of banners they have just trampled on themselves.

Yes, Mr. Frei, what is today endangered in Chile is not order and safety. What is really endangered, and what you are defending, is the power and wealth of a few who want to keep everything in their hands. It is not the Left forces or the revolutionary Left that are causing chaos, but the Yankees, the landowners, and the industrialists, who are today conspiring against and sabotaging industrial, copper, and land and cattle production. It was not the Left that sowed hatred and violence in Chile, but those who exploited and massacred the people for decades and who today have not hesitated to resort to crime or exploitation of crime in order to defend their privileges. This is what is at stake and in dispute today in Chile. . . .

The New Political Situation

The assassination of Pérez Zujovic and the political situation that was caused by it objectively defined the conflicts of the previous situation.

Taking as pretext the death of Pérez Zujovic, the dominant classes and their representative parties succeeded in obtaining what they had not been able to obtain during the previous months: their union as a class. On this basis, they started a seditious and reactionary counteroffensive against the government, the PU, the revolutionary Left, and the movement of the masses. Countless speeches, statements, and editorials in their newspapers openly called for sedition from this moment on.[3] They succeeded in raising banners disguising the real intentions of their struggle against the advance of the government and the workers. Their apparent objectives, the defense of the law, order, and safety of the Chileans, allowed them to try to drag the urban middle classes and officers of the Armed Forces behind their seditious policies.

But the essential feature was that Christian Democratic Freism succeeded in definitively imposing its reactionary policy; the Christian Democratic Party swung openly to the right and formed a bloc with the National

[3] We do not wish to miss this opportunity to answer the questions that the Christian Democratic newspaper *La Prensa* put to us some days ago. It asked us whether we had attacked some banks, stealing money, during the recent administration, and what we had done with the money. We shall answer the first question at once: Yes, Christian Democratic gentlemen! We have expropriated money in quantities that are public knowledge, but what you stole from the public treasury during your administration is still unknown to anyone. As to the question of what we did with the money, we shall not be able to satisfy your curiosity for the moment, but be assured that at least it was meant for more respectable purposes than those you used it for, many of you having become wealthy at the cost of what was the property of the whole country.

Party and the Radical Democrats, thus creating a new political situation and closing the possibility of parliamentary understanding between the PU and Christian Democracy for the purpose of progressing in the execution of the program. The alliance of the Right with Freism expressed itself in the election of the Rector of the University of Chile, in the fall of the executive board in the Chamber, in a joint list of candidates in the town council by-election in Valparaíso, etc. This is not the time to lament the swing to the right of the CD, to magnify the weight and possibilities of the Christian Democratic Left, or to attempt to hold a party sliding down the slope of reactionary politics.

All this goes beyond opinions and intentions and objectively places matters so that there is only one way to continue progressing: to recover the strength lost in Parliament by means of the mobilization of the masses.

Only an effective mobilization of the masses, in all its forms, starting with the large rural estates, factories, and settlements, for the problems specific to the masses and the struggle for the satisfaction of their aspirations will make it possible to break the hold of Freism. Only a mobilization that clearly shows the masses who are their enemies, that gives them slogans, allows them forms of struggle, and raises their consciousness and organization will be really effective. The production goal is a fair objective, as it seeks the satisfaction of the material needs of the masses. But it cannot be the only one, or the essential one. Chilean production is threatened, it does not grow, and not because of an ill design of the gods or black magic. Production does not increase sufficiently because production means are predominantly in private hands, and the big factory owners and large-rural-estate owners sabotage production. It is the responsibility of the large capitalist owners, rather than the workers, to increase production. The workers' task is not to increase production, but to control and inspect, to see that their bosses increase production; the task is to fight production sabotage perpetrated by owners, and if the owners should persist, to defeat them and make their factories and rural estates the property of the whole people. Economic and production problems are not placed above class struggle; no goals can be hoisted for the workers that will hide their enemies from them. . . .

The Popular Unity and the MIR

We have referred above to the importance we attach to an understanding between the PU and us and to the benefits this understanding has already produced. During recent months on countless occasions different sectors and representatives of the PU have critically referred to some position the MIR maintains; paradoxically, it is the Communist Party that has persisted with the greatest vigor during the very same days the Christian Democrats and the Right rushed upon the Left and the movement of the masses. At the same time, this same political force did not respond to the Christian Democratic aggression, or did so weakly. . . . The CP has persisted in its public criticisms of our policies. We have already said publicly that the moment has come to close ranks in the Left to confront the enemies attack, and we think that the ideological discussion already posed must not weaken but rather strengthen the entire Left, particularly if it is done at a level of mutual respect.

On many occasions, and recently more frequently, it has been maintained that "indiscriminate land seizures," "house and apartment occupation," and "the occupation of small industries and land properties" are reprehensible. We do not believe it would be useful to enter into combat against windmills, against positions we do not hold. We are not partisans of "indiscriminate land seizures"; we condemn "house and apartment occupation," and we do not encourage the "occupation of small industries and small land properties." It has been asserted that "the MIR should take a position"; it is not MIR but rather the CP that should take a position, not about "indiscriminate land seizures," but about whether the occupation of large factories and rural estates is not a legitimate form of the workers' struggle. The same thing must be done by the PU.

We also believe that the struggle forms of peasants and the working class must be in accordance with the present situation, with the specific experience, and the proved effectiveness or lack thereof. There are other forms of workers' struggles, apart from occupation, and we shall develop them as well. But we believe that it is a legitimate procedure, measuring the national correlation of forces at each moment and, if certain necessary levels of the workers' organization and consciousness exist, in each specific front to occupy a large rural estate when a landowner does not sow, dismisses his workers, dismantles the estates, kills animals indiscriminately, and sabotages production. We also believe it legitimate, among other forms of struggle, for workers to seize the factories of bosses who sabotage production, fire workers, or do not want to increase production sufficiently, in spite of the demand.

The experience of months of struggle by the Revolutionary Peasant Movement in the fields of the central and southern parts of the country has taught us that occupation as a form of struggle is mobilizing, provides organization, and increases the awareness of the workers. Of course there are other forms of struggle that increase the possibilities of formulas whereby workers can be mobilized. It cannot be a question of furthering the mobilization of the masses as an essential task, if occupation of factories and large rural estates is condemned in advance. The responsibility for employers' sabotage cannot be attributed to the workers struggling to make large factories and rural estates the property of the whole people, nor can the chaos provoked by plotting right-wing groups or by the bosses who seek a lack of supply and exploit the reactionary mass media.

The Tasks of the Present Moment

We believe it is necessary to preserve the understanding between the PU and the MIR. It is necessary to tighten the relations among all Left forces, especially now that ideological discussions have been publicly opened, to unite and maintain a strong unity of all the workers in the country and the city, to close ranks against the reactionary and seditious counteroffensive by the Right and Freism.

The Christian Democratic hypocrisy must be unmasked; the seditious policy raised today by the Right and Freism has to be denounced. Today more than ever, the workers must continue their advance. The mobilization of the masses, raising their consciousness and organization in factories, rural estates, and settlements through adequate forms of struggle is the basic task and is the only thing that will make it possible successfully to fight in the fundamental battle: THE BATTLE FOR THE CONQUEST OF POWER FOR THE WORKERS.

THE MIR ATTACK ON THE COMMUNIST PARTY*

ROBERTO PINTO

In what is intended to be an answer from the MIR to Eduardo Frei published in the anti-communist magazine *Punto Final,* the National Secretariat of the MIR does in

* From *El Siglo,* July 18, 1971.

fact question the Popular Unity's policy and openly attacks the Communist Party.

The MIR is an organization whose strategic formulations, political actions, and tactical operations have been proved inefficient and have been rejected by our people and defeated by Chilean social practice, except for investigation and exposure of seditious activities, where they have made their contribution.

An elemental sense of revolutionary honesty demands of people who boast of fighting for the revolution the recognition of their mistakes and consequent actions.

However, since the political and theoretical defeat experienced by the MIR on the occasion of the Popular Unity's victory, no attitude of open self-criticism on the part of the movement's leaders is evident.

Quite the contrary; they persist in many theoretical formulations and practical activities that are incorrect. And this remains clearly proved in the document of the MIR published in *Punto Final*.

Communists have no sectarian attitude toward the ultra-Left. Evidence of this is that today forty members of the MIR's "Ránquil" Movement are active in the Communist Party. These are healthy and honest people who have admitted and learned from their errors, and who today contribute to the development of the revolutionary process from the ranks of the Communist Party.

One of the most reactionary representatives of Freism, Jaime Castillo, praises the position of the MIR in the columns of a right-wing newspaper, *La Prensa*. In his analytical commentary on the MIRist document, the old Freist fox emphasizes that "the document, however, is not basically a reply to the Christian Democratic Party, to the former President, or the Right (for the MIR, all are the same). It rather means a new start of polemics with the Popular Unity forces. To be more precise, with the Communist Party." And Castillo adds, "The anti-

Christian Democratic action is, therefore, a kind of introduction, or prior safe-conduct."

This analysis by the Freist representative is not accidental. It disdains the MIR's critical judgment of the Christian Democratic administration, ignores the repeated denouncements of the anti-popular policy pursued by his colleague's government, and instead emphasizes what they are interested in—positions against the Popular Unity, the government of Salvador Allende, and in particular, the hostility of the MIR to the Communist Party.

The Communists have specified their position with regard to the ultra-Left in general and the MIR in particular, pointing out that most of that movement's activities harm the popular government. In specifying those actions, Communists have been explicit in pointing out that it is incorrect and harmful to raise to the category of a general policy line the indiscriminate occupation of land estates, grounds, factories, and dwellings.

Communists have insisted, and the facts continue to confirm their point of view, that the MIRist thesis that tends to limit the class struggle in Chile to an inevitable and desirable armed confrontation is incorrect and alien to our concept of reality.

The revolutionary process in Chile shows that the confrontation mentioned takes place every day, every hour, in the various fields of action of the masses. To evade or hide this reality means, ultimately, to scorn the role of the masses and overlook the action possibilities of the class enemy.

The MIR points out that one of the essential peculiarities that has appeared in this Chilean political process "is the understanding between the Popular Unity and the revolutionary Left."

The truth is that an understanding with honest people in the ultra-Left is in our opinion desirable and necessary, but agreement among all revolutionaries must be reached on an essential basis of revolutionary social discipline and ensuing support for the Popular Unity. These last two basic premises do not at all agree with the political practice of the MIR.

The MIR points out that the big revolutionary task that confronts our people today, the battle of production, is the responsibility of the large capitalist owners and not of the workers.

It is difficult to find a greater absurdity and a more open inconsistency with a proclaimed revolutionary position. The MIRist thesis seems to ignore the importance of the changes that have been taking place in Chile since the constitution of the Popular Unity government. The increase in production is not intended, as hitherto, to benefit capitalists, but to serve the Chilean workers, the country and its people; to contribute to strengthening the Popular Government and to assure the advancement of the Chilean revolution. . . . President Allende emphasized on the first of May that "the great combat, the great battle of Chile is now and henceforth will be production."

Complaining about the Communist criticism of the ultra-Left's positions, and in particular of the MIR, the National Secretariat of that movement claims that the Communist Party has not replied to the Christian Democratic aggressions or would do it feebly.

Such an accusation by the MIR does not stand up under the slightest analysis and exhibits ignorance with respect to the policies of the Communists. The different appraisals of Christian Democracy made by the Communists and the MIR represent different matters. The MIRists maintain that since the assassination of Pérez Zujovic a definitive turn to the right by the Christian Democratic Party has taken place, and that the possibility of an agreement with the Christian Democrats is now closed. The Communists judge that among the Christian Democrats there are forces in favor of getting the process under way in our country—together with the revolutionary sectors. The social heterogeneity of that party's membership leads to a situation, among other factors, in which the Freist sector, which occupies the controlling positions, is unable to place all Christian Democrats in the ranks of the Right.

Finally, the MIR invites, or rather challenges, the Communist Party and the Popular Unity to take a definite position on whether the seizure of big factories and large rural estates is or is not a genuine form of workers' struggle.

The "challenge" of the MIR to the Communist Party lacks all seriousness. It is merely a play on words. It is not a serious statement by revolutionaries, but a sophistry unworthy of mature revolutionaries.

In this matter, as in others, they reduce the tactic of the programmatic achievement to a merely quantitative matter regarding big or small occupations.

Communists are not *a priori* against seizures. They are indeed against them when they are indiscriminate and absurd; they are against those actions creating difficulties for the popular government and helping reactionaries. There are unquestionably real bases, very definite ones, which determine some occupations. But it is also unquestionable that for the consolidation, deepening, and progress of the revolution it is better to attempt to resolve the disputes leading to seizures, to find solutions for the problems of the masses in accordance with the popular government, and to advance in strengthening the economy of the country.

In the new conditions created in Chile it is very easy to carry out seizures. It is not difficult to mobilize small groups of workers to take a factory, a large rural estate, or some dwellings. But what is genuinely revolutionary is helping the government achieve its program and mobilize the masses in pursuit of this accomplishment. But it must be the masses and not small groups, the organized masses, the masses with social consciousness, the masses with a clear understanding of the final objectives of their struggle.

In this task, in a wide organizational policy, a policy of education and mobilization of the masses for revolutionary aims, it is possible and necessary for all those who honestly and resolutely want to consolidate and deepen the movement that leads to opening a wide channel for the coming of socialism in Chile to be under a common leadership.

CHAPTER 19

The Right

The Chilean political Right bases its politics on a spirited defense of private property. The Popular Unity is not the first Chilean government to modify in theory and fact the classical concept of private property as the institutional basis for society, and the *laissez-faire* conception of the state. The Popular Front government of 1938 redefined the function of property and enlarged the role of the state, as did each succeeding government. Many Chileans began to view private property as the root cause of underdevelopment and untenable inequalities in the distribution of wealth, privilege, and power. The Popular Unity now proposes that private property in those spheres central to the economic life of the country be eliminated and that the state assume over-all responsibility from private capital for economic and social development, while utilizing state control of wealth-producing centers to eliminate the extreme inequalities of the previous society. In spite of the gradual erosion in the legitimacy of the private property and *laissez-faire* concepts over time, Chilean conservatives still strenuously argue that there can be no freedom without private property. In their view, Chile is now headed for dictatorial, bureaucratic collectivism.

The Erosion of Private Property*

"Because of fear, demagogy, sentimentalism, or ideological confusion, we Chileans have accepted the

---

* An unsigned editorial from the conservative magazine *Portada*, February 18, 1971.

erosion of the concept of private property in deed and in right. We now see that this process inevitably brings forth unfreedom and bureaucratic tyranny."

There Can Be No Freedom Without Private Property

The Western World has known many forms of political and juridical freedom, many forms of property. The practical exercise of freedom has always been indissolubly tied to the existence of private property.

By property we mean of course more than the meagerly protected right under our present Constitution to live in one's own town house or countryside ranch.

The private-property system is one that secures for private individuals real as well as potential control over the means of production. . . .

The private-property system protects the private sphere so that the state may not be the ultimate and only employer, the only creditor, the sole entrepreneur, the only educator and sole shaper of public opinion.

No one can deny that the private-property system has its failings. Nor can anyone deny that the reduction of private property to small units, far from correcting the defects of such a system, further deprives the individual of choosing between jobs, occupation, creditors, educational establishments, and means of information, transforming him into a mere functionary, reducing his life to the frightful brutishness of routine.

A Gray Dawn

If private property were an unjustified privilege, its gradual erosion and final collapse should be saluted as the dawn of a new history for Chile. However, no free man can watch without fear the emergence of a totalitarian state, a state whose power is no longer limited by the rights of private citizens, that is, in the last analysis, by private property itself.

Claiming that the right to private property is not universal in the capitalist system, since many of its members are dispossessed, the collectivist proceeds to deprive everyone and so multiplies the dispossessed as he transforms both the rich and the poor into pariahs and bureaucrats. . . .

Confronted by an inert brand of conservatism that does not propose to resolve our social dramas with anything but monetarist rationality and public order, polymorphous progressivism has gradually turned over to the state increasing sectors of economic initiative, thus constantly reducing the sphere of activity open to the private entrepreneur. This process started in 1938 under the administration of Don Pedro Aguirre Cerda and was maintained under the successive Radical Party governments without relapse, except under Ibáñez and Allessandri. It gained new strength under Christian Democratic rule and finally found its true revolutionary form with the present regime.

Mindless Legalism

Little by little, the Chileans, so proud of their freedom, resigned themselves to losing it, choosing rather to be proud of the legal way in which it had been done, even if such a legality entailed a progressive dulling of the conscience.

Certain citizens sigh with relief when the present government proclaims that it intends to proceed with its revolution within the "legal process," even when such changes actually violate the spirit of our laws.

This distortion of the spirit of the law will soon transform itself in the new legality of statism as new constitutional texts are promulgated which aim at the suppression of private property (that is, of capital), thus greatly threatening freedom itself.

The administration of Don Jorge Allessandri felt constrained to initiate an agrarian reform aimed at the expropriation of abandoned or badly cultivated rural properties.

Let us not forget that the proclamation of the open season on private property was initiated by the Kennedy government and his idealized vision of the "Alliance for Progress." As an adversary of the United States once put it, the northern country tired of being an imperialist for the rich and chose to become an imperialist for the poor.

The majority of Chileans did not adequately take note of the fact that Jorge Allessandri's constitutional reform cast into law what was already taking place in fact: the erosion of private property. Wise doctors of the law took all the necessary precautions to allow the state to expropriate land and pay for it on credit. This did away with the most effective defense of private property. Before, the state could not expropriate private property without paying cash beforehand. By allowing certain expropriations to be made without immediate cash compensation, the way was opened for the greatest abuses.

The Christian Democratic Adventure

This, however, was a short step indeed when compared to the joyful and unpremeditated adventure of the Christian Democrats' trespassing back and forth over the constitutional text of 1925. Convinced that the time had come to besiege private property, the Christian Democratic experts put forth their long-winded and confused version of the tenth article of the tenth section of the reformed Political Constitution proposed by the Frei government in 1964, finally promulgated as law with some amendments on January 20, 1967.

We Chileans continued to live in tranquillity and legality as the Congress approved a constitutional text that turned over to the judiciary all of private property's guarantees. The state was relieved of its obligation to pay the property owner in cash before taking over his property. The legislation allowed not only the private citizen to be deprived of his property but also the determination of the procedures of expropriation, the establishment of the forms and modalities of compensation, indemnization, and appeal, finally turning over the property owner to the harsh and omnipotent grip of functionaries.

In order to facilitate the agrarian reform, the Constitution decreed that rural property could be expropriated at its declared fiscal value and compensation for it paid within thirty years. Thus, the precedent was established that later was used in other sectors of economic activity such as mining.

As the Christian Democrats' light-footed reforms kept on apace, they sustained their attacks against the defenders of private property by accusing them all of defending their wealth and class privileges.

Chilean freedom retrogressed considerably during the Christian Democratic administration. As more and more state organizations gained more and more power, more and more expropriations were used against those who defended the elementary right of the citizen not to depend on the state for each and every need.

It is only natural for a country where property owners are threatened and besieged by the judiciary process to find itself debilitated and weakened when confronted with state collectivism. Youth, intellectuals, functionaries, in a word, all those who eat their bread without incurring the risks of earning it, became militant and merrily joined the ranks of Socialists and Communitarists, who endorsed participation and whatever other ideal, well or badly understood. Thus was the prosaic conviction eroded that there must be some rich people in Chile, people with sufficient economic knowledge to rule over industries, farms, mines, commercial establishments, information media, people to control every type of instrument influencing and creating jobs. It would have been logical to demand that the rich not monopolize, not fear competition with other rich individuals from inside the country or abroad. It was illogical to proclaim their disappearance as an ideal and to celebrate the emergence of a Pharaonic state.

"Within the law" we have gotten the present political regime; "within the law" the present government has proposed a constitutional reform that puts a final end to private property in Chile. The nationalization of the great copper mines is just a pretext to eliminate all private ownership of mining property, large, medium, or small. It has transformed the owner of valid property claims into a mere concessionaire, and denied him the right to any form of indemnization. Legally acquired rights are invalidated, as are fiscal exemptions and other privileges and prerogatives which the state had earlier condoned. This casts great doubts on the state's good faith.

The Dangerous Trend Toward Dictatorial Bureaucratic Collectivism

Citizens have already conformed to the legality, even when this legality resulted in the progressive erosion of their freedom.

As freedom diminishes, the legal criteria with which to evaluate the acts of government slacken. Soon legality itself may well give way. The defenses of freedom have already fallen.

Bankers do not usually rank high in public esteem. No one defended them centuries ago when they were persecuted and condemned to their ghettos. Having first pointed its cannons against the copper-mine owners, the state now turns its weaponry against private bankers in a foolproof political shot. If by chance the administrators of private banks have been found guilty of unbecoming conduct, in a petty or a serious way, if they have transgressed one of the multitude of banking laws and regulations, then so much the better; it supplies oil for the bonfire.

Curiously, in the case of the banks the government did not even bother to request from Congress the right to expropriate. It simply presented the stockholders with its offer, while pointing out that the settlement under expropriation would be much smaller, and invited the administrators to resign in favor of persons of governmental confidence.

It was thus nothing but an act of pure bravado, counting on the fear of the stockholders, directors, and managers.

Such a tactic can of course repeat itself in other fields of activity, especially in the cases of illegal occupations by workers or aspiring property owners followed by governmental intervention, which simply puts the seal of legality on the occupations, thus completely eliminating any guarantees from the right of eminent domain.

Envious preachings against private property have gone a long way in Chile and misled us into the most dangerous of deviations, that which ultimately leads to dictatorial bureaucratic collectivism, which destroys freedom without augmenting prosperity.

CHAPTER 20

Violence

Chile's uniqueness extends to the phenomenon of violence. While Chile, like other countries of the West, does have a history of people dying unnecessarily, violence with political motives has been relatively sporadic, and then almost always associated with police and military repression of social protest. Under the previous government, of Eduardo Frei, there were several massacres of workers and demonstrators by repressive forces of the state. But even this cannot compare with the systematic killings and tortures of authoritarian regimes such as those of Brazil, Guatemala, and the Dominican Republic. However, as the social tensions have increased, the level of violence has also increased. The roots of this violence reside in two interrelated phenomena: a growing awareness on the part of poor and oppressed peoples that what the Christian Left terms "institutionalized violence"—disease, malnutrition, the poverty of underdevelopment—is not an immutable condition; and the desperation of those who, faced with a growing demand for change, would preserve the *status quo* by any means necessary. The government of Allende and the Communist and Socialist parties are absolutely committed to a peaceful transition to socialism, which they believe will put an eventful end to the institutionalized violence of capitalist underdevelopment. They will, of course, defend themselves against any counterrevolutionary violence unleashed by Chile's reactionaries and their covert foreign backers.

Since the election of Allende there have been two sensational political assassinations, those of General Schneider, the Commander-in-Chief of the Armed Forces, and Edmundo Pérez, former Minister of the Interior of the Frei government. Both were meant to precipitate a political crisis, which, if successful, could have meant civil war. The following selections provide background and reflections on this new and unfortunate turn in Chile's relatively pacific political history.

TO KILL A GENERAL*

It is not just determined persons who are guilty. An entire system is guilty. Society will continue living with these things as long as material goods and machines are central, and not human beings. What can I say in this moment. . . . The first thing that went through my mind when the attempt occurred was that it is more necessary than ever to create a human society of solidarity, a society in which all can be *compañeros*. I think that now in Chile the doors to form this society are a little bit open. Now the country has taken important steps. It is necessary to go onward. I don't want to be interpreted in the sense of personal vengeance. Certainly there are guilty persons and they must be found and judged. But most important is to change the guilty society so that it doesn't produce individuals who deny human solidarity and justice.

The ideas of my father as a military man were very clear. My father died defending the doctrine that he held throughout all his life—that the Army must maintain its professional character and not intervene. . . . Chile has

* Excerpts from an interview held by *Prensa Latina* with René and Raúl Schneider, sons of General René Schneider, just a few hours after their father's death. (Prensa Latina Especiales, SE-912/70)

its identity, but we are not in isolation, we are a part of the West and under the influence of an entire process that the West is experiencing. The West is living under a climate of violence, where the center of society is egoism, the law of the jungle. . . . Those who assassinated my father were not individuals, it was an unjust society; a sector of this society thought that to defend their interests it was necessary to kill a person and they had no scruples and killed him. . . . I say again that Chile is part of the West. . . . We continue to be a cultural colony. . . .

Raúl: Well, we all know the Right killed him. But I doubt that it was the Right alone. The Right never acts alone. It cannot live without the support that everyone knows about. The thread leads to other parts. For example, why did this Mr. Olalguiaga, from the United States, come to Chile? Suddenly a man appears handing out dollars generously. It is very suspicious.

René and Raúl: Papá always had the same position with respect to the function of the Army. One day two years back he arrived home furious from a visit to the house of a man who turned out to be from the Right. As if joking, this man said to *papá,* "And when is the military going to take power?" "I understand that you are joking," *papá* said, "but I don't accept it even as a joke. We will respect the Constitution up to the ultimate consequences." "And if the Left wins in the next elections?" the mummy asked him. "Also, *señor.* The rules of the game are the same for everybody." "No, this no," the mummy said, frightened, and *papá* left the house. Afterward he said to us, "Look at that guy; see how far they go."

Because of the rank he held, *papá* had to know many people. He withstood many pressures from people on the Right.

Once he arrived home furious. He was disgusted with a North American military man. . . . It was in those days when they assassinated Martin Luther King. *Papá* made a comment about the savagery of the crime, and the *yanqui* said, as if saying good morning, "I think that basically it was positive. He was making too much trouble. . . ."

Once, *mamá* told us, a few months ago I believe, they went to a cocktail party or a dinner at the Embassy of the United States, and two men approached him, two North American military men, and began to ask him questions, particularly questions about his political thinking. Then my father whispered in my mother's ear, "We better run; these two must be from the CIA."

THE MURDER OF PÉREZ ZUJOVIC: WHO SHOULD BE BLAMED?*

First it appeared as a beautiful idea for bourgeois-intellectual, progressive thinkers; an idea that could reconcile the progressive to the comforts of his easy life; an idea that helped silence the conscience of those indulging in the amenities of existence: gourmet food, vintage wines, sporty cars, fashionable clothes, children in private schools, in the midst of collective mass despair; a cathartic idea of redemptive, purifying violence doing away with the vices of a capitalist world, conjuring the romantic vision of the black flag of anarchism; an idea espoused by the classics of Marxism, and now upheld by its new prophets, Althusser and Marcuse. And so, the new idea, the beautiful idea, the redemptive violence of "Che," of Camillo, of the "Tupas,"[1] triumphed in the closed chapels of an emboldened bourgeoisie. Liberated priests proclaimed the new word to their scandalized/en-

---

* An unsigned editorial from *Portada*, June 22, 1971.

[1] *Tupamaros* are Uruguayan urban guerrillas.

raptured audience of perfumed ladies and pale young men of the Catholic Action.

Revolutionary artists portrayed it in posters, or sang its virtues in protest songs: "Ra-ta-ta-ta-ta" goes one, imitating the rattling sounds of a submachine gun. How appropriate! Eminent university professors, sociologists, economists, international experts, and "humanists" exalted it in their obscure but stirring jargon.

A few fog-heads did attempt to curb the threatening wave of the new idea. They pointed to the necessity of social order; they claimed that one could not at once be the jury and the prosecution; they added that the game of violence is not necessarily limited to the Left, that it may well lead to unforeseen endings. They argued that the end cannot justify the means, that one may not sacrifice the life, honor, or property of the innocent. On hearing such antiquarian scholasticisms, the condescending bourgeois smiled: "It is capitalist society which does violence to the poor." They called it "institutionalized violence." A presidential candidate, even a bishop joined the chorus denouncing this "institutionalized violence." To this *reactionary* violence, they opposed their revolutionary violence, which would give rise to the new man, the new society. Confronted with such idyllic prophecy, what could the antiquarian do but remain silent?

The gospel of violence thus first triumphed within the progressive circles of bourgeois intellectuals. From there its spark moved on to the university campus where it caught on like a prairie fire. Everything contributed to make this gospel attractive to the young. It was defended by those whom they most admired in the adult world: intellectuals, artists, protest singers, fashionable priests, the most sought-after and convincing teachers. It satisfied youth's fascination for the mysterious, the forbidden, the romantic. It answered its impatience, promising to do away, at once and definitely, with evil. Then came the "expropriations" of landed property, the looting of banks and supermarkets, the stone-throwing confrontations with the police forces, the MIR. These well-fed, well-brought-up, and intelligent youths cast their violence in a friendly mold. They saw to it that no one, or almost no one, got hurt. One or two policemen, maybe. But who cares? Are they not the prototypical representatives of institutionalized violence? The young became Robin Hoods. The antiquarians again found their speech to remind them of the sacred principles of authority. An eloquent professional phrasemaker retorted that authority can only survive if it is obeyed. Once more, they were reduced to silence.

The new idea, the beautiful idea of violence then found its new audience in the people themselves.

Unlike the intellectual, the common man does not speak harshly and act softly. His action is as rough as his speech. He does not brandish the resounding phrases of intellectuals and universitarians. He does not hold to the high canons of Marxist rhetoric. The VOP manifesto does not speak of "dialectics" or "structures," but of those who kiss the boss's ass. Ill-fed and ill-mannered, the common man plays no Robin Hood game. He does not stop midway through violence. *With rigorous logic, he brings the new idea, the beautiful idea to its fatal conclusion.*

A few days ago, a man of the people, an ordinary man, finished off a wounded and defenseless policeman and stole his machine gun. With it he later murdered in cold blood the ex-Minister of the Interior and former Vice-President of the Republic, Edmundo Pérez Zujovic.

Many who had earlier warmly applauded protest singer Victor Jara's song about the incident of Puerto Montt when he defined Edmundo Pérez as a "murderer" are today horrified, because an uneducated, uncouth man of the people believed Jara and took it upon himself to do away with the "murderer."

Tomorrow this VOPist will face the rigor of justice. Where then will be the progressive intellectuals, the fashionable priests, the progressive bishops, the candidates of "institutionalized violence," the protest singers, the professors, the sociologists, the psychologists, the economists, the international experts, the "humanists," the fans of "Che"? Where will the press of violence be with its guerrilla manuals, its detailed accounts of kidnapings and executions? Will they be there too? Who will ever repay the wretched VOPist for the mindless corruption of his heart and soul?

ALLENDE DENOUNCES SEDITION*

President Allende today denounced the rising wave in the reaction's plans to create a state of chaos in the country with the support of the rightist press and called on the workers to meet any attacks by seditious elements with firmness.

In an impassioned speech to the people gathered at the Plaza de la Constitución, across from the Palacio de la Moneda, President Allende announced a three-day period of mourning as a posthumous tribute to the detectives killed only a few hours before in a suicidal attack by one of the murderers of former Minister of the Interior Edmundo Pérez Zujovic.

The President spoke of "an incident that has shocked Chile": the fact that one of the murderers of Pérez Zujovic, an escapee, walked into the police investigation department today armed with a submachine gun and several dynamite bombs with the intention of killing the Director in retaliation for the excellent work done by the department in the Pérez Zujovic murder case.

* *Prensa Latina* wire service, June 16, 1971.

Allende said that "The action, a personal attack carried out by a terrorist suicidal maniac, cost the lives of two detectives, and a third is waging a battle between life and death."

Allende then said that there are well-founded indications that the murderers of Pérez Zujovic were in contact with foreign elements, and he added, "The opposition accuses Marxism of international links, but neither the Communist Party of Chile nor the Socialist Party of Chile has ever been involved in political crimes carried out under the direction of foreign advisers.

"In this type of crime the reaction utilizes declared elements, false revolutionaries and sometimes even infiltrated 'revolutionaries' at the service of the enemy."

With regard to domestic difficulties, the President said that, despite the trouble caused by the illegal activities of the enemies of his administration, none of these enemies have been put in prison in Chile; there are no political prisoners; and, in fact, freedom of the press has become a sort of freedom to offend.

The President then told his listeners of the relationship between a fascist terrorist group and the so-called Organized Vanguard of the People (VOP), which passed itself off as an organization of the left and which is responsible for the crimes perpetrated against the Government these past few days.

Speaking of a seditious group named the Homeland and Freedom Nationalist Front (FNPL), Allende said "How can those who murdered the chief of the Army, General René Schneider, speak of morals, order and respect for society?"

He described the members of that small group—who, in a series of expensive advertisements published in the rightist press, have called themselves "the vanguard of the resistance against communism."

He denounced the FNPL, which, together with other

groups of the ultraright, has tried to blame the government of People's Unity for the murder of former Minister of the Interior Edmundo Pérez Zujovic.

After indignantly denying the accusation, Allende said that such groups had no moral authority whatsoever. "These groups," he added, "were involved in the murder of General Schneider and are linked to retired General Roberto Viaux, now in prison for his participation in that murder and in a seditious movement against the Government.

"When Tomás Gutiérrez, a Carabineers' corporal, was murdered on May 24," the President went on to say, "we came to the conclusion that his murderers had to be elements who were passing themselves off as revolutionaries and had been infiltrated by the reactionary sectors. There was no other possibility."

Allende repeated his statement that there are those who will try to make an attack on his life, using mercenaries and criminals for this purpose, and added, "I want them to know that I am going to defend my life in order to contribute—with my attitude, my determination and my will —to the construction of socialism and the establishment of social justice in Chile.

"There could be other attempts," Allende said, "VOP might have some members who shoot at both Government and opposition politicians, but I have absolute confidence in the support of the masses and am aware that the success of our administration will constitute a guarantee against both chaos and the installation of a fascist dictatorship in Chile."

PART VII

Economic Structure and the Process of Socialization

CHAPTER 21

The Chilean Oligarchy

A handful of powerful businessmen have always monopolized the economic life of Chile, making fortunes out of underdevelopment and the dependent position of the country in relation to the international system. Some of these "oligarchs" preferred to escape from the country after the assumption of the government by the Marxist parties. This article examines three of the oligarchic clans and some aspects of their operations in Chile.

THE CLANS OF CHILE*

SANTIAGO DEL CAMPO

(with Gustavo Gonzales, Mónica Gonzales, and José Venegas)

Last September, at least for some Chileans, the country came to a standstill, it ceased to exist. From then until November, and even into December and January, the airports, seaports, and frontier posts observed an odd procession of patriots fleeing abroad "to take refuge and seek safety."

In the forefront were the ancient Grand Dukes of our economy followed by one or another paid mercenary frightened by his own shadow. Also exiting were people from the middle classes, small industrialists and mer-

* Abridged from *Ahora* I, #8, 1971.

chants who had been caught in the contagion of fear.
The sardines were climbing into the same boat as the
sharks.

Dominating this exodus was a fear patiently built up
by the oligarchy during the presidential campaign of
1970. The instigators and financiers of this fear were
aware of the fact that a popular victory in September
would put an end to their manipulations and specula-
tions.

If the historical deeds of these millionaires were classed
as treason to the country, there would be many heads
rolling among those involved in the "Great Escape." It
was they who, for more than a century, had built vast
personal empires at the expense of the nation's destiny,
always invoking Country, Forefathers, and Tradition.
Their interests, however, never coincided with those of
Chile.

For over one hundred years these men of finance
formed and promoted their fortunes with the aid of three
factors: exploitation of their employees, bleeding of the
state, and the forming of close ties with the imperialist
powers of the moment. Foreign penetration found in them
docile and obedient allies.

The advent of a popular government has signified for
Chile an end to the imperialist presence in our economy
and political life. The allies of imperialism are escaping.
It also signifies the start of socialist construction. Those
who have made a profit from our capitalist underdevelopment flee. The controlling centers affected by the measures of the new government began, also on September 4,
a gigantic sabotage of the Chilean economy. Industries
were closed down, deposits were withdrawn from the
banks, local and foreign currency was sent abroad. The
Frei government calmly watched the events of the closing
months of its reign while the Central Bank was being
stripped of dollars for use in speculation. Last Septem-

ber the Central Bank issued a total of U.S. $17 million for trips abroad. During the same month in 1969 only $5 million was issued for the same purpose. At the same time, a migratory wave began. This was formed by all kinds of people. Chamudes escaped to Mendoza and from there controlled anti-Chilean campaigns throughout the continent. Lugoze did the same thing in Miami among the Cuban *gusanos* (exiles) and "other Midases." Jaime Egaña Barahona worked with the oppressive forces of the Paraguayan dictatorship. Agustín Edwards became an executive with the Pepsi-Cola Company. In Buenos Aires, the Chilean "emigrants" went into the dry-cleaning business. Others have installed boutiques where they sell Chilean handicraft goods. What a parody! the goods they sell are imported from Chile, a country where, one supposes, anarchy and communism reign.

A phrase mentioned a few years ago by Senator Rafael Gumucio now has a contemporary sound: "A relentless capitalist will without a doubt carry out his last commercial transaction on the road between his cell and the scaffold." The actions of the present government have already started to affect monopolistic groups financially controlled, until a short time ago, by those who have decided to flee from this country en masse. For the present report, we have drawn a profile of three of these groups: the Edwards group, the Yarur group, and the group of the Banco Hipotecario, commonly known as "The *Pirañas*."[1] There exist among them and other groups such close ties that when speaking of one of them we are really speaking about all of them. It is not the purpose of this article to vilify the people who directly represent these groups. They are of no interest, nor do we have vengeful attitudes. All we are interested in showing is part of the

[1] Ferocious South American fish that attack and consume anything in the water. See also the reference to this group in Chapter 24.

enormous empire built up by the local millionaires, in collaboration with imperialism, at the expense of underdevelopment, backwardness, and the misery of the people.

EDWARDS: From One Barrel to Another

George Edwards was a humble doctor who left his native Wales at the beginning of the nineteenth century. Wales was then, and still is, the most backward part of the British Isles.

Young Edwards, like many of his young compatriots, took the only opportunity offered to him to better himself: to emigrate and seek his fortune elsewhere. Present-day Welshmen are still doing the same: Richard Burton, Dylan Thomas, Tom Jones, and Engelbert Humperdinck have emigrated.

Young Edwards boarded a ship bound for South America. Months later he arrived off the coast of Coquimbo and, who knows for what reason, left the ship. He hid himself away, inspected the lay of the land, and finally married a local maiden, Isabel Ossandón, daughter of a powerful figure of the region and recently converted Jew. She provided him with a fabulous dowry. It was the start of a great career. Almost two centuries later, his better endowed descendants Agustín ("Dunny") and Roberto Edwards Eastman inherited the migratorial urge and went into an exile of a less financially distressing nature. Agustín went to Miami, Roberto to Buenos Aires. They left behind them a country in which six generations of Edwardses had made themselves commercially and financially powerful, speculating and profiteering at the expense of underdevelopment and the misery and poverty of others. They left because the country was no longer "theirs" and the "favorable conditions" were disappearing. Democracy was in great danger. Together with other lion-hearted citizens they decided to seek new and freer pastures abroad, such as those offered by Miami and Argentina. . . .

Seventy Sly Ones

At the time of their flight, Agustín and Roberto directed and captained a peculiar sort of football team. Eleven people controlled seventy corporations, together the most formidable financial complex in Chile and, in proportion to the might of economies, one of the largest family concerns in the world. Of the seventy units in the complex, Agustín had direct intervention in nineteen and Roberto in nine. Since they were short of time, their representation in the rest was handled by other members of the team: Sonia Edwards Eastman in three corporations; Domingo Edwards González, three; Agustín Edwards Hurtado, three; Pablo Edwards Hurtado, nine; Héctor Brown Guevara, fifteen; Carlos Eastman Beeche, two; María Isabel Eastman (widow of Edwards), two; Jorge Bande Neis, twelve; Carlos Urenda Zeagers, twenty. Some of the units of this empire are the Banco Edwards, the newspaper *El Mercurio,* United Breweries, Indus Leaver, the Chilean Consolidated Insurance Co., Renta Urbana, Pasaje Matte, Lota Schwager mine, Pizarreño, Luchetti mills, Ganadera Tierra del Fuego (vast landholding in the South), Agencias Graham, The Santa María Clinic, Huecke, Dow Chemical of Chile, General Motors Chile. There was even a university—the Federico Santa María, in Valparaíso.

It is calculated that the empire had a working capital of a billion escudos. The financial dealings of the clan were controlled through the Edwards Bank. The newspaper, *El Mercurio,* created the appropriate "atmosphere." Executives of little character were the first clients to be taken in by the brainy editorials and the backslapping campaigns in favor of the Edwards interests. Some of the newspaper's executives, up until a few years ago, used to have American-style breakfasts with the President of the Republic in order to consolidate their actions. As long as the political actions of the government had backing and promotion in the pages of the newspapers, *El Mercurio*'s business protégés flourished.

Clan Versus Flan

The Edwardses did more than build close ties with other national monopolistic clans. They also looked for outlets abroad in their search for power and formed partnerships with imperialist concerns. Foreign investments abroad are closely linked with the Rockefeller group in Argentina, Brazil, and Colombia. Their Argentine business had the protection of an excellent sponsor in the person of Nicanor Costa Méndez, ex-Minister of Foreign Affairs and civil archpriest of the "gorillas." The links between the Edwardes and the Fords were channeled through the Ford Foundation. . . .

Before escaping from the country, Agustín exchanged all his national business interests for the international holdings of his brother Roberto. He bought a large holding of stocks in Pepsi-Cola and installed himself in the United States as one of the corporation's vice-presidents. Roberto, on the other hand, lives in the Argentine in a manner described as "frugal" by his friends.

The Edwardses, however, have been more than successful businessmen. There are people who criticize different aspects of the clan. They assert that the excessive mercantile voracity of the clan ultimately warped and even eliminated from public attention the valuable support given by other, not so rich or powerful members of the clan to Chilean culture and art. The well-known Joaquín Edwards Bello used to say that he did not belong to the clan but to the "Flan Edwards," the "Anti-Edwards Clan." The monarchical Alberto Edwards Vives, author of the well-known book *La Fronda Aristocrática* (The

Aristocratic Foliage), was also not considered a true member of a mercantile family, nor was he in agreement with their life style. Even Sonia Edwards Eastman professes to be inclined toward the Left ever since she was a girl.[2] She studied at the Liceo Manuel de Salas, is a psychologist, and has been present at all the electoral campaigns of the Left. The Edwardses, rich or poor, once constituted an attractive family from a human and psychological point of view. They conserved in their homes a sort of reverential cult to their British ancestry. In Valparaíso, they taught the local society manners. In Copiapó, they were miners. One of them counted Albert Einstein as one of the few people who regularly received letters from him. In politics, the plutocratic circle has always been liberal.[3] They acted on the ideas put forward by the English and American regimes of the time. There were also among the Edwardses those who have supported the enemies of the oligarchy and participated in the ranks of the Popular Front movement as Radicals.[4]

Speaking from a sociological point of view, the criticism is interesting. Agustín and Roberto Edwards head "a family within a family." The name Edwards usually conjures up an image of opulence and well-being in the public eye. There are, however, Edwardses who work as messenger boys in offices or even those who drive trucks for a living.

As in the case of the Buddenbrooks, there was also a tragic side to the family empire. An unwritten rule states

---

[2] Sonia Edwards, a Vice-President of *El Mercurio,* recently said, "The only appropriate destiny for *El Mercurio* is socialization, under control of the workers and with a regime similar to the textile firms transferred to social property." (*Punto Final* VI, №140, September 29, 1971).

[3] Liberals in Chile are conservatives of moderate tendencies.

[4] During the period under discussion, the Radical Party was a middle-class-based center-to-left-of-center party.

that the first-born male (who will always be called Agustín) will be the manager of the family fortunes during his lifetime. It has been said that "Dunny" did not want to do so, and although he was educated and brought up in a manner befitting his future role, his character and temperament were inclined toward artistic rather than materialistic matters. He would have preferred Roberto to take the tiller of the family boat.

It is probably due to this that "Dunny" introduced variations in the management of the empire. He consolidated his standing with the foreign powers and surrounded himself with young executives who were capable and daring in the true tradition of the North American entrepreneurial ethic. The empire was no longer administered and managed like a family shop. This style of thinking and acting allowed Agustín to unburden himself of actual administration and allowed him to dedicate his time to his two favorite activities: journalistic enterprise in general, and *El Mercurio* in particular. No other business received as much of his attention. This dedication to the press reached its apex when he was named President of the Interamerican Press Society.

The fall of the empire has begun. Its tentacles are so meshed with foreign concerns that no formula can be conceived to allow the growth of socialism as long as this empire remains intact. Its control over the banks, insurance, and the media, its methods of operation, and its outright monopolies (such as the beer industry) have made it incompatible with the interest of the nation.

YARUR: From Jerusalem to Glory

In the Holy Land the Yarur brothers, Juan Saba and Nicolás, traded in religious effigies carved by them, to three religious groups. In 1915 they emigrated to Peru, setting themselves up in Arequipa, where they installed a fabric store on one of the corners of Los Mercaderes

Street. Five years later, on the profits gained by the shop, they tried to import machines in order to set up a medium-capacity textile industry. The Yarurs declined to pay the required taxes and, as a result, had to leave Peru.

They crossed the border and established themselves in Bolivia. The choice of country was motivated by the fact that in Bolivia at the time there were no taxes or duties. With the blessing of the Bolivian Government, the Yarurs exploited their workers unmercifully and, as a result, their textile industry flourished and began to yield large profits. The status acquired by the Yarurs allowed them to mix easily with the oligarchy, something that proved impossible later in Chile.

When Bolivia and Paraguay confronted each other in the Chaco War, the Yarurs obtained the concession to supply uniforms and provisions to the Bolivian Army. Very soon, however, their La Paz factory was found to be serving as a front for the illegal sale of arms and munitions to the Paraguayans. Of course, they were expelled from Bolivia. This was in 1935, and here the Chilean chapter commences.

Lace and Exile

When they arrived in Chile the Yarurs had 80 million pesos. A few years later their capital totalled 1,800 million. With the backing of Arturo Alessandri's government (1932–38) the Yarurs imported machinery duty-free and set up their new factory to produce textiles on a large scale. Juan Yarur bought the land on which the factory stands today at forty centavos per square meter. Shortly thereafter he sold part of the land at two hundred pesos per square meter. After a year's residence in Chile, Juan Yarur developed considerable political influence by means of his money. His greatest dream, however, still met impossible barriers. The local aristocracy, prejudiced and arrogant, never accepted him as a member of Society

in spite of his power and wealth. He managed to become
a member of the Union Club only after paying an
enormous amount of money. Nevertheless, in matters of
business he obtained a kind of direct political influence
which gave him privileges within the banking world and,
to a certain extent, within the government. During the administration of Jorge Alessandri, Amador Yarur, the
last manager of the industry, was named Director of the
Central Bank of Chile, while he was, at the same time,
President of the Banco de Crédito e Inversiones.

At this time a scandal broke out. In certain bank accounts more money appeared to be deposited than had
in fact been deposited, in order to justify the large credits
granted to members of the clan.

From the time of their arrival in Chile until their flight
from the country, the Yarurs took pains to create around
themselves the image of patriarchs who were concerned
about the well-being of their workers. However, the treatment suffered by these workers is beyond imagination. In
the factories the Yarurs imposed a life of terror; even a
form of "militia" was set up and entrusted with "vigilance." Informers infiltrated the workers and passed any
complaint or remark onto the management. The worker
who was "disgraced" was then returned to the work-
assignment pool. The victim was usually detailed to clean
latrines, load bales, tidy salt stores, and clean machinery
parts. If the "fault" was considered severe, the unfortunate worker would be sent to "Siberia," a location within
the factory where temperatures were kept extremely low
for the preservation of raw cotton.

The Yarurs were no better in their dealings with the
state. It was always a question of obtaining the upper
hand or more advantageous conditions in the easiest possible way. It was common among the Yarurs that when
the price for a certain type of cloth was fixed by state
control they merely produced the same article but with

different designs or patterns. In this way they produced a "different" item, sometimes using less thread, and the price was not fixed.

The Empire Takes Shape

The extravagant personalities of the Yarurs led them to show off their wealth in a manner unlike that of the other millionaires. When the Yarur Textile Industry was confiscated, it was discovered that Jorge Yarur owned eight motor cars (among them one that was used only for taking out his dogs); also discovered were a hundred cases of fine whisky bottled in clay, 100 million escudos done up in 1000-escudo packets, and other choice odds and ends.

More important, however, is the structure of the Yarur empire. The family-owned Fabrilana, Plansa, Banco de Crédito e Inversiones, Yarur Cotton Manufacturers—Chile, Manufacturas Chilenas de Caucho, Juan Yarur S.A., Saavedra Benard, Radio Sociedad Nacional de Agricultura, The Robinson Crusoe Fishing Industry, Textil Progreso, and the Banco Continental.

The Dynamic Pirañas[5]

The nickname of *Pirañas* befits this group, not because of the magnitude of their business but because of their voracity, which has transformed them into the real "big fish" among the relatively "small fry" species in Latin American finance. The sixteen principal members of the Grupo Banco Hipotecario constitute the most recent incrustation in the Chilean financial oligarchy. They lived the Golden Era during Frei's government and now extend their influence through more than sixty corporations. The *Pirañas* are situated in the most dynamic centers of industry—metal manufactures, machines, and electronics

[5] The Banco Hipotecario group is also discussed by Oscar Guillermo Garretón in Chapter 24.

—without hampering their incursion into the more traditional fields of farming, cattle breeding, insurance, real
estate, transport, communications, textiles, and mining.
They are present in everyday life through Fensa re-
frigerators, Adams chewing gum, and the radio programs
of Radio Cooperativa Vitalicia. They fit perfectly the
theory of the "economic supergroup" established by the
lawyer-economist Ricardo Lagos,[6] and in many spheres
they share the honors with other clans such as the Edwardses, the Matte-Alessandri, and others.

Who Are They?

Family structures are not absent in this group, where
the components are formed by family names intermingled
with each other, such as Vial, Larrain, and Claro, with a
few additional ones that do not break this continuity. . . .
The hierarchy is led by Ricardo Claro Valdes, who heads
thirteen corporations. He is followed by the person most
representative of the group, Javier Vial Castillo (nine
corporations), and Bernardo Larrain Vial with eight.

To find out the economic magnitude of the *Pirañas*
group, a regiment of economists, lawyers, accountants,
and others would need months to sort through the maze
of balances, legal documents, tax returns, stock-market
reports, and other clues. The task is now even more difficult, since the Banco Hipotecario group have been utilizing intricate devices in their transactions to get around the
laws governing corporations.

A Few Accounts

Javier Vial Castillo is on the Board of Directors of five
corporations, two investment firms, and two insurance
companies. Between June 30 and December 31, 1970,

[6] The reference is to Ricardo Lagos, *La concentración del
poder económico en Chile* (Santiago, 1963).

seven of these companies, excluding Mademsa and Cooperativa Vitalicia de Inversiones, controlled capital on the order of 293 million escudos. During the same period of time, the profits were almost 28 million escudos. Taking a conservative estimate of 1 per cent of this amount as Javier Castillo's share, we can speculate that he had an income of 280 thousand escudos (it was probably more than this, considering the number of shares he owns), plus the amounts he received as a member of the board, for representation fees, dividends, etc. . . . The maximum salary fixed by the government for the higher ministerial posts barely reaches the sum of 192 thousand escudos per year, and it is evident that a Minister does far more than assist a board meeting or a periodic gathering of financiers once a month.

Another example is the fact that the seven members of the board of the Sociedad Anónima de Navigación Petrolera received 4,266,000 escudos at the end of 1969 for their attendance at board meetings and over 149,-500,000 escudos as their share of the profits. . . . During 1970 a laborer received a minimum salary, fixed by law, of twelve escudos per day; in other words, 4,380 escudos per year.

Founded in 1905 in Valparaíso with an initial capital of one million pesos, Fensa, under Frei's government, represented the typical emergence of the Grupo Banco Hipotecario in the world of finance, and the general control of the company openly favored the monopolistic oligarchy. In mid-1970, Fensa capital was 136,342,406 escudos including reserves, which gave them a return of just under 10 per cent, with more than 12 million escudos in profit. This capital had been almost doubled compared with five years before. The attraction of greater capital resulted in the progressive elimination of the smaller shareholders. The number of stockholders dropped from 3,647 in 1965–66 to 3,193 in 1969–70.

"The foreign license policy," Fensa states in its last Annual Report, "has allowed Fensa to take a large step forward in its technical advancements instead of a slow growth." The cost of this dependent development conditioned to foreign licenses is enormous.

The foreign influence in Fensa started in 1959, when contracts were signed with the Coleman Company and Whirlpool Corporation to manufacture heaters and refrigeration equipment. It continues with the license and technical assistance of the American Brake Shoe Co. granting them rights to manufacture brake linings for railways stock. This branch of the industry moved into motor vehicles when they obtained a License from S.A. Protto Hnos. of Argentina to manufacture motorcar wheels. They also obtained licenses from Hitachi, Japan, to construct electrical motors (1965) and paraffin stoves and heaters (1967) and in 1969 from Zerowatt e Cia., Italy, to produce washing machines.

On the International Level

The ease with which foreign influence is brought in is another characteristic of the *Pirañas*. Fensa alone operates fourteen banks, among which are the Francés e Italiano, The Bank of London and South America, Bank of America, and First National City Bank. The insurance group La Transandina links them with the telephone company (ITT), the Sociedad Renta Edificio Carrera with ITT Sheraton, and Finansa (National Finance, S.A.) with the shareholders of the First National City Overseas Investment Corporation, who own over 50 per cent of the stock of Finansa.

Finansa is one of the vehicles of foreign capital. During 1970 this firm authorized the issuance of debentures for a total of 60 million escudos. The 1971 Annual Report states, "The funds proceeding from these debentures will be invested in obtaining debentures issued by commercial, chemical, and other firms such as Wagner Stein SAI, Productores Gillette SAC, Gianoly Mustakis SAC, Franchiny Hollmart SA, Dow Chemical Chile SA, Manufactura de Metales SA, Mademsa, Antivero SAC, Industrias de Té SA, and also in the purchase of notes issued by the Compañía de Acero del Pacífico." Of these nine concerns, five are multinationals.

But now, with Allende in the presidency, the 1971 Annual Report contains a warning, which states: "During the months that have gone by in 1971, there is a tendency not to issue debentures for the time being."

CHAPTER 22

Economic Policy

Chile's economy has been beset by severe problems of unemployment, inflation, low investment rates, and slow growth. Pedro Vuskovic, Allende's Minister of Economy, analyzes these problems in terms of their structural roots in the concentration of wealth and income and outlines an economic policy for the Popular Unity that will solve the economic problems by attacking the structural roots.

Economist Vuskovic, while not a member of the Socialist or the Communist Party, is a key man in the Allende government. He was Director of the Economic Commission for Latin America's Economic Development Division until November 1969, when he moved to the University of Chile's Institute of Economics and Planning to head the group of economic experts who participated in drawing up the Popular Unity's Basic Program.

The document of the Central Bank of Chile that follows capsulizes the long-term economic goals of the Popular Unity government, as well as the short-term economic policy for 1971.

BASIC ASPECTS OF THE ECONOMIC
AND FINANCIAL POLICY OF CHILE*

BANCO CENTRAL DE CHILE

The economic policy of the Unidad Popular Government, in its fundamental approach, aims substantially at the replacement of the present economic structure with another one, which will allow the realization of a socialist and pluralistic society to begin. To attain this aim, the government will promptly start to develop the three major areas of ownership: state, mixed and private. The state area will be the prevailing one and will be made up of the existing state enterprises plus the ones that will be set up in the future, especially in certain sectors, such as basic resources, the large domestic and foreign monopolies, banking, foreign commerce and the fields that have strategic importance in the Nation's development. The mixed area will be made up of companies which combine private and state capital and which are to be administered and managed jointly. It will have a place mainly in the fields of manufacturing, fishing, mining and trade. In the private area will be left most of the existing companies set up as stock corporations, partnerships, and institutions having industrial or commercial private ownership. This general orientation will be complemented by an agricultural policy tied in to indicated transformations, the basic directives of which can be summarized as a deepening, widening and speeding up of the agrarian reform process; organized participation of the peasants both in the planning and realization of the agricultural reform and in the

* From an advertisement in the New York *Times,* January 25, 1971.

use and cultivation of the soil, looking mostly to the development of cooperative properties; changes in the commerce system through a wider intervention of the State in the intermediary field, and a strong democratization in the use of credit and in technical assistance—all this in order to strongly increase production and the productivity of this sector.

In these new conditions, the development of the Chilean economy will be guided through a system of planning with the participation of the various national sectors and (in the first place) of the workers. This will mean a change to a harmonic and balanced development of the economy from what has up to now been a cyclic and anarchistic evolution, with the resulting waste of human and material resources. The planned development, which will have as its main theme the transformation of the social relations of production prevailing today, will assure a rapid and decentralized economic growth. Within this framework it is possible for the first time, and in a real way, to solve the immediate problems of the great majorities; ensure monetary stability; defeat the great monopolies, and shift the fruits of progress to the large mass of the people, that is, to complete the tasks necessary to build a new economy and a new society.

The contradictions inherent in the present economic structure are an ever more powerful brake to our development and in the same measure, increasingly worsen the living conditions of the Chilean people. For this very reason the short-term economic policy of the Government has been conceived in order to face two orders of problems at the same time: the solution of the immediate problems, and the start of the structural changes. They both are aspects of the same unit and the Government will face them together in order to reach a solution in both fields.

Some of the most important aspects of the economic policy for 1971 are the following:

REACTIVATION OF THE ECONOMIC POLICY

The sudden rise in the levels of economic activity (which means increasing substantially the availability of goods and services) will be immediately beneficial to the growth potentials of the Chilean economy. Through it a number of programs will become reality, aiming at mobilization. Among them are to be emphasized the programs of lodging, public works, State enterprise investments and reactivation of industrial demand, widening of the agrarian reform and encouragement of exports; all this to result in a very significant increase in production.

INCOME REDISTRIBUTION POLICY

The poverty which is being experienced by large numbers of the Chilean population makes it urgent to act in several fields for the distribution of the national income in a more just manner. Finding more jobs and raising the income of the workers are two immediate objectives of the Government.

Three basic directives guide the wage policy of 1971:

(1) To recover for all workers the real wage level prevailing on January 1, 1970, that is, adjust wages and salaries to reflect 100 per cent increase in the cost of living.

(2) Give an adjustment of more than 100 per cent of the increase in living cost to the wages and salaries at the lowest end.

(3) Start a process of equalization in the family allowance which, within the next few years, should produce a single family allowance.

However, the policy of readjustment and remuneration is placed within the framework of a much larger concept of the income and income redistribution policy, of which the above mentioned policy is only a part. Measures related to a policy of non-monetary income, of lodgings, salaries, recreation, etc. fit an overall vision which assures the fullest consideration of the welfare of the entire Chilean population.

ANTI-INFLATION POLICY

Chilean inflation has become chronic. It has been a permanent characteristic of the economy since the end of the past century, with very short periods of stability in the 20's and in 1960. The annual inflation rate during the last five years has been as follows:

1966	17 per cent	1968	28 per cent
1967	22 per cent	1969	29 per cent
1970			35 per cent

The Government trusts that it will be able to contain inflation with daring and also drastic measures which will affect several complementary fields. The measures affecting the following deserve particular mention:

1. Prices

Prices will be kept stable, if necessary, by means of State control. Such policy at the same time will decrease the profit margins of certain industries deriving from a monopolistic situation.

2. Supplies

In relation to the availability of goods and services, improvement will be determined first of all by the effect that mobilization programs exert over the overall supply inasmuch as they will raise the economic activity level in general. The Government will employ all its capacity for stimulating and giving incentives to the producers in the sectors which have the slowest response or are subject to constriction and difficulties.

3. *Exchange*

One of the main components of the cost structure of firms in almost all sectors is the type of exchange. We shall not return to the policy of periodic devaluations, much more so because the foreign trade forecasts and the favorable balance of trade would render it, as it was in the past, an autonomous inflationary pressure generating inflationary expectations. However, the Government will take all measures necessary for offsetting the negative effects which this decision may have on those firms which export a substantial part of their production or those which substitute these for imports.

4. *Credit*

The credit policy will aim at the opening of new ways of financial support in line with the priorities of the production sectors and their particular type of requirements, requesting at the same time that those firms which have utilized credit in large measure increase their own operating capital.

STRUCTURAL CHANGE POLICY

To initiate the process of structural transformation in the Chilean economy is not only a necessity bearing on the realization of the Government's program (on opening the gates for the strong release of the productive energies, on the substantial modification of the productive relations and on the start of the realization of the new society), but it is above all an unavoidable requirement for the realization of the program in 1971. Therefore it is important to start this process right now.

The transformation program will start with:

a) Nationalization of the foreign banks and state control of domestic private banks;

b) Nationalization of the large mineral operations;

c) Nationalization of some large monopolies in production and distribution;
d) Decisive advances in the Agricultural Reform;
e) Widening of the State's role in foreign trade.

CHILE: TOWARD THE BUILDING OF SOCIALISM*

PEDRO VUSKOVIC BRAVO

Neither obsolete right-wing liberalism nor reformism has anything concrete to offer with respect to the way we can achieve independent, authentic, national development and destroy a structure that in its essence leads necessarily to increasing concentration of income and wealth and ever-deepening differences in economic levels and modes of life among the different sectors of the Chilean population. Under this structure, a growing proportion of the population is condemned to idleness, unemployment, and alienation, while the country's economy is increasingly turned over to foreign interests. For obvious reasons, prolongation of this system would inevitably bring about more and more dictatorial and repressive forms of government.

It is important to be totally aware of the nature and seriousness of present problems, of the extent to which they are an inevitable result of the present system, and therefore of the impossibility of solving them as long as the system is not profoundly modified. Starting from that comprehension, the strategy of economic and social de-

* This analysis is a pre-election report to the Popular Unity on the proposed economic policy. Pedro Vuskovic was subsequently appointed Minister of Economy, Development, and Reconstruction in the Allende government and his ideas on economic policy were largely implemented. Made available and translated by Prensa Latina.

velopment introduced by Popular Unity will be better understood, as will the basis of the measures planned to initiate the building of socialism in Chile. It will be equally understandable why this is the only program that responds to the genuine interests of the majority of the population and of Chile as a nation.

In general, those problems derive from the fact that the entire functioning of the economic system is now oriented to satisfy the consumer demands of a small sector of the population which controls the economic apparatus and deforms it to meet its own demands, to the detriment of the basic needs of the great majority of the population. The root of a series of interrelated problems can be found in this fact. These problems include: the growing instability and contradictions in which the system's incapacity manifests itself; the increasingly unjust distribution of income, with its consequences in terms of growing differentiations in the living conditions of the different strata of the population; the rapid increase in the concentration of property and means of production; and the already incredibly advanced surrender of the national economy to foreign capital.

The Insurmountable Instability Within the System

Some of the principal contradictions and instabilities that the present system is unable to overcome correspond to phenomena that the population perceives most directly, because they are problems that brutally affect broad sectors of our society.

Among them are the unemployment problem, the incapacity of the present system to assure work opportunities for our working-age population, and the resultant high rate of overt unemployment manifest in official estimates. In greater Santiago alone there are 232,000 unemployed, representing 21.1 per cent of the labor force. In June 1969 the proportion was 19.3 per cent, and

17.3 per cent in June 1968. These data show the extraordinarily high level of unemployment and its tendency to increase. This problem has led to the phenomenon—not measured in official statistics—of underemployment and disguised unemployment, which means uncertainty and want for thousands of families and underutilization of the country's most valuable resource: the work capacity of its population. Women constitute less than a fourth of the working population receiving an income, with the aggravating circumstance that they generally find occupation in activities paying the lowest salaries. In an incredibly unbalanced economic structure hardly 18 per cent of the active population is engaged in more or less "modern" activities of reasonable productivity, which generate 54 per cent of the national income, while almost a fourth of the population is engaged in activities that from a technical viewpoint must be considered "primitive," generating less than 4 per cent of the gross national income.

It would be naive to believe that these dramatic employment problems depend upon whether or not the owners of enterprises receive more or fewer assurances by a given government. It is the system itself that is unable to raise the rate of capital accumulation to open the way for more occupational opportunities. It is the system itself that, by orienting available resources toward the expansion of activities that respond to the demands of luxury consumption by high-salaried sectors, precisely emphasizes activities involving lower labor utilization. For these and other basic reasons, this problem cannot be solved—on the contrary, it will steadily worsen—within the framework of the present capitalist system. Not even the imported formula of birth control, which is backed by so many millions of dollars, can solve the problem.

Another manifestation of the basic instability of the system is evident in the inflationary pressures that until now have been uncontainable. So far this year (1970), the rise shown by official figures already represents 32 per cent, although there are reasons to believe that the real magnitude of the phenomenon is underestimated. If this same intensity should hold, by the end of the year a figure of no less than 35 per cent would be reached. And the process repeats itself year after year, under governments more or less conservative or reformist, while the salaried population is obliged to fight periodic battles for adjustments that only apparently restore the buying power of their salaries.

As far as government action is concerned, what has been the outcome of every promise to eradicate inflation? In less than fifteen years, three so-called "stabilization" programs, each characterized by initial success at the cost of greater distortion of the national economy, have ended in total failure. These three successive programs each gave rise to the hope that previous experience would serve to make the new program more efficient, and each employed a more refined and sophisticated use of the apparatuses of monetary policy agreed on and provided by the International Monetary Fund. The three had two characteristics in common besides the one of failure: they refused to go to the root of the problem in order not to affect certain groups of national and foreign interests, and they contributed to the even greater impoverishment of broad sectors of the Chilean population.

There also exist the increasingly unmanageable conflicts between demands for expansion of investments and public expenditure, and the drying up of certain sources of fiscal income. In Chile so-called private initiative is not characterized by its creative capacity or by its drive to open the way for new sources of production and run risks. On the contrary—and despite the frequent demagogy of its representatives regarding private enterprise and "state ownership"—private initiative makes demands of the state not only to undertake works of infrastructure that facilitate private businesses, installation and operation, but also to underwrite new lines of production that private interests can eventually appropriate. . . .

The system needs a constant increase in both general investment and public expenditures, even if only as partial compensation for the growing concentration of income imposed by the system itself. The trouble lies in the fact that, at the same time, it becomes less able to finance them under the restriction inherent in the functioning of the system. So as not to affect the interests of the dominant groups of national and foreign capital, financing restrictions on the income of less favored strata of the population are imposed—and in the past few years particularly on the middle-class sectors—through greater taxes on consumer goods, transforming temporary taxes into permanent ones, increasing the contribution rates that those sectors cannot avoid. Once again the instabilities of the system are resolved by its effects on the majorities of the national population. In a short time, the same thing would happen no matter what accounting tricks are used. In all probability the budget for 1971, soon to be sent to Congress—supposing an activity level similar to this year's, a readjustment of wages equal to the probable increase of the cost of living, and a copper price of fifty-two cents per pound—will have an implicit deficit of no less than two billion *escudos,* which again raises the question as to who should carry the weight of that financing.

For a Popular Unity government, the need for substantial extension of public activity is implicit, to attend to the urgent needs of our development as well as imperious demands for improvement in the living conditions of the population. But these won't be the means . . . employed in the past to finance these activities.

Finally, . . . there are the instabilities and contradictions that lay bare the present functioning of the system in the external relationships of trade and movement of capital. . . . The interested groups enforce a policy of importing equipment, intermediate products, parts, and accessories that reinforces the expansion and functioning of a structure intended for the production of luxuries. . . . Notwithstanding the extraordinary prices of copper, which represented an important amount of additional income, the country's external commitments have continued to increase to such an extent that the financial load prevents the design and execution of a more rational and independent foreign-trade policy. What this could mean for the future is reflected in the CORFO's calculations, according to which the amortization and interest consignments during the following six years—1971–76—would add up to over 1.4 billion. In the years 1971 and 1972 alone these disbursements would represent $285 and $283 million respectively, which, added to approximately $150 million annually of profits and another $120 million on repatriation of foreign-enterprise capital—without taking into consideration fraudulent plight of capital—would come to the enormous amount of $550 million annually of transfers abroad over the next two years; in other words, approximately half the value of our present exports.

Thus the system succumbs, a victim of its own contradictions in procuring through foreign debt the resources that it is incapable of mobilizing internally.

The Distribution of Income and the Living Conditions of the Population

Another area in which the present basic problems are situated is the increasingly unjust distribution of income and its effects, as a growing differentiation factor, on the living standards of different strata of the Chilean population.

A recent study supplies data to determine the extraordinary dimension that this problem has attained. The study shows that half of the lower-income-bracket population received only 17 per cent of the total income. The wealthiest 5 per cent of this population appropriates over 27 per cent of the income, which represents a per-capita income equal to almost thirty-eight times the per-capita income of 10 per cent of the poorer families; what's more, 10 per cent of the national income is concentrated in the wealthiest 1 per cent, which represents a rate equal to sixty-nine times that of 10 per cent of the lower-income-bracket sector. Twenty per cent of the needier families receive less than 4 per cent of the income, which means that they receive an average remuneration equivalent to scarcely half of the minimum worker's wage. Within the agricultural camp, 1 per cent of agriculture's beneficiaries in the upper-income bracket receive seventy times more than the 10 per cent of the lower-income bracket. . . .

The productivity differences and anarchy in the national wage system determine that very pronounced differences exist even within each socioeconomic category. . . .

Such income inequality explains the high degree of economic differentiation into which Chilean society has fallen, at the bottom of which is found that growing proportion of population that is marginal not only in terms of income and access to social and cultural services, but in general in all forms of life. . . .

The entire system has been functioning toward the minority higher-income-bracket sector. The new industrial initiatives and service expansions are aimed at their consumption demands, and the system's scarce dynamism ends up depending on the increase of that consumption. On the other hand, the basic needs of the majority of the population go unattended, and even the public services hold little meaning for the marginal strata; children whose minimum living demands have not been attended to cannot take advantage of educational services, nor do health services prove efficient for an insufficiently fed population. . . .[1]

The Significance of the Popular Unity Program

The system has come to this, and it is from the starting point of the accumulated problems that decisions and choices must be made. Because of its intrinsic nature and because it has already been tried and found wanting in capacity, any possibility of a reformist strategy has been discarded. The only other alternative is, on the one hand, to secure and strengthen the general growth pattern that has been taking place, with its many negative consequences for the living conditions of the population and the possibility of obtaining an independent national development; or else to drastically modify the system and determine a substantially different development strategy.

Despite the intensity of the contradictions it has unleashed, it would be wrong to believe that the growth pattern—characterized as monopolistic and dependent capitalism—has exhausted all its possibilities. But the facts show that its continuation assumes as a prerequisite the accentuation of its character even more, at the cost of even greater concentration and foreign control. It is from that concentration that more dynamism can be derived, which would increase in some measure the rates of capital formation, the growth rhythm, and occupation levels. Its inevitable counterpart would be the increase of alienation and social and economic differentiation, which would in turn have to find their own counterparts in the political field, in terms of even more dictatorial and repressive forms.

Against this choice—certainly undesirable from the

[1] Vuskovic continues with an analysis of economic concentration in different sectors—see Chapters 24 and 25 on this question—and increasing foreign investment—see Chapters 1 and 5.

viewpoint of the interests of the great majority of the population and of Chile as a nation—is the solution outlined by the Popular Unity Basic Program. In essence, it attempts to change the system profoundly, starting from drastic modifications in the concentration of property and in the distribution of income. It attempts also to determine a development strategy that signifies a reorientation of the productive endeavor toward the basic needs of the population, not assigning new resources to production of luxury commodities and even reconverting already installed capacity to other ends; toward the objective of rapidly raising the productivity of the more backward economic sectors, diminishing sectorial and regional disparities; and toward new development determined by very selective criteria of capital commodity production, basic consumption, and certain export products. The economic system will cease to operate in favor of the demands of the small sectors of high income brackets, reorienting itself to overcome deficits in the basis components of the living cost of the great majority of the population— food, housing, clothing, collective mobilization, education, and health services—as well as to lay the material foundation for an independent national development.

We count on positive factors for this, such as those derived from the very ample margins of productive capacity that the present system is unable to take advantage of and starting from which, freed from the bonds of monopolistic control and foreign interest, a substantial increase in the activity levels of Chile's economy can be obtained in a short time. The first efforts, consequently, will be aimed at this goal.

For such a substantial reorientation, we cannot rely upon the traditional tools of economic policy. Another type of guidance is required to assure the necessary changes to apply that strategy and once and for all face the chronic problems of unemployment, inflationary pressures, and fiscal unbalance that place an overwhelming tax burden on the moderate-income sectors. It is the role that corresponds to what the Popular Unity Basic Program has defined as the *"area of social ownership,"* which will constitute a dominant sector in the economy, starting from the enterprises that at present are state owned, from the nationalization of the enterprises that operate in the exploitation of the country's basic resources —the great copper, iron, and salt mines—and from expropriated enterprises, especially in the manufacturing, distribution, and finance sectors.

The constitution of that area of state control does not represent, therefore, a decision responding exclusively to political motivations; rather, it becomes the hub of an entirely new kind of economic policy. The surplus volume that will then be produced will be of great magnitude and consequently will represent the indispensable material foundation to raise the capital accumulation rate, without appealing to foreign financing or foreign capital. Aside from its quantitative importance, there is the possibility of deciding—without thinking of interests other than those of the country and the majority of the population—on channeling of those surplus goods in terms of both the ends they will serve and the combination of productive factors utilized. Therefore there is the possibility of expanding activities that will rapidly absorb unemployment and lay the foundation for the eradication of underemployment, which constitutes the only truly efficient way to solve this problem, destined to be one of the most urgent tasks of the popular government. And there is also the possibility of assuring that efforts will immediately be turned toward the sectors of commodity production and the supply of services essential to the rapid improvement of housing and other related services, especially in the marginal areas of the urban centers.

Public control of the greater part of the productive apparatus and marketing will at the same time lay the foundations necessary to end inflation. . . . Only a rational policy of production and supply will achieve the elimination of all monopolistic manipulation of prices and the effective control of any speculative aim.

Finally, the surplus derived from the social property area will open the way for a new financing of public-spending expansion. The enormous profits sent abroad by foreign enterprises today and the resources that great monopolistic enterprises appropriate through diverse methods will take the place of new taxes that would affect the lower-income-bracket sectors. It has been proved beyond any doubt that this cannot be achieved through indirect mechanisms; it must be done through the direct incorporation of these activities into a state-controlled economic sector.

In short, we are dealing with a new concept of national economic development that redetermines its objectives to suit authentically national interests and the great majority of the population. It assumes drastic modifications of the traditional growth pattern, putting a stop to the growing foreign control and to the concentration of property and income. It means new guidelines that will achieve the balance of progress of the country's different regions and the different sectors of economic activity. It means the only effective choice to overcome tensions and problems —such as unemployment, inflationary pressures, public financing—that the present system has not been able to solve. And it assumes economic policies fundamentally different from those in the past, essentially leaning on the public control of a social-property area.

It is understandable that a program of this nature should constitute the basic political commitments of the parties, movements, and independent forces that make up Popular Unity, and that it should find the endorsement and backing of both urban and rural salaried employees and of the most diverse sectors of Chile's population. All these have been suffering the consequences of the present economic system, in which the concentration process has been affecting expanding interests. For example there are the minority small businessmen, the small and middle-class industrialists, enslaved by the growing concentration in great enterprises and the increasing degree of production monopolization. The improvement of the relative position of the middle-class strata constituted by employees from public and private sectors, who benefited due to a relative deterioration of the position of manual workers, now finds unsurpassable limits. While foreign and national interest groups—which today receive the benefits of concentration—are not affected, they see themselves facing even greater tax pressures, and other mechanisms that in the past facilitated their promotion become less efficient. The minority sector of workers having access to higher production activities—where, despite the surplus appropriated by enterprise owners, they can obtain considerably higher wages than the general average—find it increasingly difficult to defend their actual income levels, faced with the growing rates of unemployment and marginalization seen in the rest of the working population.

There are, therefore, objective links of solidarity among all those sectors which ascertain the political feasibility of the substantial changes proposed by the program, as well as their active mobilization to make them a reality in a popular government that recognizes beforehand—as expressly stated in the program—that "the revolutionary transformations that the country needs can only become a reality if the Chilean people are in power and exercise it actually and effectively."

CHAPTER 23

Banks, Bankers, and Banking

By mid-1971 the Popular Unity government had achieved an important foothold in the banking sector, long a primary seat of oligarchic power in Chile. In the main, this was accomplished by the simple expedient of making it convenient for stockholders to sell their shares in private banks to the government Development Corporation.

These articles describe the background to the government's intervention in the banking system. They show both the purposiveness and the cautious diplomacy with which the government has so far pursued the completion of the Popular Unity's program. This program gave prime importance to the total socialization of banking.

BANKING POLICY*

BANCO CENTRAL DE CHILE

Banking Concentration

The Chilean economy presents strong concentration, particularly visible in several areas. In particular, the banking sector presents more concentration than the others and this has been an additional cause of the stagnation of the Chilean economy.

* First published as an advertisement in the New York *Times*, January 25, 1971.

Among the private national banks, as of June 30, 1970, three represented 44.5 per cent of the deposits, obtained 55.1 per cent of the profits and participated in 44.3 per cent of the loans. Furthermore, one bank by itself realized more than one third of the profits and represented more than one fourth of the loans and deposits.

With available precedents duly considered, it is possible to state that the concentration in the banking sector is increasing, and that some of the restrictive policies and rules for the quantitative controls of bank credit have contributed to making the situation worse.

The main problems that have derived from this situation of increasing banking concentration are:

1. Credit concentration. This bad habit has lasted a long time within the banking system. In fact, its meaning is that a group of monopolistic enterprises with strong ties in the banking system obtain the largest percentage of the credit, while a large number of medium-size and small-size enterprises have no access to this source of financing.

In addition, the conditions under which credit is given are discriminatory, as the interest is lower for the dominating monopolistic groups, which have an additional certainty of opportunity. Over the course of many years, bank credit in the Chilean economy bore a negative real cost, which has meant a subsidy from the rest of the economy to the credit users. On the other hand, the small enterprises suffer due to extended procedures, and are charged higher interest than the legal rate—through various devices, such as commissions for other services that banks render—and do not receive credit when it is convenient to them.

In December 1969, 66 debtors representing a mere 0.4 per cent of the total receiving bank loans were enjoying 28.6 per cent of the credit; and 1.3 per cent enjoyed 45.6 per cent of it, which means that 208 firms were receiving almost 50 per cent of the credit available. The other extreme was made up by 62.0 per cent of the debtors enjoying only 8.2 per cent of the credit. These figures concern those who have access to bank credit; a large number of persons who do not operate within the banking system is missing.

The monopolistic supply enterprises, for instance, grant credit to the users of their products. Such is the case for paper, concrete and steel; and in general they exact from the medium-size and small-size firm truly usurious interest, which reaches real rates of 20 per cent in some cases.

This circumstance also affects the consumers, who in theory pay a nominal rate of 5 per cent monthly, which translates into a real cost of 15 per cent, 20 per cent and more per year. In this way the distributor, who in the majority of cases is a monopolist, has had access to bank credit at an actually negative cost and has obtained 15 per cent or more in real rate of return; and this gives him a very high margin of speculative profit and leads him into larger debts with the banks.

2. The phenomenon of concentration can also be observed in the regional distribution of financial resources. A tendency toward the concentration of credit in the province of Santiago can be observed. This concentration is relatively stronger than the economic activity, employment and production. For instance at the end of 1965, 62.5 per cent of the credit was granted in the metropolitan section of Santiago in relation to the rest of the nation and this percentage increase to 66.8 per cent in June 1969.

3. If the emphasis of the banking policy is on the quantitative control, the destiny of bank credit is left to the discretion of the dominating groups, and it does not go to the sectors having priority for the development of the economy.

When a policy of selectivity was started for credit, no results came forth. Special credits amounted to 43.6 per cent of the loans at the end of September 1970. There are some lines where the selectivity is fairly strict. The total of special loans came up to Escudos 3,175.0-million in September 1970, and loans totalled Escudos 7,227.2-million. With a strict selectivity rule, it can be said that only 3.7 per cent of the credit is governed by rules clear enough to be considered really selective.

Bank Reform

The precedents we have been examining give some indications that banking activity in Chile is characterized by monopolistic practices and has been aimed at favoring the monopolistic industry's interest in the nation. The controls that monetary authorities have sought to utilize have proved inadequate to correct this situation and the faults that it produces. All this had led the Government to the conclusion that it is necessary to establish State control over the banks.

Government control of the banking system will lead to the reorientation of the credit granted by the above mentioned system toward those productive activities which have priority for the development of the economy, within the Government's plan.

Considering that credit resources are limited, they must be utilized with social criteria which are in agreement with the requirements of economic development. And this puts on us the obligation to parcel out these resources in an extremely equitable way among a larger number of users, allowing them to reach full integration with the national productive system, thereby causing considerable benefit to the entire economy.

It is also necessary to distribute the financial resources among various regions, in relation to the needs of each section and the activities that can be developed there in conformity with National Planning.

As a third consideration, with a state banking system,

it is possible to operate with very rapid mechanisms for the allotment of financial resources; and it is possible to obtain a correlation between general economic policy and financial policy, so that the latter may efficiently serve the requirements of the fields of endeavor that are to be promoted and augmented.

Finally, it is possible to relate the various sources of non-bank financing with the monetary and credit institutions, working out an overall coordinated plan, which takes into consideration all the sources of financial resources and the application of a common policy with respect to credit.

THE POWERFUL BANK OF CHILE: BATTLE OR FORMULA?*

The Banking War

On December 30, Allende announced that he would put before Congress by January 7, 1971, a bill to nationalize private banking. In the meantime, in order to accelerate matters and not to prejudice the smaller stockholders, Allende added, CORFO[1] would purchase any shares offered by these stockholders during a limited period of time (January 11 to 31) at a price that would be in excess of the market values fixed by the nationalization law. This purchasing price, offered as an incentive, would be based on the average quoted on the stock market during the first six months of 1970.

Months have gone by and the project has yet to be sent to Congress. The delay can be attributed to the fact that many shareholders, tempted by an apparently attractive

* An unsigned article from the opposition magazine ¿Qué Pasa? I, No. 14, July 27, 1971.

[1] CORFO is the state Development Corporation.

offer—prices are actually 21.9 per cent to 92.4 per cent lower than the book value of these shares—or "persuaded" by the state's propaganda, have sold their shares, causing many banks to fold. Of the larger private banks, only one—the Español-Chile—has been officially nationalized. Several others have been "intervened" by the state, namely the Edwards Bank, the Sudamericano, and the Crédito e Inversiones. These have not, however, been nationalized. The largest concern of them all, the Banco de Chile, remains neither intervened nor nationalized.

The Decisive Battle: The Banco de Chile

After many skirmishes between those concerned, the decisive battle for the Banco de Chile is about to commence. The following statistics show the importance of this bank:

—Before CORFO began purchasing shares, the Banco de Chile had over thirteen thousand shareholders from all classes, including Mrs. Graciela Letelier, widow of the late President General Ibáñez, the Bank of Bilbao, and, although holding very few shares, prominent politicians of the present government. . . .

—The holdings lodged with this bank in Chilean escudos represent 21.4 per cent of the total held by private entities. This percentage is larger than the total held by all the banks controlled by the state. Banco de Chile holdings are more than double those of the Banco Español-Chile.

—Holdings of foreign currency by the Banco de Chile represent 29.6 per cent of the total lodged with private banks and are more than five times the Banco Español's holdings.

—Profits gained by the Banco de Chile represent almost one third of the profits in private banking in Chile.

From the above information one can only reach the conclusion that, while the Banco de Chile continues as a private entity, there is no socialization of private banking.

Kid Glove Treatment?

The Banco de Chile, like the rest of the banks, has suffered from the financial restrictions imposed by the government in its softening-up campaign, such as the decrease in the rates of interest and the loss of the "brokers' market" in foreign exchange. This last measure has been a severe blow to the bank. These recent measures have resulted in extremely poor balance sheets for all banks for the first six months of the year. The Banco de Chile balance sheet for the first six months has not as yet been published, due to the fact that the bank superintendency has not approved the balance. It is supposed, however, that the results will be poor. Nevertheless the bank should, in view of its power, be able to withstand these financial blows.

In the meantime, CORFO continues to purchase shares of the Banco de Chile and now holds between 30 per cent and 35 per cent of the total shares[2]; thus the state controls between 40 per cent and 45 per cent of the votes at any shareholders' meeting, because only 80 per cent of the shareholders attend. The majority shareholders are being severely pressured to sell their holdings. One is the Banco Hipotecario de Chile, which holds almost two million shares and has had financial difficulties, making it more susceptible to pressure. Another is the enigmatic Rafael Giacamán, who alone holds over 1,800,000 shares. Moreover, CORFO is at present pressing

[2] As far as is known, no U.S. credits were given to any Chilean bank after August 1971.

minor shareholders who have not yet sold their stocks to do so. . . .

At the coming meeting of the Board of Directors, whose mandate lasts until January 1973, CORFO, with its present holdings, could take the opportunity of censuring the Board and so bring about a re-election.

It does not seem likely at present that CORFO is moving along these lines, and the government, moreover, has not brought into play one of its more formidable weapons, that of state intervention, which it has applied against other banks. The lack of sufficient reasons to intervene the bank does not explain the government's attitude, because such reasons were not important in justifying other interventions, such as that of the Banco Sudamericano.

Why, then, the apparent "kid glove" treatment toward the Banco de Chile, when this is the most appetizing pick of the private banks?

The Root of the Matter

What has in fact protected the Banco de Chile so far is that it provides a channel into Chile for numerous private external credits. These private credits are of great importance for our foreign trade, especially now, when our foreign reserves are low. The most important foreign credit to Chile channeled through the Banco de Chile to date has been an agreement with the Chase Manhattan Bank of New York. All these lines of credit would be lost in the case of intervention or nationalization, as has been the case with credit withdrawn from those banks already in the hands of CORFO, even though the amounts are not great. It has been due only to this foreign credit that the ax has not yet fallen on the Banco de Chile.

Another reason for the delay in the nationalization of the bank has been the attitude of its employees. For them, a government-owned concern would mean a threat to their Social Security. The employees fear that if the bank is nationalized, their Social Security would be merged with a state-owned system that would be more bureaucratic and poorly financed and that would, in turn, result in lower benefits for them. The employees also fear that their salaries would be frozen and leveled with those paid to employees of the state-owned banks.

Employees' positions within the bank would most likely be governed by political tendencies. Carlos Ortega, President of the Banco de Chile's union, warned that "there exists a danger that promotion within the bank would depend on whether the employee is a government supporter —of whatever government is in power at the time—and that this will affect us the same way as it has the fiscal employees who have their careers cut off with each change of government."

A Compromise Under Way: The "Tough" and the "Soft"

For these reasons, a quiet compromise may be possible between the bank and the state. On both sides there will be tough and soft attitudes. Within the bank, "tough" Vice-President Alfonso Campos has taken over the negotiations from "soft" Alfonso Vinagre. Vinagre, ex-manager and now president of the bank, was counseled by another "soft," a colleague and intimate friend of President Allende and ex-Minister of President Ibáñez, Luis Correa Prieto. Correa was named director of the bank last October, when Fernando Larrain resigned.

On the governmental side, there are also divided opinions. The president of the Central Bank, Alfonso Inostroza, of the Socialist Party, favors the compromise, while his vice-president, Hugo Fazio, a Communist, opposes the initiative. Fazio insists on nationalizing the Banco de Chile at all costs, disregarding the consequences this may have on the Chilean economy. He has tried, so far with no positive results, to stir up the unions against the bank.

Friction between Fazio and Inostroza is not new. Inostroza attempted to give the Banco Edwards an "honorable" settlement over the question of its credits in dollars to a foreign firm. Fazio, however, opposed Inostroza, who resisted, and forced the intervention of the Banco Edwards.

A peaceful compromise has a new supporter now in the person of President Allende. On July 12, he cordially invited Messrs. Vinagre, Inostroza, Fazio, the Minister of the Exchequer, and Américo Zorrilla, of the Communist Party, to dine at his residence. Several formulas of agreement were studied without a definite settlement being reached. The two formulas with greater chance of succeeding, and that also have the approval of the employees, could be either a "mixed corporation" with five directors from the private circles, five fiscal directors, and Vinagre as president of the Board, or four CORFO directors who would have executive powers in the key areas such as foreign exchange. In this second possibility, Vinagre would remain as president of the Board, since he has the confidence of the present government and also because he is a career man in the Banco de Chile who has risen to his present position through his own merits. He also has the backing and confidence of the unions and shareholders whom he represents before the Board.

Notwithstanding all that has been said on this matter, there are still skeptics who do not trust the outcome of the conversations that have been held and believe that, under the counter, the state has been steadily increasing its share holdings with the intention of launching a surprise announcement the minute they control over 50 per cent of the shares. For those who enjoy a good fight there will be no pleasure from this one. The battle for the Banco de Chile could terminate in a peace treaty, but no one knows for sure whether this will be a truce, an impasse, or an unconditional surrender.

CHAPTER 24

Industry

In each of the sectors of the urban economy a few large enterprises controlled by a wealthy family or handful of powerful businessmen effectively monopolized economic activity. Oscar Garretón analyzes the extent and process of concentration of economic power and the implications of this for such central questions as income redistribution, new forms of organization of economic life, and the direction of future development.

Now, large enterprises are passing from private to state control, but the shift in control does not mean that economic concentration will disappear in a decentralized socialism in which firms are in effect co-operatives under workers' control. Garretón argues that the state should keep large, technologically advanced enterprise intact and use its newly acquired economic power to engage in centrally planned development. Workers should be incorporated into decision making at the plant level in a process of socialization and democratization of economic life; but the state should have the final word in the economic decisions that affect the future of all Chileans. Full incorporation and participation of workers will be achieved under a state engaged in central planning that represents the interests of all workers as a class.

MONOPOLY IN CHILE AND THE
PARTICIPATION OF WORKERS AND THE
STATE IN ECONOMIC MANAGEMENT*

OSCAR GUILLERMO GARRETÓN

This exposition consists of three parts. The first is a descriptive analysis of capitalism in Chile. In the second part some implications of the monopolistic economic order are analyzed. In the third part we will observe other implications, such as the new forms of organization of the economic apparatus within a monopolistic economy. This exposition is related fundamentally to the present polemic concerning the proper way of incorporating the workers in management. This problem is analyzed in terms of the objective characteristics of the economic system.

The analysis presented here is not an attempt to reach a complete explanation. Only one part of the complex that forms the Chilean economic system is approached. Our attempt is to establish that the monopolistic character of the Chilean economy is so fundamental that an analysis centered on this aspect of reality has a truly transcendental result in the examination of the economic structure.

The descriptive analysis uses as its principal source a study made by the economist Jaime Cisternas and myself concerning Chilean corporations in 1966 and entitled *Some Characteristics of the Decision-Making Process in Large Enterprises: The Dynamic of Concentration.*

If we take the Chilean economy by sectors—the analysis concentrates mainly on the industrial sector—we

* From *Cuadernos de la Realidad Nacional*, II, No. 7, March 1971. Oscar Guillermo Garretón is Subsecretary of Economy in the Popular Unity government.

find the following result: of the total of industrial corporations of the country, only 144 enterprises control more than 50 per cent of the assets in Chilean industry. Each of the branches of industry is thus controlled by a small number of firms. . . . This phenomenon is found in mining, commerce, transportation, service industries, and banking.

It is useful to examine what lies behind this number of 144 large enterprises, because the degree of concentration differs depending on whether the 144 belong to different owners or to the same owners. For example, taking as an indicator the capital held by the ten largest stockholders, among the 144 enterprises, we arrive at the following picture: In only one enterprise do the ten biggest stockholders own less than 10 per cent of the total capital in stock. In four enterprises the ten largest stockholders own between 10 and 20 per cent of the capital. In another four, ten own between 20 and 30 per cent of the capital; in five, between 30 and 40 per cent; in four, between 40 and 50 per cent; in eight, between 50 and 60 per cent; in thirteen, between 60 and 70 per cent; in nine, between 70 and 80 per cent; in fourteen, between 80 and 90 per cent; in seventy-seven, the ten largest stockholders own from 90 to 100 per cent of the capital of the enterprises. The figures were calculated on 140 enterprises for which information was available. This means that, from the start, in more than 50 per cent of the enterprises, the ten largest stockholders own between 90 and 100 per cent of the capital of the manufacturing industries. If we project this analysis to the totality of corporations—agricultural, mining, industrial, commercial, construction, etc.—the percentage of concentration is even higher.

Thus the large monopolistic enterprises do not have extensive ownership, and in some way the fiction of the thousands and thousands of stockholders connected to these enterprises is no more than an imaginary figure.

Perhaps that number can exist, but the truth is that there are many thousands who are nothing more than fronts for the real stock controllers, while in each enterprise there are no more than five or ten persons who really control management decisions. . . . This permits us to point out that many large monopolistic enterprises have a family character. Not all, but many, of these began using the legal form of the corporation because of the tax advantages it represents, starting with the period of the Alessandri government,[1] which encouraged incorporation.

This reality also shows us that the stock market is marginal from the point of view of the operations performed in it. Its size impedes the carrying out of any important transaction through it. In fact, an important transaction implies such great variations in prices that the stock exchange becomes an inefficient mechanism for the Chilean capital market. Given such a great concentration of ownership, the possibility of controlling enterprises or of changing their ownership can be operational only through bilateral negotiation between owners and prospective buyers. Transactions are made in the stock market that may be important as complementary buying, but that in practice are actually marginal, since a large part of buying is controlled by only a few people, and the rest consist of small traders who in no way affect the policies of the large Chilean corporations.

A few enterprises have the power of orienting, controlling, and operating, with great room for manipulation, in each of the particular markets. . . . It is possible also to distinguish certain monopolistic groups that extend their control in diverse enterprises of different subsectors of the industrial sector as well as in agriculture, mining (although to a lesser degree), commerce, services, transportation, and communications. This makes it difficult to

[1] The Alessandri administration governed between 1958 and 1964.

speak of an industrial bourgeoisie, a commercial bourgeoisie, or a banking or financial bourgeoisie; in reality, it seems more accurate to speak of a large monopolistic bourgeoisie whose dominant centers invest in the most diverse sectors of the economy. This is important from the point of view of tactical action to construct a different society, because it presents us with means of judging the characteristics of the resistance that certain sectors could offer when faced with a transformation of the Chilean economic structure. Unfortunately, it is impossible here to use some of the charts that show the crossing of stock ownership in various enterprises and in different sectors and the relations of groups in different enterprises.

Intertwined within the textile sector, for example, we find that different important groups are related at the director level. Enterprises belonging to different owners have the same names repeated in their various directories. This demonstrates that beyond ownership concentration there is also regulated management by the economic groups over the dominant heights of the Chilean economy.

We will make a passing reference here to the banks, mostly with the intention of correcting common misconception. The banks appear to many as the center of economic power. They are identified as the centers from which Chilean monopoly power is managed. In our opinion, the truth is otherwise. The banks play a role fundamentally of providing cheap credit. Historically in Chile, the rate of inflation, together with fixed interest rates, has promoted negative real interest rates, and this has reverberated in a very high concentration of credit. Expressed in one set of data, from the Research Division of the Banco Central: in 1967, 2.7 per cent of the debtors, or 508 persons (both natural and legal), had credits of over one billion escudos; i.e., 2.7 per cent of the debtors command 58.1 per cent of the total credit. Furthermore, thirty-seven debtors, who represent 0.2 per cent of the private debtors, had individual credits in sums that reached 848 million escudos, or 23 per cent of the total credit. It is possible to show that this process increased over time. In fact, between the years 1965 and 1969 bank credit suffered a process of concentration that has worsened since the coming to power of the popular government. The most forcible proof of this is in the increasingly stronger and sharper pressures on the State Bank by the medium and small enterprises that previously had credit in the banking enterprises of which they were traditional clients. . . .

If we backtrack a bit to what we pointed out before, concerning the real rate of interest and the concentration of credit, it is worth while to make a short argument. If the banks themselves were heads of economic groups, their logical strategy would be to loan money to the bankers. In that way, and with a low rate of interest, the banks could consolidate their power over other economic activities. But it is clear that banks have not adopted that criterion. They have influence, they have stocks and bonds, but they do not play as impressive a role as controller. This demonstrates that they are not working for themselves, they are not taking advantage of credit conditions, but rather have absorbed these negative interest rates for a long time in order to transform themselves into cheap sources of credit for sectors that do take advantage of these conditions. It is possible to observe this by consulting bank directories. They do not form a unit in themselves, but, rather, distinct economic groups that converge toward banking activity to obtain the credit situation we have observed.

The major exception to this consideration is the Banco de Chile, which transforms its circulating assets into fixed assets by buying stocks. This policy has developed over time, and is more than a coincidence. It is due to the fact that this is *the* bank in which the banking bureaucracy or its high executive levels have an important role to play in credit policy: an autonomous policy distinct from that of the directors of other banks. The present president of the board of directors is a person who arose out of a banking career. This implies an important degree of power in what we have called in sociological terms the banking bureaucracy.

These considerations concerning banks suggest that if banks are not at the center of the most important economic groups, they do represent a source of vital support for economic power.[2] Another entity that should be mentioned is insurance. Traditionally there has also been confusion about the role of insurance within economic groups. It seems to us that, like the banks, it plays a subordinate role, because its principal function is not that of obtaining large profits within its own activity (in fact, its profits are notably low) but rather one of utilizing the reserves of insurance as a complementary means for control in other activities. . . . Insurance companies normally invest their reserves in enterprises linked to their economic groups. It is rare, however, to find any enterprise in which a certain insurance company or trust alone exercises an extraordinarily strong control.

Another facet of the operation of economic groups is the form in which they exercise their power in different controlled enterprises. And here we should make a distinction in time dating from roughly around the years 1965 and 1966. Until then and as the normal manner of operation of the groups, a type of control was used for the different enterprises that did not reflect a common coordinating center of great influence. That is to say, each group was present in the control of the different enterprises, but a central management did not exist. With a

[2] This point is disputed by other Chilean analysts of economic power. See particularly Ricardo Lagos, *La concentración del poder económico* (Santiago, 1964).

certain degree of autonomy, each activity was geared toward maximum profits (with exceptions, as noted, in banking and insurance). In this way, the group incorporated itself in the management of maximizing profit in each economic unit, but it did not exercise a very high degree of socialization in management. In practice, the decisions acted upon by the center of the economic group fundamentally concerned investment of the surplus, transferred to the group in the form of dividends. There was practically no permanent global decision concerning the totality of the investment of each economic group in itself. Starting in 1966, however, the situation changed radically, impelled by a new group, which incorporated itself in the national economy and which is known as the Banco Hipotecario or, as it is intimately known in economic circles, the *Pirañas*.[3] Its principal virtue, which has altered the forms of management since 1966, has consisted precisely in developing a form of socialized, centralized management for all its investments. In that sense, the group operates as a planning center, a center of socialization of investment decisions, or a market of capital within its own structure. How does this operate? Basically, the center of the group is not the enterprise in particular, but rather the group itself. In fact, its head is the Banco Hipotecario—at least until now. Thus the decisions made by the executives of the various enterprises, or by the directors who represent them in other enterprises, do not remain subject to the maximization of profits or to problems limited to any of those enterprises in particular; rather, the particular criteria are subordinated to the centrally planned criteria these groups utilize. Perhaps the Banco Hipotecario group's most important characteristic is its tactical capacity to take advantage of all the inefficiencies of the Chilean economy in its capital markets, with the aim of increasing its power. We mention in pass-

[3] See Chapter 21 for an analysis of this group.

ing the fact that this group started with minimum financial means. Its advantage with respect to other financial groups was its high technical capability to analyze and operate within the Chilean capital markets. This technical feature of the Banco Hipotecario group is currently unrecognized and merits more importance. What conforms more to its legend is its speculative capacity and its ability to control rapidly and in varied forms the different activities of the country. Personally, I believe that this is not its most important feature but rather its most noticeable one. . . .[4]

The Banco Hipotecario group brought a new technique to the management of Chilean capital: the portfolio of investments. This technique originated in the United States as a means for the development of the conglomerates, which make their investments to promote not vertical integration but rather integration in which they hold at the same time, for example, industries such as coal, hotels, metals, chemicals, etc. . . .

Here, in Chile, this "portfolio" technique finds a convenient milieu for its development in the conditions of the capital market. Portfolio is a technique that permits the combination of yield and risk of different stocks in order to adjust the yield of a package of securities with a certain statistically calculated risk. This form of centralized management gave the *Pirañas* group great power. . . . The more socialized and centralized form of management was extended by means of a demonstration effect on the rest of the economic groups. Other groups within the Chilean economy began to utilize a more centralized management of investments. This case is valid for the Matte group, the Edwards group, and for groups such as Ferias La Rural, etc. All these began to formulate a uni-

---

[4] Garretón continues discussing the operation of the Banco Hipotecario group in relation to the operation of the Chilean stock market.

fied management in which permanent discussion focused not on segments of the surplus but rather on the totality of the economic capacity of the group. Thus enterprises could be sold, investments settled, enterprises bought, etc., with great flexibility and taking full advantage of operating conditions.

What has happened to these groups since the election of Allende? Clearly it can be shown, after this date, that the Banco Hipotecario group has suffered an extraordinarily hard blow and that its strategy of centralized control in the large enterprises has deteriorated enormously. This has been reflected in the difficult situation of the Banco Hipotecario and has culminated in the "intervention" of this group. From my point of view, this situation is due to the fact that the triumph of the popular government has penetrated the milieu in which the Chilean monopolistic groups develop naturally. This alters their condition of operation and their whole form of development. Those most affected are the groups that operate technically, presupposing constants, assuming the institutional framework of the system. On changing the latter, reality becomes harshly transformed for them. The Banco Hipotecario group, for example, has had to confront a very high rise in risk for its operations. Part of this risk becomes transformed into uncertainty, into something incalculable; and in the measure in which the risk rises, in the measure in which uncertainty appears, there are necessarily repercussions concerning the liquidity of the group. The multiplier effect for each escudo they have is less. Risk necessarily requires liquidity in present conditions and therefore a real restriction on capacity of control. This forces them to abandon certain zones and confronts them with very great payment difficulties. This is the problem that the Banco Hipotecario group has to face now, a problem that confronts them in their mutual funds.

To a greater or lesser extent, this situation has had repercussions throughout all the monopolistic groups of the country, which obviously see themselves affected by the popular government in the measure in which they have recognized their condition of defeat. The campaign of the Popular Unity gave importance, in its economic strategy, to the attack on the forms of operation of the Chilean monopolistic groups, and the constitution of the road toward social property was transformed into a qualitatively important goal within the economic strategy. This evidently affects them in their functioning.

In summation, then, we can point out that Chile has an extraordinarily concentrated economy, in production as well as in ownership, which defines the characteristics of a strongly monopolistic economy. It will now be interesting to see, in the second part of this work, the implications of an economy with a strong monopolistic concentration for the functioning of some of its variables.

At the outset, it is impossible to think in terms of a policy of income redistribution while the monopolistic situation prevails in the form of a predominantly private economy. Every income redistribution policy will clash, in the last analysis, with this barrier in the path of its development. A highly concentrated economy with a capacity on the part of a small number of enterprises to manipulate the market means necessarily that the capacity to accumulate, the capacity to concentrate incomes in a regressive form, is a methodic and permanent reality of our economy. . . . The manipulation capacity of these enterprises in the market has as its consequence that any monetary policy becomes transformed into a greater quantity of resources, into a greater capacity for that sector to transfer its costs or directly to augment its profits. It is clear also that in some way the characteristics of production and consumption of our economy have their roots in this. Consumption is an objective reality that corresponds to the characteristics of income distribution.

Any policy for popular consumption must consider this problem. It is difficult to envision producers responding to the demand of the popular sectors if there is an attractive and secure market in the high-income sectors, while the market in the lower-income sectors is less secure. The aggravating factor of the recent inflationary process means that slowly, throughout the year, the purchasing power of the popular sectors deteriorates little by little.

It is difficult, if not impossible, to redistribute income in a stable manner while the monopolistic sector of the economy is not managed in a planned way to function in the interests of the majority of the country. This will become possible only as the monopolistic sector passes into the hands of the state. We also confront problems in the accumulation of the monopolistic sector, which transforms our development into something contradictory. The industrial sector of greatest relative growth, technology, and capacity of accumulation is the monopolistic sector. This represents a certain contradiction from the point of view of our development. In the first place, that capacity of accumulation is concentrated so that the surplus is normally destined toward investments of high capital intensity, which generate low employment. This is reflected in Chilean economic activity by the incapacity of the industrial sector to absorb even the annual growth of the active population. This becomes transformed into a structural cause of unemployment. The problem is that if this development naturally continues, if we wish to promote it, we would find ourselves with the paradox that it could only be at the cost of provoking a major regression in the concentration of income, and it would not resolve the unemployment problem. . . .

Another point of interest is the problem of dependence on foreign capital. Foreign capital has extended its domain over practically all sectors and areas of national economic activity, and is especially influential within the

monopolistic sector. Thus the role played by foreign capital in Chile is of enormous importance, because to control
the monopolistic sector means, in reality, to control the
workings of the Chilean economy. This problem also has
qualitative importance even beyond its quantitative implications. Control by foreign capital means that our own
development and growth are increasingly being determined outside the country. Investments are made by
huge international conglomerates whose headquarters are
not only outside Chile, but also outside Latin America.
This necessarily has repercussions in a greater dependence
in our decisions regarding the disposition of our surplus,
the growth of our enterprises, and the development policy
of the monopolistic sector. The policies for growth and
production are being directed toward interests outside
Chile and situated in the monopolistic center of power.
This shrinking freedom to plan our economy is aggravated
by the fact that, at present, Latin America does not
have any means of controlling or expelling foreign capital.
The question is, rather, who will grant foreign capital
the greatest guarantees? For the national bourgeoisies, the
presence of foreign capital is of vital importance. The
bourgeoisies' level of dependence means that they do not
have their own capacity or dynamism to face the present
tasks for the development of Latin America. Only the
state can provide that dynamism, under socialist forms of
state capitalism, or foreign capital. Naturally, this last alternative is the most favorable for the monopolistic bourgeoisie. . . .

Monopoly is an inherent condition in the reality of our
economy, and the problem is not one of how it can be
made to disappear. Very probably monopoly is a reality
we will have to deal with in the future, because to think
in terms of dispersing the nuclei of production would be a
utopian socialistic formula. Thus the problem set forth at
this moment is how to succeed in transforming a strongly

monopolistic economy into an economy directed toward the benefit of the popular majorities.

We must consider how to plan the Chilean economy so that the dominant monopolistic sector operates in terms of a rational allocation of resources for the majority of the country. And here arises the discussion concerning the possible mechanisms of control. The mechanisms of indirect planning that constitute the traditional production forms in Chile have repeatedly demonstrated their inefficiency. . . . Indirect planning supposes control only over the periphery of decision making (subsidy decisions, tax decisions, commercialization and price decisions), all of which undoubtedly affect the behavior of businessmen. But in the measure in which that control exists, it motivates the businessman to take action. The businessman does not accept it passively, but rather reacts in a way to try to avoid it. That is the rationality of indirect control. . . .

If one really wants to plan economic activity, it is necessary not to control the periphery but rather to truly enter into the decision making of the centers of the national economy. We think that planning will really be effective only in so far as the state participates in the production decisions. . . .

Any form of planning will be feasible only if the monopolistic centers of power of the Chilean economy are in the hands of the state and, for that reason, depend on national planning.

Another point to be dealt with here refers to the monopolistic characteristics of the Chilean economy and the incorporation of the workers in the decision-making process. We ought here to make compatible the principle of centralized planning and the incorporation of the workers. We should make clear that incorporation of workers into decision making is synonymous not with decentralization, but rather with democratization and socialization of economic and state activity. The incorporation of the workers in an economy that socializes its most important monopolistic centers is not a sole criterion, nor should it assume the same form in all economic activities; rather, it must assume different forms in the distinct sectors. In the capitalist sectors there should be no incorporation of the workers in decision making, since there the workers do not have power and any incorporation would tend to play a more formal, or mitigating, role in the workers' struggle, which in the long run would weaken them. On the other hand, in the socialized sector the incorporation must be strong, so that the enterprises are not just state property but enterprises with a real socialized management.

In the private sector, neither the forms of stock property nor the formulas of comanagement are of use to the workers. The form of stock property does not alter the manner of legitimation of power in a capitalist enterprise, whereby one participates in power not because he is a worker but because he is a small owner of capital. Stock property fundamentally transforms the worker into a capitalist, provoking confusion and a tendency to weaken his power to make workers' demands within the enterprise. Comanagement is the same. Its postwar origin in all the capitalist countries in Europe at the initiative of the social Christian business sectors fundamentally had no other object than to diminish and regulate the contradictions that surge up between businessmen and workers, with the ultimate goal of creating a kind of national consensus to resolve the problems of the reconstruction of these economies. In the measure in which reconstruction was a principal problem, certainly the formulas for comanagement had relative success. They succeeded in mediating the conflicts and in attracting the workers' sectors. Once this moment was past, however, the mechanisms of comanagement began to lose much of this function, and the objective contradictions that had been covered up by the task of reconstruction appeared. It is thus that the contradiction of class interests objectively led to the ineffectiveness of the company committees. This has resulted in the present opposition to the operation of these committees by businessmen as well as workers in many European countries. The workers oppose them because they lead to a petty-bourgeois point of view among their representatives in the different committees and because they weaken them in their long-run struggles. The businessmen oppose them because in the measure in which their co-optive strategy fails, the committees or councils of comanagement become transformed into a stage at which the contradictory interests of management and workers come face to face.

This reality has had similar repercussions in Chile, and there have been cases in which the workers have had to resort to conflict in order to bring about the elimination of this type of comanagement. We believe that neither system benefits the workers. In a capitalist economy the workers' instrument of power is the union. There the worker participates in decisions, especially in cases of confrontation. The fact that the union must be taken into account by the businessman means that it has regulation powers in decisions concerning remuneration as well as non-economic concerns. The worker is not subject to the arbitrary decision of the businessman. The union is the instrument the workers can count on in the capitalist economy, and not other instruments of power, which tend to weaken workers, which do not substantially alter the capitalist character of the enterprise, and which on the contrary can only bring about weakness in the transformations of the whole economy and the political life of the country.

In the state realm, on the other hand, the situation varies fundamentally. There, an incorporation of the workers should take place in proportion to the disappearance of class contradictions. But this does not clarify the problem of the real form of incorporation that we will propose here. In Chile, two divergent positions exist concerning this issue: the idea of central democratic planning, and the forms of co-operative management or workers' enterprises, which some call the model of self-management, referring in a distorted way to the Yugoslav case.

We believe that the model of workers' enterprises or the forms of creating co-operatives are not appropriate for the monopolistic sector, nor as the principal model of economic activity. Self-management belongs to an intermediate degree of socialization, at the level of a work collective or global social forces, and not at the level of classes, which is conducive to creating permanent situations that approach the model of private enterprise. Socialization can only be realized in the measure that it reflects the decisions of all the workers. That means that the decisions of a central government should prevail over workers' collectives or individual workers.

Objective reality offers us some important elements on which to base this judgment. In an economy with a strong monopolistic concentration, it is absolutely impossible to think of turning over the monopolistic centers of decision making to workers' collectives. That would mean turning over such great relative power to those workers that, in the long run, they would become transformed in the dominant or oligarchic circles within the economy, to the detriment of the rest of the country's workers. Thus, for example, if copper is turned over to the co-operative decision making or self-management of the copper workers, we would be faced with a phenomenon in which a small sector of the country's workers would have a dominant participation in the decision making of an activity that affects, in a permanent and profound way, all the Chilean people. The copper workers have something to say, they ought to be incorporated into decision making, but the participation of the Chilean state, of the government, must be dominant, since it represents all our workers. In this way, the copper industry can participate in national planning, with the result that our resources are used to benefit all Chileans.

The same situation can be found in the banks. It is impractical to think that the banking sector can be turned over to bank workers, organized into co-operatives, because that would mean turning over to a sector of workers something that interests and affects the whole worker population. The national monopolistic structure makes it necessary for sectors that exercise a dominant role in the whole economy to adopt a socialized form of decision making under centralized planning that does not exclude participation of workers but rather, on the contrary, integrates all the workers and not only those of the work collective. In this way, all workers, incorporated in the government, plan the allocation of those resources, and, on a lower level, there would also be preferential participation of the workers of the enterprise, incorporating them into shared decision making with the government but with the government decision always dominating in the last instance.

To insist on self-management as the principal solution to the incorporation of workers into decision making in the Chilean economy is an ideological insistence that has no foundation. . . . That insistence is no more than a search for a non-reactionary alternative in order to oppose the forms of centralized planning.

Nevertheless, we should not limit ourselves to denouncing this ideological alternative but rather try to explain it. We believe that it is logical for forms of self-management to be attractive—to the sectors with an essentially moral, fundamentally anti-scientific attitude of rejection toward the operation of capitalist forms, which constantly search for utopian solutions and goals. . . .[5]

[5] The allusion is to the Christian Democrats.

In summary, to the degree that the fundamental instrument of decision making on the level of the dominant, monopolistic sector of the economy, will be planned by the state, the important problem of incorporating the workers to power does not so much radiate around the enterprise—although there must also be participation there—but focuses rather on the state itself and its principal instruments by means of their organizations and parties. The incorporation into enterprise comes later, under the conditions already described, with a central criterion. Participation, but not on the dominant level. The participation of the state must be dominant, as the representative not of sectors of social classes but rather of the social forces as such.

The form in which this process will be constructed in practice is impossible to define at this moment, because it will become formulated as the reality dictates. We must not fall into the same error as those who developed successive co-operative or self-management forms, but rather create our own model.

The concrete experiences of interventions and expropriations that have come about, or those that will happen in the future as the program of the Popular Unity is completed, will bring errors and successes, and the forms that should be adopted, the criteria that must be corrected, the social and technical education that the workers must have, will come from that experience.

The task consists, therefore, of seeing that the interventions and expropriations do not become transformed into a mere transfer to the state, but that they remain a problem of pursuit and permanent analysis, of discussion with workers, of concrete understanding of their experiences, through which that bud of socialist society can be transformed into learning for the rest of the workers and into possibilities of success in our struggle to implant and construct socialism in Chile.

CHAPTER 25

Commerce and Consumption

The short-term effects of the Popular Unity government's economic policies with respect to wages, prices, interest rates, the tough attitude toward maintaining and increasing production levels in industry, and other fiscal and monetary measures were to redistribute income in favor of salaried and wage-earning classes and to create an upturn in the economy. Increased consumer demand, however, together with other factors which Pedro Vuskovic analyzes, quickly created supply shortages of a wide variey of consumer goods. The right-wing opposition used these shortages in an attempt to gain political advantage against the government. Women's organizations of the Popular Unity and the government then arranged a large public meeting to discuss openly the sources of the problem.

CONVERSATION WITH THE WOMEN OF CHILE*

PEDRO VUSKOVIC

Beloved *compañeras:*
My greetings go to the *compañeras* who have organized this meeting and demanded our presence.

* Pedro Vuskovic is Minister of Economy, Development, and Reconstruction. This is a somewhat abridged translation of Minister Vuskovic's talk to thousands of women gathered in a Santiago stadium on July 29, 1971. The translation attempts to retain the informality of the talk while leaving out some of the detail and repetitiveness (which the Minister used to drive home his point) of the original Spanish.

My greetings also go to the *compañeras* of Santiago who have come to this stadium to have a sincere and open dialogue with the representatives of the government of the people and to do their bit with their generosity as women helping with the tasks of this, their own government. . . .

A Right and a Responsibility

I believe, my *compañeras,* that at this meeting a right is attained and a responsibility must be complied with.

This right is being exercised: to demand that the government report directly to the people; a right to summon them to ask them for an explanation, to ask them what the government is doing. It is not the Minister who is calling you; it is the workers who are summoning and demanding the presence of government officials.

While the women of Santiago were mobilizing for this event and organizing with their government the defense of vital supplies for their homes, a Santiago newspaper took the liberty of writing the following paragraph:

"The Minister of Economy, Mr. Pedro Vuskovic, has deemed it convenient to call housewives to a stadium for the purpose of explaining the problem of lack of supplies and its origins."

I think various things must be clarified about this. In the first place, the housewives here are not meeting with any "Mister Minister": the housewives are meeting with the *compañero* Minister of the government of the people.

In the second place, it is not I who have summoned you to this event, but it is you who have summoned me to come here in representation of the government, and here I am, because the Ministers of the government of the people feel that it is their duty and their obligation to discuss problems with the people, because this government is not afraid of the people, because it is the government of the men and women of this country, and therefore, it is under such conditions that I attend.

Going Straight to the Point

We are going to speak, and it is good that we do so, of each of the problems in particular. But before we do: Why do we have to face these problems? Is it that we are producing less today, are we importing less than before? No; quite the contrary; we are producing and importing more than before. Well, then this has to be explained, because if we are producing and importing more than before, why is it that we do not have some things? Because it is a fact that we are lacking some things.

What are the factors that affect this problem? Here we have to consider the first important factor, which is behind all this: the economic policy of the government of the people has meant a substantial increase in the purchasing power of the great majority of the population.

In this there is a substantial difference with the past.

Before, the problem was one of income, of purchasing power. When there was a lack of supplies, and there was on many occasions, there was an even greater decrease in the living standard of the workers; and this meant hunger. At other times products were wasted instead of being scarce, because the families of the workers did not earn enough to buy what they needed.

That was really a crime: to waste products when there was a population that does not have enough to eat. That was the kind of problem we were accustomed to face before! Then it was easy not to have shortages of supplies. Because if the thing is to cut down on what people are earning, to increase prices again and again, until the people are not able to buy, except in very small quantities, then it is quite easy to say, "There was no lack of supplies." The problem is different now.

The problem today is that popular consumption has increased, there is greater purchasing power. And the problem is that sometimes there are difficulties in obtaining supplies of all that which this greater purchasing power permits the people to buy. Because of this larger purchasing power, which is present in each of the homes of the Chilean workers, we cannot always increase supplies as much as we would like. A higher salary alone does not necessarily make it possible to buy more meat, more rice, more oil, because, from time to time, there is one or the other thing which is not available. But the problem, *compañeras,* is that we have problems of lack of supplies to increase consumption, not to decrease consumption, and in that sense, and without denying that we must attack this problem, I could say that today we have a "good problem" on our hands. . . .

Why is it that we have this greater purchasing power? This has been attained for two reasons.

First, the government of the people defined a policy of wages and salaries different from the former one. Because it was not a question of bargaining for how much less than the cost of living wages should be readjusted, but more a question of how much above the cost of living of last year we should readjust the remunerations this year.

This year, in the public area, the minimum salaries were increased from E° 12.- to E° 20.-, without any discrimination with respect to age or sex, which represented an increase of 66.7 per cent.

The remunerations that were lower than a minimum wage were increased by 40 per cent.

The remunerations between one and two minimum wages were increased 38 per cent, and the remunerations that were above two minimum wages were increased 35 per cent.

Family allowances in the public sector were increased from E° 68.- or E° 48.- to a single amount of E° 102.-, and they were increased 100 per cent in the case of workers affected by Social Security.

Pensions were increased between 35 per cent and 67 per cent.

With all this, and if we take into consideration the readjustment obtained by the workers in the private sector, the total readjustment of remunerations has amounted to 45 per cent, compared to a 35 per cent price increase of last year.

Second, the result of price policy, of the decision to put a stop to the inflation, is that these salary increases will not vanish due to the immediate increase of all the prices. We faced the task of holding back price increases so that the readjustment of wages and salaries would actually represent a greater purchasing power for the workers and would not return to the hands of capitalists and large enterprises in terms of prices that became higher each time.

Reduction of Inflation

The results of this are well known: between January and June of last year, inflation exceeded 22 per cent; this year it amounts to 11 per cent. We have been able to reduce inflation by one half. In the first semester of last year, the salaries had been readjusted too late, about March or April, and by that time had already lost 20 per cent of their actual purchasing power. This year we did not wait until April, we readjusted the salaries in January, and the price increases have been substantially less than last year.

As a result of policies, the purchasing power of the workers has increased 30 per cent and the consumption of the whole population has increased more than 20 per cent. And at those levels of greater consumption we do have, temporarily, problems of supplies. This is a part of the answer to the question: Why are things scarce?

Of course, the reactionary press wishes to show another picture. They are not interested in this; they are interested in scandal, in making noises; they are not interested in the solution of problems, they are interested in the political dividends.

They are very happy, because for the first time they have something concrete they can hold onto; they can start again with a campaign they initiated long ago. . . .

Now they appear once again, this time carrying the banner of the consumers. This time their cynicism has reached incredible levels. When was the reactionary press ever concerned about the fact that the people were going barefoot, that they were very badly dressed? Or have they forgotten that the rate of undernourishment in Chile is, even today, a reflection of a social crime? And don't they know that infant mortality also reflects the deficient living conditions and in Chile amounts to more than eighty-five per thousand? Or have they forgotten that even during their administration they had created one bread for poor people and another for rich people and also one kind of milk for the poor and another for the rich? Then this campaign is simply unacceptable. It is a cruel and savage mockery, which the workers and especially you will be able to answer back to.

How to Confront the Problem

We are confronted with a situation we are going to correct in the right way, but under no circumstances the way they did in the past. It would be easy for those of us in the government to let prices shoot up until the workers are not in a position to buy and obtain their needed supplies, and thus exchange the "scarcity" for "too many things." But we are not willing to follow that road!

We will follow the only road we believe is correct for solving this problem: we will defend the greater purchasing power of the population and we will therefore seek production increases and not price increases. Therefore it is more difficult for us to solve this problem.

And when we are trying, *compañeras,* to solve things this way . . . it is not so easy to increase production by 20 or 30 per cent in the course of a few months. It is not so easy, because not the whole system of production is in the hands of the government of the people. Because a great part of the decisions on production are still being taken by those who are interested not in the success of the economic policy of the government of the people but in its failure, in order to be able to substitute this government for another, reactionary one.

In a nutshell, there are two ways of solving the problem of supplies.

One, which has always been used and which the reactionary sectors favor is to let the prices go, take away the purchasing power from the workers, so that no scarcity of products will be noticed (but there would be hunger and malnutrition). With the price increases, capitalists recover their incomes, and we would go back to situations like the one we encountered in 1968, when of each one hundred Chileans, the ten richest received an income sixty-nine times greater than that of the ten poorest Chileans, and this situation became worse in the following years. That is the "recipe" for avoiding problems, and naturally favors the owners of large enterprises.

The other is the way the government of the people will do it. The essential thing is to improve the living standard of the workers. If this creates temporary problems of supplies, we must solve those problems directly. The only correct solution is to increase production.

This answer to our problems involves a great many things. It involves basic change in an economy that was not at the service of the workers but at the service of the great national and international capitalist interests. Therefore the government of the people is fulfilling this program backed by the people, with their active participation.

We cannot consider these problems as completely apart from all that the government has done and will continue to do to change this economic and social system from its very roots.

Profound Transformations

There is no solution to the supply requirements, which have sprung up from an increasing purchasing power of the working class, but to attack at its very foundations all that is characteristic of the old economic system. Therefore the problem we are discussing today is not independent of the severe problems the government of the people is facing. It is not independent of the agrarian reform, because without it we would be able to solve the problem only temporarily and would have to face it again tomorrow. Agriculture has been dominated by the interests of the large landowners, who are responsible for the lack of sufficient food for the Chilean people, and it is their fault that our country has had to spend ever more dollars for importing food while the big landowners were not working the fields properly.

We then have the agrarian reform. Chile has enormous wealth in its agriculture, it has sufficient capacity to produce the food that all the Chileans need; yet each year we must spend our foreign currency to import food, just because the big landowners do not produce enough. Between 1965 and 1970, in five years, only fourteen hundred properties were expropriated. During the first year of this government more than a thousand agricultural properties have been expropriated by decisively applying the same law that already existed. Only when the process of agricultural reform has been completed, when the peasants take into their own hands, as they are already doing, the responsibility of producing necessary food for Chile, will we be able to end the miserable living conditions of our workers while also ending the expenses in foreign exchange represented by importing food.

We also have the nationalization of banks and the decrease of the interest rate, so that the small and medium producers may use our credits, as well as the small businessmen—and not just a few gentlemen, as was the case before.

We have the nationalization of our basic sources of wealth, such as coal, nitrates, and iron, and the important step for ending our dependency, for conquering our economic independence, the nationalization of copper. This is something the people and the Left have been demanding for many years, and it has recently been approved by Congress at the initiative of this government.

We have the formation of the area of social property, the fundamental basis to end the monopolies of the capitalist system and start the construction of a socialist economy: the expropriation or requisition of cement monopolies in order to permit the development of construction and the housing program, and the textile monopolies to produce the necessary cloth for clothing the people.

Together with these and other measures taken to transform the structure of the economy, to definitely resolve the problems of Chile and permit our development, this year we are starting to redistribute income to benefit the workers and the great majority of people.

To begin, we have the battle of production, involving the full participation of the workers in production committees and in the administration councils of the state-owned enterprises, as well as the vigilance committees in private enterprises.

All these things are linked and clearly influence, in various ways, the problem of supplies. . . .

Reasons for This Lack of Supplies

The first reason this occurred is precisely that the economic policy of the government of the people has permitted a substantial increase in the purchasing power of a large majority of the worker population. . . .

The second factor is that we have the deliberate maneuvers for the purpose of making this scarcity even worse. And we must consider this quite carefully. I must admit that a majority of the owners of large enterprises have responded, and production has in fact increased. As SOFOFA (Sociedad de Fomento Fabril—Society for Industrial Development) has recognized, industrial production for this year is already on a far higher level than last year. However, some large monopolies continue to interfere with it.

Several large enterprises had programmed their production to increase the expensive products and decrease those of popular use. At the state-owned enterprises we are changing this, but we still need more time to complete the process. . . .

The country learned about the indiscriminate butchering of breeding cows, which endangered reproduction levels. Also there were attempts to butcher underweight animals, which has forced us to adopt severe control measures. In addition, animals were held out of the market in order to force higher prices.

Recently, other elements have been added: a campaign to stimulate excess consumption and to hoard supplies by those who have the necessary amount of money to do it.

What are they trying to attain by all this? Why so much fuss from the reactionary press? Because what they are trying to do is to find ways of making this problem much worse. How? Among other ways, by making their people hoard products by purchasing much more than they really need. For this purpose the "telephone chains of the nice neighborhoods" go to work. All these ladies call each other asking how much Nescafé, how much condensed milk, how much oil they have been putting away. And that is one way of making the problem unnecessarily larger. For example, last week two hundred tons more meat were distributed than normally, and in many working-class neighborhoods there was not enough meat. But I can tell you that in the homes of the so-called "nice" neighborhoods there was enough meat for a much longer time than was really needed.

Then, *compañeras,* we must know that these problems do not depend only on good will, nor on managing things well. Here we are faced with political forces who are willing to confront this government with any weapons and who are not at all concerned by the damage they may cause to the people of Chile, as long as they can create situations of lack of supplies. It is through these situations that they are dreaming of regaining power and the government, which was legitimately won by the people in September of last year.

To the greater purchasing power, and the reactionary maneuvers, there must also be added some real facts of things that have happened during the past weeks.

There have been storms and also an earthquake. And without looking for excuses, they have had effects that cannot be overlooked. The Nescafé factory suffered losses. Two of its departments collapsed, one of which was the packing section, and it will take two months until it can again work normally. The result was that a production capacity of 250 tons was reduced to 203 tons per month.

The poultry farms also suffered great damage. . . .

Other activities were also affected: Rayón Said was damaged seriously, and the installations of the textile company Sedamar collapsed.

We must also admit failures, errors, and insufficien administrative capacity or lack of instruments of contro and ability to foresee needs and act in due time. We mus point out, with respect to the management of the instru ments of decision, that sometimes these remain in th hands of those who, as it has been stated quite adequately "do things the wrong way."

We Are Not Trying to Escape Our Own Responsibilities

I accept our part of the responsibilities. What is more I tell you in an open and completely honest manner tha a part of these problems can be attributed to us as offi cials; we have not been as efficient as we should be; but i must also be understood that we are just starting to man age instruments that for years were managed by a fe capitalists for their own benefit. And we will have to lear to manage these instruments not for the benefit of thi small group of capitalists, but so that they may work fo the benefit of the Chilean people. And we have to pa some price for learning these things!

We have also inherited problems such as the very lov level of stocks of important food products, which we en countered when we took over this government. At the be ginning of this year we faced very dark days at the Min istry, because sometimes whether Santiago would hav bread or not depended on a ship subject to delay. . . Stocks of grain, of wheat, were reduced to levels tha were completely and practically worthless. That is why we must produce more now, for a growing consumption and also for constituting a reserve, which in a most ir responsible manner had gone down to levels that were a serious threat to the supplies of the people. These thing must also be known. . . .[1]

---

[1] The Minister continues here to analyze shortages of meat poultry, fish, coffee, textiles, liquid gas, and other products.

Distribution

I wish to tell you, *compañeras,* that now a problem has become evident, a problem that nobody dared to face openly, and that problem is the distribution mechanism, in this country and especially in this city.

This system has been organized, designed, and directed to serve that part of the city where the rich people live and to give bad service to the people who work.

Then, besides solving the immediate problem, *compañeras,* let us also put our hands in and solve this problem at its roots once and for all!

Aside from the circumstantial problem of scarcity, the government of the people, as an important part of its program, has proposed basic changes in the manner in which the distribution of goods has traditionally been carried out among the people.

Studies of groups of essential products show the backward and class-biased character of the traditional system. . . .[2]

That is the absurd thing, *compañeras,* that things are cheaper where the people have more money and much more expensive where people have smaller incomes.

This is the distribution system you have been suffering for some time, and we must change it. This is a task we are facing. And we are willing to do everything possible and necessary to change this situation from its very roots. . . .

Speculation

It is quite certain that this scarcity will produce and increase speculation in many products, because the more scarce a product is, the more enthusiastically some dishonest people will take advantage of this situation. I realize, as the comrades said at the beginning of this meet-

[2] The Minister then details shortcomings of the retail system.

ing, that the official prices are not being respected and that meat is being sold at much higher prices than it should be. I can tell you that this is not due to the fact that the distributors are necessarily paying more. In fact, *compañeras,* this is the first time in I do not know how many years, if it ever happened before, that the price of meat during the month of July is practically the same as during the month of December.

However, we must admit that we have counted upon the honest co-operation of organizations of shopkeepers, and we know that the small merchants are also victims of exploitation. We are willing to work with them, to back them up. We wish to improve their business conditions and their profits. But, again quite clearly, we must tell them that this does not mean that we are giving them a blank check either, because some small merchants may damage the prestige of the rest and do whatever they wish, and just as we are willing to help them, we are also willing to use our full force to punish those who want to take advantage of the situation, speculating with the scarcity. . . .

Let Us Share the Responsibilities

But I believe that here we must say one thing quite clearly: if we emerge triumphant from this, if we can really solve all these problems, we will ensure an ever-increasing improvement in the living conditions of the population.

We—I refer to those of us who have administrative responsibilities: Subsecretary Garretón, the head of "Dirinco," the Minister who is speaking with you now—have assumed our share of the responsibility. But I must also tell you that we are not capable of handling this situation as if it were only an administrative, or bureaucratic, problem. It is impossible to overcome this purely by administrative means; we need others to help us out of these problems. What I want to say is this: we feel we have a right to ask that this responsibility be shared by you, by all of you.

It is the people of Chile themselves who must help to attain the success of the economic policy of the government of the people, in the fields, at the factories, in homes, and in each center of activity.

It is a problem of the entire population, of the women themselves, and they must take it into their own hands, just as we promise to fulfill our obligations.

There are practical experiences that show us how the organization and mobilization of the people resolve these problems.

We have developed several important initiatives in order to incorporate the organized people in the solution of the problem of supplies. . . .

The question is not one of a recipe. . . . But I ask you, can we develop in our neighborhoods a committee —let us call it by any name—a local source of supplies, that operates on the level of districts and neighborhoods? You can organize these! There we can get together unions, mothers' centers, neighborhood committees, sport clubs, and other organizations. Can we organize these? Are you capable of taking this thing into your hands?

Neighborhood Control

Starting from this point, if you organize this, wouldn't it be good to also organize a control of supplies? What is it that is lacking? Wouldn't it be adequate to check there the types and qualities of the products that are being sold or about to be sold? Why not control prices from there? The control should not necessarily be by quarreling with the small merchants, punishing the ones who speculate, but by patiently explaining to them that it is they who

must participate also in these supply committees, to find
out what is needed, how to work better; however, the
one and only condition should be that they work honestly. . . .

These are tasks you can do; it is you who can take this
matter into your own hands. And if you do this, if you
assume this responsibility and give it shape, we will be
able to adjust our own bureaucratic organizations in such
a way that they really serve their purpose. In some measure, we are already trying to do this.

Within the Ministry, we put together a group of *compañeras* who have the specific task of taking care of
supply problems. And we are giving this such a great
deal of importance that we are practically considering it
a rank within the hierarchy of the Subsecretariat of Internal Commerce.

I assure you that we are willing to take the control
mechanisms from the few offices in which they are all together now and to turn them over to the community. We
understand that it is very frustrating when people become desperate, because they wish to complain about
something and they find out that there are only two
phones they can call, and finally, *compañeras,* no attention is paid to them. Then people say, who will help us?
Where can we go for help? How can we solve this if we
have all the people in just one office?

It Depends on You

If you take charge of this responsibility, if you start to
organize things, we will distribute this control equipment
in neighborhoods, and to each one we will assign an official who will work with you, so that you do not have to
come uptown to pose your problems.

And I further say to you, *compañeras,* if you start
running this organization, if you put your shoulders to it

in this way, it is you who will force us to leave the enclosures of our offices. . . .

I believe, *compañeras,* that this is the only answer that is in accord with the interests of workers and the great majority of the people in the community. . . .

CHAPTER 26

Agriculture and Agrarian Reform

Chilean agriculture has traditionally been organized in *latifundia,* a system of large estates. The system is highly inefficient economically and engenders grave social injustices. For many years Chile, potentially rich in agriculture, has had to import hundreds of millions of dollars in food supplies, while the rural social structure is polarized between a few thousand rich and powerful landowners and several million impoverished and oppressed *campesinos.* The Popular Unity government has given a very high priority to a total transformation of agriculture and agrarian social structure and has made rapid progress in doing so.

Solon Barraclough's article is a rather complete treatment of land tenure systems, agricultural problems, and the need for and the nature of agrarian reform in Chile.

AGRARIAN REFORM IN CHILE*

SOLON BARRACLOUGH

As President Allende's new popular-front government begins its six-year mandate, tensions are high in rural Chile. . . . Groups of armed landlords have killed one

---

* A Spanish version of this article was published in *Cuadernos de la Realidad Nacional* II, No. 7, March 1971; the English language article was prepared by the author and abridged by the editor.

and threatened other agrarian-reform officials and say they will defend their properties by force if necessary.

The agricultural workers' federations, on the other hand, are demanding better wages and a rapid acceleration of expropriations. Many thousands of unorganized farm workers, rural unemployed, and small, subsistence farmers are expecting the new government to take immediate measures to improve their lot. During the electoral campaign the new government had promised a profound agrarian reform that would expropriate all the *latifundia,* turning the land over to the benefit of the *campesinos;* the popular front said it would also provide necessary technical assistance and credit and would completely transform the existing marketing and processing systems.

Background of the Problem

Frei was elected in 1964 with a solid majority of the popular vote. The Christian Democrats promised revolution with liberty, including an agrarian reform that would grant land to one hundred thousand of the country's some three hundred thousand landless families of farm workers and smallholders (*campesinos*). Frei's major opponent, Socialist-and-Communist-supported Salvador Allende, had received 38 per cent of the popular vote and had promised an even more drastic reform program. The moment seemed propitious to initiate profound rural changes.

Population growth had been outdistancing food production ever since 1945. Imports of agricultural products had doubled in spite of abundant land resources and a favorable climate, similar to California's. Only one fourth of the Chilean work force was employed in agriculture in 1954, which makes it one of the most urbanized of all Latin American countries. Per-capita agricultural income averaged less than one half the national average, however; the poorest 70 per cent of the peasants had incomes averaging less than one hundred dollars annually per person, even including the value of home-grown produce consumed. (This was still more than double the incomes of the majority of *campesinos* in the Andean highlands of Peru, Bolivia, and Ecuador, in northeastern Brazil, or in most of the Caribbean and Central America.) Underemployment was prevalent and one third of the farm labor force was estimated to be economically redundant. This poorest million and a quarter of the farm population bought few industrial goods. Diets were deficient, housing was miserable, and infant mortality high. Although illiteracy in rural areas was officially only 18 per cent, surveys showed that about half of the adult farm workers and *"minifundistas"* in central Chile were unable to read or write.

Over three fourths of the agricultural land held was in large estates (*latifundia*) employing more than twelve workers or tenants. Many permanent laborers received most of their pay in kind, principally the use of a small parcel of land. These *inquilinos* could be evicted at will and depended on the owners (*patrones*) for credit, markets and employment. Unions were practically prohibited and peasant political participation was minimal. Land use on the *latifundia* tended to be extensive. Despite their vast area the *latifundia* employed only 40 per cent of the agricultural work force and accounted for only 60 per cent of the value of all agricultural production. Smallholders (*minifundistas*) with one fourth of the farm population, were crowded onto 2 per cent of the arable land.

Chilean agriculture had been sluggish since the twenties, when the bottom fell out of the Chilean nitrate market and the world began skidding into the Great Depression. The growing urban population forced successive governments, radical and conservative alike, to keep food prices down and to favor urban investments. A few landlords had been modernizing their operations and were replacing a potentially troublesome labor force with machinery. Others neglected their farms and concentrated on urban activities. Many newly rich merchants and industrialists bought estates not to farm them but as a hedge against the persistent inflation and as an entry into the landed aristocracy. Some haciendas had been subdivided among heirs, small producers, tenants, or sharecroppers. A rural proletariat of wage laborers with no rights to land was increasing. Between 1955 and 1965 the number of *inquilinos* dropped by one half, the area in sharecropping increased, and the number of smallholders and landless laborers rose sharply.

An agrarian-reform law promulgated by Jorge Alessandri's administration in 1962 in response to the "Alliance for Progress" had done little to change agrarian structure. From 1928, when the first agrarian resettlement legislation was adopted, until 1964 only about five thousand beneficiaries received land.

The Christian Democrat Reform

In 1965 the new government announced its agrarian reform objectives as being (1) to grant land to thousands of *campesinos,* (2) to increase agricultural production, (3) to increase *campesino* incomes and living levels, and (4) to obtain the *campesinos'* active participation in the national society. Immediately upon taking office a committee of technicians headed by Minister of Agriculture Hugo Trivelli began drawing up new legislation. It required nearly three years, however, before the new agrarian reform law and a necessary constitutional amendment were approved by the Congress.

The law permitted expropriation not only of poorly worked estates but also of corporately owned properties and lands under single ownership of over eighty "basic" hectares (equivalent in value to eighty hectares of good irrigated land near Santiago). Compensation was set at tax-assessed values. In most instances payment would be 10 per cent in cash and the balance in 25-year bonds.

The government adopted new labor legislation encouraging farm workers' unions and declared it would enforce minimum farm wage regulations. The President said agricultural prices would be permitted to rise substantially and that credit and services would be redirected to support reform. A young agricultural economist highly influential in shaping the party's agrarian program, Jacques Chonchol, was put in charge of the agricultural development institute (INDAP). (Chonchol had been briefly in Cuba as an FAO expert and was considered too controversial to take charge of the Agrarian Reform Corporation (CORA) and expropriations.) INDAP immediately announced plans to promote unions and co-operatives among farm workers and smallholders.

By September 1970, CORA, under the Frei government, had expropriated 1,364 estates with a total area of nearly 3,433,774 hectares, 282,374 of which were irrigated. This amounts to some 18 per cent of the nation's irrigated and nearly 12 per cent of its non-irrigated agricultural lands. CORA estimates about twenty-five thousand beneficiaries are being settled with rights to land on this expropriated area—one fourth of the original goal.

CORA has discouraged subdivision into small farms, and most of the land so far has been assigned wholly or in part to co-operatives.

Production on most *asentamientos* (farms affected by the agrarian reform) undoubtedly increased. But costs were high. Cash outlays the equivalent of six to ten thousand dollars per family were made to cover investments in land, improvements, working capital, and administration, and to finance annual operating costs.

An even more serious problem was the small number of persons benefited. Over one third of the *asentamiento* labor force has no rights to the land; many of these hired workers are sons or other relatives of the beneficiaries. Only about one tenth of the potential number of beneficiaries from agrarian reform have as yet been given access to expropriated lands. Even if the present law had been enforced to the limit, well over two thirds of the *campesinos* would have received no land under the Frei government's program if the CORA had maintained its same criteria for assigning land to beneficiaries.

Probably the most far-reaching consequence of the reform was the organization of over half the *campesinos* into unions and co-operatives. *Campesino* unions hardly existed in 1964. They now claim nearly a hundred thousand members and are grouped in three national federations. Strikes are common and increasing in frequency. Daily farm wage rates in real terms are nearly double those of six years ago.

At the same time, another one hundred thousand small producers and farm workers have formed co-operatives and pre-co-operative committees with INDAP assistance. A few have gone into intensive chicken and hog production. A structure of regional marketing and processing co-operatives is beginning to emerge. One co-operative is exporting onions and garlic, previously a lucrative private monopoly.

The basis already exists for a vigorous *campesino*-controlled co-operative system. The *campesino* organizations could dominate Chilean agriculture in the future if sufficient political support were forthcoming.

The challenge of agrarian reform forced the old guard out of control of the National Agricultural Society (SNA). The new leadership is encouraging its members to modernize. The SNA no longer blindly opposes the expropriations of badly managed large estates. Many of the large landowners have responded to threats of expropriation and strikes by producing more, discharging temporary workers, purchasing labor-saving machinery.

Criticisms and Conflicts

In spite of some success in augmenting agricultural production, the government goals of increasing *campesino* incomes and participation were only partially met. Over half the country's irrigated land remains in large private estates. Smallholders' incomes have improved little, and their co-operatives are in a precarious situation. Unionized workers have higher wages. But many *campesinos* are less fully employed than before. Non-unionized workers, who number well over a hundred thousand, face especially severe employment problems and have lost most of their traditional rights to land and pasturage on the large estates. While some *campesinos* now work harder and more productively than previously, others who received work and income under the old system are now openly unemployed.

The *campesinos* in the *asentamientos* have higher average incomes than previously and more participation in management and political affairs. In some respects they constitute a new rural middle class. Many of them now feel the envy and resentment of their poorer neighbors. In spite of these difficulties, however, agrarian problems would undoubtedly have been worse without the reform.

Campesino aspirations have risen greatly during the past few years. But resentment and disillusionment threaten to divide them into conflicting groups manipulated by landlords, the government, and other outside interests unless reform is quickly accelerated and consolidated. The large commercial farmers have been quick to take advantage of this situation. Many large producers are attempting to create a common front with their workers, land-reform beneficiaries, and small farmers to oppose a more radical reform that would eliminate the remaining large private estates and benefit the poorer *campesinos*.

The biggest obstacle to meeting reform goals was the divergence of interests and objectives within the governing Christian Democratic Party itself. The rhetoric of profound agrarian reform and the Party's ideology of non-capitalist development were apparently never taken very seriously by the majority of middle- and upper-class businessmen, professionals, and politicians who were highly influential in the Party and government. When Chonchol and a group of Party technicians drew up a report in 1967 outlining what "non-capitalist" development would imply, it was accepted by the Party's governing council, but it was promptly disavowed by the government and resulted in the election of a new Party directorate. Later, under strong pressure from the Right, which was alarmed by the rapid progress being made in organizing the *campesinos,* the Minister of Interior, who was a wealthy industrialist and contractor, sharply curtailed INDAP's promotional activities in the countryside. In late 1968 Chonchol was forced to resign.

One cannot suppose, however, that merely because all the major parties supported agrarian reform of some kind during the campaign the new government will be able to implement its announced program with relative ease. On the contrary, political opposition to radicalizing the program will be strong both from the Alessandri forces and from at least a considerable part of the Christian Democrats. Moreover, even if these political problems with the opposition parties can be overcome, the Allende government confronts many similar difficulties to those the Frei government faced in implementing a major structural reform that would provide Chile's nearly three hundred thousand poor *campesino* families with land, productive employment, participation, capital, and markets.

The Allende Government's Program

The new government's goals as they have been spelled out in some detail in the popular front's program are apparently more explicit than Frei's were. Moreover, as the popular front is committed to transform Chile into a socialist society, it should be easier to agree internally on a general strategy of action. But the fact that it is made up of a coalition of six political parties, each with its own ideological peculiarities, its own organization, and each to a certain extent representing different social classes, may present great difficulties in obtaining agreement on specific issues, especially as there will very likely be much jockeying among the parties for patronage and relative influence. Moreover, the new government lacks a parliamentary majority and has inherited a public administration with all its old interests and clienteles. The task of translating the popular front's goals into effective government policies is formidable, to say the least.

The new government's agrarian reform strategy is already partly defined in broad outlines. In the first place, agrarian policies should be made within the context of an over-all strategy transforming the entire society along socialist lines. Among the twenty points specifically dealing with agrarian reform in this program, the most important include a resolve to extend reform benefits to all groups of *campesinos* and to mobilize them through their organizations to be integrated into a more unified *campesino* front to strengthen the reform. The government plans to create democratically elected *campesino* councils at local levels and also regionally and nationally to participate together with government officials in planning and carrying out agrarian programs. At the same time, it hopes to make the Ministry of Agriculture responsible primarily for *campesino* development and agrarian reform, doing away with the current wasteful duplication of functions for different clienteles.

In the future, according to the program, agrarian reform is to be planned and executed by areas instead of on an estate-by-estate basis. The intention is to benefit all the *campesino* groups who do not have sufficient productive land or by creating alternative employment opportunities in agricultural processing industries or in related activities.

In the creation of new tenure systems the program states that preference will be given to co-operative farming. Each family, however, would have the right to an individually owned house and garden plot. There will be national and zonal production plans with the aim of increasing both production and *campesino* incomes; many lines of intensive farming will be reserved for smallholders and other land-reform beneficiaries. The program promises to provide the necessary credit, technical assistance, and training for all the *campesinos* to fulfill their part of the national plan. Working capital on the large estates, such as livestock and machinery, would be expropriated in the future along with the land, to avoid the present problem of decapitalization by the former owners, leaving nothing but the bare land for the *campesinos*.

The program contemplates nationalizing existing agricultural supply, marketing, and processing "monopolies"; these are to be managed directly by the state or by co-operatives. As the private banks will also be nationalized, the entire marketing and credit structure could be adapted to achieving agrarian reform goals. In addition, the program proposes guaranteed markets and prices for all the *campesinos'* products that are produced in accordance with the national agricultural plan.

The program offers a series of social benefits to the *campesinos*. All would have Social Security coverage in the future instead of only the workers on commercial farms, as at present. There would be a national program to improve *campesino* housing. Recreation centers and hostels for the use of *campesinos* would be constructed in provincial towns. At the same time, special attention is promised for forest lands, natural-resource conservation, and irrigation problems.

The popular front proposes to initiate this strategy by a thorough enforcement of the existing agrarian-reform law. Meanwhile the new legislation necessary for completing the program would be drawn up, discussed, and approved as rapidly as possible.

Problems Facing the New Government's Agrarian Reform

The popular front's program obviously falls far short of being a clear strategy for agrarian reform. Numerous concepts will have to be clarified and many problems resolved before the twenty points just summarized can be considered a political plan of action. Even if all these issues were resolved, however, the strategy would not be complete. The essential part of any political plan must always be who (i.e., which political groups) do what, when, and how.

A. *Priorities* In the first place, the government's agrarian-reform strategy will have to give a high priority to overcoming political obstacles. The most important of these will be encountered not in the agricultural sector but in the established system of power relationships in the entire society. The success or failure of the new government's agrarian-reform program will depend primarily upon how well it is able to carry out its over-all plans for transforming the social and economic structure of which agrarian reform is only one part.

In the agrarian field, the *campesinos* will have to be mobilized at once so that they and their organizations may become active supporters and participants in the process. Otherwise the superior organization and economic power of the large landowners and allied groups will inevitably direct the reform into populist channels without changing the old power structure very much. At the same time, agricultural marketing, credit, and industrial structures, in addition to the whole public administration, must be put at the service of the reform and the *campesinos* as rapidly as possible.

The government should attempt to complete all the expropriations of *latifundia* permitted under the present law within the first few months of the new administration. Preliminary estimates indicate that from three to four thousand estates remain to be expropriated under the present law.* Subsequent legislation could then more easily be adopted to consolidate the transformation. A rapid completion of expropriations, accompanied by guarantees to small and medium-sized farmers that they would not be expropriated, at least for the present, would reduce political opposition from this quarter. The difficult tasks of economic, social, and political reorganization could then proceed more effectively.

The new government's immediate agrarian-reform priorities then should be: (1) to push ahead resolutely and rapidly with its over-all program of transforming the entire society; (2) to mobilize the *campesinos;* (3) to put the country's agricultural marketing, supply, processing, and credit institutions and its public administration at the service of the national development plan and the *campesinos;* (4) to complete all expropriations quickly under the present law.

B. *Institutional Structures* A second problem will be to define how the proposed new structures of credit, marketing, and public administration should be organized and operated in practice. Simply nationalizing agricultural industries and private banks, for example, will not neces-

* In the first two years of the Allende government, these *latifundia* were ended by the agrarian reform.

sarily change the present power relationships very much until the state becomes much more representative of the *campesinos* and their interests.

Many agricultural industries are already largely government-owned but are nonetheless the instruments of private commercial interests. The state bank and the state Development Corporation (CORFO) have not had a much better record than private lenders when it comes to strengthening the economic base of *campesino* agriculture. Many of the present agricultural co-operatives serve primarily the interests of large commercial producers.*

Vigorous action will have to be taken to assure that these banking, commercial, and industrial institutions have programs and structures that really support the government's agrarian-reform strategy after they are nationalized.

The establishment of an agrarian development fund would combine the advantages of geographic decentralization, democratic participation, *campesino* control, and purposeful national planning. It would also permit the use of the market for ensuring efficient resource allocation within the limits imposed by the development plan. This scheme would be perfectly consistent with a system of national marketing boards and state enterprises for certain key commodities, especially those important for exports and imports.

Similarly, public administration in agriculture will have to be completely transformed if it is to be an effective instrument for reform and development. *Campesino* participation in planning and carrying out reform programs will have to be real and not merely a formality. The system of individual agency clienteles will have to be abandoned—no easy task, considering that each party in the new government coalition grew up within this system

* Antonio García, *Las Cooperativas y el Desarrollo Agrícola de Chile*, ICIRA, 1970. (Preliminary)

and has its own clienteles with powerful interests. At present there are several agencies with overlapping functions, each serving their separate clienteles. This could be done by making the Ministry of Agriculture in effect the Ministry of Agrarian Reform and Rural Development.

Functionally, however, the public administration should become much more unified and centralized nationally and in each zone and area. The *campesino* organizations would participate in planning and in plan execution at the area, zonal, and national levels. The present situation, in which several national programs such as COPA's, INDAP's, CORFO's, etc. operate independently and often in competition with each other, would no longer prevail. In fact, these semi-independent agencies would tend to disappear.

C. *Guaranteed Prices and Distribution* Thirdly, a national system of guaranteed prices and markets for production in accordance with the development plan, as proposed by the popular front, is highly necessary for an effective agrarian-reform strategy. On the one hand, it is required in order to guarantee the *campesinos* markets for their products at reasonable prices so that they will have the possibilities and economic incentives to increase their production in accordance with national plans. On the other hand, such a program would help to ensure adequate distribution of essential foodstuffs to low-income groups.

In this way everyone could be guaranteed at least a minimum level of consumption; at the same time some of the most obnoxious aspects of direct rationing could be avoided while the free market could still perform its function of equating supply with demand.

D. *A National Land Policy* A fourth problem is the lack of a national land and water policy. One of the most telling criticisms of the *latifundia* system has been the irrational land-use patterns associated with it. Logically a national land policy to achieve more desirable land use in the future should be an integral part of any land-reform strategy. Little or no attention has been given to controlling the use of lands that have not been expropriated. In general, the broad land-use patterns and practices of the old *latifundia* systems have been perpetuated and sometimes even further consolidated by reform.

Water and land use should be planned in broad outline both on a national scale and for each area. These plans should be based on foreseeable needs, soil resources, and economic and ecological considerations. There will have to be adequate controls to make this planning effective in practice. Carrying out the reform by areas, as proposed in the popular front's program, would greatly facilitate such a land policy. So would the vigorous implementation of present water legislation.

E. *Land-Tenure Systems* A fifth problem is that the new land-tenure systems resulting from reform must be adequate for attaining national development goals. Land tenure is fundamentally the institutionalized system of relationships among groups and individuals in the use of land and labor and in the control of their products. It is much broader than mere legal ownership.

The new government faces the problem of devising tenure systems adapted to Chilean conditions. At the same time, these systems should: (1) ensure at least minimum acceptable levels of security, welfare, employment, and income for all *campesinos;* (2) provide for the greatest possible direct participation of the *campesinos* in decision making at every level; (3) facilitate the formulation and execution of national development plans; and (4) provide incentives for high economic performance— i.e., productivity, efficiency, investment, and growth.

The *asentamientos* formed under the Frei administration did not meet any of these criteria in an entirely satisfactory manner. They were particularly deficient in facing the equality issue. The permanent laborers on expropriated estates, and a few others who received land, obtained security, welfare, employment, and income. But more than two thirds of the *campesinos* who are *minifundistas* or unattached landless laborers had no prospects of benefiting from the reform, and many became even worse off as a result. Those few who received land had more participation in decision making than previously, although this was limited by excessive paternalism on the part of CORA, but the majority were as much excluded from political and management decisions as before. The conflicts of interests among the diverse *campesino* groups have tended to grow.

Secondly, the difficulties of administering a large-scale centralized system of state or collective farms are immense in the best of circumstances and probably insurmountable in the short run. This is in part because of a lack of experienced and adequately trained personnel; moreover, such a system could easily become inconsistent with the objective of greater *campesino* participation in decision making. In addition, many *campesinos,* especially *inquilinos*, sharecroppers, and smallholders, place a high value on land ownership as such, and it would be exceedingly difficult to convince many of them to accept willingly a system of state ownership.

In view of these objectives and limitations, the new government's proposals to carry out the agrarian reform on an area basis (presumably each area would include one or more *comunas*—roughly counties—depending on ecological factors and the farm population) and to give preference to co-operative farming enterprises not only makes sense but appears to be the most viable short-term policy. The promise to provide every *campesino* family with sufficient land for a house and garden plot of its own would ensure a bare minimum of security now lacking for the majority. The degree to which the other criteria for a desirable tenure system could be met would depend on the quality of planning and the type of co-operative organizations that evolve.

But while this proposal for agrarian reform organiza-tion by areas would mitigate the problems now created by the reform's organization on an estate-by-estate basis, it would by no means solve them. Some areas will be much poorer in resources and markets than others. Some will be relatively overpopulated and others short of workers. The problem of providing more equal oppor-tunities for all *campesino* groups will merely be removed to the area level. Its solution nationally will require na-tional planning and the virtual socialization of the in-come derived from land and capital on a national scale if the objective is really to provide the greatest possible equality of opportunities for all the *campesinos*.

F. *Financing* A sixth problem is how to finance the reform. This is not mentioned in the popular front's program but will obviously present immediate problems for the new government. On the one hand, additional resources must be mobilized to finance a massive reform. On the other hand, per-family costs of implementing the reform must be reduced considerably from what they have been during the past six years.

Mobilizing the necessary resources present a problem of fiscal policy going far beyond the agrarian sector. If agrarian reform really has a high priority, however, some way can be found to obtain the necessary funds. The agrarian development fund proposed above could prove very useful in this respect.

One simple measure that could be taken quickly to in-crease revenues would be to increase real-estate taxes sharply.

A second, complementary revenue-raising measure, which was also suggested above, would be to charge land-reform beneficiaries a tax or rent on the value of the land and capital turned over to them by reform.

The proposed nationalization of the banking system and reform of the nation's credit structure should make it feasible for the government to mobilize other, additional resources for agrarian reform. Moreover, it should explore the possibilities of obtaining new international credits to support its reform and development programs. Both the World Bank and the Interamerican Bank, for example, have on various occasions expressed their interest in making important loans to support well-planned, large-scale agrarian reforms. They may never be presented with a better opportunity to demonstrate their good intentions.*

Of course, the most important thing for both reducing costs and increasing revenues for the agrarian reform will be to increase efficiency and productivity at all levels in the process. There can be no adequate substitute for good management, rational accounting, and wise economic decisions.

G. *Campesino Participation, Training, and Education* A seventh problem that has been implicit in all the previous discussion is the necessity for full *campesino* participation. This participation presupposes effective and united *campesino* organization at all levels. As seen earlier, in spite of impressive progress during the Frei period in the creation of *campesino* organizations, really effective *campesino* participation in the reform process was not achieved.

A fundamental requirement for such *campesino* participation is to ensure that they have an important role in all stages of the reform process, making it their reform. They must participate at all levels in planning and execution. The public administration, marketing, credit, and process-

---

* All international agencies under U.S. influence have suspended all forms of aid and development assistance to Chile.

ing institutions should be controlled by the *campesinos* to the extent consistent with carrying out national development plans. The *campesinos* should actively participate in the management of the agrarian reform production units; in fact, these should normally be *campesino* cooperatives. *Campesino* unions will have to be strengthened and there will have to be more grass-roots participation in union affairs. Moreover, the unions will have to work together in support of the reform. All these objectives have been foreseen in the popular front's program and touched upon in the preceding sections of this paper. The problem is how to make this participation truly effective.

One simple measure would be for the technicians who provide assistance to reform beneficiaries to be directly responsible to the *campesino* organizations for their salaries and performance. Technicians should be recruited from among the *campesinos* and trained to provide the necessary skills for the reform's success.* There is usually no need to have university-trained professionals working directly with the *campesinos;* in fact, this usually creates a difficult social and communications barrier.

In addition to these institutional problems, however, are those of training and education. The *campesinos* can never participate as effectively as they should if they are not provided with sufficient knowledge and skills to handle their own affairs in an increasingly complex society.

Obviously, literacy and basic education should have a high priority. No one can participate effectively if he has not learned to read, write, and master simple arithmetic. Chile already has one of the lowest illiteracy rates in Latin America. Practically every *campesino* would be-

* See, for example, Jan Myrdal, *Report from a Chinese Village* (New York: Random House, 1963); William Hinton, *Fanshen* (New York: Monthly Review Press, 1966); and Gérard Chaliand, *The Peasants of North Vietnam* (Baltimore: Penguin Books, 1969).

come literate in a relatively short period if a crash program were launched. The experience already gained shows this could be done rapidly and effectively with modern methods and the full use of mass communications media.

This education cannot be devoid of ideological content. It must be consistent with the country's development goals. This implies a cultural revolution. The new government will have to mount a massive campaign to change the *campesinos'* traditional attitudes and values formed by a *latifundia*-dominated rural society.

Training in farm management, accounting, and co-operative and business management is also essential. The *campesinos* often complain now that the government technicians make all the important decisions. The only way this can be avoided even after structural reforms is to train enough *campesinos* in these skills so that they can participate in decision making as equals.

H. *A National Policy of Employment and Technology*
An eighth problem is that a strategy of agrarian reform should be co-ordinated with a national policy of employment and technology. It is unrealistic in the extreme to hope that agrarian reform alone could provide adequate employment for the entire rural work force. Historically, agriculture has been the principal employer of last resort. Chile, however, is already so far urbanized that farming is beginning to lose the possibility of fulfilling this rudimentary function.

Like previous governments, the Frei administration never faced up to the rural-employment problem. Disguised agricultural unemployment and underemployment were already estimated by CIDA at nearly 30 per cent of the agricultural labor force in 1964. Rural unemployment is almost certainly as high now in spite of the fact that agricultural production has gone up by over one fourth, while the farm labor force has remained almost stationary. Outright rural unemployment has unquestionably increased.

Full employment for the *campesino* work force will require an over-all strategy embracing the whole society. Income redistribution in urban areas would accelerate demand for many lines of labor-intensive agricultural production. This would increase farm employment, at least in the short run. Accelerated industrial production and investment would also absorb some rural labor, especially if some of the new industries could be located in heavily populated rural areas. Investment in public works of all kinds is required in rural areas. But these cannot be financed wholly or even largely from agricultural income. Schools, roads, new irrigation works, and reforestation should have a high priority in any agrarian strategy, but financing these investments is a problem for the entire economy.

A national technological policy could assure that capital and scarce foreign exchange are used to obtain the new capital goods that have the highest priorities for the success of the national development plan. These may not include some kinds of expensive labor-saving agricultural machinery now being imported until a later stage in Chile's development. The importation of many consumer durables such as private cars, etc. will probably have to be further restricted. There will have to be a well-planned policy of national industrialization, with the eventual local manufacture of many goods, especially capital goods and machine tools that are now imported.

It is idle to hope that individual farmers, co-operatives, or state farms will adopt "intermediate" agricultural technologies, even in situations in which there is a clear economic advantage for the country in their doing so if they can obtain highly modern labor-saving machinery on such favorable terms that it is profitable for them to use it. *A principal aim of a national technological policy should be to make sure that the technologies that are available and most profitable for individual economic units coincide with those that would contribute most to achieving national development goals.* This is a responsibility of the government and cannot be left to the vagaries of unregulated market forces.

A national employment and technological policy as part of a national development plan should make it possible to eliminate rural unemployment within a relatively short time. Labor shortages might even become a problem in the near future. But there is no way of solving the rural employment problem within the confines of the agrarian sector alone. It requires an imaginative national strategy. This implies dynamic planning at every level. Perhaps the greatest immediate obstacle to a successful agrarian reform is that neither the mechanisms nor the substance of this planning has yet been developed.

Prospects

The key to the future of the new government's agrarian reform will not be encountered in the agricultural sector but in the system of power relationships in the entire society. The fate of the agrarian reform will inevitably be determined in large measure by the relative success or failure of the government's over-all strategy of structural change.

Whether a freely elected "socialist" government can carry out a profound program of structural change leading to a socialist society, all within a framework of democratic institutions, remains an open question. Many maintain that it can't be done. Historical experience is not very encouraging in this respect.

The Allende government has a unique opportunity to show that an elected government can make a peaceful transition to a democratic and humanitarian social structure. Chile is one of the few countries in the world with its rural areas still dominated by a traditional *latifundia* system where a profound agrarian reform, incorporating the *campesinos* fully into a dynamic, modern, and democratic society, has some possibility of success.

If, in the end, the new government should prove to be socialist in name only, it still could carry out an important agrarian reform, rapidly expropriating the remaining *latifundia*. It would be an important "populist" reform that prepared the way for further economic growth even though it did not greatly alter the power relationships in society. Under Latin American conditions, however, without equally far-reaching reforms in the rest of the economy the reform would leave unfulfilled the requirements of the majority of poor *campesinos* for markets, credit, technical assistance, employment, and true participation.

If, on the other hand, the proposed reforms in land tenure and in the broader society are carried out rapidly and effectively, the new government could consider itself successful in carrying out a profound "structural" agrarian reform. The *campesinos* could acquire real participation in development. It would mark a milestone in the history of social change in Latin America.

CHAPTER 27

Urbanism

Environmental pollution is not peculiar to the industrial systems of North America and Europe. Destruction of the environment occurs wherever there is industrialization with no consideration of social and environmental costs, and industrial and technological development for private profit rather than social ends. This article indicates the depth of the problem of environmental pollution in Chile. Such problems are also associated with the concentration of activity and people in urban areas. One third of all Chileans live in the capital.

Santiago is an urban disaster. The city spreads like a rapidly expanding ink blot over the rich agricultural land of the province. Shantytowns constructed of makeshift materials by the increasing thousands of homeless spring up everywhere overnight. Older sections of the city deteriorate while pleasant new homes are built for the increasing numbers of the affluent. Traffic and air pollution become impossible as every middle-income family adds a car to its possessions. Chile concentrates it activity in Santiago. Such new industries as are developed usually locate in Santiago. Politics and administration spread out from the capital.

THE CONTAMINATED CITY*

LUIS ALBERTO MANSILLA

More than the smog that makes us cry and breathe with anguish threatens the health of the inhabitants of Chilean cities. The pollution of water and food, never the subject of campaigns or spectacular reports, is more dangerous and becomes more and more a dreadful enemy of life in the city.

The experts on this matter talk about ecology, which for the general public is only a high-sounding word. In brief, ecology is the adequate balance between living beings and the environment. The big modern cities, the indiscriminate use of technology, and the residue of the human conglomerate poison the atmosphere, alter the ecological harmony, and produce a series of physical and mental disequilibriums, besides damaging animal and vegetable life.

Santiago is a ghostly scene of ecological crisis. Considering the small size of the country, Santiago is one of the biggest and most densely populated cities in Latin America. In 1960, Santiago had little more than two million souls. Now the Census Office establishes that we are more than three million and that in 1985 we will be six million. This gigantic increase in population has not been accompanied by an achievement of means to take care of food, hygiene, water, and air.

Dangerous Water

We are precisely 9,280,000 Chileans: 6,550,000 reside in the cities and 2,730,000 in the countryside. Water

* From *Ahora* I, No. 15, July 27, 1971.

is essential for survival and if it is not drinkable, threats of epidemics and diseases are frightful.

Now, how many Chileans have drinking water?

The situation can be summed up as follows: Urban population of the country with drinking water in their homes: 3,900,000 inhabitants. Urban population with easy access to drinking water: 1,780,000. Urban population without drinking water: 870,000. As to drinking water in the countryside, only a hundred thousand people, living in settlements of two hundred to one thousand inhabitants, have water from pipes. Two million four hundred thousand inhabitants from the countryside do not have healthy water at their disposal.

The population of the cities that has use of the sewer systems is 2,500,000 inhabitants. There is a lack of sewers for 4,050,000 people.

Pollution by sewage is very serious. There are no adequate plants for the purification of water in any of the big cities. Most of them are obsolete or overused.

If everybody knew that the water he is drinking is polluted with human excreta, he would throw away the contents of the glass horrified. But so it is. Sewers are mistaken for water pipes and this explains many bacterial, parasitic, and viral diseases that seem at first to be of mysterious origin.

Typhus has become worse during recent years; there are between six thousand and seven thousand cases yearly; half of the afflicted are from Santiago. In many cases, vegetables are sprinkled with waste waters. Fecal bacteria do their work patiently.

Fifteen Thousand Tons of Gas

In addition to the water there is the contaminated air. All big cities suffer the same evil, but some have already created their defenses and have no problems. The human being vitally needs oxygen and a clean atmosphere. But during 1969 alone, fifteen thousand tons of sulfur dioxide fell over Santiago. This is an irritating gas affecting the respiratory tract and one of the most important agents of atmospheric pollution. Smog is part of the landscape of the capital of Chile. The city is wrapped in these winter days with fog that has no relation to climate, but is from chimneys, exhaust from cars, the indiscriminate burning of leaves and rubbish, and smoke from factories located amid very populated areas. The geological conditions of the valley that was so highly praised by Pedro de Valdivia[1] also contribute to the pollution of the air. In the long run, chronic bronchitis, lung cancer, and the death rate increase.

Be Careful with Food

The foods we normally eat can be disease carriers, starting from their very origin. Many people eat meat from sick animals and vegetables polluted with poisonous substances or harmful seeds that might be mixed with them by accident. No close and strict control exists to make businessmen comply with sanitary regulations, and they care only about what they can sell, even knowing that the merchandise is not in good condition.

Only 76.4 per cent of the total number of places in the country where food is processed or handled are considered to be satisfactory. The National Health Service examined 47,554 products in 1969 and established that 9 per cent were not fit for consumption.

The slaughterhouses that exist throughout the country (more than four hundred) lack adequate sanitary control of the meat they send to the market. Trichinosis cases are quite frequent, and last year there were six hundred cases of hydatidosis among people consuming meat. These diseases could be avoided if the "profit-making places" were under the control of appropriate specialists.

[1] *Conquistador* of Chile in the sixteenth century.

Refuse and Pesticides

The residents of Santiago and of other Chilean towns daily produce a huge amount of refuse, which has an uncertain destination. There is no place to burn garbage, and refuse is conveyed to the outskirts, generally to spots located near settlements or at heights that favor the spreading of epidemics and other calamities. The municipality's cleaning departments generally work in a deficient way. Many of these corporations do not have the means to free neighbors from the evils of refuse. The National Health Service supplies sanitary additives and recommends that all refuse collected be pressed, buried, and sealed with a layer of earth. It is no solution to dump it into the sea, because the sea food would be dangerous to consume. Lately the municipalities have agreed to ask the National Health Service to help them find a solution to this problem. All kinds of projects are studied, but we should have no illusions about industrialization, because there is no gold mine in rubbish. At the most, fertilizers can be produced that are no better than those already on the market.

Finally, there are the pesticides. Farmers need to protect their crops from manifold pests that threaten them. Cows eat grass sprayed with chemicals and the milk is contaminated. The same happens with the other animals and of course with garden produce as well. The results are alarming. Pesticides are as harmful to life and health as polluted water, food, and air.

To Avoid Diseases

One of the subdepartments of the National Health Service is dedicated to the protection of health. It is directed by Dr. Horacio Boccardo, editor of the *Cuadernos Médico-Sociales* (Social Medicine Journal) of the Medical Association. The campaigns that must be organized far exceed the lean budget they have at their disposal. Only 3 per cent of the three billion escudos for health is assigned to prevent diseases.

"Traditionally," claims Doctor Boccardo, "money has been spent in treating patients and not in fighting the causes of diseases. It is a mistake that is highly expensive and that we are now mending. The common people wisely say: 'It is better to prevent than to cure.' There is a medicine that the public does not see and that we have to put our shoulders to in the present Chilean process. The ecological crisis is an alarming result of lack of foresight. And we must learn from it. Until now, the country has paid no attention to pollution problems. Happily, a national commission against the pollution of the environment has recently been set up that intends to face the matter with all the means at its disposal and with other means sought in international organizations. But this is not all there is to fight against. Our duty is to protect the complete health of the Chilean people and to become implacable guards against insalubrity, epidemics, and all the factors that may mean avoidable disease in the future. A true scientific and socialist mentality cannot ignore the importance of the protection of health. However, those who lack foresight, and think that sick persons must merely be cured, must still be fought against. Struggle against death starts before this makes its appearance."

Dr. Boccardo agrees with U Thant, who, in calling for a World Conference on the Environment, which took place in Stockholm in 1972, made an ominous warning: "If the present trend continues, life on this planet could be endangered."

PART VIII

PROBLEMS OF TRANSITION TO SOCIALISM

CHAPTER 28

The Direction of Economic and Social Planning

The kind of socialism Chile will construct—if indeed any variety of socialism can be achieved and maintained from social democracy to revolutionary socialism—will depend in good part upon what kinds of political and developmental decisions are made in these early years. Will Chile opt, as advocated by the Minister of Agriculture, Jacques Chonchol, for a "developmental socialism," involving industrialization and building of export industries? And will this socialist industrialization follow the capitalist pattern of depending upon production of consumers' goods beyond the means of many, or even most, consumers? A simple decision of whether or not to produce automobiles for private consumption, as clearly demonstrated by David Barkin, will sharply influence Chile's social and economic future.

Chonchol also seems to advocate what some term a "technocratic" or "elitist" development path, integrating the Armed Forces into a national development effort and avoiding the mobilization of the people, especially the marginal mass of the population. Perhaps, as suggested in the second article of this chapter, socialist development depends less on economic decisions as such than on the degree to which workers themselves wrest control of the productive and decision-making processes from capitalist bosses and state bureaucrats and technocrats.

ON THE CHILEAN ROAD TO SOCIALISM*

JACQUES CHONCHOL

The accession to power of a Marxist President within the confines of democratic legality has shocked those who have tended a little too readily to dismiss the importance of the political superstructure in an exclusive focus on purely economic interests. Elected in legality, our government shall strive to accomplish its program within the narrow confines of constitutional legality. We shall strive to maintain our tradition of cultural and ideological pluralism while we attempt to expand the democratic form to the reality of democratic participation. Our road to socialism will be a Chilean road. We shall not servilely copy foreign models, but rather adapt socialism to our particular Chilean circumstances and traditions.

Clearly our economic model will be one of developmental socialism. In many years to come, we will have to stress the necessity for accumulation and strive to reinvest at least 20 per cent of our production. At the same time, we must attempt to raise the real income of the most deprived sectors of our population. This clearly cannot be done without curbing or at least maintaining stationary the real income of our more privileged middle and upper classes. Our problem is thus to realize our aim without

* This is a condensation of Jacques Chonchol's lengthy talk at a seminar on "Socialism and Decentralization," December 1970. The transcript was published in *Cuadernos de la Realidad Nacional* No. 7, March 1971. Chonchol has occupied important government posts in administration of the agrarian reform under Frei and Allende. He is also a past Director of the Center for Studies of the National Reality (CEREN), an important research and policy institution.

resorting to brutal force and repression. But no willed self-sacrifice can possibly be expected of the working class unless it is allowed to participate actively in the planning process, unless it is made to feel that it is directly making vital decisions for the good of the country.

At present, our clear class allies are the organized urban proletariat and the organized peasantry. The unorganized, marginal elements now have neither the consciousness nor the power to really support us in our program. Certain sectors of the so-called middle class are also on our side. And also the intellectuals who, regardless of their class backgrounds, have attempted to join with us in our collective struggle to build the Chilean road to socialism.

Chile has not an agricultural vocation but an industrial one. Our policy should be one of industrialization, and we should especially concentrate on those sectors in mining and forestry where we are most likely to succeed in meeting the stiff competition of the world market. Our agricultural development plan should not attempt servile copying of foreign solutions. Rather, here too we should adopt specifically Chilean solutions best suited to our particular situation. It would seem that regional planning with a combined intensive agricultural development and local industrial production would best serve the interests of the population and resolve the labor problem.

The Armed Forces can here be of great help in our collective struggle. Those who talk of the need for a people's militia are clearly unrealistic.

There can be no drastic reorientation of our economic structure, which up to now has served the interests of a minority class, without a simultaneous cultural revolution. The values of capitalism have penetrated deep into the minds of the lower strata. It is within this context that the question of freedom of the press takes on all its importance. Clearly this problem cannot be discussed within criteria of forty years ago. The information media cannot be administered according to capitalist criteria or run in defense of private interests. How to solve this problem correctly while avoiding information monopoly is of course a problem that should be confronted with great seriousness.

The road to socialism is not an easy road. The grand bourgeoisie will keep attempting to disrupt our programs and wreck our enterprise. It should not be impossible to deal with this problem, now that we have the power of the state in our hands. There is also the international situation, which may cause us some added difficulties.

Under such circumstances, since it confronts a unified Right, the Left should strive for unity and avoid unnecessary ideological divisions within the group. Not that revolutionary ideas should be forgotten. Rather, the Left should unite around a common practical economic program with tolerance of ideological and cultural pluralism. We need all the strength we can muster. Strength is found in unity. Let us all join forces and strive collectively toward our common goal, the building of Chilean socialism.

POLITICAL CONSCIOUSNESS:
THE BASE OF PRODUCTION*

L.C.

The Chilean social structure is the major obstacle to our current attempts to increase economic production. Blue- and white-collar workers presently engaged in the private sector might well suspect that our current campaign may

* The author of this article from *Punto Final* No. 136, August 3, 1971, is unidentified except by initials.

not be completely to their advantage. Should the surplus produced by their increased labor be reinvested in production? Should it be distributed? And to whom? The decision has not yet been reached, but one thing leaves no doubt: the worker will not willingly see the fruits of his increased efforts appropriated by the private owners of the means of production.

The Actual Conjuncture.

The Chilean economic structure compares favorably to that of many other nations. Added to the agricultural sector already under state control, the forthcoming nationalization of the copper industry will bring 60 per cent of our gross national production under governmental control.

Much of the industrial sector is already under the control of the state even if no more steps were taken toward further nationalization. The nationalized sector already contributes 70 per cent of our total national reinvestment.

Yet the nationalized sector still falls prey to the same mechanisms that hinder production growth in the private sector. Public ownership does not necessarily modify the social relations that prevail among workers; nor does it automatically improve manager/worker relationships. State ownership by itself is not sufficient to unleash the creative imagination of the producers, which we have been trying to encourage.

State control of certain productive sectors is a salient feature of modern capitalism. The Manchester vision is a distant memory of the past. In France, for instance, nationalized industries are numerous; in Great Britain the Labour Party has ushered through many important nationalizations; in the United States the Roosevelt administration's Tennessee Valley project was the first to challenge the sacred old principles of traditional economic liberalism.

It should therefore be clear that state control by itself is no foolproof guarantee of the people's interests.

The Chilean state enterprises, because of their insertion in a society permeated with capitalist ideology, are governed by its values and norms of conduct. A state-enterprise manager may well reproduce the prevalent capitalist ideology in his political consciousness and practical conduct.

Even the private sector is to a large extent no longer directly managed by its formal owners. Rather, it is managed by representatives of the impersonal board of directors. In the same fashion, the state, through appointed cabinet ministers, also selects its management representatives.

Mass Control.

Even if chosen for his honesty and administrative and professional competence, an appointed manager may still be unable to stimulate and put to use the worker's creative abilities. Despotic behavior, hierarchical rigidity, authoritarianism, may well thwart the active participation of the masses, inhibit the growth of political consciousness, and hinder the workers' permanent mobilization so essential for a victorious class struggle in today's conjuncture.

Recommendations.

The prevailing conditions in the private and public sectors were extensively discussed at the July National Trade Union Conference of the Socialist Party. It was concluded that clearly different strategies should be implemented in our current campaign for an increase in productivity in the private and the public sectors. The Socialist Party urged an immediate increase in productivity in the nationalized sector, while the strategies for a similar increase in the private sector were not yet defined.

The problem will be discussed within the ranks of the Popular Unity.

However, the Socialist Party has demanded that the masses play an active and determinant role in the control of the nationalized sector. Such a step is bound to have important repercussions, since, as has already been pointed out, 60 per cent of our national production is under direct control of the state. In the production of energy, in mineral extraction, in industrial production, in the fields of transportation and communication we have made giant steps forward. New factories, new plants are sprouting all over Chile, with the state Development Corporation as chief investor. With the nationalization of the mining industry, the state has become a Chilean economic giant. We already control an important segment of the banking sector. Its take-over shall soon be complete, thus putting an end to the financial monopoly of the ruling classes.

Yet, such an economic step forward is no guarantee of political and ideological progress. Such an achievement could only result from the eradication of the bourgeois ideology that still pollutes the Chilean atmosphere.

Strategic Alternatives in the Private Sector.

The private sector, now chiefly confined to the production and distribution of consumer goods, has a direct impact on the population. By preventing these goods from reaching the centers of distribution, it could willfully attempt to generate popular unrest. To prevent such a counterrevolutionary practice, the Control Committees of Production have been created.

As the national sector of the economy is chiefly geared toward exportation, it can exert little direct effect on the consumers. For this reason, the Production Control Committees can play an essential role. They can already prevent attempts to sabotage production. Yet, until a decision is finally reached as to what will be done with the surplus generated by the worker's increased labor, the Committees' task will be unduly difficult to perform.

With the exception of resentful *latifundistas* and obstinate or monopolistic industrialists, the private sector has generally responded favorably to our call for increased productivity—not, of course, responding to a patriotic sentiment, but rather enticed by the lures of higher profits. Today the profits of middle-sized entrepreneurs are higher than before. In a transition period, this should surprise no one: remember the "rich peasants"—the kulaks—of the twenties in the Soviet Union. But naturally the worker can hardly be expected to labor with increased love and care for the sole purpose of increasing the wealth of his old boss.

There is thus a contradiction between the present need to keep private enterprise going at a steady or even increasing pace, and the necessary motivation that alone could generate the fever (a specific revolutionary category) to produce more and imagine "impossible" solutions.

The Socialist and Communist parties both believe in the importance of the Control Committees of Production; they have been given an increasingly important role. However, they do not appear to be exempt from certain features of "bureaucratism," which are also present in our trade unions.

Production and the nation are moving forward. But it would be an illusion to assume that this advance automatically solves our problems. On the contrary, these assume an increasing importance: more than growth is at stake today if we are to fulfill our mission and create a truly authentic new society.

AUTOMOBILES AND THE CHILEAN
ROAD TO SOCIALISM*

DAVID BARKIN

The construction of socialism is Chile's most pressing task. Its realization will require a great effort by all Chileans and—even more importantly—a greater consciousness by individuals of their relation to the national development effort. The popular government must ensure that each new decision is consistent with its overriding objective to reshape the economy and society for the benefit of workers and peasants. Only in this way will workers be persuaded of the government's intention to break with the historical pattern of aiding the upper classes. While it is difficult to mold an economic policy consistent with the new egalitarian ethic, this task should have highest priority.

This short article describes some issues arising from a decision to manufacture a substantial number of automobiles for private use by firms financed jointly with public and private foreign investment. The decision merits comment because of its importance in the national development effort and because, by making it, the government might be closing possible lines of action in other areas. The public expenditures and increased private demand necessary to sustain a vigorous automotive sector would necessarily preclude the growth of other areas. We examine the wisdom of this choice below.

Instead of definitive answers, we suggest lines of analy-

* An original article for this volume. David Barkin teaches economics at Lehman College of the City University of New York and has done research in Chile.

sis and questions about the total impact of this decision. Doubts are raised of an economic nature—that is, in relation to the allocation of resources—as well as of a political nature—referring to the relationship of the workers to the new productive and distributive structure.

The Automotive Decision

In June 1971 bids were solicited from automobile producers around the world. The purpose was to reduce the number of different models of vehicles produced by the Chilean automotive industry and to make production more responsive to the needs of the domestic and export markets. Its goals were:

a) To produce commercial and private vehicles for mass consumption;

b) To upgrade the technology of the domestic industry and to create a technological infrastructure that would permit the development of new export industries;

c) To create, directly or indirectly, high-productivity jobs;

d) To obtain additional tax revenues and profits for reinvestment by government;

e) To balance with car exports the foreign-exchange cost that the satisfaction of the demand for automobiles requires;

f) To achieve levels of efficiency so as to be able to compete in trade with other member states of the Latin American Common Market and the Andean Pact.

To achieve these goals, production was to be limited to three models: a small vehicle with an engine of less than 1,200 cc.; a medium-size vehicle with an engine of less than 2,000 cc.; and a chassis for diesel trucks, buses, and other commercial vehicles. Production would increase from the twenty thousand units produced in 1970, to one hundred thousand units in 1980; forty-five thousand small vehicles, forty thousand intermediate, and fifteen thousand diesels were the goals.

Preliminary proposals were sought from companies willing to enter into a joint venture with the Chilean Development Corporation (CORFO) to produce these vehicles, with only a minority participation in the new businesses. Nine proposals were proffered in September 1971 to produce one or more of the vehicles; no North American firm was represented in spite of the fact that both Ford and General Motors had assembly plants in Chile at the time.

Relation to the Distribution of Income

The first question posed by many is whether an increase in automotive production is compatible with a sizable redistribution of income such as that promised by the present government. At first blush most, if not all, the answers have been negative. During the past presidential campaign, for example, Radomiro Tomic, the Christian Democratic candidate, declared, "It is a very grave error against the long-term interests of the nation to stimulate the production and sale of automobiles for the internal market. . . . The owners of the vehicles will (in 1980) barely represent five percent of the population."[1]

Household-expenditure data show that the wealthiest 5 per cent of the population, which earned more than eight times the minimum wage, purchased more than 75 per cent of all automobiles sold in 1969. It is clear that the private car remains a luxury consumption item in most cases and, therefore, satisfies the demands of only a narrow, privileged class.

From an analysis of possible redistributive programs it was determined that it would not be possible to market

[1] "Revolución Chilena y Unidad Popular," speech before the National Board of the Christian Democratic Party, May 1969.

successfully the planned production of eighty-five thousand automobiles if there were any sizable transfer of income from the upper classes to the working classes and peasantry.[2] In view of this we must conclude that *the automotive program is incompatible with a progressive program of income redistribution.*

The Automobile and Public Funds

A second widely discussed aspect of this subject is the effect that an expansion of the number of automobiles would have on the need for roads and parking facilities, especially in the large metropolitan areas. Here, too, the commentators are in agreement about the injurious effects of such an expansion. Thus Tomic noted that an even less ambitious program drawn up in 1969 would require a remodeling of all cities to accommodate wider streets, which would cost several times the actual outlays for the cars themselves. He estimated that one third of the nation's savings might be needed for such a task.

It seems almost unnecessary to detail the impact of an increase in the automotive stock from the approximately 220,000 vehicles that presently function in Chile to more than five hundred thousand in 1980 if the plan were fully implemented. Of course most of the new vehicles would be concentrated in the capital city, Santiago, and it is likely that if the new programs were to be fully implemented the number of private cars would increase from about fifty thousand in 1970 to about 250,000 at the end of the decade. To anyone familiar with Santiago, such an increase in autos holds the promise of interminable traffic delays, air pollution comparable to that of the dirtiest

[2] An analysis of the data behind these statements may be found in the Spanish-language version of this article, to be published in late 1972 by the Centro de Planificación, Universidad Católica, in a book edited by Oscar Muñoz on the distribution of income in Chile.

cities in the world, and an expensive and nerve-shattering series of "urban improvements" to permit the private car some minimal movement in the metropolitan area.

Estimates of the costs of even the barest minimum of public works—urban streets and highways—that would be required to service these vehicles without closer study are presently unavailable, but some comments are in order. Even at present there are enormous deficiencies in the road system for the basic needs of mass transportation and industrial production. These deficiencies are especially serious in the areas in which the poorest groups live. But the new vehicles would be purchased by people living in those areas that already have the best road systems and highest incomes. Even these relatively good road systems would be woefully inadequate for the proposed increase in cars. Their owners would exert strong pressures for further road expenditures in the zones that are in relatively least need of them. As in other aspects of the market economy, the tendency would be to exacerbate the existing inequalities rather than to facilitate structural change.

Regardless of the strategy followed, sizable investments will have to be made in the construction, expansion, and maintenance of the road system in the coming years. A doubt arises, however, about the size and design of the new projects. Stress should be placed on mass-transport needs. Expenditures for facilities to satisfy the demands of individuals in the upper classes for more and better roads on which to use their private cars are not consistent with the present stage of Chilean development—even if they were financed out of resources provided by the new car owners themselves through tolls and taxes.

This position is based on the obvious scarcity of resources. The decision to build a road or a building requires forgoing other facilities. There are clearly many unsatisfied demands throughout the country, and a road project would require the sacrifice of some other vital facility. The government's most important task is to establish priorities for the many demands placed on it; the popular government has explicitly expressed its intention to benefit the working classes systematically, in contradistinction to the historical tendency to channel public funds and programs toward the upper-middle and upper classes for their own benefit and that of international capitalism. Roads for private automobiles do not contribute to this goal.

A second reason for our skepticism about the desirability of an increase in production of private automobiles is its direct competition with the satisfaction of social needs. At present, mass transport is scarce and is particularly poorly designed for the needs of the working classes. There is no doubt that these services should be expanded. But the private car competes directly with mass transport not only for space on the city streets but also within the halls of power. A decision for mass transport probably requires one against private automobile production in all but the most affluent of nations.

The Economics of Automobiles

It is clear that the basic assumption behind the decision to expand the automotive industry was that its contribution to over-all growth, both through direct increases in production and through derived demand of other industries, would be substantial. This rationale emerges from the framework of bourgeois economics, in which industrial demand is insufficient to sustain an acceptable rate of economic growth; in this light, the auto industry is attractive because of the complex and numerous productive relationships it has with other industries in both manufacturing and services. It is ideal to planners, because once stimulated it then generates a pattern of self-sustained growth without the need for further bureaucratic intervention. The "demonstration effect" assures producers of adequate pent-up demand as long as some means is found to finance new car purchases; advertising and imported cultural patterns of invidious comparison assure a continued growth in demand. In this setting, the state should create incentives for industries that will generate self-sustaining growth processes.

The automotive industry offers an easy route to maintain growth while the Chilean road to socialism is being defined and the way prepared. The latent demand of elites for more cars can be satisfied with foreign capital anxious to gain a foothold in a potentially profitable auto industry; the foreign partners also will provide the technical assistance and plans necessary for its implementation. A decision to change the economic structure radically and undertake a different development strategy would require not only the mobilization of new human and material resources in an economy in which there are few reserves —especially of qualified people—but also the political power to obtain the understanding and co-operation of an important part of the society which is accustomed to the bourgeois pattern of consumption.

Finally the upper-middle income groups expect the continued production of private cars, one of their most important prestige symbols. In the present political environment, a restriction on the growth of the productive capacity of durable-goods production—for instance, autos —might be interpreted as an attack on economic freedom. The new automotive industry might be the government's way of showing its willingness to take the demands of the more affluent classes into consideration.

Some of these hopes, however, seem ill-placed. The automotive industry does not appear to represent a clear improvement over alternative investments. Its technology, for example, is too specific to have many applications elsewhere. Potential foreign-exchange savings, resulting from making a greater proportion of the parts domestically, would be more than offset by the increased use of foreign exchange due to the larger volume of production. The employment effect will also probably be less than if the resources were reallocated to other investments that utilize less capital and more labor and are more attuned to the immediate needs of the people.

The traditional approach that dictates the production of private autos can be a *dangerous* one in spite of the short-run advantages mentioned above. The expansion of the automotive industry is not a short-run decision whose effects can later be changed. It will reinforce a capitalist pattern of development—a pattern based on market signals generated by the existing distribution of income that lead to the production and consumption of luxury consumption goods at the expense of the basic needs of the working classes. In the bourgeois scheme, effective demand is the source of production decisions, and income would have to remain highly concentrated in the hands of the upper-income classes to maintain an automobile industry.

Socialism and Economic Strategy

The transition to socialism offers another alternative, which is more consistent with long-term goals: the restructuring of production on the basis of social needs rather than private consumer demand, be it actual, latent, or potential. That is, the transition makes possible—or perhaps essential—a change in the way of determining the industrial structure from one based on consumer demand and an underutilization of productive potential toward one based on needs—defined by a political process—and the full utilization of the nation's human and productive capacity.

In this new context, the political basis for the determination of productive decisions would be mass organizations that participate in the definition of a new policy for consumption. They would encourage an awareness of political power that the workers can direct. Only in this way can the population actively participate in and help implement a long-term development program that would permit high rates of investment and proper allocation of scarce resources.

This alternative might be considered complementary to one that accepted the expansion of durable-goods production. Yet, in a poor country such as Chile most of these goods must inevitably be luxuries and their production would require a diversion of resources from mass consumption or investment. Even more important, however, the consumption of these goods would perpetuate the differentiation in personal status, with the consequent heightening of conflict among groups to which such differentiation leads.[3]

It is precisely for this reason that the decision to expand the automotive industry is most incongruous. The expansion would have to depend on a high concentration of income and differentiated consumption among classes. The new government's goal is to create propitious conditions for the workers to assume power and improve their living standards, while its short-run efforts would stimulate economic activity by strengthening an industry (auto) that does not serve the workers' needs. The consequences of continuous inequality inherent in the decision are striking and in sharp contrast with most discussions of economic strategy.

[3] Given the existing distribution of power, it might be necessary to continue producing non-essential goods to accommodate existing demands and absorb some of the excess money that has been printed; this production should be as tightly restricted as possible and perhaps should be channeled toward goods for which productive capacity already exists or might be easily built, which does not require large amounts of foreign exchange, and whose illegal importation cannot be easily controlled.

A short parenthesis is needed here. The previous comments about the automobile are based on a traditional idea of its role in and distribution throughout society; we do not wish to totally disregard the important functions that individual vehicles could serve. Rather, we think that present capacity is sufficient to fill the need for vehicles in public services and to allow individuals freedom of movement in areas where public transport is inadequate or inappropriate. At a later stage of development the possibility of restructuring the distribution system to permit individuals to rent cars for short periods might avoid the stratifying effects of vehicle ownership without eliminating the benefits and flexibility it offers. For the immediate future, the possibility of restricting vehicular traffic in urban areas would contribute to a fuller use of a well-designed public transport system.

A new economic strategy must clearly define the basic requirements of the population and create the productive capacity to satisfy them. The definition of needs itself will determine the structure and the economy. In most capitalist nations real needs are determined by family incomes, materialist culture, and market structures, which often channel demands away from socially desirable expenditures; government social-welfare programs only temper the cruelty of market forces—unemployment and high prices—for some of the poorest groups. In Chile, on the other hand, the opportunity exists to make fundamental changes in consumption patterns and the basic definition of needs. With a redistribution of wealth and power to the workers, there will be greater need for wage goods—principally foodstuffs and non-durable goods—but there will also be a massive expansion of collective services.

The importance of collective services cannot be overstated. It stems from the need to provide a certain minimum to all and to broaden the area in which the workers can control their own lives. Collective services open greater possibilities for local decisions to be taken about production and distribution; these services include education, health care, day-care centers, cultural activities, and transportation, among others. Their initial organization is difficult, because the private-enterprise system generally is unwilling to divert the necessary resources to these vital areas affecting human welfare; new systems of management and decision making have to be designed and implemented.

One further area which will also require investment is housing. The capitalist economy is generally unprepared to satisfy the basic housing needs of its proletariat. Consequently it is one of the most pressing problems facing the popular government. Its solution cannot be found in the context of a bourgeois economy, where experience has demonstrated an absence of efforts to develop the needed technological innovations to produce inexpensive but serviceable housing.

This general listing of the broad characteristics of a program of mass consumption suggests that the investment program that should be implemented is very different from that of past decades. The program offers several advantages when compared with one whose point of departure is the development of the automotive industry. First, it could have a sizable employment effect, since in addition to agriculture—which any government would have to develop—a large part of the improvement in living conditions would come from personal services provided by people for each other. Housing and necessary public works would further contribute to the task of productively incorporating large numbers of people into the labor force. Second, this type of program would require fewer imports than others, since the man power and materials are available domestically and the country has an ample agricultural potential to develop.

Finally, the investment process, consciously de-emphasized during the first year of popular government in favor of income redistribution, will have to be brought to the fore. Only by gradually closing the channels for broadening consumption will the government be able to divert resources from an economy oriented toward luxury consumption to one responding to more basic needs of the entire population. This type of restriction on the availability of goods will be all the more difficult if the economy is still producing durable consumption goods in which the increases in production come at the sacrifice of heavy investments and foreign purchases for national development.

Conclusions

The decision to expand the automotive industry to produce a hundred thousand vehicles of different types by 1980 with an emphasis on the private car appears to be a grave error. Not only would it require the maintenance of the existing high concentration of income and divert scarce government funds from other areas with higher social priorities, but it would also increase air pollution and further weaken the possibility of improving public transportation.

But these simple objective criteria are less important for the construction of socialism than the considerations about the decision's relation to social stratification. We saw the difference between a program based on the production of expensive consumer durables and one based on the provision of collective services for all. The socialist alternative contributes to short-run improvements in living standards for most of the population and to a harmonization of social relations on the job and in the community. The automobile not only would be sold to the affluent classes, but its continued production would call into question the ability of the government to reduce class differences in the new Chile.

A Postscript

At this writing (April 1972) the government has decided to go ahead with the production of a small popular car known as the *Rata* (a Chilean version of the 2-cv produced in France by Citroën), to be produced by Citroën-Renault, and a diesel chassis to be manufactured by Fiat. For the time being, at least, the bids on the intermediate-size car were not accepted, and there is some ground for optimism that production of this model will either be eliminated or seriously curtailed. No details are available about how automobile production will be marketed or whether some mechanism will be created to permit a broader distribution of *La Rata*.

LA CUECA DEL AUTO*

SUNI PAZ

I tell you that the car, *compañero*, is no damn good
Your legs can take you, my friend, as far you want
And the heart works better after a walk.

The car poisons, *compañero*, our existence
Smoke in your lungs, my friend, will finish you fast
And the smog makes the cities look really bad.

A car is only a symbol of money and class
Have you ever seen a peasant, my friend, mounting a car?

Compañero, there are priorities that leave their mark
And others that only smoke up our lives

Better bicycles, my friend, than Citronetas!

* This song was inspired by David Barkin's preceding article. The *cueca* is a Chilean folkloric rhythm and dance. Suni Paz is a Latin American folk artist.

Our existence jeopardized, yes
The city gray as fog
And one can't even see, my friend, the high peaks of the
    Andes

Better bicycles, *compañero,* than Citronetas!

CHAPTER 29

Socialism or State Capitalism?

This chapter contains an energetic attack from a MIRist perspective on the "reformism" of the Communist Party of Chile. The virulence of Fernández's polemic (and the CP's response to "ultra-leftist" MIR critiques—see Chapter 18) should not be allowed to obscure the fundamental issues. Bringing Chile's natural resources under Chilean control, state control of banking and the largest industries, and other measures so far undertaken by the PU government have substantially enlarged the state sector of the economy but do not in themselves constitute what Marxists mean by socialism. The social inequalities of the previous capitalist society, though somewhat ameliorated, are still present, and the market principle governs the behavior of state enterprises just as surely as it does those in the private sector. Fernández argues that the growth of the state and co-operative sectors of the economy relative to the private sector is no guarantee of further transition to socialism, and can in fact be frozen as a system of state capitalism. State capitalism can be transformed into socialism only if political forces are committed to a revolutionary political practice aimed at destruction of the bourgeois state. The CP, Fernández argues, is not so committed. It has lost its revolutionary vision, has adopted a conciliatory attitude toward class enemies of the revolution, and seeks alliances with middle- and small-bourgeois elements which convert the Party's politics into bourgeois reformism.

THE COMMUNIST PARTY:
REFORM OR REVOLUTION?*

BY GLAURIS FERNÁNDEZ

The Communist Party's program defines the revolution as anti-imperialist and anti-oligarchic. The oligarchs are the monopolists who control various sectors of the economy in agriculture, industry, mining, etc. These are the enemies. As for the non-monopolistic bourgeoisie, the middle and small bourgeoisie, they are seen as potential revolutionary allies.

The authors of the program have obviously ignored the fundamental changes that, since the War, have completely modified the structure of the world's capitalist system. Under the hegemonic rule of the United States, the world's capitalist system has seen the growth and concentration of monopoly capital and the extension of its tentacles into the very heart of dependent countries, thus increasing the original dependency at all levels of dependent economies and preventing any possibility of autonomous capitalist development. This growing penetration of international monopoly capital into national dependent economies over the past fifty or sixty years has confronted the national bourgeoisies with a clear ultimatum: to disappear or to accept their integration into the world's capitalist monopolistic structure. This satellitization of the peripheral national bourgeoisies was made possible by the complex process of gradual hegemonic control of the technological means of production by the center. We shall not here analyze this process itself but will rather focus on its historical political consequences.

* Translated and abridged from *Punto Final* No. 91, November 11, 1969.

It is utterly senseless to propose an anti-imperialist struggle that is not at the same time anti-capitalist, when Latin America as a whole (and especially Chile, where this integration process has reached incredible levels during the past four years) faces such a conjuncture.

A viable anti-capitalist strategy cannot count on the petty bourgeoisie as a class ally. A correct Marxist strategy should rather attempt to neutralize it in order to insure a favorable transition to socialism. Indiscriminately to select the petty bourgeoisie as a class ally in the present conjuncture, and to limit the revolutionary struggle to bourgeois democratic objectives such as a mixed regime of state capitalism (the "non-capitalist" way proposed by the CP's program) is to cultivate a dangerous illusion that does not correspond in any way to the reality of our class structure. It is to transform the proletarian struggle into the utopian vision of the petty bourgeoisie.

One cannot hope to solve the basic problems that the failures of former policies of dependent development have brought upon us without putting forth a courageous program of transformations that would fundamentally restructure the productive sector, utilize the idle capacity of industries in order better to attend to the people's needs, pave the way for the production of durable goods and heavy industry, relocate in the countryside the majority of urban unemployed or underemployed, eliminate a vast sector of the useless bureaucratic apparatus that the state has supported with its fiscal revenues from the copper industry, and transform the *latifundios* into collective farms or co-operatives of production and consumption uniting the small and middle producers. In short, our objective must be to raise the working class of Chile to a position of responsibility and command in the making of a modern country, fully utilizing its resources toward the construction of a socialist society of abundance. Bits and pieces, state favors, will not do! We must also generate a revolu-

tionary international political strategy. We must plant the
seed for Latin American and Andean integration, thus
paving the way for a socialist Latin America, joining
socialist Cuba and the revolutionary struggles that are
bursting forth on the continent.

To choose any other road would be for the Communist
Party to adopt the vision of the least progressive and most
insignificant segment of the bourgeoisie: the so-called
non-monopolistic bourgeoisie. Already lagging behind the
more dynamic segment of its own class, which controls the
means of scientific and technological progress, what development strategy could the non-monopolist bourgeoisie
produce?

This is why the evolutionary stages of the revolution
envisaged in the Communist program are misleading. For
instance, we read: "We Communists fight to unite the
country's majority, victim of the capitalist regime, in this
first anti-imperialist and anti-oligarchic stage of the revolutionary struggle." With such statements, the Chilean
Communist Party foments the illusion that it is possible to
advance gradually without first attacking the capitalist
system, which is the very basis and condition of existence
of imperialism itself. The program overemphasizes the
contradictions that oppose the national bourgeoisie to imperialism. Such contradictions do indeed exist, but they
are non-antagonistic: they will disappear when the bourgeoisie finally confronts the popular movement. By pre-
senting to the masses such historically exhausted and
vacillating forces as allies, the Communist Party does not
develop popular combativeness. Even when it organizes
its festive, carnivalesque marches against capitalism, the
Communist Party does not prepare the people finally to
resolve the question of power, which is fundamental if one
is to build and live socialism. Capitalism is made to appear as a valid system so long as it is divested of its most
glaring defects. So long as the basic socioeconomic struc-

ture is not questioned, the Communist Party's program does not differ much from that of the Christian Democratic Party. The reforms proposed may be slightly more progressive. Yet the system itself is not challenged at the base, so the Communist Party's critique of reformism is nothing more than a posture. The Communist Party's leaders have no clear understanding of the nature of the transition from capitalism to socialism. This is quite obvious in the gradualist analysis they propose. They state, for example, that the anti-imperialist, anti-oligarchic revolution "will produce transformations that will pave the way for new relations of production toward socialism." They also propose that "the achievement of these revolutionary objectives, the growth of state and co-operative sectors, will permit a *smooth and continuous process* of transition from this first stage on to socialism" (emphasis ours).

But it is a well-established fact that the "growth of the state and co-operative sectors" is by itself no guarantee of a further transition to socialism.

State capitalism is today the greatest ally of monopoly capital. How then could one expect the creation of a vast sector of state capitalism to lead automatically and mechanically to socialism? State capitalism can be progressive and lead to socialism only if it is committed to a revolutionary political program aiming at the destruction of the bourgeois state itself, in its military and civilian garb, and the construction of socialist society on radically different grounds. Today's Communist parties have lost the clear revolutionary vision that sprang forth from the Third International. Remember that it was then the question of the state that divided Communists from social democrats. The latter forgot the dictatorship of the proletariat, while the former upheld firmly at the very core of their constitution the strategic primacy of the *destruction* of the state.

Is the thesis that a popular government will reach power electorally a truly Communist one? And is the proposal to maintain a regular "professional" army, thus reinforcing the state bureaucratic apparatus and guaranteeing it the greatest privileges? Is it truly communistic to maintain party pluralism without first demanding the exclusion of all bourgeois parties and their allies? Can those who affirm that such a government can pass to socialism "within a continuous and smooth process" call themselves Communists?

Were all the theoretical efforts of Marx, Engels, and Lenin in vain? Should the historical lessons of social democracy and labor governments be repressed from our memories? Should all the failures of populist/nationalist governments in Central America, the Peróns, the Vargases, the MNRs, the Cárdenases, the Arévalos, the Goularts, simply be forgotten? . . .

The True Character of the Communist Party's Program

What are the practical results of a non-Marxist analysis of Chilean reality?

a) It is clear that the Communist Party's leaders envision a popular government that would resemble not pre-Stalinist Russia or China or Cuba, but rather the Western European democratic style. This accounts for their respect for private property and opposition parties: a pluralistic vision that negates the necessity of a dictatorship of the proletariat. They write, for example: "We Communists uphold that under popular government or socialist rule, all popular currents should maintain their own identity, all religious beliefs should be respected, and there should therefore be ideological and political pluralism without hindering the pursuit by each and every one of his own personal ideals. The government for which we fight shall be the most democratic ever seen in Chile, since it will be generated by the people constituted in popular parties."

b) In spite of its "socialist vision," this proposed strategy toward a "popular government" will implant a modernization process most unlikely to succeed, since the Right always shows itself much stronger than hoped for by the Communists. Such a strategy would only result in the consolidation of the bourgeoisie, an increased governmental repression of the people, and long-lasting economic stagnation in these days of the ever-deepening crisis of Latin American and Chilean dependent capitalism.

c) The "democratism" of the program is illusory. Democracy is not liberalism. It does not merely consist of "formal" liberties but is made of *real* mass participation and power. As Marx and Engels pointed out in their analysis *The Paris Commune,* as Lenin argued in *State and Revolution,* democracy can be realized only if the masses take the most direct possible control of the state into their own hands with the least possible interference from a bureaucracy, which must be limited and restricted as much as possible. Democracy is insured by authentic popular participation in the direction of industries, communes, the state, planning, etc.

Socialist democracy can exist only when the revolutionary party (or parties) truly represents an organized political coalition of the proletariat and its class allies, so as to promote popular mobilization and the democratic rule of its dictatorship. Only the parties that support the dictatorship of the proletariat can have a right to participate actively in the shaping of a socialist democracy. . . .

The positive role that a popular government could play in the transitional process to a socialism is far from clear. It is absurd to propose that a popular government could be constituted peacefully, and even more absurd to foresee the transition to socialism as a smooth evolutionary process. We know upon what vague class analysis such a foggy conception rests. We have seen how unclear is its definition of the objective character of the transition to socialism. Such opacity only reflects the empiricism of its proponents.

d) The Party's program is thus reduced to a platform for the 1970 elections. Even if the Party insists that popular participation in the electoral process is only one of many possible strategies, it has not bothered to define any alternatives. The Communist Party's program is thus reduced to the old electoral populist rhetoric borrowed from the nationalist bourgeoisie.

The CP of Chile can now be seen waving high the rotten banners of bourgeois development at the very moment when bourgeois oligarchs and imperialists attempt to bring to final completion the process of dependent development that has brought to Chile and Latin America only stagnation and frustration, strong governments, and popular repression.

e) The CP of Chile has emphasized the need for redistribution. Such a program could not allow for the tremendous growth of productive forces, which alone could secure our economic development. As it reflects the reformist demands of the petty bourgeoisie seeking to protect its interests threatened by the necessary process of capital accumulation, as it proposes to grant some concessions to the middle class and to some privileged sectors of labor, the Communist program is not even a viable economic development program.

With so many allies and so few enemies, with such vague objectives, the basic interests of real revolutionary classes are veiled and transformed into such grand generalities as "the interests of Chile" or "the unity and common action of all the forces that oppose the fundamental enemies of the country," etc. In the name of "the interests of Chile," the Communist Party leaders openly support a *"modern, patriotic, and popular conception* of the defense of our national sovereignty that guarantees *to all sectors* of the Armed Forces the *material and technical means* necessary to fulfill their *specific mission,* which requires guaranteed economic security, professional training, and rank mobility to *all officers and troops* by means of adequate remuneration compatible with their qualifications and needs during service as well as in retirement. We support the *professional* character of the Armed Forces . . ." (emphasis ours).

As for the "professional character" or the "specific function" of the Armed Forces, only petty bourgeois reason is unable to understand that there can be no apolitical "professionalism," that the bourgeois's notion cannot be that of the proletariat, and that bourgeois domination rests securely behind such mystifying veils. . . .

f) Finally we must discuss the Party's conception of popular unity. While it is true that unity must be achieved and that sectarianism opposing allies must be curbed, it is also true that there can be no true unity without a common goal. Only a truly revolutionary unity that refuses to make any concessions on matters of principle, only a unity that seeks not to reform but rather to deepen the system's contradictions, must be sought. Popular unity for its own sake can be of the gravest consequences. Blind enthusiasm for abstract unity or the politics of extensive coalition, which, for instance, seeks an alliance with the so-called non-monopolistic bourgeoisie, middle bourgeoisie, or small bourgeoisie, casts aside along the road the very foundations of true revolutionary working-class politics. To insist on the "decisiveness of unity" always leads to the complacent adoption of bourgeois reformism, to concessions to the Right, and to the exclusion of those whom the Party then chooses to call "leftists."

But how does the Party define these "leftist" elements? Are they not part of the people? Why then does the Party not seek to persuade them to adopt its platform and join its politics of unity? Simply because one cannot mix Greeks and Trojans. One cannot unite bourgeois reformists with revolutionaries. For this reason broad unity turns into its opposite: division. What matters is not unity for its own sake, but rather unity of whom and for what. The Party's popular coalition politics excludes many segments of the Left that in spite of previous errors (and who has not committed any?) are truly revolutionary forces. By condemning as "anti-Communist agents of imperialism" all those who favor popular insurrection without allowing any discussion of their position, the Party has clearly adopted a Stalinist posture. Such a stance clearly betrays the weakness of its position and its fear of confronting any opposition from the Left. The militants of the CP well realize that a workers' party is not necessarily a party of the working class, as European social democracy and the British Labour Party rule have already amply demonstrated. To be a Communist does not mean to agree with a party that calls itself Communist.

Especially since the Cuban Revolution, the Communist Parties' monopoly of the Left has been called into question. Since Marx and Lenin, to be a Communist has always meant to act as a revolutionary. Today in Latin America, to be a Communist is to form a vanguard in order to prepare and organize the masses militarily and politically for the revolutionary conquest of power by the people and the victory of socialism. This is what defines a Communist. Not a Party membership card.

CHAPTER 30

Populist Reform or Mass Revolutionary Mobilization?

The Communist and the Socialist parties of Chile have long been extremely energetic in defending and promoting the interests of the organized workers of the mines and large industry. Their roots among the unorganized workers and peasants, however, are extremely tenuous even today. The Christian Left and the MIR have seized the initiative from the traditional Marxist parties in recent years and succeeded in mobilizing large numbers of agricultural workers and Mapuche Indians into farm workers' unions and land invasions. MIR, followed by the CP, has also been active in community organizing in urban settlements. For the most part, however, unorganized workers in medium and small industry and commerce and the impoverished inhabitants of urban *callampa* (mushroom) settlements lack organization and political consciousness (see Chapter 10).

It is clear that many orthodox Marxists of both the Socialist and the Communist parties, as well as certain non-Marxist theoreticians of the PU such as Jacques Chonchol (see Chapter 28), write off the great mass of unorganized workers as a potentially organizable force to construct Chilean socialism. Moreover, the government becomes extremely nervous when peasants and settlement dwellers engage, with increasing militance, in agitation and direct action. In part, this is due to the political vulnerability of the government owing to the potential alienation of non-proletarian sectors the PU is trying to win over or neutralize and to the strong right-wing reaction to such action on the part of the masses. Mass mobilization could lose the PU support among equivocal sectors or even precipitate a counterrevolution or sufficient chaos to force a military intervention. It is also the case that the PU conceives of socialist construction as a controlled process. Most farm workers, poor settlers, and unorganized workers are not under control of one of the main PU parties—and their situation is so desperate that political mobilization can generate demands the PU cannot satisfy. Julio Arredondo, however, argues that only mass mobilization can transform populist reform into revolutionary socialism.

OUR STRUGGLE CAN ONLY BE A MASS STRUGGLE.*

JULIO ARREDONDO

The accession to power of the Popular Unity government has sharpened the ideological differences between PU partisans and the revolutionary Left. Class unrest is growing throughout the country, while the Right has taken over the political offensive. Recent polemics have not always helped to clarify our ideological differences or generate a common revolutionary strategy. We must unite, and to do so we must speak our mind clearly.

Let us start by taking a close look at the Popular Unity's program. Large farmholdings, national and international monopolies, and the imperialist penetration of our economic structure presently hinder the adequate development of our productive forces. The labor and commodity markets cannot adequately supply the needs of our population. We must therefore immediately initiate the proc-

* Translated in somewhat abridged form from *Punto Final* No. 134, June 7, 1971.

ss of transition to socialism, which alone can resolve the present crisis of Chilean dependent capitalism.

The Popular Unity's program recommends as first steps toward this goal the expropriation of *latifundios*, the nationalization of private banks and external commerce, and the state take-over of our raw-materials resources and commercial and industrial monopolies.

The expropriation of large rural estates will free the economic surplus presently appropriated from the peasantry in the form of land rent. The nationalization of industrial and commercial monopolies will then turn over to the state the economic surpluses that are presently either exported abroad by the imperialists or else consumed internally by the capitalist class. Through centralized planning, this generated surplus would then be reinvested in the manner most appropriate for an enlarged reproduction of our economy. Furthermore, full utilization of our productive resources coupled with an increase in our labor productivity would solve our unemployment problem while creating the base of a real income redistribution in favor of the popular sectors.

Within the class struggle, the Popular Unity defines "imperialists, landed oligarchs, and the monopolistic bourgeoisie" as the enemies of the revolution, while the working class and the peasantry are seen as the major supportive sectors of an alliance that includes the middle and small bourgeoisie as well as radicalized intellectuals. The mission of this alliance is to insure the implementation of the above-described "democratic-national" program, as it has been called by some members of the Popular Unity coalition.

The revolutionary Left actively supports the goals of the program; it is its duty to join forces with the class coalition seeking to strengthen the nationalized sector of the economy in order to destroy imperialism and the agrarian oligarchy. However, the revolutionary Left must also ask if the class strategy of the Popular Unity coalition is adequate to the tasks it has set itself to perform.

To bluntly affirm that the process of nationalization and expropriation will automatically lead to a consolidation of state capitalism at the expense of socialism seems too rigid a position to take. Indeed, the maintenance of a private and mixed economic sector within an expanding state-controlled sector could well be a step forward in the construction of socialism, provided that the working class gains control of the state power in order to direct the capitalist relations of production and process of circulation in its own interest. Moreover, to focus on this problem at this stage is completely unwarranted. The state economic sector must first be built and consolidated, a process that can result only in sharpened class conflicts. Will the class strategy proposed by the Popular Unity permit facing adequately this deepening contradiction? Will it insure the consolidation of proletarian hegemony within a strengthened state?

To answer these questions we must first analyze the contradictions that will be generated by the Popular Unity's strategy. Control of the economic surplus is the real bone of contention—a state control that must be achieved within the framework of a peaceful bourgeois democratic alliance with the small and middle bourgeoisie politically neutralized and economically strengthened.

How is this likely to affect the Popular Unity's program? First, there is the copper problem. The nationalization question has now been transformed into a struggle between the Chilean and the American governments. If Chile nationalizes the copper interests without indemnization, we will face temporary difficulties in the international market structure, thus reducing our economic surplus. If, on the other hand, we agree to pay indemnizations, then we will again see our economic surplus significantly reduced.

As for the internal economic surplus, it is clearly generated from the economic exploitation of the peasantry and the proletariat. The surplus value appropriated by the monopolists is a direct function of real wages. A redistribution of income will clearly, in the short range, diminish the economic surplus. Furthermore, the present legal parliamentary maneuvers of the monopolists successfully delay the time when the state will finally take control of the surplus. Delays which already result in the sabotage of production further diminish the surplus.

Through fiscal measures, credit favors, and price controls, the alliance with the small and middle bourgeoisie not only maintains but actually in many cases strengthens the bourgeoisie's control over the economy.

It is obvious that to augment simultaneously the income of the working and propertied classes at a time of diminishing governmentally controlled surplus can lead only to a rupture of economic equilibrium. The working class will rightly feel entitled to a rise in income, while the bourgeoisie will insist that its participation in the coalition be rewarded with cheap credit, guaranteed demand, low costs of raw materials, etc. . . .

The alliance of the peasantry and the rural and urban proletariat must be strengthened economically and politically if it is to succeed in neutralizing the bourgeoisie. The nationalization process must be accelerated in order to avoid production sabotage and reduction of the economic surplus. This should be done now or not at all.

The Popular Unity's Position on the Worker/Peasant Coalition

An acceleration of the nationalization and expropriation process will result in a sharpened class struggle requiring the strengthening of the rural and urban mass coalition. The peasantry and the urban proletariat must become the hegemonic class within the revolutionary alliance. This can result only from the inclusion within the struggle of the non-organized masses. For while the Popular Unity's program theoretically recognizes that the proletariat and the peasantry are the main wings of the revolutionary forces, let us see which peasantry and which proletariat are actually included within its ranks. As we know, the peasantry is not a homogeneous class within our social formation, nor is the urban proletariat. Recognizing this situation, the Popular Unity has chosen to include only certain sectors of the rural and urban proletariat within its class strategy. *Compañero* Jacques Chonchol, for instance, in his analysis of the Chilean road to socialism defines the organized rural and urban proletariat as the support of the revolution. The unorganized workers, he tells us, are in no position to join in the struggle. Chonchol's conception of the revolutionary process is peculiar indeed. He defines the rural and urban proletariat's participation as supportive of the revolution, but it is not clear just what they support. Is it other classes? Or maybe a revolutionary project that is not of their own making? In either case, the revolutionary process is defined as escaping their direction. Chonchol excludes the non-organized peasants and urban workers. Since only 30 per cent of the rural population is organized and since close to 50 per cent of the urban working class is presently employed in shops of fewer than five workers, we have a clear idea of whom he means to include in the revolutionary struggle.

Compañero Jorge Insunza's argument, couched in more clearly Leninist language, is even less persuasive. He tells us that "certain deformations are emerging that threaten our struggle for power." What deformations? From what direction? Insunza adds, "The rise to power of the present government has provided a great impulse to the organization of non-organized workers. This is an extraordinarily auspicious sign. The popular government must respond positively to such a tendency and support those nuclei in their attempts to join the class struggle. It is only natural that anarchistic tendencies would manifest themselves in these new sectors inexperienced in the class struggle. This, however, should not prevent the leaders of the labor movement from giving them active support. On the contrary, they should devote special care to the political education of these workers who until now have been the most oppressed of the working class."

From this we may conclude that the Popular Unity has no intention of denying to the unorganized rural and urban proletariat their role in the revolutionary struggle. However, the Popular Unity leaders' attitude is politically ambivalent. On the one hand the active integration of the unorganized workers into the political process is deemed auspicious, while on the other hand integration is simultaneously defined in ways implying contradictory strategies. Should these new forces spontaneously emerging from below be guided into the revolutionary struggle? Or should they rather be contained and controlled from above? The same phenomenon is seen as both auspicious and threatening. The allusion to "anarchistic tendencies" and the paragraph title "social discipline" clearly reveal this fear. Behind the Popular Unity's rhetoric, it is obvious that the poorest sectors of the rural and urban proletariat, defined as "anarchistic," are excluded from the hegemonic control of the class alliance. It is also clear that the Marxist parties participating in the Popular Unity's coalition have no clear strategy for the integration of the unorganized sectors within the peasant/worker alliance.

The Revolutionary Left and the Peasant/Worker Alliance

The revolutionary Left affirms the urgent necessity to incorporate these most impoverished sectors within the revolutionary struggle, and demands that these spontaneously emerging nuclei be encouraged and guided within the process. This is absolutely essential if the successful socialization of the economy is to be accomplished. The organized proletariat presently employed within the nationalized or the soon-to-be-nationalized sectors does not suffice. The immediate incorporation of the non-organized masses into the collective struggle is essential if workers control and an end to production sabotage are to be achieved. Clearly this strategy would sharpen the class struggle and could lead to a face-to-face confrontation with the small and middle bourgeoisie. Such an incorporation would also increase the pressure on the economy because of the demands that such new sectors would make. But it is also quite clear that inclusion of these disfavored groups within the class struggle would serve to curb the demands of the bourgeoisie on the state economy.

It is impossible at this point to measure the economic impact of such a strategy. It is clear, however, that it would strengthen the peasant/worker coalition. This is what really matters at this point in our struggle for power.

The immediate objective is not to take over the property of the small, the middle, or even the grand bourgeoisie, but rather to augment the social, economic, and political control of the revolutionary masses so as to prevent the propertied classes from strengthening their political base.

Let us speak clearly: the inclusion of the small and middle bourgeoisie within the ranks of the Popular Unity coalition is not what should worry us at this point. We should instead turn our energy to strengthening the peasant/worker alliance with the inclusion of the non-organized sectors. Such an integration would serve to neutralize the strength of the propertied classes within the coalition in preparation for the moment when the class contradictions will reach an antagonistic level.

Tactical Implications of the Revolutionary Left's Strategy

This neutralization is economically and politically essential because of our attempt to strengthen the state sector within a capitalist structure of production and distribution, which can only increase the struggle between the state and the private sector of the economy as they compete for the appropriation and distribution of the economic surplus.

At what level should the growth of the private sector be curbed? What proportion of the economic surplus should it be allowed to appropriate? These are the fundamental questions, which can only be answered, of course, at the "actual moment" of the conjuncture, when the power struggle for control of the state apparatus becomes acute.

What then of state capitalism? The Popular Unity program clearly envisages state capitalism as a stage leading to socialism, in its distinction between the three economic sectors, public, mixed, and private. Private ownership of the means of production and capitalist relations of production would persist in the mixed and private sectors, while all three sectors would be included within the capitalist process of circulation. The socialization of the entire economy would be inconceivable without this transitional mixed-economy stage for lack of adequate means of technical and administrative centralized control.

Thus, state capitalism is itself a necessary transitional stage. What is at issue, however, is the class struggle itself, that is, the question of who shall benefit from and control the over-all economic process. There are two possibilities. Either the state wins in the struggle with the private and mixed sectors and becomes the chief instrument of economic accumulation, thus ensuring the progressive socialization of the total economy; or the state loses the struggle and transforms itself into the tool of the

private economic sectors, thus ensuring the transition to
a new stage in the development of national capitalism. In
the first case, the proletariat would utilize the state as an
economic and political instrument to promote in its favor
the process of economic accumulation and the development of the productive forces within a capitalist structure
of relations of production and circulation in order to ensure the progressive elimination of the mixed and private
sectors and the socialization of the entire economy.

On the other hand, state capitalism could strengthen the
hold of the bourgeoisie over the economic process in the
private and mixed sectors, thus allowing it to gain a new
and absolute control over the state and creating the conditions for a new growth of Chilean capitalism. For this
reason, the neutralization of the small and middle bourgeoisie within the Popular Unity coalition is essential if
the state is truly to become the political and economic
base of socialism. To achieve such an end, it is essential
to allow the peasant/proletariat alliance to become the
hegemonic power within the revolutionary class coalition.

The small and middle bourgeoisie form the spearhead
of the social, political, and military domination of the
grand bourgeoisie and imperialism. It must be neutralized
if the state is successfully to oppose the bourgeoisie/im-
perialist cohort. However, to prevent this political neutralization from adversely affecting the economic growth
of the nationalized sector and impeding the rise to power
of the peasant and urban proletariat, the entire urban
and rural masses must be incorporated into the struggle.

The state itself must actively favor the mobilization of
the masses, support their economic demands, and find
ways to strengthen their participation in this struggle for
power.